Praise for *The Trouble with Harry Hay*

"Hay's colorful personality and turbulent life are portrayed in a book written with a verve worthy of its subject."   *—Publishers Weekly*

▽

"This engrossing, well-written book rescues Harry Hay from the realm of myth and also recovers large chunks of gay history. On both counts, it is a solid, praiseworthy achievement."   —Martin Duberman

▽

"Timmons's biography of Harry Hay will be one of the most important contributions to gay history to date. It is my hope that this book will find as many readers among lesbians as it will among gay men."
      —Feminist Bookstore News

▽

"There is no 'Trouble with Harry.' His determined caring and searching shine like a diamond through his life. We need a lot more like Harry!"
      —Del Martin and Phyllis Lyon

▽

"Hay had the audacity to see that we gays were an oppressed minority and that material and spiritual politics and community were the answer to our isolation. Harry's 'trouble' still irradiates the gay condition." *—The Advocate*

▽

"The first biography of a major figure in gay history. Ever controversial, Hay isn't interested in observing gay proprieties: he's been kicked out of gay parades for representing subgroups deemed embarrassing to mainstream gay interests. He loquaciously assisted in the book's preparation, often contradicting others' versions of events — a circumstance that considerably enlivens Timmons's effort."   *—Booklist*

▽

"A detailed, informative biography that covers Harry Hay's turbulent forty-year career as actor, writer, activist, Communist, and, ultimately, 'the Father of Gay Liberation.' Timmons provides a very readable and educated perspective not only on Hay's life but also on the Gay Rights Movement's political backdrop."   *—Kirkus Reviews*

"Reading this amazing profile in courage often brought tears to my eyes and will, I think, deeply move a new generation."   —Jonathan Ned Katz

The Trouble with Harry Hay

Founder of the Modern Gay Movement

by Stuart Timmons

Boston: Alyson Publications

Alyson Publications
40 Plympton Street
Boston, Mass. 02118

Distributed in England by GMP Publishers,
P.O. Box 247, London N17 9QR.

First edition, first printing: November 1990
First paperback edition: December 1991

ISBN 1-55583-111-7

Editing: Sasha Alyson
Cover design: Catherine Hopkins
Book design and production: Lynne Y. Fletcher
Proofreading: Tina Portillo

Library of Congress Cataloging-in-Publication Data

Timmons, Stuart, 1957–
    The trouble with Harry Hay : founder of the modern gay movement /
by Stuart Timmons. — 1st ed.
    p. cm.
    Includes bibliographical references.
    ISBN 1-55583-111-7 : $12.95
    1. Hay, Harry. 2. Gays—United States—Biography. 3. Gay
liberation movement—United States—History—20th century.
4. Actors—United States—Biography. 5. Communists—United States-
-Biography. 6. Mattachine Society—History—20th century.
I. Title.
HQ75.8.H39T56 1990
306.76′ 62′ 092—dc20
[B]   90-45443
                                                                          CIP

Urning men and women, on whose book of life Nature has written her new word which sounds so strange to us, bear such storm and stress within them, such ferment and fluctuation, so much complex material having its outlet only in the future; their individualities are so rich and many-sided, and withal so little understood, that it is impossible to characterize them adequately in a few sentences.

— Otto de Jeux,
Love's Disinherited, 1893

For everyone who became an activist.
And for everyone who will.

Contents

▼

Acknowledgements

▼

Sasha Alyson and Richard Labonté first proposed this biography; it would never have reached completion without their patience, encouragement, and support.

Many others deserve my sincere thanks. They include: William Alexander, Robert Balzer, Albert Bell, Phyllis Bennis, Kate Hay Berman, Ruth Bernhard, Allan Bérubé, Betty Berzon, Martin Block, Joan Blood, Phillip Blood, Blue Sky Butterfly (Walter Blumoff), Joe Breyak, Peggy Hay Breyak, Peter Brocco, James Burford, Jean Hay Burke, John Burnside, Joey Cain, John Cage, Tracy Cave, John Ciddio, Kay McTernan Cole, Craig Collins, David Cohen, Josie Cottogio, Katherine Davenport, Tom Dickerson, Dimid, Ben Dobbs, Sandy Dwyer, Alan Eichler, Arthur Evans, Harry Frazier, Elizabeth Freeman, Fritz Frurip, Rudi Gernreich, Sandra Gladstone, Al Gordon, Eric Gordon, Helen Johnson Gorog, Lacie Gorog, James Gruber, Pat Gutierrez, Manly P. Hall, David Hawkins, Jack Hay, Jean Hay, Dorothy Healey, Tom Heskette, Bill Hill, Evelyn Hooker, Luke Johnson, Jorn Kamgren, Jonathan Ned Katz, Walter Keller, Jim Kepner, Morris Kight, Chris Kilbourne, Ronald Kirk, Reginald Leborg, Dorr Legg, Gene London, Alejandro Lopez, Phyllis Lyon, Del Martin, Lin Maslow, Bob McNee, John McTernan, Harnish Mearns, Alma Meier, Joan Mocine, Mary Mocine, Jim Morrow, Hannah Hay Muldaven, Irv Niemy, Chaz Nol, Alan Page, Frank Pestana, Stanton Price, Shane Que-Hee, Angus J. Ray, Silvia Richards, Ben Rinaldo, Martha Rinaldo, Florence Robbins, Earl Robinson, Bradley Rose, Charles Rowland, Sai (David Liner), Pete Seeger, Al Sherman, Michael Shibley, Dan Siminoski, Joel Singer, William Lonon Smith, Konrad Stevens, William Stewart, Mark Thompson, Dale Treleven, Jacques Vandemborghe, Frans Von Rossum, Mitch Walker, Donald Wheeldin, Walter Williams, Raven Wolfdancer, and Martin Worman.

For providing information related to Hay's background, thanks are due to Sarah Cooper and Mary Tyler of the Southern California Library for Social Research, and to Sandra Archer and the cheerful staff of the Academy of Motion Picture Arts and Sciences Library. James Kepner's International Gay and Lesbian Archives contain many original documents related to Hay and the Mattachine Society; special thanks to Kepner for allowing me to examine his personal correspondence with Hay and his unpublished historical writing. Thanks also to James Broughton for kindly allowing me to preview a section of his unpublished autobiography, and to Gerard Koskovich for sharing an unpublished interview with Hay and for information about Stanford in the 1930s. Rudi Gernreich preserved his notebook of early Mattachine Society meetings, and Oreste Pucciani allowed me to study it. Thanks also to Dr. Robert Christianson, Dorothy Doyle, Hal Fishman, Mike Furmanovsky, Sue-Ellen Jacobs, Don Kilhefner, Dorr Legg, Freddie Paine, Miriam Sherman, and Don Slater. Will Roscoe spent entire days photocopying notes from his personal archives; for that and many hours of manuscript review and suggestions, I am deeply indebted. For sharing with me her notes and original source material on Will Geer, as well as her thesis on him, special thanks to Sally O. Norton.

This book absorbed hours of editing time. For their sound suggestions and support, thanks to Sasha Alyson, John Burnside, Craig Collins, Dorothy Doyle, Anthony Duignan-Cabrera, Fritz Frurip, Mike Furman-ovsky, Bill Hill, Henry Holmes, Sue-Ellen Jacobs, Gerard Koskovich, Richard Labonté, Craig Lee, Joel Lorimer, Jim McGary, Jim Morrow, Carter Rose, Brad Rose, Peter Sigal, Faygele Singer, Bob Stacey, Mark Thompson, Joyce Timmons, Emily Timmons, Neal Twyford, Mickey Wheatley, and Walter Williams.

For sharp wits I often feared dulling through overuse, Devon Clayton, Bill Fishman, Jim Kepner, and the incomparable William Moritz have my sincerest gratitude. Those four taught me as much about friendship as about writing.

Thanks for sustaining encouragement to those mentioned above, as well as to my friends from the Radical Faeries, A Different Light Bookstore, and to gay community writers; to my mother, Joyce Timmons, who took me to my first protest in a stroller and has grown nearly as much as I have; to John Callahan, Bill Capobianco, John Fleck, Felidae Nemo, and Adrian Rodriguez, impeccable friends; and to Carter Rose, who showed me, finally, the Eros of my ways.

Introduction

▼

I met him at a Radical Faerie gathering in the spring of 1980. He cut a dramatic figure, his tall frame draped in a pale shawl and topped by a broad-brimmed black hat that might have belonged on a Quaker elder. Harry Hay spoke dramatically, too, about maximizing the differences between gays and straights instead of downplaying them. *Maximizing* differences? This was utterly contrary to the conventional wisdom — and completely intriguing.

His large hands grasped both of mine when I approached later to say how honored I was to meet him. Gay men who, like me, have been aware of him for years, shower Hay with these earnest introductions. But on each occasion his dome-like brow furrows with concentration, and he holds the hands or shoulders of the individual, staring fixedly into their eyes. An intense personal bond is quickly cast, into which Hay often injects a challenging statement. In my case — as a college junior approaching an offbeat intellectual nearing seventy — he said, "You know, you probably wouldn't be talking to me at all if we were back in *their* world, at some gay bar. Remember that when we go back." With only the wilderness and gentle gay men around us, and given my uncertainties about what life held after school, his words struck deep.

To tease him and perhaps to break the poignance of the moment, I snatched his hat and put it on. People began to chuckle; in a micro-drama, the twinkie had stolen the crown of the father of gay liberation, as Harry Hay has come to be known. Not missing a beat — or the attention of the audience — he smiled. "That's my founder-of-the-movement hat. You may wear it, but be careful with it. I'm not through with it." The laughter of the Faeries deepened, with Harry adding his baritone chuckle. Harry often says that gays have a special talent for affectionate mockery, and we all enjoyed the moment.

Little did I imagine that seven years later I would be writing his biography. It was an intense project, which created a deep and sometimes explosive relationship. Here's an example: After more than a year of intimate interviews and plans for the book, we got into a scrap about homophobia in the Communist Party. He got upset seemingly because, though he had suffered prejudice at the hands of his former C.P. comrades, his loyalty to their shared ideals survived. With great emotion and conviction, he declared that "homophobia" was not a word, or even a concept, at the time of his troubles. When I failed to appreciate this, he stood up from his kitchen table, shot me a withering glance, and growled, "I'm not sure we are able to communicate at all!"

I saw a year's research crumbling over what seemed a semantic quibble — or a test of my fortitude. Calculating, I scolded him. "Perhaps it'll take some work before I can talk about this issue without offending you. But I thought you invited me over today to begin that process, *and* that we'd do it politely."

I had miscalculated. Harry drew himself up to his full height of six-feet-three, his intense anger setting in motion the earring by his white mutton-chop sideburn. Flinging his index finger toward the front door of his rose-colored, book-lined cottage, he proclaimed, "You are *un*invited!"

We quickly made up — and resolved the problem — but I learned the contradictions of a committed life. Harry is an anti-patriarchal patriarch, a future-looking visionary ruled by nineteenth-century manners and ethics. The mix of Communism and homosexuality may be his most volatile contradiction, and it is at the core of his existence. The skills for organizing and belief in revolutionary change he acquired during his years in the Communist Party USA fostered Hay's founding in 1950 of the Mattachine Society, the underground organization acknowledged by historians as the starting point of the modern gay movement.

That organization was so effectively underground that Harry Hay, a social reformer of tremendous and long-reaching impact, was for many years scarcely known. This is partly by design; in spite of his flamboyant character, he and his gay compatriots vowed to remain anonymous. The extreme repression that homosexuals faced then made such tactics necessary. The year 1948, when Hay first attempted to organize gays, was "a very painful time for homosexuals," said Quincy Troupe, poet and friend of James Baldwin. Troupe emphasized, "You weren't just in the closet, you were in the basement. Under the basement floor."

Hay's radical politics and equally radical sexuality contributed to his remaining buried for decades. Though multitalented and gifted with a magnetic personality, he remained obscure while a number of his friends became famous.

In the seventies and eighties, gay historians delightedly "discovered" Hay and told the tale of his founding of the American gay movement. Still, most of his story, which neither began nor ended in the fifties, has not been told. In his youth he protested fascism and agitated for trade unions, first on instinct, then as a dedicated member of the CPUSA. Even in that context, Hay obsessively studied and decoded folk music as a language of the oppressed, to be used against the oppressors, and quietly discerned shreds of gay history as well by "reading between the lines" of standard texts. Through the sixties, seventies, and eighties, his progressive instincts asserted themselves in the Traditional Indian movement, the Gay Liberation Front, and more campaigns leading up to Jesse Jackson's Rainbow Coalition.

Since his values are group-oriented, Hay himself has never ballyhooed his status. He prefers to be thought of as a person of ideas rather than credentials, and sees himself as a figure of today rather than a relic of yesterday. Further, he understands that the gay movement is constantly being *lived,* no matter who founded it. But his status as the founder of the modern gay movement is an inspiring highlight of a fascinating life. His friend Jim Kepner explained that it took determination and guts to create that breakthrough: "Many people thought about gay organizing, but were never able to sustain the interest of others. It was like getting a periodic fever," he explained. "Sooner or later, you got better."

The trouble with Harry Hay was his refusal to adapt to a reality he found unacceptable. He made trouble for anti-gay attitudes in an era when most homosexuals bore, according to Allen Ginsberg, "that wounded look." It took quite a person to do what Harry did. I wanted to know what kind.

"Harry is an enthusiast," said his friend Earl Robinson, the well-known composer who, along with Pete Seeger, worked with Harry in the forties. Robinson also called Harry a "behind-the-scenes person"; others have called him a dreamer, an administrator, a brainstormer, a daredevil, and, most frequently, a visionary. That intense personality was key to Harry's accomplishments. Robinson continued, "I can see his face light up about things I wouldn't get so excited about — a bit of historical information, or an action of Pete's at a hootenanny. I remember Harry's manner of putting his whole self into whatever he was excited about at the time. There was a sense that you *had* to listen to this man."

The good fortune of having a living biographical subject demanded that I listen to Harry a lot. Over a period of nearly three years I recorded almost sixty hours of tape, took seventeen tablets of notes, sorted through approximately three filing cabinets of personal papers, and talked with him on a weekly basis for countless hours. I interviewed more than fifty of his associates, including his children, siblings, former lovers, friends, adversaries, political comrades, and all but one of his surviving Mattachine Society co-founders.

The bulk of material in this biography is from original sources, though I also did considerable library research; all sources are documented for the use of the future researchers that Hay and the gay movement deserve. It should be noted that a number of people who knew Hay declined to be interviewed, either because of his Communist background or because of his homosexuality. Noteworthy in another way is that Hay's memory checks out with great detail and accuracy. Since, when Hay recounts his memories, tenses frequently shift between past and present, in this text, with his approval, tenses have been aligned for the sake of consistency and clarity.

Also adjusted, though in this case against his wishes, is Hay's capitalization of terms denoting gay people. In writings as early as the late 1940s, Hay capitalized every term he used in his activism: *Androgyne, Homosexual, Homophile,* even *Minority.* This was Hay's way of promoting respect for gays, and is a campaign that follows the paths of Jews and Chicanos who also fought the lower-case syndrome. The challenge this poses to the rules of grammar and to the shifting nature of conventional usage, Hay argues, is insignificant next to the physical reminder of self-affirmation.

Hay insisted that I see the context of gay life as he lived it. He regularly challenged me to understand the enormous changes in gay culture since his first awareness of it in the 1920s. His distress over my usage of the contemporary word "homophobia" is one example. Another time, early in the research, I asked about gay lifestyles in the thirties. Harry rolled his eyes and groaned, "Honey, we didn't *have* 'lifestyles' in the thirties."

Various readers may be challenged by parts of this biography. One day when glancing at the obituary of a classical musician who had lived in Los Angeles, Harry sighed and said, "He was *so* handsome." When I asked if he knew the man, Harry screwed up his face, obviously searching for words, and finally said, "I didn't know him well. But I knew him often." Some nongay readers have expressed puzzlement over the sexual abundance that was a hallmark of Hay's youth, especially in contrast to his deeply sentimental emotions. Gay readers, on the other hand, understand. In many instances, I have reported rather than analyzed.

Harry Hay is determined to express himself on his own terms. Given that and his imaginative and far-reaching mind, Harry sometimes wandered far astray from a narrative sequence, often with seeming delight.

Whenever his tangents got long and, for my purposes, pointless, I would wait for him to take a breath (often an amazing period) and slip in a polite "May I ask a question?"

His reflex answer, always with a smile: "You can try."

In the end, and indeed throughout the process, the effort has been worthwhile. Beyond his driven and effective activism, Harry Hay deserves recognition and study as an innovator and potent thinker on the fronts of gay politics, historical research, philosophy, and spirituality. He has labored for forty years to probe the depth and breadth of the culture of gays as "a separate people" and to create a theory for the existence and nature of gay people. Mark Thompson, editor of *Gay Spirit, Myth and Meaning,* credits Hay with forming the only "unified theory" of gayness.

There is much of Harry's busy, complex life that I was not able to cover or definitively assess in this book. Only time will tell if his founding contributions to the Radical Faeries or his writings on the relationship of "gay consciousness" to humanity will outshine his work in the fifties. Many of his achievements, theories, and opinions —and opinions are something Harry is never without — await another examination; after all, he has not stopped moving, thinking, or agitating.

His legacy, however, is clear. As well as serving as its father figure, Hay has given the once-faceless gay populace a series of fabulous mascots: the masked Mattachines; the mocking Fool, who requires wit to play his part; and the luminous Faerie, who does good deeds at whim. Hay's own symbol, which often guides his actions with uncanny effectiveness, is the benevolent Troublemaker. Like the sacred Contrary of Native American societies, the Troublemaker upsets the order of things, shows new possibilities, pushes the agenda. And in so doing, he is a balancing force for the order of life.

Behind Harry's achievements of stirring things up, blazing trails, and calling forth movements, there is a kind of life story that is rarely told — a gay life story. If everything doesn't at first appear to be there, do what Harry does: Read between the lines.

THE TROUBLE WITH HARRY HAY

·1·

From the best of families

Our beginnings cannot know our ends.
— T.S. Eliot

He was born a sissy, with a delicately imperious streak that surfaced when he was just two.

That was in 1914. Harry Hay, his ten-week-old sister, and mother Margaret lived in Worthing, his birthplace on the South Coast of England. One fine spring day, Miss May Pittock, the nanny, was preparing to take the children out.

"My new sister was already bonneted, frocked, and bundled into the big, luxurious pram that stood in the vestibule waiting to be wheeled out into the bright afternoon sun," Hay recalled the story as it had been told to him. "My lovely young mother, then twenty-six, stood nearby, wearing a light blue, loosely fitting peignoir of heavy Chinese silk. Soon she would be dressing to receive visitors for afternoon tea. They were all waiting for me to come downstairs, either to ride in the pram also or to walk beside it, holding nanny's hand."

Little Harry, thus nicknamed to distinguish him from his father, appeared on the landing. He was handsomely dressed in a white twill coat with collar, white trousers and shoes, and a white linen hat that covered his soft curls. He would not, however, come down the stairs.

"Where my gubs?" the child demanded.

Miss Pittock protested that she had looked high and low for the little gray suede buttoned gloves but had not found them. She glanced anxiously at Harry's mother.

"It will be all right, dear, to go without them today," Margaret said, offering reason to her firstborn. "It's a lovely afternoon, and quite warm."

"I not go out," he announced firmly, "'out my gubs."

As an old man, Harry was amused at his early willfulness. "I knew I was causing an immense fluster. Nanny couldn't leave my sister, now wheeled out into the garden. Mother was behind schedule in dressing herself and arranging her hair. The downstairs maid was already polishing the service for today's tea-time. It was the upstairs maid's afternoon off."

In the end, the cook had to go up and find Harry's gloves.

No one in 1914 could have suspected that this patrician will would throw its force behind many of the century's most radical causes. But for Harry Hay, propriety was always something he himself defined. His founding of the American gay movement, a thing that was nearly inconceivable for the first half of his life, was his most astonishing achievement. He called that movement the product of "total allegiance to high purposes, tenacity of vision, irrevocable resolve, and above all else, audacity."

What shaped the singular and audacious character of Harry Hay ran deep and started early. He often spoke of his gay society as his primary family, but his blood relations mattered greatly to him. He was fond of retelling their stories to illustrate the qualities he inherited and admired, and also to preserve their memories. Harry became the family historian of his generation, but he was selective about his heritage; what Harry consciously laid claim to was as important to him as anything in the genes.

The traditions of the Scottish Highlanders were his preferred heritage. They were individualistic and egalitarian, yet devoted to their clans. The Highlanders were noted for socially progressive values and emphasized education for all, operated by consensus, and tended to split from authority over moral issues. The Hay family crest showed three shields and three ravens, topped by an oxbow, because a millenium before a Highland ancestor and his three sons had played a major role in routing invading Danes by swinging the oxbow and fighting with ploughshares and scythes. In gratitude for their valor, each son was granted as much land as a crow could fly over in a day. "We are the descendants of the old man and his sons," Harry's father told him. The Hays did not, however, identify with the motto on their crest, "Serva Jugum," which means "To Serve the Yoke."

Harry's grandfather, William Hay, had a twin brother who became a prosperous farmer, but William made an exception of himself and studied law at the University of Edinburgh. After a few years as an apprentice barrister, however, he became greatly dissatisfied. According to family legend, William discovered that the purpose of being a lawyer was "not to uphold the majesty of the law but to help the wicked man discover how far he could go." He wanted no part of it, and as soon as possible, he sold his position in the law office and left for New Zealand, then a British colony. Over six feet tall and with a beard and long hair he never cut after leaving Scotland, Grandfather Hay was suited for the farming and sheep-ranching this frontier offered. Grandfather Hay's moral stubbornness in forfeiting his profession, and his independence at finding a new livelihood, made him Harry's favorite ancestor.

Within three years of arriving in New Zealand, he married Helen MacDonald, another Scottish emigré. Her descendants quietly referred to her as the love child of a farm servant and a woman promised in marriage to a man twice her age. This illegitimate daughter became a devout Christian, and severely respectable. She always dressed in black, and wore only simple jewelry if any at all. At four-feet-seven, she was dwarfed by her huge husband. They addressed each other only with the formal "Mr. Hay" and "Mrs. Hay," and taught their only daughter never to raise her eyes to a man. Harry's niece Jean Hay, the family historian of the modern generation, noted that this emotional chill persisted. "The whole family, going back to Harry's grandparents in New Zealand, seems to have been rigid, cold, unable to express basic love and affection — let alone sexuality," she said. By modern standards, she perceived the family as "wounded." She explained, "I don't think any of them grew up with the minimum of self-confidence that comes from having loving, accepting parents." In a story Harry wrote in 1937 about a Hay family reunion, he himself observed a family whose tenderness was restrained by "tight leashes around their hearts."

Helen MacDonald Hay's stern propriety may have been exacerbated by her membership in a strict religious sect, the Plymouth Brethren, a mid–nineteenth century Anabaptist group related to the Mennonites, and known for their fervent evangelism and stance of non-resistance to per-secution. That Harry Hay, who was often described as "evangelistic" in his gay organizing, had a missionary grandmother would not surprise many of his friends.

The Hays flourished in New Zealand. They had one daughter and seven sons, the eldest of whom was Harry's father, born in 1869. In 1879 they decided to go to America, perhaps, as Harry's Aunt Alice told him, because Helen MacDonald had always dreamed of having an orange grove in California, or perhaps, as her New Zealand descendants indicate, because the Plymouth Brethren planned to establish a settlement in California. Whatever the reason, Harry's grandfather bought a parcel of land in California sight unseen, on which they planned to build a cattle ranch. But when they arrived, they found that they had been swindled; the California land was in Baja California, Mexico, a region long stricken by drought. Suddenly poor, the family moved to the Los Angeles area where they rented a dairy near Long Beach.

Six years later, in 1885, Grandfather Hay bought a cattle ranch in Hernandez, in a beautiful valley in the San Benito Mountains of central California. There he devised a practical plan to ensure the fortunes of his sons. He took each, one at a time, into a three-year partnership. The young man would learn everything his father knew about farming and ranching. Each brother went through this process except for the third youngest, James, who ran away to sea, and Harry's father, Henry, who aspired to education and the professional classes. He studied mining engineering at the University of California at Berkeley, quickly prospered, and ultimately bought his mother her orange grove. "He was ambitious to fulfill her dream," recalled Harry. "He was her boy. He was her Henry."

Harry is a diminutive of Henry, and the Hay family tradition held that the name means "mother's steward." (Its original German meaning is "steward of the estate.") The son named Henry, to the Hays, was the spokesman for the family matriarch. Harry's father took the role seriously and protected his mother's interests. Harry himself shepherded his own mother's affairs, and publicly he carried that meaning a step further, speaking for the disenfranchised as a progressive. Eventually, Harry applied the role to all gay people, saying they were stewards of the great Mother Earth.

Harry's mother's side of the family, the Nealls, were a good match for the roving Hays. The Nealls also were strong-willed, and many achieved social distinction. Although they had lived in the United States longer, they moved often, and their web of movements and sagas are slightly dizzying. Margaret Neall was born at Fort Bowie, Arizona Territory, in 1886, when her father, a military man, was stationed there. But her pedigree was refined, and her family included Corcorans (of Washington's Corcoran Gallery of Art), Anna Wendell (an aunt of Oliver Wendell Holmes), and the Van Rensselaer family, who were among the first land-granted Dutch "patroons" of New York. Margaret's stuffy Aunt Kitty researched a genealogy to show that the family had no interracial "shadow" in its background and thoroughly documented generations of social prominence.

Harry was often compared, in both face and temperament, to his maternal great-grandfather, General James Allen Hardie, who was appointed by President Martin Van Buren to West Point Military Academy.

There his classmates included Ulysses S. Grant and William Stärke Rose-crans. Hardie was a sensitive, scholarly man who became a breveted Civil War officer, but his highest honor was his appointment by President Abraham Lincoln to be Secretary of War during the temporary absence of Edward Stanton in 1863. After his death, the government published a biography commemorating Hardie's military career.

Harry rebelled, however, against Hardie's bloody politics. Among his many military campaigns, Hardie served as an officer in Colonel George Wright's war against the Spokane Indians in 1857, and Hardie introduced the newly invented long-range rifle in the "highly successful" slaughter. His son, Francis, then carried the Third Cavalry flag at the notorious massacre of Indians at Wounded Knee. This "shadow" in his family background haunted Harry, and perhaps partly in compensation, he cultivated a lifelong relationship with Native Americans.

Harry's grandfather, John Mitchell Neall, married General Hardie's daughter. He was also a West Point graduate and served as a cavalry lieutenant, first at Fort Davis, then at Fort Bowie. Neall became a captain of the Fourth Cavalry at the San Francisco Presidio, but abandoned his military career to teach mathematics and mining engineering at the University of Nevada. No one in the family understood the reason for the change, but, as with Grandfather Hay who quit the bar, this revolt against the establishment impressed Harry. He suspected a connection with Neall's service at Ft. Bowie as one of the young officers sent to negotiate the surrender of the Apache warrior Geronimo. The commanding officer in this action, General George Crook, had nearly negotiated a successful arrangement when the jingoistic press called for his sudden replacement by the ambitious General Nelson A. Miles, who broke all promises and subdued Geronimo by force.

When the sixteen-year-old Harry wrote his Grandfather Neall in 1928 to request a recommendation for appointment to West Point, he received a furious reply. "Grandfather said he would see to it, if he possibly could, that no blood of his ever went to that school again. He said that at one point the U.S. Army stood for honor and dignity, but as far as he was concerned it had become a sink of corruption." Margaret was shocked; she had known that her father wanted out of the military years before he made his final severance, but she had never known why. Neall's anger had simmered long and quietly.

Harry's parents were brought together by mining engineering. At the turn of the century, that profession was booming as minerals and metals were discovered around the globe. Grandfather Neall and Big Harry, along with scores of other mining engineers, heard the call of British financier and colonist Cecil Rhodes in South Africa. Rhodes, then at the end of his long career, headed the largest mining operation in the world, encompassing diamonds as well as gold. Though associated with enlightened scholarship, Rhodes had the Western-supremacist ambition of uniting the English-speaking countries of the world in domination over the rest. "Equal rights for all civilized men" was his motto, and he was known to be ruthless in business and politics.

Big Harry was intelligent, capable, and strikingly handsome. These qualities may have encouraged his bachelorhood until age forty-two. His boss Rhodes never married and was known for his love of decorating and antiques — and for handsome male employees. When Harry told his mother about his own homosexuality in 1951, and speculated how shocked his father would have been over it, she replied, "Your father knew Cecil Rhodes," and never again referred to homosexuality.

When Big Harry joined Rhodes's employ, he quickly became a member of the inner circle, sporting with the American men in Johannesburg and even winning a shooting trophy. In a short time, he was named manager of the Witwatersrand Deep, the mine that ultimately produced half the world's gold. This paid so well that he made yearly visits by steamship to his parents in Southern California during which he bought the house with the orange grove for his mother and made a series of real estate investments for himself. To be at the center of the international market, he also established an office in London at 7 Old Jewry Road, which he shared with, among other American mining engineers, Herbert Hoover. Their social acquaintance helped establish both Henry and Margaret as lifelong Republicans.

Harry often described his father in physical terms: stone-faced, ham-handed, and massive of body. Indeed, Big Harry's education and professional success did not disguise his ranch rearing, and he stayed earthy and athletic well into his forties. Success suited him. The eldest son of farmers, now a rising executive, he developed a commanding, authoritarian air. Harry always remembered his father roaring and stamping about, and described him in a short story as "tyrannical" and "filled with heaven-inherited principles and wisdom." His lordly demeanor intimidated relatives and especially cowed his immediate family. Big Harry's relationships with all three of his children were distant, and with both of his sons they were downright chilly. An especially deep hostility eventually developed between Harry and his father, though they shared many qualities, including managerial prowess, iron will, and self-reliance. Despite his rebellion against the class of his parents, their status was not lost on him; Harry knew, as his own children would know, that it "meant something" to be a Hay.

Though in her later years she acquired the pinched face of a pioneer woman, young Margaret Neall was admired as one of the beauties of the American colony in Johannesburg. A local painter became infatuated with her and, as the social custom of "good families" dictated, was unable to ask Margaret to sit for him, so he painted her life-size portrait from memory. Margaret's strict mother also forbade singing lessons, though her daughter had a three-and-a-half-octave vocal range. By the time she was a debutante, however, Margaret was allowed to take piano lessons and to sing at "home entertainments" in private drawing rooms. She was cultured and could be a lively conversationalist, refinements she passed on to Harry.

After approximately ten years in South Africa, Big Harry set his sights on Margaret Neall at the formal dances, lawn tennis, and similar social occasions sponsored by the Martha Washington Club for American women in South Africa. Few stories of their courtship survive, save that Margaret's parents disapproved; there was a seventeen-year age difference between the couple, and Hay was not Catholic. They may have also worried that despite his already accumulated riches, the demanding life of the ambitious, 42-year-old man would be taxing to whomever he married. In fact, he had just been offered the job of opening new gold mines in the uncolonized district of Tarkwa in the Gold Coast. But Margaret knew her own mind and was herself ambitious. Her military family had been genteel but never affluent, and when the handsome, wealthy man proposed, she accepted. As part of the arrangement, Big Harry converted to Catholicism and agreed that any children would be raised in the Catholic Church.

They married in Johannesburg on April 29, 1911, and set sail on an extravagant honeymoon. In Madeira, the newlyweds bought linens and lace, and in Paris and London they attended the opera. On the final leg of their tour, a pilgrimage to the Hays' ancestral Scottish Highlands, they were joined by the groom's sister, Alice, and their father. Henry had sent them passage from California, so they could meet his bride. After visiting the old-country relatives, Big Harry and Margaret ventured north to the Trossachs, the part of the Highlands that Sir Walter Scott dubbed "peculiarly adapted to poetry." Margaret particularly wanted to visit these romantic heathered lands, and it was there that Harry was conceived.

Before leaving Europe to commence their new life in the wilderness of Tarkwa, where they would be the first white people, the new Mrs. Henry

Hay faced a test: She needed to plan and order all the necessary supplies for her isolated household. The white managers would expect every European accoutrément, and it would be a full year before she had another chance to purchase anything she forgot. She packed what "essentials" she had acquired on her honeymoon, including three sets of silver candelabra, Royal Doulton china, Steuben crystal, and a Gorham silver service for sixteen. From Fortnum and Mason she then ordered an entire boatload of supplies, including linens, clothing — and enough food for three meals a day plus the formal dinner parties that would be held for the white managers at least once a week for a year, each including the proverbial soup to nuts, with caviar, anchovies, champagne, second wines, dessert wines, and sweets! She interviewed and hired English servants and bought a houseful of furniture. Harry always thought that the calm efficiency with which Margaret collected and transported this ménage was her initiation into "maintaining empire" by bringing the artifacts and practices of culture to the outskirts of civilization, a lifelong mission that lasted all the way to her final outpost in the provincial town of Los Angeles.

The harbor at Tarkwa was too shallow for a barge to come closer to shore than one hundred yards, so Big Harry and Margaret, along with their boatload of goods, came ashore on the backs of Africans, Big Harry on the shoulders of a young African man, Margaret in a rig known as a "Mammy Chair," which was carried by several men. With the exception of white neighbors, the Hays wanted for nothing. A symbol of their privilege was the piano Margaret brought to the jungle. It was not just any piano. Since the tropical climate would warp wood, she had, back in London, commissioned a piano made entirely of metal. Big Harry arranged for an electric generator to constantly burn a light inside it to keep the felt on the hammers free from mildew.

During more than seven months of her pregnancy with Harry, Margaret worked, entertained, and toiled to help establish the settlement. But since Tarkwa had no medical facilities and Accra, the largest city in the colony, offered little improvement, she set sail in March to give birth in the safety and comfort of England. Henry was unable to leave his work, but his office in London arranged for the rental of Colwell, a large Tudor-style house in Worthing, an exclusive seaside resort not far from London and close to Brighton. There, on Easter Sunday, April 7, 1912, Henry Hay, Jr., was born.

Harry, as the new arrival came to be called, was reared in the shadow of the Victorian and Edwardian worlds. With her husband on intermittent short visits home and an English nanny to look after Harry, his mother spent the three happiest years of her life in the heart of polite Edwardian society. During her weekend visits at the elegant English country manors to which she was invited, Margaret was frequently asked to sing, and her voice always made her popular. With the baby in the nanny's charge, an afternoon's train ride brought Margaret to the opera, the theater, and the fulfillment of all of her dreams — she attended every performance of the famous coloratura contralto Clara Butt, whose voice so resembled Margaret's own. She could stay the weekend in a hotel and be back in Worthing to make sure the staff of seven had instructions for the following week. She considered that time in England to be the peak of civilization, and adopted it for her own. The writer Philippe Jullian characterized Edwardians as valuing nothing more than their comfort and discreetly ignoring each other's indiscretions, which may account for Margaret's quiet acceptance of her son's unorthodox life.

The Hays' son grew quickly. His characteristic large forehead and deep eyes were already evident in a photographic portrait taken at age six weeks. Frequent snapshots and formal sittings documented his rapid growth for his father in Africa. Baby Harry had an unusual expressiveness in his broad face, with hints of knowledge and opinions already formed. One photograph taken on the beach in Worthing shows the toddler confidently holding the hands of two older, passive-looking children. Little Harry is clearly in control.

As the Tarkwa mine became established and began to run smoothly, Big Harry was approached by the Guggenheim family's Anaconda Company and offered a high management position in the copper mine at Chuquicamata in the Andes of northern Chile. He went to New York to sign the contract, then proceeded straight to the Andes, leaving his wife to continue her Edwardian idyll — and her second pregnancy. In February of 1914, Harry was given a sister, named Margaret Caroline but always known as Peggy. Margaret rented a different house in Worthing called Placilla, which had more rooms as well as a garden for the children.

When the Great War broke out that August, Big Harry wired his family to join him in Chile. For six weeks, Margaret once again crated possessions and ordered provisions. Though practiced at moving, she found it particularly hard to leave England. Their departure was delayed for two weeks by submarine blockades and air raids. Decades later, Harry still remembered the scream of the sirens.

Another clear memory of his English infancy was downright lustful — or so he slyly insisted at many tellings. It took place on an afternoon when May Pittock, the nanny, took Harry to Waterloo Bridge, which all the soldiers crossed on their way to Victoria Station en route to the battlefields of France. Miss Pittock joined the crush of British patriots waving good-bye to the young men. Harry clearly remembered himself as scarcely more than knee-high, and earnestly recalled that while "Nanny looked into the faces, I looked into the crotches. Scores passed by. I was fascinated. I remember their legs, with the puttees wrapped from their knees to their ankles. I remember the belts, and the water bottle bouncing at the hip, and long knives, perhaps bayonets. Lots of clank and dust. And that mystery behind the baggy pants."

▽

Margaret told her children that they caught the last American transport ship out of Great Britain. It was a dramatic trip. German U-boats patrolled the Atlantic, and though all torpedo attacks were supposed to be preceded by a ten-minute warning so that women and children could board lifeboats, the passengers knew that some ships had already been sunk without such warnings. To prepare for the worst, Margaret arranged two large baskets, one for each of her babies. One half of each basket was packed with food, clothing, and medicine; the other half held bedding and the child. Margaret and Miss Pittock slept fitfully in deck chairs, their hands always near the basket handles. The calculated zig-zag course and the regular precaution-ary cutting of the engines extended the voyage from its normal three weeks to six. When their ship docked for two days at Barbados, Margaret noticed that it listed severely to one side. She must have felt elated with relief when they neared South American shores.

The new country filled Little Harry with fantastic sights and sounds. At Guayaquil, the boat went upriver into the jungles of Ecuador, reverberent with screams of monkeys and birds. In the pallid ocean at Callao, Peru, he saw beautifully hued Portuguese men-of-war. At Antofagasta, Chile, near their new home, the ceilings of their hotel were higher than any he had ever seen and were decorated with elaborate iron filigrees. From the east window of their hotel room, Harry saw two high volcanoes, one pouring forth smoke.

The twin volcanoes were also visible from the arid mountain where his father had been set up in a one-story house. Only one other house was higher up the slope, that of Fred Hellmann, the general manager of the three Guggenheim mines in the area. Hellmann and Hay had already worked together at the Witwatersrand mine in South Africa, and their wives had been socially close there. The Andean job involved adding an underground mine to the existing open pit, and Hay had mastered underground mining in Africa. Because of the war, the price of copper had skyrocketed, so the Chile Exploration Company, a subsidiary of Anaconda, paid Big Harry a yearly salary of $50,000 — a staggering sum in 1914.

Chuquicamata, or "Chuqui," as the family would always refer to it, sits on a dusty slope 11,500 feet in the Andes, in the Atacama desert region of northern Chile. The dry, rainless climate eliminated the need for Margaret's metal piano to have a light burning in it; instead, a dish of water now kept the felt from turning to dust. A shantytown for the miners spilled down a fold of the mountain, out of sight of the executives' houses at the top. There was a general store and a large hospital, and managers could play tennis on a red clay court, where they used weighted tennis balls to counteract the effects of the thin atmosphere. At the foot of the slope, also out of view, lay the mine itself. Railroad cars, some on elevated trestles, brought the ore to a noisy crusher, then to a tremendous smelter.

The Hays' house was much smaller than their previous homes — and was made of tin. Its great luxury, two four-foot by two-foot strips of lawn at either side of the front door, had to be kept green by buckets of water hand-carried up the arid mountain. The Hellmanns' home conspicuously outdid all others; it was made of brick and centered around a fifteen-foot square of grass contained in an atrium stocked with tropical birds. This oasis became the playground of the executives' children.

Harry's recollections of his early surroundings suggest a surreal capsule of Edwardian manners in the mountaintop desert. Margaret even brought an artificial Christmas tree, under which she arranged the presents bought the previous summer in England. The residents of this small colony had weekly dancing or bridge parties, and Harry remembered watching couples waltzing by candlelight when he was supposed to be in bed. One night, he recalled his mother entering his room to check on his sleep. "Mother, wearing a pink taffeta dress with sparkling stones on the sleeves, looked over my crib. She apparently found me playing with myself and, horrified, cried, 'Dirty, dirty boy!'" After much consternation, she consulted a doctor who prescribed a nighttime restraining device: White gloves were fitted for Little Harry's hands, then taped and pinned to the corners of the bed. He slept thus for four years, long after his family had returned to America, but he learned to play with himself secretly in the daytime. And as soon as the restraints were discontinued, he resumed the practice at night.

Miss Pittock instructed the children to call their parents Mummy and Daddy. All their behavior was strictly taught. "When a nanny brings you up," Harry's sister Peggy explained, "you are expected to know table manners by the time you sit at the table — about age six." Harry was presented to his father for one hour in the afternoons, and he spent little more time than that with his mother. His parents bestowed physical affection only occasionally; he recalled being "kissed at the proper time" by Margaret. On treasured rare occasions, he was allowed to spend an entire morning with her, watching her have breakfast in bed, then play the piano.

Most of Harry's time was spent with Miss Pittock. She taught him French phrases, and during his visits with Margaret, he recited his lesson and she corrected his pronunciation. He also picked up some Spanish, which all of the servants (except May Pittock) spoke. Harry loved to visit Francisco the cook, a Spanish-speaking Chinese man, who made him treats and showed him his braid, normally coiled under a black silk cap. He arranged for Harry to ride the llama of the man who brought produce down from the mountains, which so excited the child that he wanted a llama of his own — until the creature spit a foul-smelling excretion at Miss Pittock.

Talents emerged early in Little Harry. His lifelong affinity for music started almost at birth. In Worthing, Margaret had held him on her lap as she played the piano. In Chile, Harry remembered listening raptly to recorded pieces of music for the first time. At night, his father played opera arias and waltzes on the Edison cylinder phonograph in his room. One was "The Staircase Waltz" from Franz Lehar's *The Count of Luxembourg*. It became a favorite piece throughout Harry's life, partly because he discovered it behind his parents' closed door.

Another piece of music came to him one night in the room he occupied alone. It began with drum beats — faint but clear. He peeked through the covers into the dark; everything was black except for a faint, pale light that sifted through the east window. He could barely discern the silhouettes of the two volcanoes. A shrill flute wrapped around the staccato drum beat, which was backed by low chanting. Then came another sound, a woman's voice that modulated from a low growl to a high, soaring peal. Entranced, he listened to the music till sleep overtook him. The next morning, Francisco explained that the songs had announced ceremonies of the Quechua and Aymara Indians in faraway villages. Harry talked about that singing long after he arrived in America, and thirty years later he would run into similar music under dramatic circumstances.

When Harry was three, he came down with bronchial pneumonia. His mother was terrified; though Chuqui had a hospital, in the era before antibiotics the disease was a feared killer of children. The doctor wrapped

Harry in a mustard plaster from neck to navel for six weeks and he recovered, but his lungs suffered permanent scar-tissue damage. On the doctor's orders, Margaret dressed him in a quilted shirtwaist every winter until he was seven.

May of 1916 saw the completion of the Hay family with the birth of John William, henceforth known as Jack. It also saw labor trouble at the mine. Prior to the First World War, the status of Chilean workers was little better than that of medieval serfs. Chile's harsh land created such tough economic conditions that a large class of day laborers wandered in search of work and sustenance. These desperate nomads, called "Los Rotos" (the Broken Ones), chewed coca leaves to numb their misery. As the mining industry grew, a class of workers developed who gained just enough comfort to lose their numbness. They were influenced by European radical economics, and more recently by news of the Mexican Revolution. Quickly, they realized that their greatest national asset, copper, was being sold cheap to American companies. Popular discontent grew and strike forces gathered at the Chuquicamata mine. Big Harry led the forces that put it down.

One day in mid-June of 1916, while Margaret was still in the hospital with the newborn Jack, Harry's father was inspecting a work site. From an elevated trestle-track nearly a hundred feet above him, a one-ton carload of ore, bound for the great crusher, suddenly fell. He jumped, but his right foot and leg were caught and smashed. Surgeons quickly arrived from Antofagasta and Santiago, but though Big Harry escaped death, he lost his leg below the knee.

Harry understood that something serious had happened and knew that he was to be brave. Nanny took him to visit his mother and baby Jack and, in a different part of the hospital, his father. He recalled only sharp details of the screened veranda that served as a waiting area: people sitting in chairs, visiting quietly, the light from behind casting them in silhouette, like paper cutouts. He recalled having oyster crackers with lunch on the veranda — but he could not recall seeing his parents or his new brother.

Mr. Hay's uncertain condition required that he leave his job at Chuqui and seek further treatment in America. Margaret hurriedly recrated her household, leaving behind the metal piano. The family set sail for Southern California aboard the Grace Line steamship S.S. *Chile*. The captain personally invited Margaret and Harry to tea and extended special sympathy to his little passenger, and when they were invited again, Harry's favorite tea cake was waiting for him, courtesy of the captain. Amenities notwithstanding, bad weather bedeviled the trip, and at the Gulf of Tehuan-tepec a hurricane tore off the gangplank.

Harry's first view of his new home was blurred by fog; the ship had to wait two days in San Pedro Harbor (then just a breakwater) before the weather was clear enough to anchor. There was no dock yet, so while Harry's father, mother, Miss Pittock, and the babies were lowered over the side on a baggage crane, Harry had to climb down a rope ladder into a waiting boat. The ropes had been sturdily knotted, but the swaying terrified him. The ladder swung away from the dull metal side of the ship, and Harry thought he would hit the ship, lose his footing, and fall. He remembered his panic while climbing down the seemingly endless rope ladder, and he also remembered being aware that he must say nothing about it. Already, the four-year-old had learned that he must hide his feelings and rely on his own strength.

·2·

The example

We have been naught, we shall be all.
— Eugene Pottier, "The Internationale"

Big Harry's accident altered the life and plans of the Hay family enormously; Margaret's dreams for Little Harry's private education in Switzerland and the University of Heidelberg evaporated. His spare new circumstances helped to develop the strong intelligence, the will, and the complex personality that would serve Harry as an adult. But in the short run, his greatest challenge was learning to get along with his father, since their time together was now greatly increased.

Although a series of painful operations eventually resulted in the amputation of his right leg at the knee, Big Harry made a remarkable recovery. He insisted on driving a car, which was possible only by manually lifting his top-quality prosthetic leg from the gas pedal to the brake. The Guggenheims offered to retain him as a mining consultant at nearly as high a salary as he had earned in the field, but he bristled at that notion, saying that he would not accept the "half job" of an office-bound bureaucrat.

Upon landing in Long Beach, California, the Hays lived in a rented house for six months, then moved to Tustin, an inland town to the southeast in staid Orange County. Big Harry knew the area; he had visited it on the trip from South Africa when he bought the house and orchard for his mother in the town of Charter Oak. Now he bought himself a large, idyllic house surrounded by twenty acres of orange trees. Harry spent the last of his childhood here. As a six-year-old, he frolicked with chickens and rabbits in their pens and played in a large flower garden, which became a stage for the drama of his imagination. That garden provided the setting for a story about childhood that Harry wrote later, imagining that its giant dahlias could bend down and talk to him and that he could climb up inside them.

One night when he was ill, Harry's parents came into his bedroom to give him medicine. He still slept with his hands tied to the corners of his bed, and he recalled that as his father leaned over the bed, "his thin cotton pajamas parted and I saw his genitals. It was the first time I had ever seen a man's genitals, and I thought they were the most beautiful sight I'd ever seen. And at the same time that this feeling of appreciation filled me, I knew that I must not show any sign of it, to anyone." He referred to this as a "beautiful vision" and as a "knowledge" that he carried with him throughout an increasingly rancorous relationship.

In February, 1919, the family moved to Los Angeles, then a growing town with a population just under half a million. Big Harry bought a large house that still stands at 149 South Kingsley Drive, a wide, quiet street south of Hollywood. Taking up the family tradition he had previously rejected, Big Harry became a farmer. Upon his recuperation, he bought thirty acres on Azusa Avenue in Covina, twenty miles east of L.A. With newly developed citrus stocks from Luther Burbank's Experimental Farms in Northern California, Big Harry began to grow "first-quality" lemons and Valencia oranges, which he sold through the new Sunkist Co-op to the Eastern hotel market.

He also invested in the burgeoning stock market, and continued adding properties to those he had bought in the teens. This real estate included a block of stores in Pasadena, a farm which filled a valley north of Sunset Boulevard (now a priceless tract called Beverly Glen, which Hay sold to the Janss Company for $100,000 in 1920), some large rental houses near Lafayette Park on the outskirts of downtown, and three storefronts on elegant Hollywood Boulevard. The elder Hay did well in his enterprises. As a teenager, Harry typed his father's tax forms, and recalled that in 1927, seventeen months before the stock-market crash, Big Harry was worth almost $750,000.

Despite his ample wealth, Big Harry developed a miserly caution. Never again would he allow money for the luxuries to which the family had grown accustomed in the early years. Many of their fine possessions shipped from Chuqui and Worthing were stalled in wartime shipping delays and because of exorbitant accumulated tariffs, he forfeited them. Though the family never lacked for comfort, Big Harry kept Margaret on a strict budget that curtailed her high social aspirations; though her china had been smashed in a Chilean warehouse, he wouldn't buy her another good set for ten years.

Little Harry was hardest hit by the change in the family fortunes. Big Harry bore down, putting him to work early and making him earn every penny of his spending money. Jack and Peggy were given an allowance, but never Harry. As the eldest, his special responsibilities were held sacred. "I was to be the example," he often recalled, and his behavior was sternly scrutinized. In any argument with his siblings, he would be found at fault, because, as eldest, he was expected to prevent squabbling. And no matter how hard he tried, or how successful his efforts, he never felt that he could please his father. When he was enrolled in Cahuenga Elementary School, Little Harry's precocious intellect and a near-photographic memory landed him in the fourth grade with children three years older than he. Yet his father would complain: "If I made a B in school, it should have been an A. If I made an A, it should have been an A-plus." Those strict standards remained fixed in Harry's mind long after he escaped his father's house and rules. In his youthful roles as student, musician, or ranch hand on the family farm — and later, in his more rebellious roles as bohemian, Communist, or homosexual, Harry conscientiously strove to be a model.

Big Harry's disability aggravated his authoritarianism. The self-made man was unaccustomed to being helpless about anything, and he forced his limits. He even took to the tennis court, but, despite hours of determined practice, he could not force his body to be agile. The more he failed in his physical struggles, the more he turned angrily on his namesake, enforcing a code of perfection with verbal attacks and frequent physical beatings. Harry sometimes said that he lived his life deliberately in opposition to the way his father had lived, and that even his politics were motivated by a "personal hatred" of his father.

Years later, Harry's favorite opera would be Wagner's *Parsifal,* the story of a land made barren by a wounded king who can be healed only when a knight pure of heart goes on a holy quest. Though Harry took little stock in psychology, the wisdom of myths fascinated him, and the tale of heroic redemption in *Parsifal,* for which he would name the inner circle of Mattachine, must have resonated with his own struggle against the wounded patriarch who brought him up.

By the time Harry was eight, his father was taking him to work in the Covina orchard. Though others were hired to do the same work, such labor was expected of Harry and treated as a routine chore. Even the simple tasks of pruning and hoeing brought friction, for Harry was left-handed, a condition his father insisted on correcting. Whenever Big Harry found his son holding an implement in the "wrong" hand, he would whip the boy. Since school officials shared Big Harry's opinion, Little Harry was forced to write with his right hand, though he reverted in adolescence and remained a lifelong southpaw. At home as well as in the orchard, Big Harry inflicted cruel punishments, including such frequent ear-boxings that Harry sustained permanent hearing damage in one ear.

His father's harshness, Harry later suspected, may have been partly due to the fact that "my father began to know what he had spawned — a big sissy." What Harry called "the traits" of flamboyance and sensitivity began showing up as early as the years in Chile, and by the time he was six or seven, he showed a distinct preference for staying indoors and putting on plays and "operas" in which he enlisted his brother, sister, and the cook to act; Harry *always* directed. He later said that his father had "tried to beat the sissy out of me." In any case, distance grew steadily between them, and by the time Harry prepared to leave for college, the few letters his father ever sent him read like business memos.

Margaret, on the other hand, was a fountain of acceptance. Of her children, she loved Harry most, to the point of having what Harry called a "fixation" on him, and her influence, since she survived her husband by almost forty years, was ultimately more extensive. Thus, during his childhood, something of an unspoken struggle ensued between the parents for the soul of Little Harry, with Mr. Hay determined to bring out the macho man and Margaret quietly cultivating the parlor gentleman. She arranged for seven years of piano lessons, beginning when Harry was eight. The teacher told Margaret her son had strong musical aptitude, and Mrs. Hay spent many hours at the piano supervising his practice and singing with him. When he was a teenager, she enrolled him in ballroom dancing lessons, and Harry felt "more comfortable on the dance floor than anywhere else," but when his teacher, Mr. Smart, rhapsodized over young Harry's potential for "fancy dancing" lessons, as ballet was referred to then, Big Harry put an immediate stop to it. Harry sensed the tension between his parents. "Sometimes at the dinner table," he recalled, "Father would start to say something and Mother would shoot him a glance. They had agreed never to argue there."

Harry and his mother had identical tastes. He was the only one of her children who would eat Limburger cheese, shad roe, sweetbreads, and other exotic specialties she favored. She loved him all the more for it, and once when Peggy and Jack were safely out of earshot, Margaret muttered to her favorite son, "Sometimes I wonder where those little peasants came from!" Margaret's aristocratic pretensions tended to surface in times of stress, most noticeably when visiting her cattle-farming in-laws in rural California or Nevada, and the accent she acquired in her years in South Africa and England suddenly starched her speaking.

Two family members aside from his parents were especially significant in young Harry's life. One was his mother's Aunt Kate, a small but independent woman who had been a schoolteacher in Virginia City, Nevada. Having retired, she visited the Hays for long periods at a time, and Harry called her Aunt Kate too. Harry felt closer to her emotionally than he did to either of his parents. He prized her as much for teaching him to read as for being the only person in the house who dared stand up to the strict Republican views of Big Harry.

The other significant relative was Margaret's brother Jack Neall, a dashingly handsome lifelong bachelor who served in the Royal Air Force during World War One. Although he had studied chemistry, Uncle Jack favored a dilettante's life of investments, art, and the company of theater people — in Los Angeles the Belascos, the Pantages, and the Wilkes, all theater owners — as well as the pre-eminent acting family, the Barrymores. Harry always remembered how his Uncle Jack spent half his salary on clothes from Bond Street in London, buying only such high-quality items as ostrich-skin shoes. For extended periods in the twenties, Jack lived with the Hay family, and Harry spent hours looking reverently at his uncle's library and his wardrobe, and absorbing Jack's lectures on music, theater, and art. Harry later pegged him as a "gay snob," but no mention was ever made of his possible sexual proclivities during his lifetime.

Little Harry's intelligence distinguished him early in school. In 1921, he was among the first children tested as gifted. Though Harry favored English and music, and grew close to several teachers in these subjects, he seemed to excel at every academic subject as well as in drama and art. Remembered Jack Hay, "My brother was just very brilliant. Everything he did was outstanding." He sensed these multiple talents burdened Harry: "He was such a genius, he'd just fumble around with it."

Whereas he flourished in the classroom, Harry suffered on the playground. Not only was he bright and therefore labeled an apple polisher, Margaret dressed him in velvet suits with short pants and ruffled collars. These outfits — more suited to a lad in Edwardian England than Los Angeles in the twenties — sealed his doom with the schoolyard bullies, who ordered him to kneel before mud puddles and admit he was a sissy. When he stubbornly refused, they pushed his face in the mud and tore his Irish linen sleeves. When her bruised and bullied son came home, Margaret vaguely counseled him to "find nicer boys to play with." Big Harry said nothing, but one afternoon he brought home a set of boxing gloves, tied them onto the boy's hands, and started to spar.

"My hands went up immediately," Harry recalled, "and Daddy said, 'That's right. Protect your face. And when you get the chance, you try to hit my face.'" This command only bewildered him. "I couldn't. I could not hit my father. I felt immobilized, as though iron bands were squeezed around my head. I couldn't even tell him why I couldn't do it." As his father dodged, thrusted, and insisted Harry hit him, he came close to tears. In exasperation, Big Harry untied the gloves and threw them down; Little Harry had failed this litmus test of manliness. While he reeled from the humiliation, his little brother Jack, a scrapper of a boy who would go on to play college football, dashed down from the porch where he had been watching and eagerly took up the gloves. Harry often cited this incident as an illustration of his belief in an essential "anti-aggression" trait, a difference between gays and straights that transcends sexual expression.

At age nine, in a backyard fort of blankets and tall grass, Harry was initiated into sex play by a twelve-year-old neighbor named Calvin. He told Harry how he secretly got together with some of the other older boys. "Calvin sneered, 'But all they do is jack each other off. I'm going to show you something that's much more interesting than that! Now, you lie here and you put your head here, and I lie here and put my head there and then I'll put it in my mouth and you put mine in your mouth, and then we suck.'

"'What do we do that for?' I asked, and Calvin told me I would see. It felt really nice, and I liked it. He obviously liked it too. 'It's real daring,' he said. 'It's much more daring than the other boys'll do.' Though we weren't very good at baseball, we could sure do this!" They called this prepubescent sixty-nine "doing it." Since Calvin always invited Harry to stay for supper and then treated him to a movie afterwards, Harry joked for years that he was "kept" at an early age by an "older man." Harry and Calvin "did it" for six months until Calvin was felled by appendicitis, and graduation from Cahuenga Elementary separated them.

One evening that summer at the Hays' proper dinner table, Big Harry made a remark about the history of Egypt, a country he had visited while working in Africa. To Little Harry, who had just that day been studying a schoolbook by the Egyptologist James Breasted, the statement sounded incorrect. What he recalled with his photographic memory contradicted what his father had just said, and with total conviction, he announced, "You're wrong."

Margaret, seated at the other end of the table from Big Harry, audibly gasped. Everyone suddenly fell silent.

"Harry," she said, "your father is waiting for you to apologize." The boy had broken two sacred rules: Besides the custom of no arguments at table, the master of the house was never to be contradicted. He blithely continued, "Because Breasted says..."

Before he could finish, Mr. Hay pulled his son from the table and marched him, boxing his ears all the way, to the garage behind the house. There he had a set of thick leather razor strops, one for every day of the week, and with this cat-o'-seven-tails, he began to whip his son, waiting for him to recant. But the incident stalemated him in a brutal standoff. "He was a Scotsman. I was a Scotsman," Harry recalled. "I wouldn't say I was wrong." Big Harry finally stopped the whipping and sent his son to bed without supper. When all was quiet, a sore but defiant Harry crept from his bed to his schoolbooks, opened his James Breasted book, and confirmed that indeed he had been right and his father wrong. "Mother came up later with a plate of supper," Hay remembered, "and found me looking in another book, one my Aunt Kate had left for me. It was a book of quotations that she had drilled me on, and I was looking for one now, which went, 'This above all, to thine own self be true.' I didn't really ever 'get' it till that night, when I earned it."

This incident set off a chain reaction in Harry's mind. "If my father could be wrong, then the teacher could be wrong," he realized that night. "And if the teacher could be wrong, then the priest could be wrong. And if the priest could be wrong, then maybe even God could be wrong." It was to this experience that Hay always traced his lack of guilt over his "deviance" in thought and action.

As an adult gay speaker, Harry invariably told this tale of dinner-table drama when asked if he ever felt depressed over his homosexuality during his repressive childhood. The series of realizations became a litany, always dramatically rendered. His eyes would grip his audience, and his voice would fall to a staunch whisper, so that one strained just a bit to hear the moral. Because of this separation from trust in his father and other mainstream values, Harry concluded, "the voice of dissent began that night," the night of the beating.

By this early age, Harry began to develop a defense that he felt was common to all gay people. He called it "the mask," a set of different personalities one instinctively acquires to greet and relate to different people — and to substitute for one's real, forbidden identity as a homosexual. During the twenties, as Harry was growing up, most Americans either thought that homosexuality was a fiendish affliction or, more commonly, were completely ignorant of it. Two heterosexual contemporaries of Harry's explained that in their youth, the concept of homosexuality was "less unmentionable than unmentioned" and stated that their mothers, like Queen Victoria, did not believe such a thing could exist. As a protective survival strategy, Little Harry developed different personae for various occasions and acquaintances — one day he might be a sensitive, isolated dreamer; the next, a team player; later, a know-it-all. Little wonder, then, that the personality beneath, once it emerged, turned out to be so strong.

▽

In the early twenties, the sprawling, rustic city of Los Angeles still had the rough edges of a frontier town. The desperate and unemployed as well as the polite and prosperous flocked to its welcoming clime. But the society was not welcoming to all. L.A. was known then as the "White Spot of the Nation," meaning that it was unspoiled by union shops and fair wages. This state was secured by the billy clubs of the Red Squad, an arm of the Los Angeles police force that Harry would tangle with as soon as he grew up. Though unions were not tolerated, citizen vigilante groups were. One day in 1924, while driving from their orchard through El Monte, Harry and his father were pulled to the side of the road by men from the local Ku Klux Klan and forced to witness a cross burning.

What Harry loved best about the city was the nature that coursed through it and surrounded it. The wilds of L.A. became Harry's primary escape from the stresses of his youth. The air was smogless and sweet, Harry recalled, with the perfume of orange blossoms. He scouted the great lowland plateaus pleated with canyons and watercourses (now vanished) and played in vast poppy fields where today stand the skyscrapers of Century City. He spent weeks at a time in the wilderness, and of all his writings over the years, some of his best passages are descriptions of natural settings. His eldest daughter, Hannah, had the impression that her father was "more interested in nature than in human beings."

Harry developed a particular love for hiking the pastel-toned San Gabriel Mountains, which form the rim of the Los Angeles basin. Every summer, he trekked to the far-flung campgrounds of Big Pine Flats, Chilao, and the high plateau of Deer Flats, usually with his friend Stanley Mitchell (who, thirty years later, would join the Denver Mattachine chapter). An experienced outdoorsman by age nine, Harry guided a party of adults visiting his parents on an expedition up Mount San Gorgonio, an 11,500-foot peak behind Redlands, near Big Bear Lake.

The best channel for his backpacking passion was a boys' group called the Western Rangers that Harry joined at age ten, shortly after enrolling in Virgil Junior High School. It was an offshoot of a nationally popular boys' group, and run locally by a man named Harry James. The group combined nature with male comradeship. Little Harry Hay couldn't get enough of its corny clubbiness, evident in its anthem:

> Up in the mountains far and free
> Where the pines tower to the sky,
> Or up on some canyon rising sheer
> Or where desert sands are dry.
> There's a camp of husky manly boys
> And it's most beyond belief,
> How they hop to attention while they hark to the words
> Of the heap big Chief.
> Each group of boys has its chief, Tony or Al or Chuck,
> And all Western Rangers obey commands
> And they never think to buck,
> They will rustle grub or scour the plates
> And it's most beyond belief,
> How they hop to attention while they hark to Harry,
> The heap big Chief!

Harry's participation in this group sharpened his outdoors skills, introduced him to a lasting relationship with American Indians, and provided him with warmth that was not forthcoming at home. As the first male brotherhood Harry joined, with its emphasis on personal ethics and natural harmony, the Western Rangers influenced him strongly and fore-shadowed his models for the Mattachine Society and, later, the Radical Faeries.

Patterned on Indian braves and forest rangers, the Western Rangers named its councils after Indian tribes. Harry's was the Shoshone. The Rangers took regular hikes and camp-outs and had a complete philosophy and structure of government. Harry James worked out an elaborate per-sonal-development program for his charges and coached a balance of physical culture, literature, science, crafts, and self-sufficiency in the wilderness. James's unique character made him as important a teacher as any Harry had in school. Hay said of James, "Most of us had a reverence for Harry." He remembered him as a slender, youthful man, refined, yet burnished blonde and tan from his devotion to the outdoors. He studied American Indian life and had been adopted by the Hopi early in the century. He drew on many Indian motifs, traditions and prayers in his lessons for the boys; the Great Spirit, not Jesus, is mentioned in his handbook. Later, Harry recognized James's style as based on Hopi methods of government and arbitration.

James took a group to the Hopi reservation in Arizona every year, and though Harry desperately wanted to go, he was dependent on his earnings and could never afford the cost. He did, however, meet Indians visiting California in 1925 and again in 1927, when groups of Sioux and Hopi made pilgrimages to the Pacific Ocean. James directed his charges to form a circular cordon at the entrances to the beach where the Indians went to perform religious ceremonies. Afterwards, at a feast at James's home, the boys were enthralled by the Indians' songs and dances.

Harry made his first Indian studies in James's extensive library of Native American books and materials and was also absorbed with James's tremendous collection of 78-rpm classical records. James took a group of boys to most of the classical concerts staged in Los Angeles during the 1920s; the boldly experimental, like Erik Satie, as well as Bach. When the Denishawn Dancers came to town, a group of Rangers went to see them too. James encouraged a level of sophistication and even sensitivity; in fact, Harry recalled once sobbing over an aesthetic revelation of Leopold Stokowski, and borrowing the handkerchief of fellow Ranger Kirbey Schlegel. "The sprinkler," as Harry called his weepiness at music, was one of the few emotional responses he could never control.

James's interest in boys was suggested to have been more than just spiritual. In the spring of 1925, he was accused of having an affair with a handsome blond Rangers counselor of eighteen. Harry recalled hearing that Ernest Thompson Seton, the founder–chief of the Woodcraft Rangers League of America, the progenitor organization of the Western Rangers, huffily withdrew the charter of the group from James's purview. So many of the boys and their parents backed him up, however, that after a quick marriage to Miss Grace Clifford (whom Harry described as a "larger, older spinster") James formed a nearly identical group that he called the Trail-finders.

Whatever James's private life, Hay stressed that the Western Rangers was completely oriented toward "normal" boyhood. Nonetheless, the group undoubtedly provided an erotic charge for any young gay boy. Harry recalled that whenever groups of Rangers went skinny-dipping, his glance would discreetly linger on the exposed flesh. He was extremely attracted to several boys in the group, and at least one, he suspected, had similar feelings for him. But despite a feeling of "straining against bonds within," Harry made no move. "My hands were at my sides and they didn't move," he said of his adolescence. "There was a lot of that."

He wrote moody poetry about nature, which his teacher encouraged and his mother criticized. (Thereafter he simply did not show her his poems.) In the schoolyards of Virgil Junior High, he found that the treatment from his peers changed from overt bullying to silently but systematically pushing him off the end of the bench. During recess hours, his refuge became the world of books, which he consumed voraciously, sequestered in the embrasured windows of the school building. Much of his reading came from James's carefully chosen list, and Harry also read historical novels that Margaret handed down. Unsatisfied with what seemed left out of these accounts of the adult world, he systematically read through the school library, boasting that he started with the A's and read through the Z's.

The most significant work he found was a volume by Edward Carpenter called *The Intermediate Sex*. This book brought an "earthshaking revelation" and lasting change to Harry's life. Carpenter, a nineteenth-century poet and scholar, published prolifically on radical subjects including women's rights, animal rights, and, most daringly, homosexuality. A friend of Walt Whitman and E.M. Forster, Carpenter was the model for the title character of Forster's novel *Maurice*. Carpenter's work was largely out of print from the 1940s until the 1980s, when its visionary acuity was rediscovered in a new wave of appreciative articles and republications.

When eleven-year-old Harry was employed as a delivery boy for the Acme Grocery Store on Cahuenga Boulevard, he spent his spare hours at the public library branch on the corner of the block. As at school, he read everything except a few volumes in a locked glass case; its key was kept in the drawer of the elderly librarian. Harry noticed a book with the word "sex" in large letters on the spine and grew convinced that the books in the case held pictures of naked men. Determined to see them, he befriended the librarian, and one day he saw his chance. She wistfully mentioned the new marcel wave process advertised by the hair salon up the street, but alas — it had the same hours as the library. Harry earnestly insisted that she should get the marcel, and extolled the difference it would make. The checkout desk, he offered, would be safe in his care during her absence. Under her supervision, he stamped books and made change for overdue fines. After a week of this, she made the appointment.

As soon as the librarian left, Harry took the key from the place he had spied her hiding it, unlocked the case, and made a beeline for *The*

Intermediate Sex. He found no naked men in it, but he did find something equally, mysteriously provocative — the word "homosexual." When he went to the dictionary to learn its meaning, it was not listed. Still it had an impact. "As soon as I saw it, I knew it was me. So I wasn't the only one of my kind in the whole world after all, and we weren't necessarily weird or freaks or perverted. There were others, the book said so [Michelangelo, Shakespeare, Sappho, Whitman] and even named some who believed in comradeship and being everything to each other. Maybe, someday, I could cross the sea and meet another one."

The Intermediate Sex is a remarkable book even today, but in 1906, when first published, it offered a uniquely positive view of homosexual identity. A genteel but forthright discussion of people with "Uranian temperament" and the "homogenic attachments" between them, Carpenter's work is distinctly gay-positive, scholarly, and concerned with understanding the roles gay people have played in relation to their surrounding culture — a progressive view then as well as now. Carpenter saw "Uranian" people primarily as intermediaries or catalysts, mostly in religion but also in other aspects of culture.

"The homogenic affection is a valuable social force," he wrote,

> and in some cases a necessary element of noble human character ... The instinctive artistic nature of the male of this class, his sensitive spirit, his wave-like emotional temperament, combined with hardihood of intellect and body; and the frank, free nature of the female, her masculine independence and strength wedded so thoroughly to feminine grace of form and manner; may be said to give them both, through their double nature, command of life in all its phases, and a certain freemasonry of the secrets of the two sexes which may well favor their function of reconcilers and interpreters.

Harry was so engrossed in his reading that he did not look up when the librarian approached, wearing a new hairdo and an expression of horror at the book in his hands.

The impact of these passages on the eleven-year-old was cataclysmic. Carpenter's writing inspired a vision within him — a heartfelt awakening to the knowledge that love was possible to him as a gay person, both in finding an "other" and in affirming his own value. With his discovery of Edward Carpenter, gay relationships would become for Harry more than immediate physical stirrings, and he was set on his lifelong course of persistent detective work to find clues to gay history in obscure books.

That vision was one that Harry often described. In a 1977 speech detailing a unique potential consciousness in gays, he recounted that day:

Suddenly my world was transformed into a whole wonderful, different place because my night-dream and day-dream fantasies from then on would always include HIM — the one who was going to be everything to me, as I naturally would be to him. And he would have been bullied on the school grounds, just as I had been. He would have run away into the woods, and often in the darkness wept with loneliness and terror, just as I had. But now, when I went to the woods, he would be there waiting, and he would say, "catch my hand," and we'd run away to the top of the hill and see the sunrise. And now, we'd never have to come back again, because we'd have each other.

But that perfect other was long in coming, and the real-life candidates he found were often less than ideal. There was a man at the Bimini Baths, an indoor spa in Los Angeles with separate pools for men and women, who dove between Harry's legs and nibbled at his genitals. Though the advances were unwelcome, he knew instinctively not to tell on his "elder brother."

All that Harry found to live on was the sublimated romance of close friendships. One of the fondest of these was with a cherubic boy named Bobby Marks, whose broad, clear features entranced Harry and defined a lifelong type he called "flower-faced boys." They visited during lunches at Virgil, and Harry often had dinner at the Markses' home. Bobby's mother, an opera singer who performed in the San Carlo Opera Company, would sing private concerts for the boys afterwards. But once when Harry returned the hospitality, Margaret told him that "Bobby would not feel comfortable visiting here again." The reason, she explained, was that Bobby was Jewish, and "those people preferred their own kind."

Anti-Semitism was widespread in Los Angeles at the time, as the very name of the Social Purity Club of Pasadena attests. Restrictive covenants in sales agreements often prevented Jews from owning property in many parts of the city. When Jewish neighbors moved in next door on South Kingsley Drive, Mrs. Hay sent over a casserole and chatted over the garden wall, but she would not invite them to visit and refused to let her children do so either. She likewise restricted Harry when he made friends with a Negro boy. Such edicts "broke my heart," Harry said, but he obeyed them.

During their first three summers in Los Angeles, Big Harry packed the family off to a nearby resort called Forest Home. Rather than patronize the overpriced store and restaurant there, he and his son spent four hours meticulously packing the family car with provisions. Then Big Harry drove them out, dropped them off, and returned to work in his orchard. To Margaret's disapproval, Little Harry took to the large dance floor in the lodge and learned the Hoochie Coochie and the Turkey Trot, but when someone he did not approve of danced with Peggy, Harry cut in brusquely, pronouncing, "My sister dances only with gentlemen!"

In 1922, Big Harry decided the family should have a more rustic summer experience and he dropped them off at his father's ranch in Hernandez, near the Central Valley. All the Hay children learned to ride; Harry learned to shoot a moving target while riding and to "roll," or fall with his horse so that neither would be hurt. An anthrax plague swept the ranch's cattle that summer, and Harry was given the grim job of preparing sagebrush pyres on which to burn the infected carcasses.

The following summer, a ranch hand at Hernandez gave Harry step-by-step lectures on how to make love to girls, and warned the youth of "morphodites." These, he explained, were "men who would do low things with other men." He offered to show the boy certain bars over in Salinas, where he had seen them hanging around. "Lot of them morphodites in Salinas," he said. Even more than the message of the book in the glass case, the cowpoke's slur was a miraculous message of acknowledgement. The other homosexual wasn't only across the sea. He was as close as Salinas.

▽

When he entered Los Angeles High School, Harry was twelve years old and six-feet-two. With deep-set, dark hazel eyes, thick, curly dark blond hair, and a cleft in his chin, he was only slightly aware that he was becoming a handsome young man. As well-to-do and responsible citizens, his parents began preparing him to enter the ranks of Los Angeles society. Peggy, Jack, and Harry, along with the rest of the children of the elite families of Los Angeles and Pasadena, participated in bimonthly Friday night dances at the Beverly Wilshire Country Club. These formal soirees required evening gowns and corsages for the girls, dinner jackets and pomade for the boys. Parent–chaperones included Mrs. Harvey Mudd, Mrs. Doheny, Mrs. Chandler, and Mrs. Henry Hay.

The less-than-elegant tuxedo that Harry self-consciously wore bespoke the difference between the ways of his family and his friends. He lived in a strange limbo between privilege and parsimony, magnified by his sternly monitored position as "the example." In 1926, the Hays moved to 940 South Windsor Boulevard, in a genteel neighborhood bordering exclusive Hancock Park. The house was larger than the last, and had such amenities as a maid's quarters, a tennis court, and a turret, which Big Harry immediately claimed for his study. But while Harry's friends were given fat allowances and even cars, Harry washed dishes in the school cafeteria to pay for his lunches.

At L.A. High, some of the same teachers that had taught his father forty years before taught Harry. The school overwhelmed Harry as a freshman; though tall, he was younger than most other students and felt less mature. As always, he excelled in classes, but much of his education came from outside the classroom through a series of mentors. First were a childless couple, Dr. and Mrs. Wood, who lived a few doors up Windsor Boulevard and welcomed Harry to use their large library and to stay for talks about literature. Dr. Wood introduced him to many authors, including a new writer called Virginia Woolf, as well as to Yeats, John Synge, and Will Durant. Another mentor, the father of a high school friend, introduced Harry to European literature and drama. Harry's most serious mentor was a Jesuit priest who invited him for weekly tutoring sessions on philosophy and religion, hoping (unsuccessfully) to persuade young Harry to take the cloth.

His zealous studiousness both in and out of school was supplemented with a growing love of theater. Harry was delighted whenever his mother took him to a show or opera, and he ushered for every drama production at L.A. High, in no small part to see the boys in the Shakespeare plays wear tights. His theater obsession may have caused his parents some worry about the "normality" of his development. Peggy suspected that Big Harry had definite concerns in that direction. "Father had grown up around ranches and ranchers," she said. "He wanted to get Harry away from music and literature and that sort of thing, and get him around ranch hands and so on." At the end of his first year of high school, when Harry was thirteen, his father sent him off to work for the summer in the hay fields on his cousin George's ranch in Western Nevada, to toughen him up. Whether or not the experience was targeted necessarily to "cure" Harry of his homosexuality, it followed the practical family tradition. Big Harry's farming skills sustained him after the accident, and his cousin George, who still farmed in the fertile Smith Valley of Western Nevada, could pay Little Harry as well as teach him.

Harry, who had never taken a long journey away from home alone, was put on a train that took him into the rural inland area, where the transportation ended. From there, a relative drove him to the family farm where he was immediately set to work pitching and stacking hay. It seemed impossible. The hot Nevada sun forced the workers to strip their shirts, but exposed skin quickly blackened with mosquitos. Rattlesnakes were also plentiful, even in the hay fields. Because his muscles had not caught up with his height, the field labor brought Harry the worst fatigue he had ever felt. The physical exhaustion combined with homesickness and anxiety to make his first two weeks miserable. He recalled that at first, "everything ached. I was so scared that my peripheral vision often went black. I remember just holding onto the back of the wagon and letting it drag me."

Help arrived from his hay-pitching partner, a middle-aged Washoe Indian named Tom, who quietly picked up those hay shocks the youngster could not keep up with. After Harry adjusted, he began picking up Tom's shocks and doing both their work. This turnabout seemed like showing off, and offended the older man; Harry apologized. That summer he learned the manners of the workplace, to drink coffee, and even to drink Nevada's bootleg brew, which he said tasted like coal oil. And when he went out with the haying crew on Saturday nights, he always somehow managed to avoid going to the whorehouse, which the field hands called the cribs, thus evading the coarser aspects of his father's toughening plan. As if to subvert that program, Harry discovered a collection of opera records owned by cousin George's mother, Aunt Laura, and spent his spare hours at the ranch house, listening to opera and discussing music with his aunt.

But his most complete subversion of Big Harry's scheme was in becoming a socialist. The agents of this were men from the local labor pool who were miners part of the year and worked on the ranch during the summer. Many were members of the Industrial Workers of the World — the Wobblies — and were veterans of that turn-of-the-century labor movement. They had known the great songwriter and organizer Joe Hill, who had been martyred only ten years earlier, and taught Harry some of his songs. Their politics never flagged, and, out in the field, they casually talked about "the corrupt bosses." Their young comrade Harry was all ears.

On the hay wagon, they tutored Harry with Marxist literature, often turgid booklets translated from French and German. Among the greasy, thumbworn pamphlets, Harry remembered Karl Marx's *Value, Price and Profit* and *Wage-Labor and Capital*. By day, they drilled him in the principles of exploitation, organization, and unity. By campfire, they told him stories. "I was immersed in the first great railroad strike of 1887, the Haymarket Massacre, and the dreadful Ludlow Massacre, where Rockefeller goons gunned down fourteen women and children in the snow on Christmas Eve, 1913." This political baptism by the Wobblies made a powerful impression, and for decades afterwards Harry politicized young people by telling thrilling historical tales.

Despite their warm slogans of "One big union" and "One for all and all for one," Harry felt a chill when they warned him against homosexuality. "There were many variations of a story about how miners would have to bunk together, two or more to a bed. It always ended, 'Anyone who couldn't keep his friggin' hands to hisself got thrown out the third floor window.' I heard that dozens of times." That particular folkloric chastity belt signaled his first awareness of the rift between progressive politics and his inner nature.

The Wobblies provided Harry with a clear initiation to the working class. Though he had already been earning money for several years, and the silver spoon of his infancy had long tarnished, he now had words to identify himself as "a working-class kid." He played down any class rebellion on his part, and said that his new politicization merely gave a theoretical basis for his personal hatred of his father's staunch conservatism. The Wobblies' praise for his honest toil strengthened this new political bond, and each winter he eagerly awaited the return of summer and their companionship.

Another unusual event happened that summer, quite outside the realm of doctrinal politics. It began near the end of his stay, when his hay-pitching partner, Tom, approached his Aunt Laura in mid-August with an invitation. "Tomorrow we have fandango. You bring boy. We dance. You bring boy two o'clock." Harry was curious. He had already met Hopi Indians through Harry James and the Western Rangers, but knew little about the local desert Indians. His aunt was also curious, and remarked to Harry that few non-Indians received such invitations. She trusted Tom and assured her nephew that it would be worth his while to go.

The next day, in Laura's open-top 1924 Buick touring car, they drove towards the north end of the Smith Valley. They turned onto a dirt road and entered a tall thicket of mesquite and willow, where some Indian women took Harry and promised to return him at eight o'clock. They led him to a camp enclosed by a thick wall fashioned of willow and brush. Once inside, Harry saw thatched structures and a central area where a group was dancing and singing around a small pine tree that appeared to have been brought from another area. He smelled food, and noticed women tending a series of cooking pits, where their beat-up pots sat on stones in the fire. Harry also noticed a frail old man sitting on a raised platform of woven willow, on piles of blankets woven from strips of rabbit fur. The old man appeared sightless, for when he was speaking with people, he constantly touched them with his hands.

The Indian boys engaged Harry in the game they were playing, gesturing and speaking in Washoe to explain it. As they struggled to converse, one of the women returned and told him their "sacred old man" was with them. "He knows you are here," she said. "He would like to speak with you. Is it in your heart to speak with him?" Harry agreed to accompany her to the willow platform. Up close, he saw that the old man's skin was weathered like dried parchment, and deeply wrinkled. "She said something to him. Then he said something to her and then she asked me to give him my name and where I had come from. Then he didn't ask me direct questions any longer. He ran his hands over my face and over my head and across my forehead and back to my temples again and down the sides of my face. Then he felt my mouth, he felt my nose." He repeated several phrases in his own language, then became tired. Harry was excused.

Harry asked the woman what the old man had said. "We are to treat you well. We are to feed you well," she answered, "because someday you will be a friend." Harry asked about the gestures made over him, and was told simply, "He wished you well." Harry returned to play with the other boys. After dinner, though the late summer sky was still light, they took him back to his aunt. When later telling the adventure to his friend Tom, he learned that the "well-wishing" gestures were a formal blessing given in friendship, and that the old man was a medicine man known as Jack Wilson.

For more than forty years Hay had no idea how special this experience had been, but in 1969, he learned that Jack Wilson was the Anglo name of a famous Paiute Indian better known as Wovoka.

Wovoka is recorded in most Indian histories as the greatest mystic and prophet of his people. His doctrine of nonviolent transcendence of white oppression spread across the country, and he is still referred to as "the Red Man's Christ" or "the Ghost Dance Messiah." During a solar eclipse in 1889, Wovoka had a vision in which the Great Spirit taught him a new religion. It involved renunciation of war and alcohol, and promised that all Indians who practiced a dance he had learned in his vision would be restored to their youth in a world full of game and free of white men. The Ghost Dance religion, as the new faith became known, quickly spread to most Indian nations, and proved to be a watershed in Indian history. In a tragic misunderstanding, the new nonviolent religion was interpreted as a "disturbance," and directly led to the massacre at Wounded Knee two years after Wovoka's vision. Especially in view of the Indian-slaughtering activity of Captain Francis Hardie, Harry's great-uncle, who had carried the flag at Wounded Knee itself, Harry felt astonished at having been blessed by such a noted spiritual Indian as Wovoka.

In 1969, when Harry learned the identity of Jack Wilson, he was working with the forerunners of the modern Traditional Indian movement; a decade later, he would play a pivotal part in stopping a dam that would have extinguished some of the most ancient pueblos in New Mexico. Indeed, Wovoka's words had been prophetic.

Hay's account of that August afternoon in 1925 has been extensively researched and a footnoted account of it published by Will Roscoe, a historian of Native American and gay studies. In this account, Randy Burns, a founder of the organization Gay American Indians and himself a Paiute, states that he had seen elders of his tribe touch the face and head in the manner Hay described as a means of blessing or of transferring power, and verified many other details of the encampment. Burns also suggested that the frailty and blindness were really the temporary effects of a peyote trance.

Harry made countless references to this incident, and his gay movement friend Jim Kepner ribbed him about the story, dubbing it "the visit of the wise men." But the bestowal of a blessing in the warmth of a charismatic, personal bond stayed with Harry, and throughout the years, many gay seekers would ask for, and receive, his blessing.

▽

At the end of his second summer in the Smith Valley, Harry complained about the high cost of getting back home to Los Angeles. The Wobbly field hands gave him an I.W.W. card and directed him to go to the Embarcadero Union Hall when he got to San Francisco. The card would allow him to sign up with one of the tramp steamers that brought cargo to coastal towns that lacked harbors.

Though Harry was fourteen, at six-feet-three and 175 pounds he easily convinced the union officials that he was twenty-one. He was duly signed to work a trip south. The steamer left Alameda harbor and anchored at a roadstead in Monterey Bay. After the unloading, the crew went to a Monterey saloon and Harry showed off his new adult drinking style. He stayed sober enough, however, to discreetly avoid the obligatory trip to the cathouse, an evasion he had perfected in Nevada. Once he was back on the steamer and the dark maw of Monterey receded, he retched the liquor overboard and was dimly aware that one of the sailors helped him to his bunk.

That sailor, Harry learned the next day, was a merchant-seaman who had already traveled to seaports throughout Asia, Africa, and Europe. He was a gracefully muscled young man of about twenty-five, with dark coloring. Harry sneaked looks at him and found brilliant blue eyes and a gentle smile looking back. His name was Matt. When Harry shuddered in response to Matt's inquiry about why he hadn't gone with the others to the cathouse the previous night, they agreed to explore Santa Barbara's beach after work had finished.

As they walked alongside the moonlit ocean, Harry was swept up by bracing physical sensations. His mouth was dry, his flesh tingled, Matt's hand dangled near to his. When he clasped it, he momentarily feared that the sailor would respond violently. Instead, Matt pulled him close and kissed him. They headed to a grove of trees and, with awkward but driving passion, fourteen-year-old Harry discovered his first adult lovemaking. Afterwards, between kisses and sighs, he unthinkingly admitted that he had little experience and was, after all, only fourteen. Matt jumped to his feet in a panic, explaining that he could be sent to jail for twenty-three years if he were caught with an underage person. Harry desperately persuaded him to stay — to hold him and talk.

Reassured, Matt told Harry that they were members of a "silent brotherhood" that reached round the world. "Someday," he explained, "you will have wandered to a strange and faraway place. You'll not know who any of the people are there, or whether they mean you good or ill; you'll not hear a single word or a sound you can recognize. And then suddenly, in that frightening and alien place, you'll look across the square and you'll see a pair of eyes open and glow at you. You'll look back at him, and, at that moment, in the lock of two pairs of eyes, you are *home* and you are *safe!*" They slept in a lifeboat on board the steamer that night, and Matt gave Harry more tips about how to take care of himself in the world that lay beyond family and school. These ideas — that there was a culture of "people like us" in many cities of the world and that they shared signals by which to recognize each other — inspired Harry almost as vividly as the erotic memory of Matt.

When in later years he told this favorite coming-out story, he referred to it ironically as his "child-molestation speech," to make the point of how sharply gay life differs from heterosexual norms. "As a child," he explained, "I molested an adult until I found out what I needed to know." He recalled that Matt's promise of a new world and a future served as a life raft during the isolated period of high school. Far from being an experience of "molestation," Harry always described it as "the most beautiful gift that a fourteen-year-old ever got from his first love!"

The following year, a rapidly maturing Harry broke with the Catholic Church. Like his father, he was not particularly religious to begin with, but he attended mass regularly at St. Gregory's, at Ninth Street and Norton, to perform his bass solos in the choir. "When the soprano was absent, I could use my counter-tenor high head-tones to sing her part. Since the congregation sat in front of us, nobody noticed that it was me. For the same reason, they didn't notice when I slipped under the seats with the nice-looking tenor, George, and kissed during mass."

The Saturday afternoon before Easter of that year he waited, with many of the other parishioners of St. Gregory's, to endure the twice-yearly confession. "Almost everyone in the congregation was there," he recalled, as the priest, Father Follen, took the confessions one by one. When it was Harry's turn, he made his confession, but "instead of telling me a penance, Father Follen asked, 'And now, my son, have you thoroughly searched your soul and confessed to God all the sins you have committed for which you are truly repentant?' I said yes, I was finished. It did fleetingly cross my mind about George and me, but already I was thinking that this was something that was not a sin, and was not wrong, and was beautiful, and some day I would find the words to tell people. So I said nothing more.

"Suddenly, there was an abrupt drop in the temperature. I could feel it through the screen. His voice came back very low and very cold, and he gruffly repeated, 'Have you finished?' I said, 'Yes.'

"'You have not!' he said. I realized in that instant that Father Follen knew who I was, which he was not supposed to — and that George had talked.

"'Are you going to say you are sorry?' he asked. I wasn't sorry, and there was nothing for me to confess. There was a moment of strained silence as he waited, then I heard him putting on his vestments. Before I knew what was happening, he reached into my side of the confessional, grabbed me by the collar and by the back of the belt, and, in front of all those waiting people, marched me to the front of the cathedral, kicked open the door with his foot, and pushed me out, shouting, 'Don't come back until you are ready to say you're sorry.'"

Harry never did. But when, during the Depression, he visited home from college, he sometimes went to St. Gregory's, not as a parishioner, but as a musician, to play an occasional mass. "From the pulpit, Father Fallon would thank me for the music, then invite me to the sacristy, where we would finish off the sacramental wine. Then the old hypocrite would chase me around the table. But I never let him catch me. I was very wise by then."

·3·

A toe in the mainstream

The good are attracted by men's perceptions,
And think not for themselves;
Till Experience teaches them to catch
And to cage the Fairies & Elves.

— William Blake

When, after three years, Harry was ready to graduate from Los Angeles High School, his father pressed him to choose a profession so that a suitable college could be chosen. Big Harry insisted his son study only a field that would lead to money; medicine was permissible, but his own profession, engineering, was preferred. Harry balked at all of them. Despite the tensions at home, he re-enrolled for two more years of high school.

Those fourth and fifth years proved to be his happiest at L.A. High. He had completed his requirements, so he had time for elective courses, extracurricular activities, and developing himself as a grand young fellow. (One friend wrote in his yearbook, "Mon Homme — You told me to call you that, so there it is ... even though I'm always scolding you, I'm very fond of you.") He was in a poetry group called the Ink Beasts, was state president of the California Scholarship Federation, and president of the school's debating and dramatics society, the Forum. Winifred McPherson, daughter of the legendary evangelist Aimee Semple McPherson, was a fellow member; one day when Winifred could not make it to a Forum meeting, Sister Aimee had a messenger deliver a handwritten excuse to Harry. He learned parliamentary procedure "backwards and forwards, to the point where I could blind anybody." This early practice would come to serve him well, as he easily mastered any procedural system that came his way.

To escape the horrors of gym class, Harry joined the Reserve Officer Training Corps. There he met his closest high school buddies. One was the fair-faced Al Cronkite, known as "Handsome Al" in the yearbook. Another, Robert Balzer, who went on to become a respected wine critic, recalled Harry's "very military bearing," though Harry himself flippantly described ROTC as "sashaying around with our caps and ceremonial sabers." (And sashay he did; ever the show-off, he choreographed un-authorized surprise formations with extra fillips and flourishes for the precision drills the ROTC performed, outraging the principal while im-pressing the school assembly.) In his senior year Harry became a captain. Over long lunches in the cramped officer's quarters, the officers formed a band of little hell-raisers they called "the Gang."

Every Friday night, in their formal military dress uniforms, they met at a member's house for dinner. Within earshot of any mother, they acted most dignified. But immediately after dinner, they transformed; first by changing into a "civilian uniform" of yellow corduroys, white shirts, black bow ties, and signature blue school sweaters. After a movie, their weekend mischief consisted of soaping or setting firecrackers on the tracks of the city's Red Car rail line, stealing the velvet queue ropes from cinemas, and once, absconding with an entire silver tea set from the Ambassador Hotel (returning the pilfered items, neatly boxed, before the next dawn). Their worst prank was snatching red glass kerosene lanterns from street work sites and placing them on private homes and churches, thereby converting them to "red light district houses" — whorehouses. At all such shenan-igans, the boys in the Gang laughed their sides off and never got caught.

The price tag on this male camaraderie was the attendant heterosexual peer pressure. The Gang dated heavily and as a group, so Harry swallowed his distaste and followed suit. He met the challenge by careful observation and charades, "watching what Bob would say to Betty and how she responds, then saying the same thing to get the same response." Thus he passed for a horny hetero teen — until a girl his age invited him to her house a few doors up Windsor Boulevard when her parents were out, and did her best to seduce him. After some light necking, Harry realized that "the more I tried it, the more I didn't like it," and stopped.

He didn't tell the Gang about this, nor about the hoop skirt he had fashioned from scraps of wire stolen from his father's workshop. He explained this project to himself as the product of a developing aesthetic and historical interest in costume, though his homemade endeavors were frustrating. "When our parents occasionally went out, I'd put on the frame and pin up every bedspread in the house — but the result always looked wrong. The material never hid the wire stubs from the frame, and none of the hoops were completely round."* He perused better-made period garments than his hoop skirt at Western Costume Company, which supplied the movie studios and the public. Harry wanted to rent one of their Elizabethan outfits for the Junior Informal's annual costume ball, but, too poor, could only dream about it.

Sometimes dreaming paid off. One Friday, in the spring of Harry's senior year, his Solid Geometry teacher assigned a theorem to be proved in class the next Monday. It was particularly complex, but the teacher offered a strong incentive: Those who wrote a complete proof would receive an A and a reprieve from the rest of the class. Harry labored futilely all weekend, then, Sunday night, awoke from a vivid dream in which the proof was revealed. For the rest of the year, he went to the beach instead of to math class.

Around the same time, Harry became eligible for the Southern California Oratorical Society Contest. His speech instructor, Miss Whitman, arranged for him to be coached by the previous year's winner, a prodigious L.A. High student named John Cage, later renowned as an avant-garde composer. During Harry's speech, "a vaguely poetic World Friendship kind of thing," he noticed for the first time that his audience was listening, rapt, waiting for him to continue. "I had them, and made them wait three beats more than Miss Whitman had rehearsed me to see if I could hold them. I could." It was a thrill that surpassed winning the competition — and a trick he never forgot.

When he graduated in the class of 1929, the issue of his professional future flared up again. Big Harry still insisted he become a mining engineer, or, to offer a choice, an oil geologist. Harry insisted the opposite: "I wanted nothing to do with the sorts of people Father had worked with." He attempted instead a career in paleontology. The study of fossils had held no particular interest for him until he chose it as a project for a science fair. His well-crafted fossil facsimiles attracted the attention of a paleontology professor from the California Institute of Technology, who offered Harry a scholarship. Big Harry forbade it.

---

* Only once did Harry actually get up in full drag, for the San Francisco Beaux Arts Ball in 1931, when he dressed as Sarah Siddons, a British actress of the eighteenth century. He chose her because she was over six feet tall, like he was. He selected as his outfit the tragic muse costume she wears in the Joshua Reynolds portrait that still hangs at the Huntington Gallery in San Marino, near Pasadena.

A compromise was achieved: The solid profession of law seemed natural for such an articulate, argumentative young mind as Harry's. Big Harry arranged for a job in the office of a friend, Walter Haas, whose partnership, Haas and Dunnigan, was a prominent downtown firm specializing in water rights. Harry's work there was unpaid; the entrée that such service provided into the lucrative field was considered compensation enough. In between his official duties as a process server working throughout the city, Harry helped the reserved, whispering secretaries with the switchboard, but during most of his spare hours he read legal texts in the office library. In the eighteenth-century law book *Blackstone's Commentaries,* Harry found references to homosexuality, but "only the negative stuff," which further dampened any interest he had in law.

At the end of October, after just two months on the job, Harry made a delivery on Spring Street, the financial center of Los Angeles. He saw little activity on the normally busy street that day, except for well-dressed men talking quietly in doorways. Inside the office, he found the receptionist on the floor, weeping. She explained that the stock market had collapsed and that, like many others, she was suddenly impoverished. Mr. Haas shut himself in his office, and that night at home Big Harry slammed the door of his turret and stayed there for weeks. More than half of his nearly million-dollar fortune had been invested in the market, and what was left began to dwindle as other markets, including citrus and real estate, slowly unraveled. Before long, his tenants began to falter in their rent payments. The Great Depression gradually wiped him out, just as it put a third of Americans out of work and devastated millions more. Through those long years, Margaret quietly sold off pieces of her English silver and even rare books to make ends meet. A shrewd businesswoman, she held on to her husband's worthless stocks and built them up to a sizable nest egg over the next twenty-five years.

Life and Harry's job continued. He commuted to work at the law office for the remainder of the year, and found that the Pacific Electric Red Cars connecting the Southland provided an unexpected benefit: cruising. "Matt had told me that I would discover the eye-lock and that it would be unmistakable." It was, though none of the young men who met Harry's gaze actually met him. Unexpectedly, he made contact one day while serving papers at Los Angeles City Hall, then still under construction. A large mass had gathered for a public demonstration, and even in a crowd, tall Harry, in his scarlet sweater, salt-and-pepper knickerbockers, and knee socks, stood out. A hand from somewhere groped Harry through his knickers. The older man who had done it pressed against him again, taking full advantage of his sudden erection, then led him up some stairs. Harry followed with urgent desire to the unfinished seventh floor of City Hall. There, amid the plaster and planks, he got a head job. The anonymous man fled immediately, and the thrill sank to a feeling of unpleasantness.

It was time to find out about meeting people; a way that was less a matter of chance. His only clue lay in stories he had heard about goings-on at the large, landscaped grounds of downtown's Pershing Square. These ranged from tales of people who had "gone in and never come out" to what an ROTC friend told Harry, that "men met each other there and did things." He told his mother he was going to the library one night after work at the law office, and instead he went to the park. "In those years, Pershing Square had great bushy trees and clumps of overgrown bushes. The paths that crisscrossed in the center were unpaved, and some of the paths actually (and obviously) ended *in* the bushes." He walked around, anxious and uncertain, and to escape his mounting nervousness, went into the restroom. Men were concentrated there, too, and he found himself with "a full erection and a cold sweat" when the man in the adjacent toilet stall started moving his foot. Harry gingerly followed suit, unaware he was answering a homosexual pickup code. "I couldn't tell much from the shoe about the person wearing it, but I knew something was happening. I wasn't sure what, but I sensed I had passed the point of no return." They touched shoes, met face to face, and left together.

Harry's new friend was a man in his mid-thirties named Champ Simmons. He was unemployed, recently arrived from St. Louis, and no matinee idol — Harry described him as "the most un-Champ-like person you could ever meet," phlegmatic and lisping. He was nervous about Harry's inexperience and his being underage, but made a date for the next day. During an extended lunch hour, they met at Champ's sister's house and went to bed. In one golden afternoon, Harry learned "all the positions a homosexual boy needs to know."

Harry saw Champ twice weekly for half a year, until he left for college. The young law clerk felt embarrassment when his paramour visited him at the office; Champ, with his lisp, seemed "obvious." Hay's opinions about such appearances changed drastically over the years, to the point where he himself felt embarrassed if he was *not* obviously homosexual.

As Matt had done, Champ Simmons brought Harry out to many arcane elements of gay culture, relaying bits of information the youngster absorbed like a sponge: There was a place in Denver called Cheseman Park where "people like us" met each other. In San Francisco, at a series of sentry boxes, the guards were "haveable" at certain hours. Harry learned these euphemistic phrases — deliberately vague to protect against the severe harassment that could come with being identified as a "deviant" — from Champ and his friends at parties they occasionally attended as a couple. The euphemisms made up a veritable gay language. Men under twenty-eight years old were called "belles." Up to thirty-five, one was a "queen"; anyone older was an "aunt." The words "gay" and "homosexual" were not used; "sophisticated," "temperamental," and "that way" were.

Champ enjoyed another particularly significant link with the gay world; a former lover of his had been involved with a homosexual group set up by Henry Gerber in the 1920s in Chicago, which was shut down by the law after a few furtive weeks. Champ sternly proclaimed that the former lover warned him that such groups had always been dangerous and brought everyone in them to bad ends. Still, the notion of an organized group of "temperamental" men fascinated Harry, and the idea took a deep hold.

After nearly a year at Haas and Dunnigan, Harry was admitted to Stanford University. He decided to study international relations. His father did not object, but neither did he contribute money to his son's education, and the financial assistance Harry won proved crucial. To orient himself, he arrived a week before classes began. His first impression was of isolation. The 8,000-acre campus was located amidst ten times as much undeveloped farmland; in fact, it had been Governor Leland Stanford's stock ranch before the university was founded in 1886, which earned the school its nickname of "the Farm." Harry observed that the fraternity system wielded inordinate influence in Stanford's decidedly macho power structure. By his second day on campus, he was alarmed to hear stories, similar to those he had heard from the Wobblies, about "queers" getting beaten up and thrown out of third-story windows for making advances on dorm-mates.

Stanford in the early 1930s stressed its professional schools: Law, Medicine, and Business. It had "almost no liberal arts," according to poet–filmmaker James Broughton, whom Harry met there the following year. Broughton explained, "Stanford was a rich man's school. The emphasis was on sports and dances and beer busts — all that Joe College stuff. A small group of us pretended to be smart about music and ballet, and the majority of the student body ignored all this and us too." Poetry flowed from Harry's pen that year, and an early droplet was inspired by a display at the Leland Stanford, Jr., Museum, which was filled with the personal effects of Mrs. Stanford, Sr.:

> How nice — the "Frosh" can go on Sundays
> To see the founder-lady's undies.

Though unsophisticated, Stanford offered splendid environs and the freedom to explore them. Nearby Palo Alto was picturesque and neighborly, and San Francisco, "the City," was only an hour north. College also offered friends. In Encina Hall, the freshman dormitory, there were other men from L.A. High, including Bobby Balzer and "Handsome Al" Cronkite from ROTC. Harry suspected that Cronkite was "that way," but he acted increasingly shy and nervous. Another familiar face that surprised Harry was Bobby Marks, the Jewish "flower-faced" lad whose friendship had been forbidden during junior high school days. Bobby, grown up and "breathtakingly beautiful," never acknowledged Harry when they passed each other, and quite suddenly during that fall semester, he died of meningitis.

In Encina Hall was a pale blond boy named David Hawkins, who became Harry's closest college friend. Cerebral and courteous, David had much in common with Harry, and the two developed a great mutual affection. Hawkins recalled that "Harry could talk about any subject with verve and wit," and they talked almost eight hours a day. David was also a music lover, though not as accomplished as Harry; he was in awe of Harry's sophisticated knowledge and credited Hay with having started his musical education. As a ritual, every day after class, they played Ravel's *Bolero* (the first recording conducted by the composer) on Hawkins's wind-up phonograph. This daring work, which had had its American premiere only a year before, wove its slowly building, repetitive theme through a four-record 78-rpm set, and after a few weeks of hearing it, others in the building started making threats to "break that record you keep playing over and over again." Harry reveled in *Bolero* anyway and said it opened the door to his understanding of modern composers like Satie, Debussy, and Poulenc.

David and Harry hiked in the countryside, listened to music, and talked away their afternoons. Hawkins recalled the time as leisurely exploration with "eyes wide open on the world" and did not recall Harry as having a fixed political viewpoint. If such tarrying left little time for study, Harry found he didn't really need to study anyway. He made mostly A's, except in biology. "That I couldn't figure out by Socratic logic," he said, "or bluff my way through by what I had read," as he could with most other classes. His only C's were in science courses.

Alphabetical classroom seating brought Harry a new friend who shared his name, a spirited girl named Jean Hay who had masses of pretty red hair. They could trace no blood relationship but liked each other well enough that they called each other "cousins by preference." She already knew David Hawkins, and together they became a threesome. They often escaped the boredom of Palo Alto in Jean's secondhand Chevy roadster, heading for a lodge in Santa Cruz that featured ballroom dancing contests. Their practiced steps of Fred and Adele Astaire, whom they had seen in San Francisco, invariably won first prize. The trio visited the City often for madcap adventures. One involved going to the Mark Hopkins Hotel on the night the newspapers had announced the French ambassador was due. Penniless but determined, they dressed in their evening clothes, Harry wearing a red sash and all his ROTC medals, and took a ringside table at the Top of the Mark. Harry blustered in Spanish and the others spoke French. Deferential waiters brought them caviar and champagne, and when the orchestra played a waltz, Harry and Jean made an expert tour of the floor. Harry's scrawl on the check seemed to satisfy the maitre d', and as soon as it was signed, the students scurried to the old roadster, parked blocks out of view. A week later, Harry said, he read about the "incident" in the San Francisco papers.

That year, Stanford set up a pilot project called "the Oxford program," named for the university whose visiting fellows administered it. Harry participated with independent study courses in English, history, and political science. The program required strong personal interest in a subject and voluminous reading in primary sources; grades were given on the basis of interviews and a term paper. (One of Harry's papers was called "The Rise of Benevolent Despotism," an early study of the fascist movement in Europe.) This experience secured a life pattern for Hay of being a "free scholar," able to comfortably work in uncharted territory. This freedom, however, seemed to curtail his maturity in academic discipline, especially in written expression.

"Experimental" was the byword of Harry's education and developing worldview. As a young observer near the turn of the century, he saw old forms, both empires and ideas, falling apart, and new forms taking their place. From Stanford's library, he checked out a book about the recent imagist literary movement, which rebelled against romanticism. He bought Stephen Crane's naturalistic poetry volumes, *The Black Riders* and *War Is Kind,* and carried them wherever he went. Harry was tremendously excited to see the German avant-garde dancer Mary Wigman when she performed in San Francisco. Harry could not, he admitted, shake a deep sentimentality; "down to my last quarter, I would buy a pack of Camels and a bunch of violets." But in art and ideas, the new world appealed to the rebel in him and took precedence.

An important chapter opened in Harry's life when he chose the drama elective that first year. Though he was at first unconfident, his performance during a class exercise soon won him admiration as a natural actor, and he was asked to be in many student plays. "Everyone suddenly realized that I was an actor. It surprised me but made everything come into focus about where I really belonged." His early love of theater revived, and international relations quickly dimmed as his career of choice. One scene he had played, Chekhov's one-act *Swan Song,* was selected as the best student production of that year, and with Harry in the lead, it was performed for the public of Palo Alto and, later, at the Geary Street Theater in San Francisco. From then on he felt that "the theater was definitely it for me."

During Christmas break of 1930, he returned to Windsor Boulevard. While visiting old friends at his former high school, he chatted up a decidedly savvy student who told him about a speakeasy where there would be a New Year's Eve party for "people like us." On the appointed evening, Harry made his way to the bar, called Jimmy's Back Yard, on Ivar Street near Hollywood Boulevard, a district he would later know well as a glamorous cruising ground. He spoke the name of his friend at the door and joined the crowd of more than two hundred, all of them, apparently, that way! He was happily stunned. Harry's young friend fetched him to a table and introduced him to an older man he was involved with. "This fellow told me that since I was so near San Francisco, he knew someone there, Dr. Frank Fenton, whom I should meet." Harry agreed to look the man up, and again was lost in his fascination with the homosexual speakeasy. Never had he imagined anything like it; men were dancing with men and women with women. At midnight, a handsome Negro took him in his arms. They welcomed the year 1931 with swooning kisses.

As soon as possible after returning to school, Harry made his San Francisco connection with Dr. Fenton. The doctor, a cultured, sociable English professor, happily introduced the handsome and precocious Harry to San Francisco's gay society. His favorite boîte was Finnochio's, at Bush and Stockton Streets, which during World War II became a burlesque and drag saloon and a San Francisco landmark. Harry recalled Madame Finnochio, the original owner, as "a gigantic lesbian who dressed in feather boas and huge picture hats and surrounded herself with equally statuesque femmes." She presided over the cash register. However, Roy, the maitre d', was the real power broker of the place. Because of the double jeopardy of being a gay bar during Prohibition ("social" touching and cross-dressing were as illegal as booze), the door had to be carefully protected. Harry made friends with Roy, who reserved tables, managed the dinner service, and carefully assessed and screened the clientele, recommending hours when they might be more likely to find compatibles. This gave the establishment the flavor of a cultured, companionable salon. For younger patrons like Harry, Roy assumed the balance between a nanny and a Madam, offering counsel when a drink or an entire bottle was sent as a proposition. A nod from Roy instructed "go" or "stop." Harry saved his money for adventurous weekends at Finnochio's as often as he could.

One Friday evening, a British gentleman with slick hair and suave manners sent an expensive bottle of champagne to Harry. Roy signaled him to refuse, but a combination of curiosity, vanity, and lust got the better of Harry. He went to the man's table and then accompanied him to his hotel, the swank St. Francis. While his admirer was preening in the restroom, Harry observed an insignia on his dressing case. "It was the crest of the royal house of Windsor; I guessed that he was the then-unmarried duke of Kent and always assumed that this was the social height of my one-night stands." But the date went downhill fast. The following morning, "after a night of not-very-good sex," the Englishman informed him that the rest of the weekend would require several changes of formal wear. When Harry explained he had no other clothes, he was thrown out. Harry sheepishly begged Roy's pardon and learned a lesson about how more experienced gays could help protect the younger ones.

One of the more free-spirited San Francisco crowds to which Fenton introduced Harry centered around a pair of brothers, Richard and Robert Gump. Sons of the founder of San Francisco's famous stores, the Gump brothers delighted in the experimental and the exotic. They set up a warehouse art gallery frequented by "sophisticates" and concocted unusual mixes of people and art. At different times, Harry recalled seeing paintings by Miro, Matisse, Gaugin, and Cezanne, small ones priced at fifty to seventy-five dollars and large ones selling for one to two hundred. The brothers traveled between high society and bohemia. Once they brought a Polynesian princess and her troupe of male dancers to a gallery opening, where everyone got tight on bootleg liquor. "If I ever attended an orgy, it was at one of their affairs," Harry said, "though we usually drank too much to remember."

The hedonistic stimulation of San Francisco fired up Harry's confidence and activities back at Stanford. When, as part of a hazing tradition, boys were "forced" by upperclassmen to dance with each other at the Freshman Bonfire, Harry thoroughly enjoyed it. He began meeting one of the boys from his dorm for assignations in the bushes. But quite suddenly, Harry fell in love. Like all freshmen in the third quarter, he had to join one of the university's eating clubs, and was sponsored by a young man named Smith Dawless to join his club, El Tigre.

After the first evening's meal, Dawless suggested they take a walk around the campus. As they strolled the moonlit fields, they talked mostly about the poetry Dawless wrote. Harry remembered, "We lay on a hill, and I started chewing on a long piece of hay. Smith picked up the other end and chewed that, and we wound up in his room, which was one of the few private ones. The next morning, I woke to see Smith pulling foxtails that had gotten stuck in my college sweater the night before. The sight of that made me want to shout my love from Hoover Tower." Dawless was equally enraptured and dubbed Harry "Python Coils," a poetic intimacy about a creature whose strong clinch had no beginning and no end. "Discovery," an obliquely erotic poem Dawless wrote about their affair in the spring of 1931, won a contest that year and was published in the mimeographed *Yearbook of Stanford Writing*.

Harry's roving eye, however, led him to on-the-sly trysts with a ballet dancer named Horace who lived in San Francisco. Bereft, Dawless joined a summer-stock company as soon as school ended and announced that he could not return. Harry's straying, moreover, strained some other relationships. "Because of my 'irresponsible' flirting while I was coupled with Smith, I got a bit of a rep in certain Stanford circles. This didn't mean that the fashionable 'in-group' at the time was monogamous — only that they were ingenuous. Deceivers, but discreet about it. In the beginning, I was neither!" Harry worried more about the poet than about his own reputation. But from small theaters across the country, Dawless wrote a stream of sentimental letters, all of them beginning, "Dear Coils."

▽

Harry found a summer job as a clerk and part-time musician at the Housekeeping Camp and Hotel of Fallen Leaf Lake. Armed with his new knowledge of adult affairs, he grew his hair long, hoping to catch the attention of young men among the guests and staff. Instead of love, however, he ended up with a taste of worldly dissapointment. The family-run resort was tightly run, and since jobs were scarce during this Depression time, no one dared question the lack of privacy. One employee professed his crush to Harry but, terrified of being "suspected," he refused to touch him, even in a rowboat in the center of the lake. Ironically, Harry was even enlisted to quash the gay trysts of another employee who was being talked about and was in danger of losing his job.

Harry's attempts at romance that summer were a series of discreet failures. The most stirring was with a Hollywood actor named John Darrow. The Eastern-born Darrow had interned in Washington as a congressional page and, according to his press kit, was voted "handsomest pageboy" on Capitol Hill. He rose rapidly as an actor and played the young pilot in the silent classic *Hell's Angels,* which Harry and Frank Fenton had viewed repeatedly. Darrow had come to the lake with a male friend, but he made it a point to befriend his obviously love-struck young fan. Though they remained platonic, Darrow was the first person to tell Harry that in the film colony, there were temperamental friends all around — if one looked carefully and followed the rules. The summer job was cut short when Harry badly sprained his ankle.

Harry returned to Stanford walking with a cane but otherwise sure-footed, a tall, handsome, and brainy college man, with formidable confidence. As one of his lovers said about him, "Harry knew everything — which was intimidating, because he really did!" Harry joined the Glee Club and was invited to join a fraternity. In the shower after gym class, a beautiful diver smiled at Harry frequently and introduced himself as Pete. Pete was one more reason Harry looked forward to a fine year.

But life was not entirely happy. His best friend, David Hawkins, had found a girlfriend, and to double-date with his friends, Harry fell back on his high school practice of playing it straight and dating women. On campus, his secret affairs with boys proliferated, and he often pursued more than one at a time. On top of that, he hopped north as often as possible to the delights of San Francisco's gay scene. Maintaining these multiple lives involved keeping his sets of friends separated, sometimes by making up several sets of alibis. At one point, he miserably confided his problems to Hawkins, who had a tendency to juggle more than one girl at a time. David, who already knew Harry's secret, suggested that since the two of them spent so much time together anyway, perhaps they should fall in love and live together. "The problem was that he was really straight," Harry said. "I told him it just wasn't that easy." The challenge of keeping track of his alibis became nerve-racking: "I couldn't remember to whom I had told what. I felt almost as though I was going mad. I couldn't stand it any more."

To make a clean sweep, a few months into his sophomore year, Harry came out on campus, systematically declaring his homosexuality to nearly every student he knew — in his eating club, in the Glee Club, and to dorm-mates in his new residence hall, Branner. This was an outrageous action, one that completely destabilized the polite, established order. Harry described his motive as both the simple desire to "see what it meant to live as a homosexual" and as the only escape from his desperately stressful web of lies. Most reactions seemed mild. Jean, like David, held the attitude of "so what else is new." A member of the Glee Club (which he sensed was almost entirely "temperamental") told Harry that many of them "might feel very understanding," though none of them could ever say so openly. No one in his eating club seemed concerned. But the fraternity told him firmly that his membership would not be a good idea, and Pete the diver, with whom he had finally made a date, suddenly severed all contact. As the weeks went by, Harry found that many of the people who said they didn't mind seemed to be going out of their way not to be seen in his company.

"The problem," he commented, "was that I came out at a time when that was unheard of. Had I waited to be brought out, I could have joined all those circles." But Harry couldn't wait.

Not all doors to romance, however, were shut. In gym class, Harry noticed "this perfectly darling fairy two rows away." He was just seventeen years old, a year younger than Harry, and was new at Stanford. He had a broad face set with large, intense blue eyes and wide, dark lips. His name was James Broughton; in later years he would gain fame as a prize-winning poet and filmmaker. Young Broughton's fey, flirtatious personality perfectly matched his elfin features. Smitten, Harry plotted an approach. First, he memorized the number Broughton stood on in the gym, which yielded his name from the class roster. From there, the student registry revealed his residence hall. One night, Harry followed the perfectly darling fairy to his dorm, but before a word could be spoken, the quarry shut the door. The next morning when he left his room, Broughton recalled, there stood Harry, who invited him to have a Coke and talk. "About what?" Broughton asked. "About you!" Harry replied.

"Harry had a bearing," the poet said by way of summation. He found it both alluring and intimidating. He described Hay as "determined" and even "ruthless" in his courtship. "He gave it to me as an ultimatum. I *had* to go with him. The persistence was what made him attractive — you knew he really wanted you." Though not inexperienced in matters of sex, Broughton felt overwhelmed by Python Coils, and their brief affair was passionate. For their first date, Harry somehow contrived an elaborate high tea, complete with a tea set and all the proper cakes. On the next, all Harry could offer was saltines, ginger ale, and a private reading — in bed — of *Hassan,* a play set in romantic Arabian fantasy by British author James Elroy Flecker. Written in somewhat campy verse, it follows the transformation of a spurned lover into a thoughtful pilgrim seeking "the golden towers of Samarkand." A bemused young Broughton listened to the verses and watched the clouds roll through the afternoon sky.

Broughton played down the affair in a 1986 interview, but his 1931 love letters confirm strong feelings. He wrote, "If I could only regain the carefree aspect of that first afternoon of ours, when you were so tender, so illogical, so gay, and lovable." He also betrayed a sense of their incompatibility. "Science and mathematics have made you too practical, and being very empty-headedly romantic myself, I long for the freedom of that love, which lives for nothing but the gaiety of the moment." With the self-effacing persona that was to become his lifelong trademark, Broughton offered "to take you out of that baffling self and into little unbaffling me." They recommended William Blake and imagist books to each other, and exchanged poems and letters.

But, quite suddenly, the romance ended. Harry recalled that Broughton's friend Neal Berry approached him to break off the relationship. "He explained that James had been in 'this sort of trouble' before and that his conservative family was capable of cutting short his education — and all other funding — if it happened again." In this light, Harry's status as Stanford's most visible homosexual made him a particularly grave social liability. Berry ended this petition with the suggestion, "If you care about him, make him be the one to end it. And you must not let him know I spoke to you." Sadly but dutifully, Harry decided that he would be honorable about his "responsibilities" for the younger person, and called Frank Fenton to plan a tour of the seamiest bars in San Francisco, the better to appall the tender seventeen-year-old. Loud drag queens, "rough trade," and other coarse aspects of the gay demimonde, they imagined, would be sufficiently distasteful.

Late that Friday night, after the gritty trip, they returned to the house of James's parents, who were gone that weekend. Harry had planned to stay, "but James said, 'I think we better end it now.' He didn't even give me time to say good-bye, to hold him in my arms one last night." Though he had deliberately provoked an authentic break, Harry still felt miserable as he took the lonely train back to Stanford. On Sunday night Broughton wrote him, "Do you want me to return your letters? ... I want this adventure to end as pleasantly and friendly as possible, for I like you too much as a person to want to be unreasonably unkind. I am sorry that you asked me not to speak to you when I see you in gym or elsewhere." He arranged to return shoes, a package, and a library book. Monday, he wrote, "I had dinner with Neal this evening. I shall never be able to thank you adequately for your superb fineness, your kindness, to me. I have been bitterly unhappy all day." Broughton burned Harry's letters and sent him a William Blake print. A sonnet about James Broughton remains in Harry's papers. But they did not encounter one another again for fifty years, when they met under the sympathetic circumstances of a Radical Faerie gathering.

Harry's flood of college poetry, which both Smith Dawless and James Broughton encouraged, was sometimes whimsical, but his most common theme was of bittersweet longing. A few of his poems appeared in student publications and more were published in arts journals later. His poems were often strongly homoerotic; one begins,

> When with your milk of manhood I am drunk,
> and feel your flaccid muscles turn from me,
> I know what want you had of me is shrunk,
> (the bird is preened and hungers to be free).

Another poem in his notebook is titled "Sodomy," later changed to "Sodom," and its lines about "womanless lusts" include:

> hide your honey-sweetness of narcissism,
> else I press the great thighs to my mouth,
> else I draw you wantonly through my lips.

Harry's outer confidence and social brashness masked his substantantial insecurity and loneliness during this time. Such melancholia is betrayed in his poem "Hell's Patterns," published in the 1931 *Yearbook of Stanford Writing*, about the end of another affair:

> Black and white flung on my window...
> And me the prism of a tear...
> I am trapped in the web of your sequence
> And yet I may not come near.

> Black and white splashed on the ceiling
> And me the hull of the stair,
> And if the black lengthen and deepen
> I shouldn't be there.

> Black and white patterns in magic
> And me the mind that is chained
> And what is an altar to God
> When the cloth has been stained...?

Harry admitted that his coming out had backfired. "I loved sexuality very much, but I was always looking for a sort of idealism as well, and the guys I was meeting in San Francisco were into sex and that was all. I felt like I had given away the glow and the idealism for sexuality. I thought I would be going into greater realms of spirit, and it turned out that I seemed to have closed the spirit off."

The emotional stress of that could not have been easy to bear, though Harry was alternately taciturn and blithely dismissive on the subject. David Hawkins and Jean Hay recalled that it was a deeply serious issue for him, and both were aware of a heavy gloom settling over him. These friends were questioned by Stanford counselors about what Harry called his "complex" — Harry had made some "joking references to suicide" as a solution to his identity dilemma. Hawkins cited a "terrible need to be open" in Harry, and aside from his intimate life, his future was torn between his plans and his father's. Specifically, his proud assertions of homosexuality stood in scandalous opposition to his role as "the example" of the Hay family. His failure to pledge a fraternity had him worried that he was already disappointing his parents. The strains on "the baffling self" James Broughton had identified made a crisis inevitable.

It happened one February morning in the winter quarter of 1932. "I had just passed the end of the second week, the point of being able to drop courses without being penalized, when I woke up one morning with an absolutely shocking headache. I had never had this before. The first few days I sort of staggered through it, took lots of aspirin, and even [used] a hot water bottle. By the third day I got to the infirmary." There he was diagnosed with a massive sinus infection and was immediately hospital-ized. Yards of gauze soaked in an anesthetic cocaine solution were packed into his nasal passages, which deadened the pain, but only for a while. His doctor ordered him to forget school for the rest of the term and go to a dry climate. His cousin George's ranch in Weeks, Nevada, was ideal, so Harry made arrangements, packed his clothes, and stored his books and tea set, anticipating a return he never made.

David Hawkins surmised that Harry's premature departure from Stan-ford may have had something to do with his daring homosexual declara-tions, and called the end of Harry's studies "an unhappy time for him, and I think partly the fault lay with the university's inability to deal with the kind of person that he was." James Broughton remembered that Harry left under a cloud. Both Harry and his brother Jack, however, insisted that his reason for leaving Stanford was purely medical, and that his not returning was due only to tight finances. Whatever Harry's innermost feelings were, the pressures against boys with bright futures going homosexual at that time were unbearable for many. Within a few years, his school chum

"Handsome Al" Cronkite, whom Harry always suspected could not face his own homosexuality, committed suicide.

By the spring, Harry was sleeping outdoors in a tent and working with the ranch hands, cutting hundred-pound slabs of ice from the Carson River and hauling them to the ranch cellar. Such simple, rugged work and the familiar associations of ranch life occupied all his physical and mental energies and proved the perfect cure. He even helped forge metal tools in the ranch blacksmith shop. The beauty of that familiar countryside warmed his spirit, as did the simple camaraderie of working with a team of men. He was happy and stayed nearly a year.

It was while living this idyllic, rustic existence that Harry woke up in the middle of the night in his tent with a sudden insight. Though he had always felt shoved to the edge of the socialist utopia because of the anti-homosexual threats of the Wobblies, he realized that if the teams were entirely "temperamental," it would not matter: "If we cared about each other, we could be unbeatable as a work team, and no one could criticize us when they'd see what we could produce." Like reading Edward Carpenter when he was eleven, this insight sparked a gay communal vision that survived through Hay's life.

This long-term gay vision would probably never have crystallized had Harry completed the university. The homing instinct that directed him to Weeks is hinted at in a story he wrote a few years later called "Loveliest Spring," about a young man whose college plans break down.

> He had done all this [coursework], just as he had been told, until the preceding winter. And then, practically invalided with sinus, and lonely for the one place he'd ever wanted to call home, Ellis had turned tail just before final exams and made tracks for his cousin's place on the Carson.

The predestined life of an establishment scion faded into the distance. Though he intended at first to continue his classes by correspondence, the environment in Weeks was isolated and earthy, not conducive to study. Eventually, Harry learned that his Stanford jobs were unavailable and that his parents, badly battered by two years of the Great Depression, could no longer afford to make up the difference.

Before he returned to Los Angeles in the fall of 1932, his friend Jean Hay came with her parents to visit Harry at the ranch. The "cousins by preference" walked in a field, and Harry made a garland of wildflowers to set atop her thick auburn curls. In a shy, wistful moment, he blurted, "If I ever grow up, I might ask you to marry me."

She answered, "If you ever do, I might say yes."

▾4▾

An actor's life

He's learned the English tradition well, and Harry's very believable under amber spots.

— Will Geer

Los Angeles in the thirties was a city still teetering between the rough frontier and the stodgy Midwest. A powerful elite exploited the land and its populace. Police chiefs quickly burned out if they were honest, and those that stayed provided cover to vice operations and gangsters. After the stock market crash, Los Angeles police chief "Strongarm" Dick Steckel, at the urging of such anti-union businessmen as Harry Chandler of the *Los Angeles Times,* earned Los Angeles the title "citadel of the open shop." Early demonstrations of the unemployed were met with police violence and police broke up meetings of Leftists so routinely that L.A. Reds took their activism to neighboring cities. "Angel Town," city of oranges and wealth, was a city of double standards between the haves and have-nots.

Among the greatest have-nots were homosexuals. Moral outrage escalated because of a series of scandals that rocked Los Angeles in the twenties, such as the murder of director William Desmond Taylor. That crime was not solved for six decades, because Taylor, one of Hollywood's classiest film directors, was gay, and homosexuality was a greater scandal than an unprosecuted murder. In such a moral mire, gays served as the perfect scapegoats in crackdowns and arrest sweeps. Harry recalled with annoyance that before every mayoral or city council election, the parks where gay men met for midnight trysts were raided so that politicians and police could brag of "cleaning up the riffraff." Only public decency had rights. The front page of the *Times* in 1930 blared that when the body of a murdered boy was found, the house of "every known deviant" was searched.

It was to this appearance-conscious, nosey city that Harry returned in September of 1932. Physically restored from eight months in the hay fields, he was also wealthy — the summer haying paid him a Depression fortune of two hundred dollars. But once home he hardly knew what to do with his life. As befits a young man of twenty, he went in many directions at once: In the early thirties, Harry pursued writing, acting, dancing, politics, and a dizzying flurry of what he called "love affairs."

These increased through a kind of cruising that was a step up from the streetcar. He discovered it one Friday night around eleven, while waiting for a bus at Hollywood and Vine. A surprising number of handsome cars, he noticed, circled the corner. "An almost new Cadillac sport convertible stopped right before the bus got there, and with old-fashioned courtesy, the driver asked if he could drive me home. In the course of that ride, I got to know Joe McManus, a well-to-do businessman who lived with his mother. And I learned what the other circling cars were all about."

He visited McManus often, and met his coterie of conservative European emigré friends. But Harry was looking for zestier companions. These he found in the close-knit world of Los Angeles artists. His introduction came, ironically, from his conservative mother. Reading the *Times,* Margaret noticed the return from Europe of John Cage to his prominent Eagle Rock family. At her prodding, and himself curious about how his high school tutor had grown up, Harry telephoned. Cage remembered him and invited him to afternoon tea, beginning a fascinating episode.

Cage would later attain world fame as a composer, author, and iconoclastic philosopher. His renowned intellect pursued many of the 1930s experimentalist notions that old cultural forms were becoming obsolete, and the frontiers he chose to expand were of music. As a composer, he "deconstructed" music by introducing silence, "prepared" instruments, and the element of chance as the basis of many of his compositions. Acceptance of detachment in both art and life, he believed, would break down the boundaries between the two and hence was the wave of the future. Such ideas earned him a reputation as master of the American Zen gesture. Cage pioneered electronic music, composed a noteless score in which the pianist sat silently at his instrument, and for many years collaborated with choreographer Merce Cunningham on experimental dances. By the 1980s, Cage was internationally revered as the grand old man of the avant-garde arts.

In 1932, at the age of nineteen, he had just dedicated his life to music. After graduating from L.A. High, Cage went abroad to study painting and architecture, and in Paris met a young American artist named Don Sample, also known as Don St. Paul. They traveled south together to Majorca, where they lived for six months, and finally drove from New York to Los Angeles in a Model T Ford.

John invited Harry to tea at a Spanish baronial–style house in the Pacific Palisades neighborhood of West Los Angeles. "It was the second house of John's Depression-stricken parents, Milton and Crete," he recalled. "They had put it on the market, so it was stripped of furniture, save a few tables and daybeds the boys covered with blankets and weavings they had bought in Greece and Majorca. In such a big, high-ceilinged place, the effect was very bohemian."

His hosts were unforgettable characters. "John was at first very New England, very formal and buttoned-down in his three-piece suit and tie. His blunt face revealed very little smile and very little charm. He didn't say much. I always had the feeling that he was afraid the bottom button of his vest would pop open and you might see his belly button, and it would give you the wrong idea — whatever that wrong idea was."

Sample, on the other hand, was freewheeling. "Don had bright, mischievous eyes in a scholarly-looking face. He wore little glasses and had a shock of lank hair that kept falling over his lenses; he looked very boyish, pushing it back all the time." The more secure and verbal of the two, Don fired a steady stream of cultural questions at Harry, but criticized Harry's responses in a bewildering manner, one that "made me very aware of the mud under my shoes." When Harry remarked, for instance, that he had enjoyed a performance of *Carmen* he had seen in San Francisco, Sample laughingly pronounced that opera passé. However, when Harry mentioned having seen and liked Mary Wigman, the Isadora Duncan of Germany, Sample approved. Other questions and answers followed in this cross-examination pattern. By the time he left, Harry felt "like a bug on a pin."

During the hour-and-a-half streetcar trip home, his humiliation simmered into a resolve never to return. But when he walked in his door, Margaret was just putting the phone down, and told him insistently to call Cage. He did so diffidently, and was told, "You've passed the test — you're one of us. There's plenty of room, so when can you come back?" When Harry returned that night, he found Cage and Sample completely welcoming, and they made no mention of the tense tea. Over the next six weeks, a "totally sharing comradeship developed between us, to the point of swapping each other's freshly ironed shirts." The insatiably cultural Sample took the role of instructor. He located, for example, new buildings by Internationalist-style architects R.M. Schindler and Richard Neutra (both Austrian emigrés) and the boys drove around to view them on weekends. Back home, they checked the Bauhaus catalogue Sample had brought back from Europe for commentary on furniture and design detail.

As their friendship deepened, Harry's hosts showed him a slim portfolio of the homoerotic photographs by Baron Wilhelm von Gloeden, and an edition of stories by the artfully perverse British author Ronald Firbank. At Sample's prodding, the three friends even camped around the house with what Harry described as "merry drag performances." Behind closed doors, Cage seemed to drop his reserve; he seemed both bonded with, and in thrall to, Sample's adventurous spirit.

One warm day in early October, the three stopped to invite a friend named Maddie to join their beach picnic. She was at the piano, practicing the accompaniment to a song called "At Dawning" by Charles Wakefield Cadman. Harry commented that he had sung that song in his high school Glee Club, and Maddie begged to hear it, which did not go over well in all quarters. "Such emotional hearth-and-home songs were exactly what those two detested, so Don quickly started picking up our bags and beach umbrella. The pleading of Maddie and then John made him relent. She started the introduction and I sang it. Afterwards, when Maddie was thanking me, John interrupted, 'You never told us you could sing like that.' And Don said, 'Migawd, Honey, that's a first-class voice. Come on, guys, we've got work to do!' 'But what about the beach and all this food?' the others asked. 'That was before Harry sang,' Don said."

Cage had scheduled a concert the following month, an experimental bill of music by Poulenc, Hindemith, and Honegger, as well as two of his own compositions. It was to Cage's work that Sample wanted Harry to perform the vocals. One was a setting of Greek odes from *The Persians* by Aeschylus, the other based on "At East and Ingredients" by Gertrude Stein; both were especially challenging. Sample rigorously coached Harry in the Greek alphabet and pronunciation, as well as in German and French for other songs. The Greek finale, about the death of Xerxes, had special effects and costumes — Greek blankets and stark makeup. Harry joked that he looked like "Diogenes just crawled out of a barrel." He continued, "The blankets I was wearing were white, and a sort of lampshade shone colored patterns onto me." Cage's father, an inventor, had devised a fluorescent light source over which Sample laid a piece of vellum painted with designs in oils. "It looked very good. The thing got so hot the designs began to run, but that only made it better." But the audience, the Santa Monica Women's Club, seemed more challenged than impressed, and managed only strained applause. Still, somehow, the performance was engaged to be repeated the following spring. Harry called those concerts the out-of-town tryouts for Cage's career as a composer, and surmised that he was probably the earliest stage performer of Cage's music, a claim undisputed by Cage's biographer, Franz Von Rossum.

Harry continued to see Cage and Sample often during the next year and a half. In the summer of 1933, Harry helped Cage prepare a series of classes in modern painting and music for the local matrons, who formed his base of support. The lectures, based on an art history text, were sold door-to-door for twenty-five cents each. Harry searched thrift shops for art prints to use as illustrations. "We could get them for a nickel that way," he recalled. "If we didn't have that much money, we'd just swipe them." The next spring, Cage and Sample left L.A. to visit photographer Edward Weston and his wife Flora in Carmel, then went on to further travels, leaving behind Cage's stave-written scores from the concert. Harry kept and treasured them for years.

Sample returned alone that June and was promptly arrested in Delongpre Park in Hollywood on a morals charge. After his release from jail, Harry encountered him and was appalled by Sample's malnutrition-induced skin sores. Knowing Margaret , would insist on taking in such a waif, he brought Sample home, and indeed Margaret fed and nursed him for several weeks. Harry and Don remained friends for most of the thirties, but the friendship with John Cage soured. When the composer returned in 1937 he brought back a wife, Xenia Kashevaroff. Harry went to the family's home in Eagle Rock to pay a social call, but "John would not let me in and would not say why. He spoke to me at the back porch. It was very awkward, and I finally left. I could only guess I looked too — obvious." Cage's marriage ended in 1945, and he remained unmarried and guarded about his private life.

In May of 1933 Harry met Paul Mooney, the lover and ghostwriter of romantic explorer Richard Halliburton, and the son of anthropologist James Mooney, who coincidentally wrote an original study of the Ghost Dance religion of Wovoka. Paul Mooney was a handsome Lothario, with beautiful young men trekking up and down the hill to the house he shared with his lover in Laguna. While Harry was not his physical type, they were mentally well matched, and talked till dawn many nights. The friendship that blossomed proved important to Harry. "Paul was my first gay 'big brother' who seemed to understand my thinking and interests. It was during our talks that I first heard about Robert Briffault's six-volume study called *The Mothers,* which was the basis of my historical materialism work a dozen years later. Paul also told me about the black ghetto nightclubs on Central Avenue, where boys could dance together."

While Harry was looking for work that spring, sharp-eyed Margaret noticed another newspaper item: A newly arrived theater troupe would stage a dramatization of Charles Dickens's *A Tale of Two Cities* at the Hollywood Playhouse. Noted English actor Philip Merivale headlined George K. Arthur's International Group Players, but local actors would be cast in minor roles. Harry immediately went to audition. "It was a cattle call of hundreds of unemployed actors," he recalled. "All of them were gripped with the Hollywood fever: 'I've got to do something on stage — someone will see me!'" The director, E.E. Clive, singled Harry out from among the throng and gave him the part of Citizen DeFarge, who, during the French Revolution, led the yells at the guillotine while his wife counted the tumbling heads by the stitches in her knitting. The play opened as a Hollywood society event, with Clive Brook, Fredric March, and Dolores Del Rio in attendance. Harry was entranced with the company, which had most recently performed at the Copley Square Theater in Boston but had toured provincial England for years before that. The Players continued performing "well-made" drawing-room dramas to showcase themselves for the movies, and from its ranks, Laird Cregar, E.E. Clive, and Arthur Treacher launched film careers.

When Treacher received a sudden call for a film role during *A Tale of Two Cities,* Harry got his understudy break. He was given a single afternoon to learn his part, but Laird Cregar and his boyfriend gave Harry coaching and moral support. The scene was opposite Merivale, the big star, and Harry, though terrified, exited to applause, and was later hired as the company's male understudy. "There were about twelve men in the company and male roles were often doubled, so I was frequently employed. I had to be ready to go onstage in any one of eight men's parts," he said. A quick and somewhat arrogant study, he deliberately strayed from the scripts to test his improvisations — and the patience of the company. The eight years of stagework that followed barely paid for his lunches and streetcar fares, but it had a lasting effect on his ability to communicate.

If he was not already beyond caring about his son's career, Big Harry must have been furious. The stage was never a practical career choice, and was especially bleak in those years. Several major Los Angeles theaters became casualties of the Depression while Harry was away at Stanford, and even before the crash, actors all over the country suffered cutbacks in work. Still, Harry took delight in his apprenticeship. As an eager new member of George K. Arthur's Players, he was liked. An older actress named Elspeth Dudgeon, called "Dudgey" for short, taught him classic makeup techniques, how to place himself in the light, and how to project his voice. In roles ranging from juvenile to senile, he got typed as a character actor. Will Geer, whom Hay met later in a production, pitched him to a Universal Studios director, saying, "He's learned the English tradition well, and Harry's very believable under amber spots."

He lived backstage as much as possible, and learned to appreciate the almost tribal theater culture the other players seemed to represent. He was particularly intrigued by the second-class, "not respectable" reputation of theater folk, and their proximity to the twilight people — homosexuals. Backstage was where Harry learned to camp, which he saw as having the social responsibility of making light of a serious problem, and so gently bringing it into awareness. (Harry invariably isolated a high-minded tradition in any aspect of the gay world, and he always distinguished "camping" from "dishing," the harsher version of gay banter.)

As a backstage name, the Britishers dubbed Harry "the Duchess." He said on different occasions that it was shortened from the affectionate "Duchess Theodora Beara" and "the Duchess of Devonshire." Whatever the case, it so aptly connoted the high dudgeon to which he was given that "the Duchess" became Harry's lifelong drag name.

Acting consumed Harry for the first half of the thirties. He even wrote to one friend that he planned to pack off to Broadway. When he perforce took other jobs, they were cultural, like carrying spears in visiting operas and reading for radio plays. His ear for languages got him work as a freelance dialogue coach among Hollywood's foreign colony of expatriate royalty. These were mostly Hungarians, White Russians, or Czechs, dukes and countesses who scraped along as dress extras in the costume epics of Hollywood's golden age. Harry explained, "Josphine Dillon, the other game in town, never could get Hungarians to say 'jam and pajamas' on radio. Of course she charged fifteen dollars a lesson and I charged only five ... when I could collect in anything besides trade, which was *sometimes* a meal at some Ladies' Club luncheon."

He continued to write poetry, which occasionally got published (though never for money), and started collecting rejection notices for short stories he wrote. His steadiest work was as a screen extra, often as a stunt rider for Republic and Monogram westerns. (Riding tricks he'd learned as a teen in Nevada now paid off.) And when female impersonator Ray

Bourbon performed in his Sunset Strip nightclub, Harry worked for him as a shill.*

He also sang. Through an ad, Harry joined a Latvian Choir which performed Russian Orthodox hymns in churches throughout Southern California, and he developed a novelty act by singing duet with his mother, continuing their long tradition. Hay composed arrangements for the German, English, and California-Spanish songs they sang, and devised a unique professional gimmick. "Mother and I would sing behind a screen. I would play piano or she would, but no one could tell what the combination of singers was." Margaret's "woman's baritone" so matched Harry's bass that their voices were almost identical. "It sounded like a man and another man, and when we came out from behind the screen we surprised people." They performed for banquets of the Los Angeles Masons, and occasionally appeared on amateur talent radio shows, where an announcer once said to the gasping studio audience, "And you'd never believe this is mother and son!"

As a sophisticated bohemian and a young man new to gay life, Harry discovered a new dimension to Los Angeles. At dusk and after the theater let out, young men without cars would amble elegant Hollywood Boulevard in search of "friends." During this leisurely street cruising, "we would stop in the best tailor shops, handling everything, buying nothing. If someone had a red tie or a lavender handkerchief, he might be — interesting." A more secure Harry than the nervous underage pickup of Champ Simmons returned to Pershing Square and also found out the charms of Lafayette, Delongpre, and Echo parks. As Paul Mooney had directed, he found the speakeasies of Central Avenue, the Harlem of Los Angeles, where indeed, "gays were permitted to come and be easy with themselves and maybe even dance together — cautiously, to be sure, without upsetting people too much."

In 1933, when Prohibition was repealed, speakeasies turned into nightclubs. "Before 1933, these places were raided, the patrons booked, shamed, and publicized because of the Volstead Act. After 1933, in our places, the same routine continued *because it was queer!* Freddie's had a new opening about six times a year. It was Freddie's and Jimmie's and

---

* This campy, outrageous comedian traveled the vaudeville circuit in the twenties and thirties, then starred in Mae West's stage shows in the forties. In the 1950s, he became known as "Rae" by undergoing one of the first sex-change surgeries, immortalized on the record album *Let Me Tell You About My Operation.*

Johnny's and Tessie's and Bessie's. More established places like Maxwell's downtown would get knocked over and close down but pay off the cops and not move out."

One night, while cruising one of the parks, he ran across a familiar face. It was George, the boy he used to neck with during mass at St. Gregory's. "'Fancy meeting you here,' I said. 'I see you've quit the Church.' He looked quite annoyed at me and said, 'No. Why should I do that?' 'So you wouldn't have to be a hypocrite,' I answered. That upset him, and he said, 'I don't have to give up my faith because I happen to — know what I like.' 'What's that? Sucking cock in the bushes?' He turned purple and hissed, 'Must you be *so vulgar?*' and huffed away."

Like many of the Depression generation, Harry lived at home until he married. While in the house he politely adhered to his parents' rules, but as a sign of adult independence, he moved from the room he shared with Jack to the maid's room after she was let go. Big Harry's outrage shifted to concern. One morning at the breakfast table, he announced that he had signed a 99-year lease with the Ritz-Carlton Hotel for one of his Hollywood Boulevard properties. "We'll have a guaranteed income for life," he said. "And of course we'll have to take care of Harry because he's the dreamer and he'll never make any money." The Depression undid that plan, but even without a guaranteed income, Harry continued to dream.

$$\triangledown$$

It is hard to keep track of youthful Harry's restless affairs. In fact, he once said that he must have had "two or three affairs a day between 1932 and 1936." But the sexual flurry did not preclude several ongoing relationships. One lover was a blue-black Afro-Cuban man named Luis Rosado who worked as houseboy for screen actors Bebe Daniels and Ben Lyon; another was a conservative, scheming Hungarian count.

But the most important relationship of that time was with an actor he would meet backstage in an antique melodrama, *The Ticket of Leave Man — or — Falsely Accused*. This first production of the new Tony Pastor Theater on Sunset Boulevard, the Los Angeles branch of a famous New York house, was the pet project of producer John Decker. The entire theater was modeled after the conventions of the nineteenth century, a beer hall with "meller-dramas" and variety artists. The 1933 handbills advertising *Leave Man* deadpanned: "Hitch up the old gray mare and come over and hiss the villain!" (This formula was later used to greater advantage by *The Drunkard,* L.A.'s longest-running stage production.)

Harry was hired as the comedy lead, a part that was later cut, so he played several bit parts and worked as assistant stage manager. The cast of *Leave Man,* like the George K. Arthur Players, consisted mostly of performers over forty who had spent years touring. One of the younger members was particularly interesting. "The guy who played Honest Bob Brierly, the lead, was a big, slightly awkward-looking man. Seeing him rehearsing, I was immediately aware of a dynamic sexual presence. He was not classically handsome, but was very arresting, with powerful, quiet eyes. Our glances met during that first meeting and held for a moment too long. My throat went dry and I knew I'd made a connection." This was Will Geer, known to modern audiences as "Grandpa Walton" from the famous 1970s television series. Then a thirty-year-old actor, Geer had already spent half his life on stage, with experience ranging from tent and riverboat shows to playing Shakespeare on Broadway. He had only recently arrived in Los Angeles and was seeking film work.

The two young actors made a point of avoiding each other for the six weeks of rehearsal, but shortly before the opening, Harry learned that the charismatic and urbane Geer loved nature, and invited him hiking. "I took Bill — he was not known as Will then — to White's Park and Creek, in what used to be known as the Santa Ynez Mountains. We came in from the Valley side because the mountains in front were part of the Rindge Ranch. There were wonderful geological features to be seen in White's Canyon. Many birds hunted there temporarily on their way south in fall; there were salamanders in the creek, and thick herbal growth along the banks." Geer, who had a degree in botany, wasn't familiar with many of the wild plants of the area, so they filled a knapsack with cuttings to ask about at the next ranger station. Harry stayed with Bill that night in his room at the Mountain View Inn on Hollywood Boulevard. Many days of vigorous hikes, and blissful nights, followed.

It was Will Geer who introduced Harry to the Left-wing community of Los Angeles, and eventually to its Communist Party. This started over coffee klatches between Geer and Maude Allen, an older actress who lived at the Mountain View and was also in the show with them. They hashed over the anti-socialist Palmer Raids made by the federal government in the 1920s, the Sacco and Vanzetti trials, and various strikes — fascinating stuff to this young man. Around Geer's room lay pamphlets and leaflets similar to those the Wobblies had shown Harry in Nevada, but newer. He read them all.

Though new in town, Geer had already earned a reputation as a radical Leftist. He produced fund-raising and entertainment events on a regular basis, sometimes in conjunction with the John Reed Experimental Theater Club. In fact, the proprietor of the Mountain View was a Leftist who gave Geer a free room in exchange for political spoofs to be staged in the parlor every week. These had names such as *The Siege of El Monte— or— 1000 Armed Reds March on Raspberry Fields* and *Today We Fascist.* Geer produced other skits and plays around Los Angeles, including *Stevedore,* which united trade union and racial struggles.

As an active Leftist, Geer often approached wealthy sympathizers for contributions to campaigns and productions. Geer mentioned to Harry two sympathetic heiresses, Kate Crane Gartz of the Chicago steel and iron fortune, and Aline Barnsdall, daughter of an oil driller. Barnsdall lived in Hollywood in a superb Frank Lloyd Wright house atop an olive-planted hill she later gave to the city as a park and museum. Around the base of her huge lot were large signboards supporting radical causes such as Free India, the Scottsboro boys, the eight-hour day, and the Free Tom Mooney campaign. Harry was never taken to these private pitch meetings, but recalled that many times he trimmed the threads off Geer's well-worn coat sleeves to make him look presentable.

Geer plunged Harry into hard-core activism: demonstrations for the benefit of the unemployed, for the wretchedly exploited field workers in the Central California Valley, for labor unions in need of lawyers. The radical young actors once even handcuffed themselves to the wrought-iron lamp posts that flanked the main entrance to the original campus of U.C.L.A. (now Los Angeles City College) to pass out leaflets for the American League Against War and Fascism. The police soon cut them down and dragged them away.

One afternoon, Geer sent Harry to downtown L.A.'s Bunker Hill district to observe a demonstration. It grew rough and became one of his favorite stories. "The Milk Strike," Harry recounted, "was an action called in 1933 by the wives and mothers of the poor and unemployed to make the government stop allowing surplus milk to be poured down the storm drains to keep the price up. They wanted it for the needy. A crowd of thousands turned out downtown in the shadow of the newly built City Hall." Harry wore his best clothes that day. "If you were very well dressed in Hollywood then, you wore a very white shirt with a starched collar and tie, probably a black tie. And if you were a Hollywood actor, you wore a black silk hankie in your pocket to match your tie. Of course, I was being a bit of a nonconformist that day, and was wearing an ascot with a stickpin. Not many people wore ascots in those days. There would have been Nils Asther and David Niven — and Ray Milland — and me."

Looking up, he saw machine guns atop nearby buildings. Violence had broken out in many cities over human needs, and the local government was prepared for the worst. He backed away from the quickly growing crowd when he saw mounted police charging through the thick of it, swinging their clubs at people's heads. "This was a dramatic scene! Women were grabbing and shielding their children, and every so often you would see someone go down with a bloody head. The police were being absolutely brutal, without provocation. I think they may have wanted to incite a riot so they could clear the crowd."

With his hands behind him, Harry backed up to the open door of a bookstore, where stacks of newspapers were held down by bricks. He found his hand resting on a brick. "I made no conscious decision, I just found myself heaving it and catching a policeman right in the temple. He slid off his horse and a hundred faces turned to me in amazement. No one was more amazed than I. Always before, I had been the one who threw the ball like a sissy. This 'bull' was my first bull's-eye ever!"

Sympathizers murmuring in Yiddish, Portuguese, and English grabbed him. He heard, "We've got to hide this kid before the cops get him." Hands led him backward through a building connected to other buildings — a network of 1880s tenements that formed an interconnected *casbah* on the slopes of the sprawling old Bunker Hill quarter. He was pushed through rooms that immigrant women and children rarely left, across catwalks and planks, up, up, hearing the occasional reassurance, "Everything's fine. Just don't look down." Once out of the structure, near the top of the hill, he was hustled to a large Victorian house, where he found himself standing, dizzy and disoriented, in a living room full of men drinking coffee. In the center, cutting a cake, was a soft-featured man in women's attire. The man gestured theatrically when he spoke, and everyone addressed him as Clarabelle and referred to him as her. So did Harry: "Clarabelle had hennaed hair that was pinned up, and a blouse that was pulled down around the shoulders, gypsy style. I could tell by the condition of the skin that she was somewhere in her forties. 'My dear,' she said to me, 'we saw what you did, knocking that old cop off his high horse, and it should have been done years ago. We'll have to hide you; they'll be after you soon. Cup of coffee first? No, no time. They're already on their way.'"

Harry had heard of Clarabelle as one of the most powerful of the "Queen Mothers" who traditionally oversaw the temperamental comings and goings in the districts of town where they lived; Harry felt that such figures formed a regional network of salons among some pre-Stonewall gays. "Clarabelle controlled Bunker Hill and had at least a dozen 'lieutenants' covering stations, one called the Fruit Tank — that was our nickname for the jail cell for queers. Clarabelle was legendary, a Mary Boland type who really knew how to pin a curl while giving an order." She ordered Harry to be hidden in her basement, and a lieutenant led him down five flights of stairs to a room storing Persian rugs, concealed him in a carpeted cave, and promised him coffee and a fried-egg sandwich in due time. "After several hours, someone finally brought me the coffee. It turned out to be Clarabelle's nephew. A cute, sort of V-shaped young man who just loved sixty-nine. He stayed for hours. I never got the egg sandwich, but I didn't much care."

After his feat with the brick, Geer recruited Harry to help with his agitprop work. "Bill had an entire repertoire of five-minute plays, recitations, and dialogues that made Leftist propaganda points. He needed a fall guy to feed him his lines and make these things work, so I was happily drafted. To be honest, at that point, I was more interested in being around Bill than in the politics." They performed at all the demonstrations and benefits, and most often spontaneously in the streets, which served as Harry's next important training ground.

Throughout his long participation in the Left — indeed throughout his life — Hay kept alive Geer's training in agitprop, as he defined it, "a responsibility for keeping spirits high at picket lines and keeping attention focused at large meetings." Most often, they performed in the "Free Speech Zones" of Los Angeles, such as Westlake Park, where ideas could be freely expressed without risk of persecution. Geer had arranged for a van and driver. The back doors of the vehicle opened into a black-painted interior, which served as a stage. The actors entered and exited by turning flashlights on and off under their chins.

Harry shouted setup lines. "Time: From the Boom Days to the Dog Days! Place: All over the United States of America!" Their sketches discussing social reform were meant to be "sort of comforting, speaking the words of the oppressed in ways they couldn't speak for themselves." Over several months, "We did a whole flock of these and we got a pretty good reputation for ourselves." At another Free Speech Zone, the old church plaza on Olvera Street, protection was regularly ignored by the police. Mindful of this, they designed the van to close up and pull out fast, but if the crowd was too dense, the actors fled on foot. "A Chinese restaurant in an alley off the plaza, Jerry's Joynte, used to hide us. It was owned by an old Red who put us in his pantry and sent back plates of spare ribs. Once he dressed us in Chinese robes and false moustaches and hid us among the patrons!"

Harry and Bill's relationship went through a change after about four months, when Geer recommended an education class in the Hollywood section of the Communist Party. Harry found the sophisticated level of theory fascinating and bewildering, and he stuck with it mainly "out of my love for Bill." His older, more world-wise lover, however, was often called away to work in the Central Valley and other areas, and though Harry's involvement with the Party eventually became passionate and dedicated, it was hampered at the start by feelings of abandonment and resentment at what he called Geer's "total immersion" method of recruitment. These stresses made already challenging material even more difficult. "It was disorienting to sit there with urban people, mostly film workers, discussing rural worker models of Marxism," he said. His first teacher, Lillian Asche (who later became a friendly witness to HUAC), was also intimidating. "When I asked about the recent purges of Lovestone and Muste, I was harshly criticized as a reactionary. I simply shut my face. I felt I was in an intellectual prison. I couldn't find a link to any other theory I understood. But my imagination was caught, and I was madly in love with Bill." Several years later, this political deadlock would break, but because of it, 1933 was "a miserable year," even when Geer returned for weekend hikes. "I wasn't going to tell him my bewilderment — or that I knew *he* couldn't sort it all out either," Harry said, and as they drifted apart, he determinedly completed the class and signed up for another.

Harry found more than an ideological catalyst in Will Geer. Geer provided an ideal model to which Hay could aspire. He embodied the seemingly opposite directions of culture and radical politics through a persona of self-reliant, almost transcendent optimism. (Geer once said that his greatest fear was "people who believe you can't change human nature.") While remaining earthy and folksy, he could be cultured and refined. Neither his gardening trowel nor his progressive politics were ever retired, and his family referred to him until his death as "the world's oldest hippie." As he aged, these same descriptions fit Harry.

Harry credited the final step in his radicalization to the weekend he spent with Geer in San Francisco during the General Strike of July, 1934. Centered around a maritime strike which shut down the waterfront, the action lasted two months, involved 120 local unions, and became one of the largest and most dramatic actions of the modern labor movement. Governor Frank Finley Merriam, only six weeks in office, threatened to call in the state militia. During a period when *Leave Man* was closed for rewriting, Hay and Geer drove up the state, stopping regularly to gather donations of food for the strikers. Once in San Francisco, Geer was in heavy demand to speak and to attend various meetings. Sometimes Harry accompanied him, but other times he was assigned to type, translate, or in some other way help with the fervid activities of the hour.

Merriam did call out the guard, which opened fire on a crowd of more than two thousand. Harry was there and remembered hearing a bullet zing past his left ear. Two men were killed, eighty-five more were hospitalized, and *News-Week* headlined, "Blood Flows in San Francisco Streets." At the massive funeral procession that followed, Harry recalled, "As the two flag-covered caissons passed, drawn by horses slowly high-stepping to funeral music, a posse of dock workers knocked the bowlers off the heads of bankers who refused to show respect. It was pretty damn impressive." And it had a lasting impact. Hay told historian John D'Emilio, "You couldn't have been a part of that and not have your life completely changed."

Against such economic battles of hungry people versus greedy businessmen, the Communist Party exerted an urgent pull. Communists felt they were riding with the tide of history, and the Party offered a program of practical action that was global in scope. More personally, it held out a surrogate for Harry's aloof family — chosen comrades who had similar values. Mostly, it appealed to his deep idealism. C.P. historian Joseph Starobin describes the Party as "a community that went beyond national boundaries and differences of race and creed: it was driven by the certainty that man's sojourn on earth could be happier if only his social relations were transformed from competition to cooperation." To hundreds of thousands of Harry's generation, Communism represented something between opportunity and destiny to change the world for the better. At twenty-three, with his whole life ahead of him, he was caught by what he called "the siren song of Revolution."

For Harry, this passionate political enlightenment also marked the start of a protracted alienation: The Party strictly prohibited homosexuals from joining and did not acknowledge homosexuality as anything more than the degenerate phase of a decadent system. They were not a group who could have rights. Harry naively brought up his idea of a "team of brothers" to Geer, who would not consider it. "I said I'd wanted to get a society of 'just us' together. Bill argued that that was the theater." Harry countered that the theater milieu did not involve political discussion. "But what's to talk about?" Geer asked, exasperated. The only person who encouraged Harry's idea of organizing homosexuals was old Maude Allen. While Harry once argued the notion to Geer, she broke in that "this was possible, but you might have to start it yourself." Over the next twenty years as he occasionally proposed the concept of a gay political identity, Harry rarely got any more encouragement than that.

Still, for a spirit like Harry's, the Party was the future. "We were involved in organizing the unorganized; the CIO [Congress of Industrial Organizations] had a wide open field on the West Coast. Along with the waterfront, the newspaper guilds began to organize, as did the department stores." It was a dangerous and circumscribed world, which added to the thrill. "We were automatically afoul of the law. The Los Angeles Police Department's Red Squad was always ferreting out the agitators to see if they could expose them." Oppression was so intense, Harry recalled, that people who went to the one progressive bookstore in Los Angeles would barely look at each other for fear of provoking an undercover policeman. The Red underground demanded extreme discretion. False names were often used. Over the years, Harry would ponder how in the gay world many of the same practices were necessary.

▽

While his underground radical life flowered, Harry busily developed his paying careers. Hazel Harvey, an aspiring Hollywood photographer who rented a studio from his father, recognized Harry as another temperamental type, and they met regularly to drink coffee and trade studio gossip. She took a number of soulful acting portraits of Harry which emphasize his cleft chin, broad jaw, and high forehead with the deep wrinkle he called "the dent." They also show a remarkable resemblance to the popular thirties actor Charles Bickford, whom he hoped to understudy. Harry did get frequent studio calls, but only to act as a nameless extra.

Besides acting, another promising avenue in movies was writing. He had gained some experience working with Ole Ness rewriting the outdated material in *Leave Man,* but his film opportunity arose when a man who picked him up at Hollywood and Vine talked about a problem he was having in a movie scene he was writing. "I made some stage business suggestions, and between the two of us, we completely readjusted the sequence. From then on he almost always had some script hot-spot that needed operating on. For these ghostwriting tussles he would give me fifteen to twenty-five dollars a hit."

Harry's new friend was George Oppenheimer, a writer–director at MGM whose screen credits included *No More Ladies* and *A Night At The Opera.* An urbane New Yorker, he mixed business and pleasure and sent late-night taxis for their private dates. Occasionally, he introduced Harry to the lavender network in the film industry, about which John Darrow had spoken earlier. But the entrée was severely limited, and Harry learned that ghostwriters were among Hollywood's faceless, and were never publicly acknowledged.

The industry had many positions suited to the talents of gay people, and many had come West to fill them. "There were hundreds you would know —or sort of know—once you were inside the gate," Harry said. But staying for more than a short visit was difficult, and this network was by no means "out." Discretion was the byword, and exclusive cliques the rule.

In the mid-thirties, Harry's sometimes-clique was a group of chorus-boy types. Evenings, they cruised quietly around the fresh art deco facades of Hollywood Boulevard, and weekend mornings they met for coffee at its open-air cafés. There they gossiped about the "stables" of George Cukor and others, and snickered at "movie people parading in their Daimlers and Packards with exotic white panthers in the back seats." Of course they went to films together. "Once we all went together to see the new Fred Astaire movie called *Flying Down to Rio* at the Egyptian Theater. We sat in the tenth row center and just screamed when we recognized friends. Lots of 'We know that one,' and 'Get *her*,' and so on." On Mondays they scanned "Hedda and Lolly" (Hopper and Parsons) to see who had been censured in blind items for appearing in queer company over the week-end. Inhibitions were stronger in the thirties than in previous decades, since scandals and marketing strategies forced the private lives of film actors to fit narrow standards. Hollywood institutions that were later refined, like the publicity date and the "beard" marriage, were in those years just starting to be enforced.

In times of trouble, the network might offer help. Harry recalled hearing, for example, that costume designer Walter Plunkett often provided bail money when unfortunates were entrapped on morals charges. Friendships among industry gays were often lifelong and helped many people get their start and remain employed in the competetive, conservative industry. George Oppenheimer told Harry about a dinner party for MGM's wunderkind producer Irving Thalberg, who numbered the discreet Oppenheimer among his "bachelor company." Hay was thrilled at the possibility of meeting Hollywood's most powerful producer, but Oppenheimer regretfully nixed the plan. "I'm sorry," he told Harry, "but you're too obvious."

Harry could scream with his mouth shut. He often wore the crimson peasant shirt he had acquired for the Latvian choir while strolling Hollywood Boulevard. The attention it attracted was not executive, but it could be well worthwhile.

Harry had flings both short- and long-term with various aspiring matinee idols. Among them were Willy Wakewell, Phillip Ahn, and Hans Von Twardowski, a handsome German emigré. Harry felt very strongly for blond, green-eyed Roy Rattibaugh, renamed Richard Cromwell for films, who was briefly married to Angela Lansbury and committed suicide in the 1940s. From a night at a bar that would turn into a weekend affair, or a crowded party that would turn into an evening's duet, Harry saw the inside of many Hollywood bedrooms.

Even among the largely apolitical society of actors, Harry persisted in discussing a gay utopia. At one party when he broached the subject, his date cut him dead with the remark: "My God, you *are* degenerate!" But at another party, at the Santa Monica Canyon home of stage manager Tom Turner, Harry's notion fared better. He and the host "got to talking about dreams of what we wanted in our lives. And I must have talked about some of my dreams of a team of men like us.

"Following up on the writings of Edward Carpenter, I wanted to discover who gay people were, and what we had contributed, and what we were for. I wanted a way for us to show 'the others' how beautiful our dreams really were. Several of the most hardened, experienced queens started to laugh and taunt me. Suddenly Tommy stood up and said, 'Stop it, all of you. Because of his dreams this boy has a long, hard, and rocky road ahead of him. We all had dreams like his once, too. We've lost them, traded them away for trash, or even betrayed them. So leave him alone. Be glad he's got his dreams. Maybe someday, if he's lucky and brave, something will come of it. Something good for all of us.'"

▽

"We are living in a time when new art works should shoot bullets," wrote Clifford Odets of the thirties. In 1935, at the age of twenty-eight, Odets wrote a machine gun of play about unionization called *Waiting For Lefty*. It was immediately performed by the Group Theater of New York, and its dramatic muscle and timely demand for a living wage drew a fabulous critical success, and led to Odets's Hollywood screenwriting career. *Lefty* was the most militant attraction of the Leftist theater movement, and its powerhouse ending had audiences on their feet nightly, joining with the actors to shout, "Strike! Strike! Strike!"

The same year *Lefty* premiered, the Hollywood Theater Guild assembled on the West Coast to produce it. Harry recalled, "Bill Watts, the director, Scott and Georgia Landers, Don Sample, and I put that organization together to perform *Lefty* for trade union groups and strike line entertainments." Harry volunteered to search for a headquarters and found a mansion for rent on Harold Way in Hollywood, which had belonged to Lloyd Pantages, son of the legendary theater owner. The Guild included actors Peter Brocco and Marc Lawrence, who later succeeded in films, and Will Geer, who returned to town and couldn't resist getting involved.

Because Odets's play was a success in New York, Geer found a New York "angel," Jay Kaufman, to put up the $35,000 needed for the West Coast productions. Harry recalled Kaufman as "fat and sad — sad because he already knew this wasn't going to be the box office hit it was back East." Nevertheless, the show went on, and everyone in the cast became a member of the Guild. The villain of *Lefty* is a corrupt union official named Harry Fatt who needs an armed guard to protect him from the union he purports to represent. Those members who rebel against their substandard wages are Red-baited by Fatt, but a series of dramatic sketches reveals the injuries caused by "the Bosses." In the end, every man becomes a militant, and the union triumphs.

Harry played Dr. Barnes, an old hospital administrator who resists supporting socialized medicine, then endorses it after admitting the human debris left in the wake of the medical bosses. Since *Lefty* lasted only about an hour, it was coupled with another short Odets play, the anti-Nazi *Till the Day I Die*. In that, Harry played Adolph, a Nazi soldier who is homosexual. The part was written as a broad villain — Adolph helps an S.S. officer ("a man like Goering," say the stage directions) to torture Communists. Later, he cries after the S.S. man rejects his advances. Though the part exploited the stereotype of homosexuals as sadistic degenerates, Harry always considered it a backhanded honor to have given an openly gay stage portrayal so early. One reason that he got the role was that no one else in the Guild would touch it, less because of the Naziism than the queerness.

The production played out of town at first, in San Diego, Santa Barbara, and Laguna, where it was threatened with closure. "John Law and the American Legion threatened to break up the show and throw the cast in jug," reported the March, 1935, New York *Weekly Variety*. Right-wing Legionnaires "demanded the deletion of the Communist propaganda and police ordered the profanity in the play eliminated."

Opposition escalated just before the play opened at the Hollywood Playhouse, when Will Geer was attacked. His swollen face, bandaged and grimacing from a hospital bed, appeared in local newspapers with the caption "U.S. Nazis Try Hitler Methods." Geer's attackers were members of the Friends of the New Germany, Los Angeles Nazis upset about the final scene of *Till the Day I Die,* in which a picture of Hitler is ripped from the wall. The day Geer was beaten, they posted at the theater a note marked with swastikas and skulls which warned: "MANAGER — YOU KNOW WHAT WE DO TO THE ENEMIES OF THE NEW GERMANY — IF YOU OPEN. F.N.G."

Peter Brocco, who got the best reviews in *Lefty,* recalled the intense pressure from all sides. "I got a telegram from my union telling me to get out of that Communist play. Then Geer came around with that bandage on his head. On opening night, it was pretty scary going on." Geer's injuries from the beating kept him from continuing to direct, so a film director from Universal Studios was brought in to help tighten up the plays before opening.

A small, loyal audience of brave film industry progressives could not counterbalance the weak reviews, and the show ran only four weeks at the Hollywood Playhouse. For Harry, the highlight of the Hollywood run was the night Edward G. Robinson, known for his patronage of progressive artists, came backstage. "He told me that a middle-aged actor named Roman Bohnen was playing the part of old Doctor Barnes in the New York production of *Lefty,* which he had just seen. And he told me that I, at twenty-three, had done it better. I was so pleased."

The perfect clubhouse for Harry sprang up across the street from the Hollywood Theater Guild, when devotees of the new camera arts formed an organization called the Hollywood Film and Foto League. Part Left, part art, part commune, the League documented demonstrations and social unrest on film and had a counterpart in New York. Like modern video activists, they used their footage to defend progressives victimized in police riots, and to inspire public campaigns for social redress. To keep afloat, the Film and Foto League rented studio space and living quarters in a large complex of buildings which included a main house, a carriage house, and a barn.

The main house had a huge dance floor and a stage. It had previously been a White Russian nightclub, with murals of giant flowers in Russian folk decor style. These were whitewashed so that experimental films — such as Sergei Eisenstein's *Ten Days That Shook the World* — could be projected on the walls each weekend. More than a dozen dancers, sculptors, and other artists pooled their relief checks for rent and communal meals. Some identified as Reds, but many were completely apolitical. One tenant, a sculptor, was unable to raise his rent, so he camped under a tree in the yard. Whenever people got jobs, the house went untended; when they were out of work it was clean but they were hungry. Its nickname, hence, was the Filth and Famine League.

Harold Way became Harry's home away from home, and he frequently escaped the stuffy air of Windsor Boulevard to spend his free hours there, talking politics, enrolled in classes the dancers offered, or simply hanging around. The Film and Foto League was not necessarily Communist or "temperamental," but plenty of such people could be found there without much looking, and it was here that he met many of his best friends for the next fifteeen years. Among them were photographer Roger Barlow, dancer Bruce Burroughs, sound engineer Burton Perry, and a vivacious young dancer named Helen Johnson.

Johnson described the anything-goes ambiance: "In those days, in the circles in which I moved, gays and straights were not so separated. A lot of people at that place swung a bit both ways. It was taken for granted that Communists were around; they were scattered in the Filth and Famine League like raisins in a cake. There was a woman named Adele whom we thought was a Communist agent because she never mixed with anybody. Bea, an older lady who ran the place, was always looking to lay the younger men who were there. There was a Hungarian who we found was stealing typewriters and reselling them; he also taught fencing to famous Hollywood people. I had a room over an old stable, next to a guy who gathered rusty old files and tools and soaked them in a big vat of acid to clean them up for resale — he always shook them in the middle of the night!"

Distinguished European musicians who happened to be Leftists were among those who gave concerts at the building when films were not being shown. Visitors covered the social spectrum, and one of the more glamorous was Richard Buhlig, a renowned Viennese pianist who was a teacher to John Cage. Buhlig invited the young people from Harold Way to his own house in Los Feliz. "Buhlig's big distinction was that he had an affair with Isadora Duncan," recalled Helen Johnson. "He was gay, but I guess she was just too good or too famous to pass up. He had a wonderful large house with a front room that was completely unfurnished except for his grand piano. I remember his playing, and Harry and I would dance together. That was something. Harry was a very good ballroom dancer, and with Buhlig playing, it was glorious."

Sometimes the kids from the Filth and Famine League would go hear Harry play the organ for the Los Angeles lodge of the Order of the Eastern Temple, or O.T.O., Aleister Crowley's notorious anti-Christian spiritual group. Based on the Order of the Golden Dawn, a secret society concerned with the use of ritual sex in magic, Crowley's society was not so secret and was known to have created homosexual sex–magic rituals. The O.T.O.

motto, "Do What Thou Wilt Shall Be the Whole of the Law," inspired the name of its mother church, the Abbey of Thelema, which in Greek means "will." The original Abbey was in Sicily, but the Los Angeles chapter also called their meeting place Thelema, although the smallish quarters were in the attic of a four-story house in Hollywood.

Regina Kahl, with whom Harry had acted, was high priestess of O.T.O., and she hired Harry to play the organ at services. In keeping with the times, no one was openly gay, but the lodge was run by a frail man named Wilfred Smith, who often performed "exorcisms" on attractive young men. Kahl, whom Harry described as "the biggest lez you ever saw," and two older women known as the Wolfe sisters were priestesses. The Wolfe sisters wistfully hinted that sex–magic rituals would be nice if enough people ever joined the L.A. Temple — but enough never did.

When the services were to start, remembered Harry, "a gong sounded and we'd get to the chapel by ladder. The congregation sat in pews facing a sarcophagus behind a gauze curtain. Regina, in a flowing robe, slit the veil with a sword and out came Wilfred wearing a snake diadem and a red velvet cape made from a theater curtain. 'I am a man among men,' he would say. Then, taking Regina, who towered above him, he'd say, 'Come thou virgin, pure and without spot.'" Many visitors had trouble keeping a straight face. Harry mischieviously slipped "Barnacle Bill the Sailor" or "Yes, We Have No Bananas!" slowed to dirge tempo, into the contrapuntal themes he was hired to play. Frequently, he dropped into his former Catholic church to play a mass earlier in the day — just to balance his sacrilege.

In late 1935, Harry landed a good part in *Clean Beds*, an American adaptation of the Gogol play which was directed by a Russian emigré named Vadim Uranieff. The drama was staged at the Holly Town theater, owned by Mae West's long-time manager James Timony. The lead was played by young Anthony Quinn, whose sex appeal, Harry recalled, "nailed you to the wall, but he was so hetero it hurt!" As second lead, Harry's portrayal of an impoverished newlywed pleased the crowd, and one night it brought backstage an admirer whose interest increased once he saw Harry out of makeup. Stanley Mills Haggart was nearly as tall as Harry, with curly blond hair and an open, handsome flower-face. Harry fell for him instantly "with a chemistry the like of which had never happened before." It seemed immediately to Harry "very likely that our relationship could become permanent."

He faced, however, a formidable barrier: Stanley's mother. Jane Lawrence Haggart reminded everyone that hers was the premiere family of

Lawrence, Kansas, even after she moved to California. Helen Johnson, also a friend of Stanley, described Mrs. Haggart as a variation of Margaret Hay, "beautifully mannered but a real pain-in-the-ass." Stanley and his mother had a business of buying, refurbishing, and selling houses. (Eventually she pioneered the tourbook series *Europe on Five Dollars a Day* and bequeathed the publishing contract to Stanley.) She was also involved with the British-based Oxford Group, which was concerned with morality and meditation but is often remembered for its pre-war dealings with Adolf Hitler.

Stanley suggested that he and Harry move in together at one of the properties they were restoring. Mrs. Haggart was as displeased as her son was happy, and shortcut his plans by suggesting that she and Stanley move to England to join up with the inner circle of the Oxford Group. A skirmish of letters between Stanley, Harry, and Mrs. Haggart in the spring of 1936 tells of the growing strains. On March 23, 1936, Mrs. Haggart wrote to Harry, "Stanley is not strong, and goes much of the time on nervous energy, and the long and continuous late hours with you have been very hard on him ... I don't mind admitting to you that I have felt a growing resentment for you on this account."

In late April, six months after meeting Harry, Stanley disappeared. He sent Harry a letter from Central California in which he spelled out his capitulation to his mother's position: "Our close contact in early youth has cemented a bound [*sic*] not broken by our seemingly different views and aims in life. [But] you have gone a way which neither I nor my associates who know you approve ... Physical relationships that are not normal make me have a repulsion toward you." Something drastic had happened, for during their last visits, Stanley had been anything but repulsed.

Mrs. Haggart assured Harry that Stanley would return to Los Angeles soon, then shortly afterwards, she left town herself. Harry wrote dozens of letters and received no reply. Certain that the Oxford Group would be able to fix her son's "problem," Jane Haggart took him to its bosom. Harry jokingly referred to himself as a "bereaved widow," but Stanley's departure was probably as difficult for him as a death, and seems to have significantly damaged his hopes of finding happiness in love. The following October, he would receive a parchment invitation to Stanley's wedding, in England, to a Miss Phyllis Ward. Taking no chances, Mrs. Haggart posted it a safe two weeks after the ceremony had taken place. Emotionally thwarted, Harry fell deeper into politics.

▾5▾

Which side are you on?

Communism is Twentieth Century Americanism.
— Earl Browder

Nineteen-thirty-six was a year of changes and decisions. President Franklin Roosevelt and his New Deal of progressive reforms were up for re-election. The Communist Party sanctioned the Popular Front, a coalition of progressive causes, and modified its own program of immediate revolution in favor of pragmatic reforms. The new agenda was to unite with trade unionists, socialists, and liberals to stop the rise of fascism abroad and at home. In many elections, the Party ran candidates who openly campaigned for the Communist platform of "Jobs, Security, Democracy, and Peace." During this Popular Front era, which lasted till 1939, the CPUSA expanded more rapidly than ever before. That expansion caught Harry in its sweep, but not immediately — he was still having fun.

Though he did not attend many Party meetings in 1935 and 1936, he participated in a series of urgent fund-raisers and demonstrations which addressed the Communist concerns of protesting Franco's Fascist rise in Spain and the Nazis in Germany, forming trade unions, and promoting the civil rights of Negroes. From 1936 to 1938 he volunteered regularly for various progressive organizations, including the E.P.I.C. campaign (End Poverty in California, Upton Sinclair's near-miss at the governorship), the Hollywood Writers' Mobilization, the Hollywood Anti-Nazi League, the American League Against War and Fascism (primarily reacting to the troubles in Spain), the Mobilization for Democracy, the Workers' Alliance of America, and Labor's Non-Partisan League.

A promising business relationship also came to Harry that year. At the end of 1935, Harry's boyfriend Gabor de Bessenye (the Hungarian count) had introduced him to a Viennese gentleman named Reginald LeBorg. A small, immaculately groomed film director, LeBorg sported continental manners and an accent that were as natty as his ever-present ascots. "Reggie" moved to Hollywood, spelled his name backwards (in Austria it had been Grobel), and by the time Harry met him, he had come under tenuous contract with MGM to direct his specialty, second-unit opera and ballroom scenes. LeBorg spoke shaky English but he wanted to write a futuristic screenplay about a man who saves the world with a death ray. This, he hoped, would be his ticket to steady first-unit directing. As a studio sales strategy, the sci-fi script would first have to be written in novel form, and for this he needed a ghostwriter. During Harry's affair with George Oppenheimer, he had learned that ghostwriting was a thankless end of the business to start with, but that, if he could prove himself indispensible to someone, he might be "carried along inside the gate" to become a fully credited screenwriter. When LeBorg offered him the chance, Harry took it.

The unwritten but firm rules of ghosting required that Harry attend clandestine story conferences at LeBorg's Fountain Avenue apartment. "I usually arrived after ten at night and would hide at the end of the hall until the coast was clear. My presence would have been unexplainable to any 'legitimate' industry contacts he had." LeBorg, who died in 1989 after directing forty-three films and nearly one hundred television shows, recalled his partner's credentials. "Harry impressed me as a well-educated man — knowing literature. And I liked his work." Talent aside, however, LeBorg felt that Harry's passionate idealism barred him from a film industry career. "He was too stubborn and had too many opinions. He would never compromise, and you have to compromise in the industry."

Shortly after New Year's Day, 1936, they signed an agreement to co-author the novel, to be titled *The Death Ray*, later changed to *Tide Rises*. LeBorg was granted controlling interest and first billing, because he said he wanted only "polish" from his co-author. But Harry's touch marks the entire story, the only novel he ever wrote. In the spaciousness of the speculative genre, his political and social theories took flight, making *Tide Rises* part science fiction and part political prognostication. It has some remarkable accuracies. The story is set in the distant years of 1975 to 1980, as America falters. Government and industry have become so corrupt that foreign investors make easy prey of the once-great nation. A dome over a ballpark collapses, illustrating the breakdown of the American spirit. Japan, which has come to dominate the world economy, finally launches an invasion of the United States, whose weak leaders fail to repulse the takeover. But a state-by-state folk uprising builds, as Hay phrased it, to "rehearten the urbanites by showing the rising tide of the simple decency of the American people." LeBorg's gimmick plays when the hero steps forward at the crucial moment and drives back the Japanese with his death ray.

A New York literary agent with the promising name of Henrietta Buckmaster represented the novel, certain that its social criticisms would find a place in the liberal press. For several years Harry hoped something would come of it but, perhaps because it was too radical, no one would publish it. Such issues gave rise to frequent arguments within the partnership. "We had fights over commerciality and politics," LeBorg confirmed. "Our protagonist was a money man, and Harry painted him as very greedy, the bad man, the bad boy. He said my ideas were too fascistic, too Right-wing." Whatever their arguments, at the close of each conference the continental Reggie offered liqueur, cake, and a handshake.

They worked on several other projects, including *Largo,* a feature-length script based on the life of eighteenth-century composer George Frederick Handel, with a fictional love interest built around one of his compositions. Harry happily dove into the research, combing the vast collections of the Central Library in Los Angeles and the Huntington Library in Pasadena, producing rich historical detail with which to embroider the script. *Largo* might have made a perfect period costume epic in the style of Irving Thalberg, who was exactly the person LeBorg had in mind for the project. LeBorg had social connections with British actor Basil Rathbone, and had tailored a role for him so as to help sell the package. When an interview with Thalberg was granted, LeBorg was confident. But, "the day I was to see him, his secretary called me and canceled the appointment. Mr. Thalberg had fallen ill. Three days later, he died."

Largo never sold, but their next (and last) project did, with rather extraordinary results. It was another classical composer story, about Handel, Haydn, Mozart, and Scarlatti (this time convening in the hereafter), and naturally called *Heavenly Music.* Harry remembered pitching nine concepts, and that only that one caught MGM's attention. "They thought it was a cute idea, and told LeBorg they would buy it. But as the studios always were, they had a couple of people they were interested in pushing who changed two lines and got the job based on that. It was basically my script. In the end, LeBorg got original story credit and I remained anonymous. Imagine my surprise a few years later when the damn thing won the Oscar!" LeBorg, for the record, denied Harry had any part in the writing of *Heavenly Music,* the winner of the 1943 Academy Award for best short subject. Harry had suspected as much; it was part of the ghostwriting game. And as Reginald LeBorg's career slowed to directing such films as *The Zombie's Ghost* and *The Black Sleep,* it was his highest honor ever.

$$\triangledown$$

The Left's anti-fascism was not based only on the eruption of the Nazi and Fascist Parties of Germany, Italy, and Spain. Harry believed that fascism could take hold anywhere, and that many established interests, particularly large businesses, would support it. As if to bear this out, some American companies did business as usual with the Third Reich until war was officially declared in 1941. When the U.S. sent athletes to the 1936 Olympics in Nazi Berlin, Communists were among the few who protested in Los Angeles. The clandestine Friends of the New Germany, which had beaten up Will Geer, and its public counterpart, the German-American Bund, advocated the "benefits" of Naziism for the U.S. Harry often helped round up crowds to loudly protest outside its Washington Boulevard office.

The strongest organized local response to Hitler was the Hollywood Anti-Nazi League, organized that spring of 1936 by Dorothy Parker, Oscar Hammerstein, and writer Donald Ogden Stewart. Harry described the League as geared toward the film industry, particularly actors of conscience. (Paul Muni and Boris Karloff were among those on his list of League supporters.) For three years the group aided refugees, found funds for their transport, arranged American sponsors for them, and organized a boycott of German goods. In the League's office on Yucca Street, just north of Hollywood Boulevard, Harry spent regular shifts folding, stuffing, and stamping mailings about the emergency in Europe and its Nazi supporters in Los Angeles. The Anti-Nazi League was a typical mass organization, which, while independent, relied heavily on leadership from the CPUSA and served to introduce sympathetic people to Marxist principles and to the Party. The structure of the Mattachine Society, fourteen years later, was strongly influenced by this model. The League lost most of its support in 1939, however, with the signing of the Hitler–Stalin Nonaggression Pact.

What was then "the Jewish question" abroad and at home concerned Harry deeply. In Los Angeles, he was appalled by the reluctance of the strongest Jewish leaders to become active. The Hollywood Anti-Nazi League, he said, was not welcome to make presentations at local Jewish temples and synagogues concerning the persecution of Jews becoming apparent in Germany.* Many Party members were Jewish, often immigrants who had been involved in European Marxist movements, and the Jewish community in the Boyle Heights area of East Los Angeles was the heart of what Harry called the "Cultural Left," so his concern over anti-Semitism deepened as Naziism played out its horrors. Additionally, several of his romantic involvements were with Jewish men, and he probably identified with Jews as a people separated from the mainstream by a profound difference, and subject to severe prejudice and ostracism because of it.

Between bouts of activism, Harry still sought the comfort of gay bars. He emphasized that gays were only tolerated, never truly welcome in such spots, which were invariably "sullen basements with a pall of smoke, a bare bulb on a string, and smelly floors." People of the same gender could find each other there and, as he noted in a story he wrote in 1936, coyly shout, "Well isn't this gay!" while nursing a beer, the longest, cheapest drink available. His favorite spot during the mid-thirties was on the north side of Hollywood Boulevard, just off Highland, and its brightly painted entrance earned the name the Red Door. "The whole place was hardly big enough for two dozen people to squeeze into," Harry recalled fondly, "but some of us managed to convince the proprietor to stay open late and serve beer and sandwiches after the theater let out. Most of that group happened to be queer, so the Red Door became a temperamental clubhouse." The proprietor, an older heterosexual man, was delighted with the steady business and asked no questions. He later opened a larger bar nearby, the Cherokee House, on the street of the same name. With its gold-flecked mirror over the bar, Harry recalled this as the first "elegant" bar for gays in Los Angeles — at least the first one he saw.

Often, after the show was over and after whatever passed for the bar was closed, Harry cruised Hollywood Boulevard until the last bus came. If he was distracted or determined enough to wave it on, he would spend the wee hours in Delongpre Park, then walk home, watching the sun rise over the east end of Hollywood Boulevard. Other times he would take late strolls in vacant lots, such as the top of Kirkwood Canyon, Lookout Mountain, the Shakespeare Bridge in Los Feliz, and the Cerro Gordo water tower in Echo Park, places where he often found other single men — also out for late strolls.

---

* For more on this, see Neal Gabler's *An Empire of Their Own: How the Jews Created Hollywood*, New York: Crown Publishers, 1988.

And with certain of his randier pals, Harry often went south to Wilmington on what was known colloquially as the Milk Run. "That was notorious. The word would spread like wildfire that the Navy was in, and hundreds of families, friends, and 'well-wishers' — like us — welcomed them. The lineup around the pier was four to five deep and the more expensive your car the better chance you had of offering someone a ride." That Halloween, Harry and his lover took a weekend oceanfront cottage in Venice, to offer a place to sleep to passing sailors. He recalled, "I had been working in the orchard for my dad that fall, but had made him promise to give me the weekend off. At the last minute, that Saturday morning, he reneged and demanded I work. There was a confrontation and I informed him then that not only was I not going to work for him that day, but I would never work for him again. *And I never did* — until he was in the hospital and his crop was freezing."

Harry liked to analyze the gay social scenes then. "Gay life was not so much a life as an aggregate of cliques," he observed, cliques which he found insular and isolated. Several times, when he introduced friends to a favorite bar, they met co-workers there whose homosexuality they had never suspected, despite long work days together. "The little pockets existed," he explained, "and either you were lucky enough to fall into them or you could go your whole life and not know about them. The close-down, the terror, was so complete that people could remain ignorant, unsocialized, and undeveloped. 'Communities' were the little groups that formed by accident. And with lots of restrictions. Tiresome bitchiness and boasting predominated. To find someone whose sensibility was more wide-ranging was relatively rare."

There were other restrictions. At the Red Door, he made friends with a good-looking young man named Wynn, who was being kept by the president of a major record company. Wynn and Harry had a frustratingly discreet affair. "He so wanted for the two of us to go away together so he could be *himself*—a bright young man in love, and not the handsome, kept plaything whose patron required that he dress well, sit still, and look pretty. It was during this time that I let myself be 'kept' in the same social clique." This mostly symbolic episode started when Wynn introduced Harry to Hal, an older, heavier man whose family owned several large national corporations. Hal wrote for radio, and he and Harry found each other pleasant and witty in conversation; soon Harry was always welcome for dinner or to help at script sessions. An affair developed, and when Hal invited Harry for an all-expenses-paid vacation south of the border, Harry accepted, thought better of it, and left early, never again to flirt with such bourgeois compromise.

It would be easier to go straight, and there are several mentions of a "best girl" in Harry's papers from that spring. He had never discussed his true intimacies with his parents, who must have experienced tension as their eldest remained unattached. There was no shortage of women interested in him, and he dated several. One close brush with hetero-sexuality started when his friend Hazel Ito was trying to put together a two-couple professional waltz team for a possible film extravaganza that summer. "She was having trouble keeping men who were willing to train rigorously, and someone suggested me. I was happily partnered with a handsome woman with a broad forehead, cool, blue-grey eyes, and silver blonde hair that she always wore straight back in a knot, pulled tight so one could see the design of the comb. She always looked equally at home in the saddle, on a tennis court, or on the dance floor." Her name was Edie Huntsman, and she and Harry made dates to go swimming or riding together. When they began bumping into each other at political events, she introduced Harry to smart-set progressives.

One of those people was society girl Janet Riesenfeld, the daughter of prominent conductor Hugo Riesenfeld. She was a Spanish dancer who felt passionately about the anti-fascist cause in Spain and raised money for it through her performances. She and Harry made a sport of rounding up one hundred people between them to cheer at demonstrations for Free Spain, and a few dozen to attend the monthly Rhumba Cotillion held by L.A.'s Cuban families to rhumba up funds for the Spanish Loyalists. A gaggle of music-loving progressives frequently gathered to listen to Janet's father's tremendous collection of 78-rpm records. "A man named Bill Miller, who later went to Spain, was in that group, and so was Janet's friend Selma, who decided that she and I were cut out for each other." Though Harry had other ideas, Selma was the first woman to lay him. "Selma did everything she could to get me into bed and finally did. That was my first sexual experience with a woman. When it was over I blurted out, 'I certainly hope I never go through *that* again!' She was a very nice girl, and I immediately felt sorry, but I just couldn't help it." Even so, Harry pursued the woman he really liked, Edie Huntsman. When he told her that he wanted to see more of her, she shocked him with the reply that she was dying. Cancer claimed her within a year.

The happily torrid consummation he finally had was with another member of the waltzing team he had joined in the springtime — the other man. "Beautiful Antti Halonen," a Finn, had come to dance in Hollywood movies, and his thick blond hair, blue eyes, and dancer's physique gave him an edge. He was frequently picked out off the beach for background in other people's photo layouts, but his Hollywood break was slow in coming, so he lived at the cheapest room available, upstairs at the Melrose Baths. Harry and Antti had a pleasant summer affair, but the relationship ended on a sour note. Halonen wrote Harry a blistering letter expressing resentment over his "sophistication and critical mind" and "big words" — words that he accused Harry of using as an emotional shield. Still, Antti suggested they continue to see each other.

Harry turned him down and took up another steamy and ultimately strained romance with Walter Keller, a young man he met that autumn. Keller was of Russian-Jewish heritage, seventeen years old, and resembled a young faun. They met at one of Don Sample's parties in "Homo Hollow," a house Harry's old friend rented on Lower Laurel Canyon Road. It had been painted by a Hollywood set designer to look like a crumbling ruin and was a well-known party spot. "Don had cultivated a salon of all sorts of people — from the adventurous to the pretentious," recalled Helen Johnson. "Parties there would start Friday night and end sometime Monday or Tuesday, whenever people had to crawl off to work. That house had great suspended ceiling beams, and I remember Don walking barefoot across them every time he got drunk enough."

On this particular night at Homo Hollow, Keller was with Kenneth Hopkins (gay but married to a lesbian), a successful hat designer whose clients included Hedda Hopper. "Kenneth warned me that Harry was experienced, and could sweep pretty young boys off their feet." Walter, however, was ready to be swept. "Harry was being fascinating," he recalled of their first meeting. "He was tall, thin-faced, balding. He had piercing eyes and this cynical mouth that twitched a little bit." The pretty young naif was smitten by the college dropout who poured on the sophistication. "He made you feel he was very smart and had very important connections. And if it worked out between you, you'd have a perfectly fascinating life."

Keller looked up Harry's phone number and dropped everything in pursuit of a relationship with him. ("I gave up Homo Hollow for Harry," he said.) The Kellers lived in Sierra Madre, near Pasadena, and were remarkably accepting of their son's homosexuality. He was consequently well adjusted and secure for his age. They began to see each other, and late at night, Keller would park his Model-A Ford near the Hays' house, walk the last block, and throw pebbles at Harry's ground-floor window. If they had argued, Hay might lock Walter out. "I would cry outside his window," Keller recalled. "I could never resist that," Harry said. In the mornings Keller always left by five, before anyone in the house awoke.

Once, as he tiptoed out, he was startled by Margaret, who was "tall, pale, and disapproving." Harry made an excuse to her later, and she did not pursue the subject.

Harry saw Walter for almost a year, but the relationship, though passionate, did not last. There was a harsh legal reality: "If Harry had acknowledged me," Keller said, "he could have gone to jail. I was under-age." Even had they been able to move in together, they would have had a hard time surviving the hostile Depression economy. Worse, for Harry, was their political incompatibility. Keller was not susceptible to even the suggestion of going to Party classes — he did not trust the C.P. and was politically moderate. Harry feared that a relationship with a non-move-ment person would force compromises and stifle his growing radical zeal. Ideological problems intruded frequently. "I got him to go to a play once," Keller recalled, "the WPA production of *Johnny Johnson* at the Mayan Theater downtown. I was going on about the power of theater when Harry said, 'That's just a snobbery of yours. The movies are a much more important art form.'" That was a Communist Party line, to which Harry already adhered.

The gap between Harry's politics and his gay friends widened, al-though he sometimes attempted to bridge it. In the fall of 1936, a clique of "rather shallow, listless, and pissy queens who lived in southeast L.A." threw a costume party for Halloween. Harry, thinking politics, decked himself out as the spirit of fascism. "I wore lots of black tulle and horren-dous scarlet, a black Charlemagne-type cardboard crown topped with a huge swastika, a belt and wristlets of chain. Did I clank!" Though Keller remembered the costume as "Spain in Flames," referring to the Spanish Civil War, Harry was certain he was spoofing Germany and projecting the demise of Naziism. "Everyone in that group was being very nonpolitical," he said, "and I was doing my best to rouse people into action about what was going on in Germany." Finding little sympathy at the party, he "trooped the Boulevard." There, dressed as Fascism, he scored.

The best-preserved image of Harry Hay from that time survives in New York's Museum of Modern Art on an experimental film he made with LeRoy Robbins and Roger Barlow, friends from the Hollywood Film and Foto League. Hay oversaw the script; Robbins and Barlow, both WPA-trained photographers, handled the filming; and all three acted. Their black-and-white, sixteen-millimeter movie is called *Even — As You and I.*

Though they were financially strapped — between them they barely scraped up the budget of twenty dollars — they were lavish with their imagination. The story was a self-reflective imitation of life, in which a trio of poor scenarists enter a "shorts" film competition. Conventional story lines bore them, but a magazine article on surrealism inspires them. They make a film called *The Afternoon of a Rubber Band,* where trick photography spoofs surrealist cliches and classic avant-garde films, the best being when Harry's eye fills the screen, à la Bunuel's *Chien Andalou,* and a straight razor hovers menacingly, then slices a boiled egg, a cow's eye from the butcher, and finally passes Harry's eye and neatly shaves his cheek. Bohemian wags that they were, the filmmakers constructed the climax to parody the famous "Odessa Steps" sequence from Eisenstein's *Potemkin:* Crosscutting between a steam roller and a snail results in a scream and dough smashed under a rolling pin. Harry, as director, looks like a mad queen with his black beret and excited gesticulations.

The three filmmakers entered this group project in the Liberty–Pete Smith short film contest. Though *Even — As You and I* did not win — Harry heard that the film was judged too professional and was thus disqualified with a backhanded compliment — the film was recognized as an unusually early and skillful experimental film (it has been called the first surrealist film made in the United States) and was shown at the Los Angeles County Museum of Art as part of the Bicentennial program of 1976–1977. It was also shown at U.C.L.A. in 1987 in the presence of several of Hay's political comrades from the Mattachine era. When it was announced that the film was silent, his friend Don Slater cracked, "Silent? Then how will we be able to recognize Harry?"

▽

Early in 1936, Big Harry had a stroke that paralyzed the entire left side of his body. As with his accident in the Andes, he hurled his will into recovering, but this battle was far tougher. He was incapacitated for months, and Harry often entered the sickroom to find his gruff father weeping in frustration. Bit by bit, he regained some muscle function. To compound the family's troubles, Bob, the youngest of Big Harry's brothers, became ill with pneumonia and was brought to Los Angeles for treatment. His grave condition merited permanent residence at St. Vincent's Hospital. One afternoon in January of 1937, he seemed to be improving enough that his doctor allowed him to join the family for dinner at Windsor Boulevard. To join him, Big Harry made the now rare and exhausting trip downstairs for the last meal the brothers ever shared.

The younger Harry, dreamer or not, now had to bear the somber adult responsibility of medical decisions, which Margaret deferred. On top of that, a record frost threatened the orange grove, and he dutifully stayed up night after night during the worst of it, burning smudge pots to protect the new growth. He was so exhausted that his birthday, normally celebrated with faithful lavishness by Margaret, passed unnoticed. One afternoon Harry was called to St. Vincent's because his uncle's condition had worsened. Gangrene had set into his legs, and his lungs, crippled by pneumonia, required an oxygen tent. The nurse told Harry there was no chance of improvement, and that the supports that had been Bob's best hope for a time now prolonged his excruciating death. She recommended that he allow his uncle to die naturally, which meant disconnecting the oxygen. The 25-year-old stood by the bedside, watching the old man's agony at every breath. After an eternity, he consented to disconnect, watched the nurse carry out the procedure, and held his uncle as he died. He drove his father's car a few blocks away from the hospital, wept, then went home to tell his parents.

Harry's responsibilities extended to shipping the body to Hollister, where many of the Hays were buried. Harry drove up into the San Benito Mountains with his old spinster aunt Alice and was greeted by the entire Hay clan. Harry's bedridden father was the only member absent. This was the third time all the Hays had assembled in fifty years, each time for a funeral, which so fascinated Harry that he wrote a funeral story he called "Flight of Quail," referring to those birds that shun formation and scatter in different directions when taking flight. He admired the "golden apple handsomeness" of his clan and observed the accompanying aloofness: "To look at them you would think they were attending a lecture ... no head hung, no shoulders twitched."

Harry returned home restless. No plays were on the horizon, and he was tiring of the uncredited and underpaying writing work he had done for Oppenheimer, Hal, and LeBorg. At the end of May, he arranged to live on his grandfather's ranch at Hernandez. Harry decided to study and collect the folksongs of the area, a high-minded purpose that masked his need for the refuge that ranch life represented. He intended to live there for several years, which suggests that his urban life, with its urgent activities and social circles, had become unsatisfying.

One summer was all he stayed at the ranch, but he packed it full of adventures. One Saturday, his relatives went to a large Fourth of July rodeo some fifty miles away, leaving Harry alone at the ranch to care for the animals and to do other chores. He had begun to bring in the newly mown hay from the fields to the barn when, while unloading his first wagonful, he heard the chattering noise of a rattlesnake. He had known since his youth that rattlers sometimes hid in shocks of sun-warmed hay and could be unwittingly harvested. Now it had happened. "I was standing hip-deep in hay, and looked around for the snake, when suddenly I knew exactly where it was! It was hanging from my jeans, its fangs all the way into the flesh at mid-leg." The snake let go and Harry watched dumbfounded as it slithered away.

Since his arrival in Los Angeles, Margaret had had him carry a small vial of permanganate of potash, a chemical used for snakebite. For the first time, he used it, pouring a small handful into the open wound he made with his knife, then tearing up his underwear to make a tourniquet. That, however, was only a stopgap. He was thirty miles from the nearest ranch, sixty miles from town, and far from anyone he knew: His situation was as perilous as the climax of a Technicolor western. He hastily fed the animals, mounted a horse, and rode all night to the nearest ranch. The next day, when he was taken to the doctor's in Hollister, his leg was bluish-black and swollen twice its normal size. The wound took an extra week to heal, because Harry had applied a handful of potash where a few grains would have sufficed, and inflicted severe chemical burns.

As soon as he was ambulatory, he helped plan a dance for the locals, the first in years. Harry collected his first songs as he played the piano for the crowd. In the following weeks, taking advantage of the quietude of the ranch, he poured forth half a dozen short stories, some about recent experiences, some of earlier times. In an ambitious list of story sketches of which many were completed, Harry outlined a search for himself. One set of nine tales was to be called *Stories of Hernandez*; another set was titled *The Dempster Cycle,* using Harry's code name for the Hay family.

At the beginning of August, something arrived in the mail, a letter from the long-departed Stanley Haggart. Harry had waited a year and a half. The letter read: "Harry, you win. I have learned my lesson. May I write? I have so much to say. There is a chance of my returning soon." Those five lines made Harry abandon his new home on the Hernandez ranch. He wrote Stanley a stream of encouraging letters and went back to L.A.

He returned to a home immersed in a new crisis: Big Harry had suffered a second stroke that paralyzed his other side and revoked all the function he had recovered. Completely confined to bed, he was unable to bathe or shave himself and required steady nursing care. His deterioration was not only physical: After twenty-six years of marriage, he was suddenly obsessed with the idea that Margaret was trying to poison him, and he would not let her feed or touch him. A male nurse was hired to perform most personal duties, but the old man allowed only Harry to shave and groom him. This was emotionally very taxing. As Big Harry conceded to despair, he seemed, in his misery, to be reaching out to the son he had so completely rejected. But the suggestions of trust and love he now displayed were too late to transcend the old barriers. During the days, Harry waited on his father and quietly worried about Stanley, who had not answered his letters. To get through the nights, he went to a makeshift bar on Western Avenue. The Twin Barrels, as the place was known, was run out of a first-floor flat and served beer. A musician friend of Harry's often played Helen Morgan torch songs like "More Than You Know," and "Can't Help Lovin' Dat Man," or Noel Coward's lyric "Mad About the Boy" (which, the temperamental crowd gossiped, the Englishman had penned for his Hollywood matinee idol lover). Sometimes, when it was late and the offendable (straight) patrons were all gone, Harry would sing along at the piano.

After months of silence, thick letters from Stanley began arriving at the rate of nearly one a day. Stanley poured his heart out in this vivid and rapturous correspondence, a testament to an ultimately tragic affair. On October 23, from the honeymoon shipboard of his arranged marriage, Stanley wrote,

> You know me well enough to know that I will go to any lengths if I feel I am right — if I feel I have something to do. A few weeks ago my latest effort was to marry Phyllis Ward. Does that shock you to know this — and that I am now crossing the Atlantic with her — married to her? My awakening has been horrible and the agony had been almost more than I can bear. To go back a bit, I got your letter 2 days before the ceremony. Your letter has struck deep down into the very depths of me — has cut through all pretenses ... To think it had to take a marriage with its wedding night experience to show me where my real affinity lies. Every cell in me screamed out in protest at my desecration of my body. At that time I knew that I belonged to you and you to me. ... I need your help in straightening this mess out. And it is a mess — frightful. Phyllis loves me terribly and is such a fine girl. I told her yesterday of my feelings for you and she realizes from my behavior that a part of me which she had wanted for herself belonged to you. Our marriage was and is a perfect set-up ... wrong in every way. The reason is that I belong with you, and you with me. Neither of us seems able to help it. Goodness knows I have done everything possible to keep us apart. Why? I don't know. But I'm trembling now over the thought of being with you soon.

Stanley explained that the marriage had been encouraged by a doctor in England who counseled the couple. "He wanted to know whether I was homosexual through birth or if it was acquired. Phyllis (not her fault) made him decide that I could be 'normal' and he urged our marriage. Just because of this lack of truth, this mess has come about." He fretted over Phyllis's future, and her need to get away from her restrictive family in England. He also worried about his and Harry's prospects as a couple. "I know the difficulties in our way if we go onwards together. I will have none of my present life to back me up — all will desert me. My life with you would have to be enough so that I would not care — would willingly abandon everything for you. But my darling I have that sweet certainty that if we were close enough together nothing else would count." In closing, Stanley warned Harry to be discreet. "News travels fast and I want to have our times together unbothered."

After arriving in America, Stanley wrote again, this time from his brother's house in Lawrence, Kansas. Stanley planned to visit a doctor in Kansas City at the insistence of his mother, who would soon arrive from England to find her scheme unraveling. His brother Robert suggested the doctor appointment. "He would like a diagnosis of me, feeling that backed up by a medical doctor, a psychologist — the battle will be easier with my family. I will tell him my history if necessary, and my love for you, and that will serve to convince him. I know within myself and am seeking ways to help others to understand."

He reported that the doctor seemed understanding:

> After two hours of cross-questioning, he said, 'You know yourself what the answer is. Without the slightest doubt, you are an innate homosexual. If you had acquired it, there might be some hope of change but ... being as you are, your marriage is absolutely impossible.' ... He pointed out three alternatives: (1) A married life as at present — with an outward appearance of unity; (2) A life of complete homosexuality; (3) Complete abstinence of sex. He said that the solution was really up to me ... All this I knew without asking, but I did it for the others' sake.

But when Stanley told this to his wife Phyllis, she crumpled. "She sobs for hours and last night and tonight I have given her sleeping pills. It is a horrible sight to see such suffering. I must be careful, for I may ruin her life by an unwise move," he feared. "I talked to my brother Robert today and he told us both in his simple, loving way that he felt our marriage was wrong ... he thought we should go separate."

A few days later, a note announced that loving brother Robert had reversed his position. "Sweetheart — I left Lawrence yesterday and am halfway across Kansas — on my way to you. Society has already begun to collect its price for our love. I was forced to break with my brother and his wife and the hurt of it sends me to you with tears in my eyes. I'm crossing my bridges to you my beloved — and my eyes are steadily on you — my heart is with you." More letters followed, mixing anxiety, hope, and poetic devotion. "Some of my thoughts today went into song — and lifted an untrained voice up to that level where one exists when inspired. For I love you, Harry." In another letter, he wrote, "I gasp with expectancy over the thoughts of our being together in a home — for ever. That's what I want. Every nook and cranny of the rooms will be inspired. The walls will burst and surge with the vibrations of our merging."

As Stanley made his way across the country, Harry began his own trek into a new set of political contacts and circumstances. He reconnected with the film industry progressives to whom his late friend Edie Huntsman had introduced him. Among these, Lillian Hatvanyi, a successful vocal coach, became enamoured of Harry's good breeding and sharp, progressive mind, and put him on the guest list for her continual weekend open house. She mixed social occasions with politics, and Harry played piano, badminton, and the social network. "There were a lot of good-looking, well-appointed fellows with various Hollywood ambitions at those affairs," he recalled. Most of them "would joke and play, among themselves, but their eyes were on the prize, so they were not interested in developing a relationship with anyone who hadn't any money." Harry knew by now that he was the romantic type, and such climbing "was beginning to curdle my blood a little too much. Progressive or not, everyone was peddling someone at those parties, and always themselves."

While charting Stanley's progress, Harry met a Brazilian man named Gilberto. "He was slim and cute and wrote publicity releases for the Brazilian press. We were attracted on more than a political level and went out for a drive on several occasions," Harry recalled. "But once, while we were kissing, Gilberto said to me, 'You really don't want to know me. I'm an awful person, and can't be trusted.' I knew instantly that he meant he had been an informant. 'Will you turn me in to the FBI?' I asked. 'No — but sometimes I get very hungry and I need to sell a story.' My eyes filled a little, and he saw that. 'I'm not as bad as I make myself out,' he said, 'but I got caught once and I have had to pay ever since.'" As well as a romantic disappointment, this incident may have symbolized for Harry the fate of a temperamental radical. He had witnessed such plights before, and would see gay men blackmailed again and again.

Late in 1937, Viola Brothers Shore, a progressive screenwriter, invited Harry to a Marxist discussion group held at the home of the popular film director Frank Tuttle. The group was active in a popular campaign to recall the corrupt Los Angeles mayor Frank Shaw, who ultimately left office for

Las Vegas. As a result of that effort, Harry was invited to a deeper level of study in Marxism offered by the Party. Known as the Beginners' Course, it was attended largely by film industry workers. The course was based on new translations and refinements of Marx and Engels that made the complexities easier for Harry's theory-oriented mind to grasp.

He had a revelation. "Suddenly it all made wonderful sense. I began to understand. I was turning on right and left." (This sort of enlightenment was not unique. Writer Arthur Koestler described a similar breakthrough with Marxist theory: "The new light seems to pour from all directions across the skull.") Not only did the structure of Marxism and the Communist Party make sense, in contrast to the difficulty he had in classes four years earlier, but the underlying ties between his various political experiences began to come together. To Harry, this was "wildly exciting," and his excitement was strengthened when he joined a Hollywood writers' discussion group, which included people he had known from the Hollywood Anti-Nazi League and other campaigns. If his emotional experience in the General Strike at San Francisco made him become a Communist, this all-encompassing conversion of mind and spirit pushed him the next step, and kept him a Communist through a long and difficult period.

In November, Stanley returned to Los Angeles and a passionate reunion with Harry. Phyllis remained in Kansas, but in early 1938 she came to Los Angeles and Stanley found lodgings for her with a family of Oxford Group followers. "Harry let me know that his true love was coming back and he was all excited," remembered Helen Johnson. "Phyllis, it turned out, didn't have a clue about what was going on — with Stanley and Harry or with much of life. All she wore was gray stockings, which meant she was *very* provincial."

Between Harry and Stanley arose the old bugaboo of political incompatibility. While Stanley did go to a few Party meetings, Harry discovered that "in attitudes towards struggle and revolution, he just wasn't there." And after a few weeks Harry saw another problem. "Stanley had not made it clear to Phyllis that he wanted a separation ... which meant he hadn't told his mother." Exasperated, Harry took the matter into his own hands. He told Phyllis that Stanley had not outgrown his homosexuality or their passionate involvement with one another. Since Stanley was not willing to face reality, Harry abruptly ended the affair himself. "I just stopped taking his calls. The maid would come outside to where I was on the tennis court and announce that Mr. Haggart had called again. I didn't answer."

Though Harry insisted that it was Haggart who was acting dishonorably, Helen Johnson called Harry "ruthless" in his abandonment of Stanley. Stanley, she said, felt the same way. "Stan was like a big wounded bear, in just terrible pain. I was also on the rebound from a broken relationship with a man, and we commiserated together and made friends ... Harry's life and Stanley's didn't touch after that second breakup, but Stanley was always keenly interested in what Harry was up to over the years. He always asked if I had heard anything at all. Despite a new lover, which was a life-match, he always carried a bit of a torch for Harry."

Walter Keller also felt discarded, and so hurt he needed "years to get over what Harry did." For Harry's part, he anguished that two possible life partnerships were not going to work out. "I was caught up in the Marxist notion that 'man makes himself.' The simple involvements of domesticity, which both Walter and Stanley insisted upon, were simply *not good enough!* On this point, all of my lovers and I (except for Will Geer and three others I would meet in the future) were at loggerheads. Perhaps I was insisting on the impossible, but I kept on insisting."

The twilight world of the temperamental people could seem flimsy next to clear-cut political urgencies. Toward the end of the year, it was apparent that Franco's Fascist forces were going to triumph in Spain. "We had lost," Harry said, "and Czechoslovakia was next." The urgency of the world situation, and his increasing grasp of the power of Marxism, weighed upon his conscience.

For Christmas that year, Harry carved a lineoleum block from which he printed holiday cards. It showed a handsome, strong-jawed man in profile, reaching with fingers that radiate light toward a Star of David. Large letters spell the name HAY, 1937. Graphically and politically, Harry allied himself with enlightenment. But in the stormy, mysterious, war-brewing future, light and dark would trade places.

·6·

Married man

Gide told him everything with the precision of a scientist and the frankness of a confessional. The doctor responded to this revelation of confidence with complete cynicism. "Get married. Get married without fear. And you will realize very quickly that everything else doesn't exist, except in your imagination."
— Francois Fonvieille-Alquier, *André Gide*

O ne of Harry's favorite lovers was a ballet dancer with a wife and two children. "Kirk was compact, with a profile from a Greek coin, dancing black curls he must have combed with an eggbeater, and startling, brilliant blue eyes. I met him at rehearsals for a play I was in, and he dallied with us at the Red Door afterwards. Kirk was a wonderfully passionate poet, but his poetry had a nasty meanness to it — like fairy gardens that suddenly dissolve into furious landscapes with vipers. Likewise his love-making was lustfully delicious at one moment and hysterically demonic the next. About a month after we'd met, his wife forbade Kirk to leave the house *ever* except for work or school. We never saw each other again."

Kirk was a harbinger of Harry's own future; within a few years of their affair, Harry too would be married, cut off from the society of men, and plunged into dark moods and tensions. His marriage,* which lasted from 1938 to 1951, seems like a major contradiction in someone so passionately

---

* For various reasons, chiefly respect for her privacy, Harry rarely discussed his marriage till after the death of his ex-wife in 1983.

gay, and it confounded many of his later gay comrades when they learned of it. A complex mix of political and emotional reasons prompted the marriage; paramount was his inability to find a male lover who tolerated the progressive movement — and a progressive movement that would tolerate his having a male lover.

Marriage was common for both male and female homosexuals of Harry's generation. The most famous modern homosexual, Oscar Wilde, was married with children. Matrimony, in one of Harry's more philosophical letters, seemed "the casting couch for society." The homosexual, he observed, is "pressure-driven by home, Church, college, and community requirements to marry and multiply in order to place (let alone compete) in any profession." Kirk wasn't the only of Harry's lovers to follow this rule: Will Geer and Stanley Haggart married, and Smith Dawless and James Broughton married twice.

The "community requirements" Harry mentioned could be as important to the gay person as to the dominant straights. Harry knew that professions that tolerated relatively obvious homosexuals — fields like dance, theater, dressmaking, and design — tended to be surface-fixated, apolitical milieus that would have frustrated his driven social conscience. Though he ultimately described his thirteen married years as "living in an exile world," to live as a homosexual in 1938 would have meant exile from the worlds that held all his other passions. His friend James Kepner concurred: "In the forties, for many gays who wanted to be socially productive, marriage was a necessity. It seemed inescapable." This extended, even, to the realm of gay politics. Kepner thought that if he himself wanted to educate and organize for gay rights, he'd have to look neutral — "and that meant getting married."

The policies of the Communist Party influenced all Harry's decisions at that time. By 1938, he had made a full commitment to the Party, and the Party held a firm position against homosexuality. It had not always been so. After the Russian Revolution in 1917, homosexual acts were legalized by the Bolshevik government, following, according to one Soviet government pamphlet published in 1923, "the needs and natural demands of the people." But by 1928, homosexuality in the U.S.S.R. was described as a "social peril," and in 1934, Stalin introduced a new federal statute that criminalized such acts as part of a broad policy of "proletarian decency" and gave rise to a righteous, puritanical ethic for Soviet Communists. (The repeal of legal abortion swiftly followed, in 1936.) Since the Soviet Party set the tone for the CPUSA, a severe "Party morality," which forbade adultery as well as homosexuality, followed for American Communists.

When Harry's marriage ended, his wife charged, with no small amount of truth, "You didn't marry me — you married the Communist Party." Getting married certainly made it easier for Harry to work comfortably in the Party, though it would be unfair to say that he married solely for that reason. After the ragged edges of his relationships with men, political involvement seemed his greatest hope for a meaningful life. To come into the CPUSA, he explained, involved almost religious feelings: "Joining the Party actually was like joining the Holy Orders in earlier centuries. Party ways and outlooks dominated your everyday consciousness from then on. Except that instead of manifesting the City of God on earth, you were creating the International Soviet, that shall be the Human Race, as one sang in the final line of the 'Internationale.'" In the future, observers would comment on the similar evangelical fervor with which Harry approached building the Mattachine Society.

The Party, on the whole, had a missionary nature, and the relationship with the group was primary: Some Party psychiatrists even argued that the group relationship of social responsibility (including baby-making and family-based citizenship, as well as work) was basic to mental health.

Harry credited a psychiatrist instead of the Party as the catalyst for his thirteen-year experiment with heterosexuality. He visited the therapist for one afternoon at the referral of his personal physician, Dr. Saul Glass.* While visiting Glass, Harry had poured out his heartache over Stanley Haggart, and the doctor made a medical referral to his brother-in-law, who had recently graduated from the Jungian Institute in Switzerland. Psychiatry, which would soon become anathema to the Communist Party, was even then an idea Harry strongly disliked, yet he kept that one appointment.

He told the psychiatrist of his despair "in not being able to find a flower-faced boy who was a Marxist like me, who would stand with me in the class struggle against oppression." The analyst suggested that the problem might be solved if he stopped discounting heterosexual relationships. He asked if Harry had ever looked for a young woman who could see his point of view. Next, the doctor asked, "Maybe instead of a girlish

---

* Harry was participating in an experiment Glass conducted in the late 1930s, looking for physiological indicators for homosexuality. Harry was in a group whose blood and urine samples were tested against a pool of homosexuals in the "Fruit Tank" of the county jail. Glass, H.J. Deuel, and C.A. Wright published the result of the research, "Sex Hormone Studies in Male Homosexuals," in the journal *Endocrinology* in 1940.

boy, you're looking for a boyish girl. Do you know one?" Harry did. There was a tall girl whom he had seen at all the picket lines and demonstrations. As Harry spoke about her, the doctor encouraged him to pursue a relationship. But Harry worried: Could compatible personalities conquer sexual differences? He voiced serious doubt that he could sustain a physical relationship with a woman. The therapist assured him that he could. "He told me that all I needed to do to change my orientation was to deliberately close one book and open another."

Harry believed him — or wanted to — and set about opening the new book. He sought out the tall girl, whose name was Anita Platky. She was twenty-four years old and from a large Jewish family, which had moved from New Jersey to Los Angeles shortly after the stock market crash of 1929. An athletic girl interested in acting, Anita had tried to get work in movies as an ice skater and was once cast as an Amazon in a stage play. Anita was slim-hipped and strong-jawed, described by many of her friends as handsome and by some, even, as masculine. She did her best to make her outstanding height work for her by cultivating a regal style in clothing and movement, but she was always self-conscious. One of her favorite things about being married to six-foot-three Harry was that she could wear heels and still be no taller than he. She was also smart, as pointed out by the class anagram from her high school yearbook:

> Anita's
> Nice smile
> Is good to see.
> Tall?
> About six feet!
>
> Plays ball
> Longer than
> Anyone else.
> To increase
> Knowledge is her desire.
> You know these intelligentsia.

Helen Johnson, Harry's friend from the Film and Foto League, was Anita's best friend in the class of 1931 at Beverly Hills High School. Anita was gifted with fine intelligence, humor, and style, Helen said, though because of her appearance she lacked self-confidence. Other of Anita's friends shared that impression. "Anita really was attractive and had a lot of style," Helen recalled, "but she was dark, and, as my mother would have said, 'foreign-looking' — which meant Jewish-looking. In the thirties, if you weren't five-foot-two-with-eyes-of-blue, you didn't feel so pretty." But to Harry, Anita's Party membership outshone all else. "She had already gone through the classes I was involved in, and had read the right literature and knew all the right people." It seemed like the start of a beautiful relationship, free of the deadlocks he had faced before.

He contrived to meet her at his birthday party that April. Leroy Robbins's wife, Florence, threw a dinner, and Harry asked Helen to invite her tall girlfriend. That night, Harry remembered, "we discovered we liked each other." They found they thought alike and shared a sense of humor and an interest in the arts. Harry recalled that at political meetings, when slogans were being composed for protest signs, he would start a slightly wicked, sophisticated one and Anita invariably finished it. Harry once said, with awkward sincerity, "If she had been a boy, we would still probably be together." During the course of public protests and family dinners, they fell in love. He noted, "Anita and I loved each other dearly and had a wonderful time doing anything together. We rarely quarreled because I usually understood her point of view. Most of her family and friends thought we were a perfect match — I never looked at another woman. (But oh *the men!*)"

Within a week of their meeting, Anita invited Harry home to meet her mother. Harry fell in love with the Platky matriarch, too. She provided something his parents never had, a warm home and an open mind. "Annie Platky was an absolutely grand woman — warm, intelligent, cultured, *and* progressive. She was the first mother I had ever met who understood and supported her kids' being Communists." A favorite family story (recalled by the Hays' daughter, Kate) told of how Anita and her brothers once met a woman registering voters on the street. "Anita decided to sign up. When asked what party she wished to register, she said, 'Communist!' The woman nearly died, but everyone else got quite a kick out of it."

The more he learned about the Platkys, the more he liked them. Of Polish and French background, they came to America with their family business — boar-bristle brushes — but were prosperously diverted into the clothing trade. In the 1890s, Annie bore a son and daughter; then, when middle-aged, she surprised everyone by bearing three more: Adolphe Kasimir, Joseph Edouard , and Anita. (The boys changed their names. As Hitler rose to power, Adolphe became Ae. While in the Party, Joseph Edouard proletarianized his name to Joe Ed; when he left the Party, he jettisoned the names "Joe Ed" *and* "Platky" and became John Storm.) The family was educated, with a background Harry called Biedermeier

(Germany's sensible equivalent to Victorian style and mores), and sufficiently well off to maintain a staff of servants. During the Depression, however, "this family was really poor," remembered Helen Johnson, "so poor that they stayed in bed all day in the winter because there wasn't any heat." They survived their leanest years peddling homemade noodles Annie cut with her sewing scissors; what they couldn't sell, they ate. Marked by these experiences, Anita and her brothers joined the active Left, but eventually all dropped out. Anita retained a strong social conscience, and spent the last decades of her life working at Valley Cities Jewish Community Center in the San Fernando Valley. Her lifelong friend Helen felt that Anita was at heart less a radical than "a bourgeois Jewish girl with very traditional family values."

Harry told Anita about his homosexual past. She assured him she understood, that she already knew several men who were "that way." At least one of Anita's few boyfriends before Harry had also been gay.

The higher purpose of "building the movement," as Anita phrased it in a letter, colored their romance. To tip the balance, the *Largo* screenplay seemed likely to be sold soon, and Harry felt confident that his work with LeBorg would finally result in a steady job at MGM. He began to think about marriage. "I thought that it could solve a lot of my problems. Things would all come straight and fly right if she and I could find a working relationship." Anita wrote to Harry later that summer that she thought the same way:

> You say in your letter you can see no reason we can't be married shortly after my arrival. Since I can't either, shall we do the plunge act up good and plan in that direction? Somehow we can get enough to pay the first month's rent and from then on we can do something. Hell, darling, I do want to be with you, work with you, and live with you — start our job of building together, and I can build without attaching paramount importance to sex. I'm pretty sure I can, and you can too ... Certainly our involvement and our desires to work in the groups we are working in is that much in our favor. So many of the people getting married these days have not that mutual interest to use as one brick in the foundation.

Ironically, the same day that Harry began courting Anita, Stanley Haggart (evidently unaware of Harry's new path and impending marriage) took a final bow in Harry's life. He seized the occasion of Harry's twenty-sixth birthday to condemn his ex-lover by running away from their relationship and, ultimately, from himself. "You have absolutely no humility," he wrote, and warned Harry that without the ability to admit his human frailties, he would face a life of heartache. "Two years ago," he concluded poignantly,

> I told you 'no,' and four weeks ago, you told me 'no' ... We are both human and have our human needs, and since I am denied a life with you, I will most naturally accept substitutes — physical. None of them shall take my separateness from me. None of them shall be entangled in my life or shall rob me of my newly found strength. I imagine it is the same with you. Quite by accident, I discovered Jay Britton, the chap you had an affair with in the hills. [I] picked him up in some park ... [He] served beautifully. He has taught me how to have an 'affair' without any emotional attachment. It is strange to have affairs without one's heart being involved. New to me.

Protesting too much he concluded, "So, you see, I'm quite detached from you in all ways."

▽

Marrying a Jew was quite an escalation from making Star-of-David holiday cards. The Hay family, especially purebred Margaret, must have been torn between feelings of relief that their eldest son had finally found a girl, and alarm that she was Jewish. Helen Johnson called it "a bitter pill for Mrs. Hay to swallow." It was typical of Harry to counterbalance the most traditional, mainstream event of his life with a strike at his family's bigotry. Once the vow was made, however, mother and daughter-in-law were faithful to it and remained friends long after Harry and Anita were divorced.

Less than a month after his introduction to Anita, Harry went to the downtown headquarters of the Southern California branch of the Communist Party and formally applied for membership. The officials there knew about his checkered past, and he informed them of his decision to marry, which everyone involved accepted as a permanent change. He had occasional qualms about this step, but was reassured as his Party work began to fall into place almost immediately.

The couple wooed in the milieu of L.A.'s Left-wing culture. Anita and her brother John were involved in the Contemporary Theater of L.A., which produced working-class revolutionary plays. Harry also saw Anita at dance classes and screenings at the Film and Foto League. Anita introduced Harry to her circle of friends, young progressive straight couples who became their friends for many years. They went out frequently, "when going out meant going to rent parties, picket lines, and demonstrations."

They spent a great chunk of their courtship working on an anti-Nazi demonstration produced by progressive Jewish women connected with the film industry. As the group's agitprop consultant, Harry suggested it somehow dramatize the atrocities in Nazi Germany, which were still largely unreported in America. Sympathetic studio carpenters and wardrobe seamstresses created the props: dummies burning at the stake, hanging from yardarms, piled high like refuse under the banner of the swastika. These displays, mounted on trucks, became gruesome 'floats' beside which walked demonstrators costumed in Eastern European folk dress, who handed out leaflets from French and British newspapers documenting Hitler's crimes. The procession, which paraded through wholesome areas of Los Angeles like the Farmers' Market, must have been a jarring sight. They did this for more than a week, and Harry scheduled the cross-town logistics of the troupe and kept long vigils, because of arson threats from the German-American Bund. Despite extensive exposure, the event was never mentioned in the papers.

Harry's gay life ground to an abrupt halt. He shed old friends and haunts, though he still picked up news from the circuit, such as the arrival of W.H. Auden and Christopher Isherwood from England. Though their life was not dissimilar to the one he had admired in his friend Paul Mooney in 1934, Harry now dismissed the Britishers as decadent: "They had a sycophantic group of younger, attractive men around them to whom they provided a place to sleep, shower, shave, and eat, along with a lot of bon vivant–type conversation." The tang of sour grapes in this description fits with Harry's pain at severing his ties with the bohemian and temperamental worlds he had so loved. He maintained in later years that he then thought gay life was "all very beautiful still, but perhaps it was something that must be laid aside, as you lay aside things you love for civilization, for maturity."

Shortly after the wedding date was set, Anita's mother, Annie, had a massive heart attack. She was hospitalized, then had a second attack and died. Anita accompanied the body east to help make funeral arrangements. Her brother John and his wife Reat attended, as did Anita's older siblings, Ira and Mina. The latter two were outspokenly anti-Red, and while Anita stayed at her sister's Manhattan apartment, she kept quiet about her politics.

In Hollywood, Harry madly finished writing the *Largo* screenplay. Anita wrote him almost daily. "Went to the movies, saw *Three Comrades* and *Kidnapped,* neither of which helped me to forget you." She dropped occasional references to politics — "you should collect two bucks for that subscription to the *People's World* from Sylvia" — but her recurring theme was love:

> At first I didn't go to the door twenty times a day to look for mail, but now I'm lucky if I get away with fifty. I didn't used to feel like spending every minute of the day and night with a pen in my hand trying to write you, but now I feel like starting again as soon as a letter has left this floor via the mail chute. I didn't used to sink inside when I saw how happy John and Reat are together. I didn't used to want to turn around and go back to L.A. I didn't used to feel a whole lot of things. Oh but I do now.

Her letters were filled with the big city: The Harold Rome labor musical *Pins and Needles* entranced her, the quantity of comrades encouraged her, and she had never seen so many kinds of restaurants. With such enticements, she suggested Harry move east after their marriage. Her brother John had landed a job at Crown Publishing Company, and she thought that might help Harry: "John pointed out that he will be able if not of a certainty, to get any novels you may write read at Knopf's, at least to secure you a good agent who may be able to do something about your shorter stuff. All of which may turn out to be sumpin'." She planned her return west and asked Harry to find "a room, bath and kitchen for about 18 to 20 bucks a month" for the period before their marriage. She also made several mentions of Harry's growing participation in "the world fight," dizzily mixing revolution into her sentimental billets-doux. "I'm so terribly, terribly thrilled at each piece of news of your further activity in the Party work and am horribly eager to pitch in and join you." On a personal note she promised, "I'll try not to rob you of your independence."

Anita returned in late August and resumed wedding peparations. After Harry announced his intention to obtain a double bed, his mother took him aside. "Are you sure you don't want twin beds?" she queried. "The only reason your father and I didn't have them at the Kingsley house was the room wasn't big enough." The first weekend in September, a family friend threw a stag party which Harry called a "ghastly jollity" complete with cigars. "What presumably marked the groom's last night as a 'Wild Free Blade' was all pretty much sham and difficult pretending," he reported. "My brother was away on a job at Hoover Dam and the rest of the 'men' I knew, right up to, almost, the day of being hitched, were not exactly the 'Smoker' type." Among these were Anita's brother Ae and John Storm's brother-in-law, who had just come back from working with Trotsky in Mexico City. "These well-meaning guys really didn't know very much about sex, and of course, it would not have been politic for me to share the considerable amount that I knew about male sexuality." He ended up slipping off to spend that night with a former lover, an assignation, he insisted, that was "the best sixty-nine I have experienced before or since. That," he added, "was my real farewell to bachelorhood."

The Hay–Platky vows were exchanged on California Admission Day, September 9, 1938, in the backyard garden of Ae's home in downtown Los Angeles. The crowd of fifty faced the bride and groom while the minister performed the ceremony with his back to the crowd, a deliberately unorthodox touch. The Jewish bride and the Catholic groom stood before their Unitarian minister, Steve Fritchman, who obliged their wish to omit any "God stuff." Their honeymoon was spent in the hills above Laguna Beach in a cottage overwrought with mother-of-pearl decorations. Snapshots taken there show Anita radiant, while Harry offers a strained smile, and stands, as if metaphorically, half in shadow.

That week, Big Harry suddenly died. The honeymoon was cut short, and the young couple returned to Windsor Boulevard. Harry sang at his father's funeral. He and Anita moved into their first apartment, a twenty-dollar-a-month flat on North Robinson Street in Silver Lake. Harry planned carefully to be employed long enough to be able to secure the apartment, then arranged to be laid off to qualify for Relief and a job in the Works Progress Administration.

With Harry's assistance, Margaret Hay set about liquidating her late husband's properties and building a new, smaller house. She bought a site on Oakcrest Drive in the then-quiet Cahuenga Pass canyon between Hollywood and the San Fernando Valley. Harry told her that the shape of things to come was the Bauhaus-influenced International school of architecture and recommended a young protégé of Richard Neutra, Gregory Ain, whom she hired as architect. As a result, the grande dame of Edwardian tastes spent the rest of her years in a modular box of wood and glass. (Harry's advice was on target: Ain's Hay house is featured in modern architectural guidebooks.)

In October, Margaret took the couple on a late honeymoon trip in her Hupmobile Sedan to the Pacific Exposition in San Francisco. They returned to newlyweds' poverty, surrounded by lovely appliances and dishes, but not much food. Anita canned everything she could get her hands on, and even made jam from turnips. By December, she found work as a receptionist for a short-lived progressive-artists' gallery on Sunset Boulevard. About a month later, Harry's WPA application was accepted, but instead of getting the Theater Project job that he wanted, he was assigned to the Historical Records Survey, cataloguing Orange County's civil records. Shortly, he rose from a $55-a-month clerk job to earning $85 dollars per month as a supervisor, and was made responsible for Los Angeles County probate records as well.

They did Party work as a couple, undertaking a photo exhibit on poor housing conditions in the Los Angeles area. With no training and only a Brownie camera, they surveyed the dilapidated Victorian mansions that made up the city's worst slums, such as the racially restricted areas of Chavez Ravine, South Central Avenue, and Bunker Hill. One picture shows the single-faucet outdoor cold-water pipe that supplied twenty-four houses. Their project was part of a city-wide campaign to pass housing subsidies, which landlords argued would penalize taxpayers. To combat that argument, Harry and Anita compiled statistics documenting taxpayer costs incurred by the slum environment, specifically crime, ill health (mostly tuberculosis), and juvenile delinquency. They showed how subsidies would, in the long run, save money. The exhibit was popular and toured the city and state, but was repeatedly vandalized because of its political ramifications: Several city councilmen insisted that there were *no* slums in Los Angeles and that all talk of federal subsidies was "Communistic."

As their first anniversary approached, Harry showed a happily married surface, but he harbored serious misgivings. The stress of repressing his homosexual impulses aggravated his lifelong tendency to sleepwalk and have nightmares. He remembered, "The whole time I was married I dreamed the same dream over and over. I am in my father's car. He is driving, but something happens and he can't get his wooden leg from the gas pedal to the brake and we're going to crash. I would thrash around in the covers trying to move the leg. Often it was Anita's leg I'd be holding."

His homosexual urges didn't diminish, though he waited for them to. By the spring of 1939 he was seeking quick sexual encounters, usually in a park about once a week. His sexual tensions remained so high that on the WPA job he escaped to the lavatory to masturbate daily, a pattern that continued till the end of the marriage. And Party meetings, which ended late at night, provided a perfect opportunity for him to walk through Lafayette Park, which he had known as an active cruising ground for years. What physical relief his solitary sexuality or fleeting "quickies" offered was offset by a sense of emotional misery, and constant danger.

One night in Lafayette Park, he was stopped by a policeman for violating a curfew aimed at controlling such activity. Harry was certain he would be booked and his marriage and public life would be over. But somehow "I managed to pop my shocked and innocent eyes at the cop.

'You mean, officer, that people are not supposed to walk through the park at night?'" he began, and spun a yarn about walking for inspiration for song lyrics he was writing for church socials. "'Oh — you mean it's dangerous?' I went on. 'Oh my goodness, officer, I never *guessed!*' Boy, was I relieved when he let me go home. I didn't go again for several months."

▽

A year after their wedding, the entreaties of Anita's New York relatives began to sway the newlyweds' thinking. Although Harry had tried out for hundreds of stage and radio parts over a period of several years, and submitted his writing to countless magazines and publishers, none of it had come to much monetarily. Moreover, his laborious investment with Reginald LeBorg — his best entrée into the film industry — collapsed when they broke relations in an angry exchange of letters about writing credit and money. When Harry was offered a job as scriptwriter for his old Filth and Famine League buddy Roger Barlow (now director and editor at the Educational Film Foundation at New York University), the California couple decided to make the move.

At their farewell bash, the tennis court of the Windsor Boulevard house spilled over with friends talking excitedly, gobbling down enchiladas (the specialty of Florence Robbins), and weaving in square dances. The dance music was distinctly Harry Hay in inspiration — "We took revolutionary songs and put them to a square beat. It horrified some people, but we did it, and it was fun."

They sold his car and drove hers on the long cross-country trip. Although this was Harry's first drive across America, he experienced frequent and eerie déjà vu. Arrival in Manhattan plunged them into the logistics of the present. Roger and Louise Barlow welcomed them into their already cramped one-room Greenwich Village apartment and for several weeks the couples traded off sleeping on the mattress or the bare box springs.

The script work for Barlow paid five to ten dollars a day and was intermittent, so Harry immediately played his ace, an appointment with Harry Guggenheim at his Pine Street office. Margaret had secured this by a letter of introduction in which she reminded the wealthy man of the faithful service rendered the worldwide Guggenheim ventures by Big Harry two decades earlier. Amazed by the scale of Mr. Guggenheim's office and impressed with the implications of being allowed into it, Harry felt briefly hopeful, but after a few moments of chatting across the wide polished desk, he realized that nothing more than cordialities would be offered, despite Margaret's certainty that her son could cash in on the connection. It was, Harry realized, a dozen years too late.

So the Hays were poor in New York — work was never steady for Harry, and when he worked the pay averaged only thirty-five dollars a week. As in Los Angeles, Anita was the first one to land a job, joining her sister, Mina, as a telephone solicitor at *Cue* magazine, and shortly afterward she was hired as a typist–receptionist at the World's Fair for the "World of Man" display of the World Health Organization. She kept that job for the duration of their stay. Within a few weeks they found a sublet on the twelfth floor of a tall building near Sheridan Square. Because of his sleepwalking, the height terrified Harry.

While the couple was still adjusting to their new city, Harry's mother came for a six-week visit. Margaret's modernist house was still under construction in Los Angeles, so she had taken to travel. During her visit, she bought Harry two expensive new suits, the better to impress prospective employers — of which there were many.

His first steady work was through a progressive contact, Alfred Baruch, an industrial engineer who, with his fabric-designer wife, Frieda Diamond, marketed new types of textiles. They hired Harry to plan marketing strategies in twenty large American cities, complete with a handbook. After that, he was a service manager in Macy's toy department, a product demonstrator, and an actor in the brief run of an off-Broadway play, *Zero Hour,* by George Sklar. But this was Harry's sole stage work in New York, and for much of his two years there he had no job at all. Frequently, when he applied for clerk positions, "they told me I was too well-spoken and would scare the customers away."

But Harry and Anita signed up with the New York C.P. office almost immediately, and Party activities kept him exhausted. He was assigned to the Artists' and Writers' branch and enrolled in the regular regimen of meetings, committees, and ever more complex classes in Marxist theory. In New York, however, Harry became a Party functionary with the Theater Arts Committee for Peace and Democracy, a major Left-wing group, so his position in it signified an advancement within the Party. He also worked on several strike committees and attended the unceasing flow of demonstrations and fund-raisers relating to the Party and its many issues of concern.

One of Harry's nonpolitical adventures took place at the upstairs gallery of Gimbel Brothers department store, where an estate liquidation sale was taking place. While perusing the shelves of unusual books and art works, Harry came across a slim volume of picture writing labeled "Old

Indian Manuscript." He recognized it as an old Central American codex (a classic manuscript volume), and suspected that it might be quite valuable. He ran off to scrape up the fifty-dollar price, but when he returned with the money, the item was gone. Later, he read in the papers that Manly P. Hall, a philosopher of the esoteric sciences, had become very wealthy from the sale of such a codex, and Harry suspected for years that he had been the purchaser. Hall confirmed that he had indeed purchased three antique volumes of that description from Gimbel's gallery at that time. He added that he published one of the texts, with a monograph, through the University of New Mexico Press, under the title *Codex Hall*. (Hall did not comment on the economic value of the books he bought, but evidently, the world did come close to having a *Codex Hay*.)

Such heady brushes with fortune, rather beyond the ken of Los Angeles residents, were common occurrences in New York, the cultural capital of the world during the forties. Although poor, Harry and Anita scraped together the means to visit the many museums and, less frequently, to attend the Metropolitan Opera. They saw flamenco artist Carmen Amaya, American bard Carl Sandburg, popular Brazilian soprano Elsie Houston, and mime Agna Enters. With money Margaret sent him for his birthday, he took Anita to see the original Broadway production of Saroyan's *The Time of Your Life*.

The simple fact of being in New York made even everyday events take on a more vivid quality. "Every Sunday there was a parade somewhere or other," Harry recalled, "parades for various saints of the Catholic Church, for local candidates, for the neighborhood junior high school. If we wanted to have a parade that was important to the Left, we'd have to check with the junior high first." The Hays frequented parades. "In 1940, I bought Anita an Easter bonnet, a huge cap of woven jute, in a lovely sulphur yellow color, to which I added more than a yard of yellow tulle, tied in a huge bow. We went from watching the large Easter Parade to walking in it, and with me at six-three and Anita, with that hat, even taller, we became a separate section. We were giggling because of the impropriety of Leftists in such activity." They marched quite properly in the thousands-strong May Day parade that year. As it entered Chelsea Square, Harry recalled, "Everyone was singing the Leftist anthem, the 'Bandiera Rossa Trionfera.' It echoed through the canyons of the city. People were hanging out of windows singing. You'd really think the whole of Manhattan had signed up with the Party."

As Harry immersed himself deeper in the Party, he began to observe a paradox. Though the C.P. was officially opposed to homosexuality, a fragmented, unofficial subpolicy existed beneath the surface. For certain homosexuals, Harry saw exceptions made. "I knew a number of black and white men from the performing arts in the Communist Party who were gay, but the Party didn't seem to suspect. I realized that since they weren't that unnoticeable, certain Party people saw the necessity of tolerating and covering for them." He elaborated that the Party officially knew of homosexuals only if they were arrested and exposed — in which case they would invariably leave the Party — or if they were "star exceptions," like Marc Blitzstein, the Leftist composer of *The Cradle Will Rock*. Though Harry never met Blitzstein, he knew the married Marc was homosexual, but also knew that because of his value as a famous and effective cultural worker, Blitzstein remained secure within the Party. His own political zeal fulfilled Harry enough to comply with the Party's double standard.

In comparison, other issues pressed hard and urgent. In May of 1940, Harry, along with a black married couple and a single white man who were progressives, drove to Chicago for a conference of the America First Committee. On the way there, in Gary, Indiana, an incident took place that Harry recalled years later:

> It was just after daybreak and we stopped to go into a busy all-night diner. The stoney-faced middle-aged waitress took our orders at the counter, then as she served coffee to me and to the other white man, she turned to the side cupboard and took out a self-standing card runner. Dusting it off with the pleats of skirt which covered her voluminous ass, she noncommitally set it on the counter in front of the cash register: "We reserve the right to refuse service to customers whose patronage is unwelcome," and so neglected to put the thick white coffee cups in front of our Black comrades who sat between us.
>
> The other guy and I nudged each other, drained our cups, got refills and gave them to our friends. We waited quietly until our Denver Omelettes were served us, complete with checks from the waitress's pad. Then we pushed off our stools, deliberately ground the meal-checks firmly into the food so that the plate could not be served again, and all four of us wordlessly stalked out, clumsily knocking over the "Refuse to serve" sign as we left. It was the limit to which we could protest this act of Jim Crow in those years. The Black couple held themselves tightly throughout all of this, saying nothing to the waitress and nothing to us, just waiting to see what we'd do.
>
> They didn't signal they wanted special personal reassurances, but I've never forgotten the silent tears that overflowed. I felt it too. It wasn't fury which I suffered, but a frighteningly quiet grief too deep for words. I remember thinking, "Someday those tears are going to have to be paid off.

Like the taunting and rough handling Queers get on the same streets by some of the same rednecks. Someday, someday, there's going to be a reckoning if I can help it." But this last part, personal only with me, I couldn't share with the others.

Overwhelmed by the unrelieved flatness of New York and the New Jersey skyline, he expressed homesickness for the Sierra mountains of California, so some of Anita's high school friends, who were now also young Reds, took them on a picnic to Mount Orange. Several weeks later, the group had an all-day picnic in a wooded Catskill park surrounding an abandoned marble quarry near Peekskill, New York. Harry and Anita brought along Anita's sister, Mina, and her son, Peter, a Harvard freshman home for Easter holiday. Peter was eighteen years old and just out of prep school, but he was still adolescent, overweight, and clumsy.

They decided to explore the quarry. Harry, the most experienced outdoorsman, gave careful instructions for the others to follow his movements: Crouch to keep the center of balance low, and move slowly. This was especially important because the marble faces were often slick and slanted, and slipping would be dangerous. But teenage Peter brashly stood up and jumped from one ledge to another. He landed on his feet but lost his balance. Anita reached out but failed to connect with his hand. Falling from the ledge, Peter injured his head and died shortly thereafter. Mina, who had so recently lost her mother, was naturally in despair, but Anita and Harry were also devastated. Many of their new friends stepped forward to comfort Mina and the Hays; nevertheless, for many years afterwards, Harry sensed that Mina blamed him for the tragedy. "I always felt haunted by that," he said.

$$\triangledown$$

That spring, summer, and fall, Harry cruised regularly in Central Park. These encounters generally took place, much as they had in Los Angeles, on the walk home after C.P. classes and meetings. One popular spot for sex was called Sheep's Meadow, which was so wide and shadowed that it sheltered couples in the center. Another was a large, lake-bound rock accessible over a Japanese-style footbridge. In the warmer months it was overrun all day and early evening by necking heterosexuals, but on cool nights, after ten o'clock, it was gay. Now in his second year of marriage, Harry's involvements with men were increasing to full relationships, which also put him in jeopardy with the Party, with its demand for an upstanding public image. He confided to no one about his silver-lit cruising in Central Park.

Such surreptitious meetings gave way, in the winter of 1940, to his first actual affair since his marriage. He was at Macy's demonstrating celluloid closet compartments to protect furs and woolens from moth damage when a handsome young blond man watched his pitch for a longer time than usual. The man expressed interest — though not in the product. His name was Barry, and he had an apartment where they met, but that affair ended when Barry brought along a friend named John Erwin to meet Harry at Macy's for lunch one day. John, a medical student at Bellevue, had beautiful skin and eyes and, as Harry noted years afterward in a fond recollection, "a mouth that begged to be kissed again and again." Their involvement lasted several months, though often they could do no more than sit together at lunch hour in Central Park, because John lived with an older man who paid his medical school tuition, and Harry lived with Anita.

One thing they discussed was Harry's dream of homosexuals getting together and understanding themselves. John suddenly commented that at Bellevue Hospital, research on that very subject was being conducted by a doctor named Alfred Kinsey. John had met lots of interesting people while waiting in the Bellevue lobby — would Harry consent to be interviewed? The introduction was made, and in a little office at Bellevue Hospital, Harry Hay added to the statistics that would greatly influence his own destiny when the *Kinsey Report* was published eight years later.

One night John and Harry went to the Metropolitan Opera to see Wagner's *Parsifal.* "The standing room gallery was unheated," Harry recalled, "and very cold. The room seemed to be completely male, and considerable sexual activity was going on underneath the overcoats. The smell of sex must have been apparent even in the loges!" *Parsifal's* theme of sacred brotherhood would become important to Hay's later ruminations about gay organizing, so this stray memory, in such a homoerotic context, is especially intriguing.

In the spring of 1941 Harry met a man who nearly jarred him loose from marriage and political commitments. It started while Harry was in the Village, looking for a new apartment for Anita and himself. "I was walking down Morton Street, east of Canal, and stopped to look at a building when this handsome, pixieish face peered out the window. He motioned me to come up, and, thinking he was the manager, I did. When I got to his apartment I realized he wasn't the manager but I didn't much care." The handsome pixie, William Alexander, was a rising young architect and a protégé of Frank Lloyd Wright. Harry recognized that the chairs in his apartment were by Charles Eames and was quite stunned to see a painting of Paul Mooney, whom he had known years before in Laguna. When he mentioned that he had known Mooney, Alexander explained that he and Mooney had been lovers — but Mooney had embarked on a voyage in a Chinese junk with adventure writer Richard Halliburton, and all hands had been lost in a storm. "When Bill told me that Mooney had been drowned on Halliburton's last ego trip, I was crushed and had to sit down. Bill got me a drink, and as he leaned over with it, he kissed me."

Their relationship lasted for more than seven months. "I came close to leaving Anita and the Party over Billy," Harry said. "In so many regards he was the person I wanted to share with." The youngest son of a large Russian immigrant family, Bill Alexander was independent and highly cultured. In the 1950s, he abandoned his successful career as an architect to found a West Hollywood gallery and boutique called The Mart, providing an oasis of aesthetic imports during Los Angeles's provincial decades. He loved music as much as Harry, and introduced him to the Fifth Symphony of Russian composer Dimitri Shostakovich, which was an appreciation of the Bolshevik Revolution. ("You listen to the first and last movements and you can *see* it," insisted Harry.) It became Harry's favorite, which he played every time he visited Bill, and it was the first record he bought upon his return to Los Angeles the following year. Every day after work he played it, doubtless reveling in its associations of his affair with Bill.* But since Shostakovich was a leading Soviet composer, Harry's appreciation of him could appear as simply progressive zeal.

Bill Alexander returned Harry's affections. "Harry was warm and lovable. It was pleasant to be together, shopping, doing anything," Alexander said in 1987. He even gave Harry occasional jobs in his architecture and decorating company, handling everything from accounting to furniture finishing. But Harry's anxiety over being spotted by a C.P. associate dogged and constrained him: "Bill and I went around only in his immediate neighborhood. I was always concerned that I might be recognized. As a married person and as a Party person, it was impossible to be seen with anyone who was not my wife and not directly involved with the movement. The Party taught us early to be careful of appearance and association in public." Despite this dilemma, Harry wanted Alexander to accompany him to demonstrations and become more politically involved. But the architect refused. "I knew endless people in the C.P.," Alexander explained. "I never went to any of their meetings, but I sympathized with what they had to say."

---

* It was one of the many times Harry used music to express his gay yearnings — from that time on, he associated a song with each of his lovers.

Once again, the conflict between political commitment and personal freedom posed a barrier to Harry's intimate relationships.

For most of 1941, Harry worked as interim head of the Left-wing New Theater League after its previous chief, Ben Irwin, was hired as a screenwriter in Hollywood. The N.T.L. encouraged both theater talent in various unions and use of theater as an educational and organizing tool. As shop after shop signed up for the unions, Harry recalled, "Somebody would eventually say, 'Jeeze, somebody ought to write a play about what we went through ... If we told our story, other shops could learn from us.'" Trade union theater became an organizing, unity-building, and educational technique of unionism. "To be sure, the material was crude, obvious, heavy-handed, and even occasionally obnoxious. But for the most part, union audiences didn't care. It dealt with what was on everybody's lips and immediate to their needs, and what they might do to improve their lives."

In his capacity as director of the N.T.L., Harry was the contact person for all the community and trade union theater groups, and offered advice to unions that wanted to set up theater groups. To fund such activity, twice a year the N.T.L. director was expected to organize a fund-raiser. Harry's benefit concert in the spring of 1941 featured the likes of blues great Leadbelly, Burl Ives (years later, after Ives was a friendly witness before HUAC, Hay always referred to him as "that drunk"), and Aunt Molly Jackson, and was presented at the Auto Workers' Hall in Lower Manhattan.

He also taught, with a woman named Mary Tarcai, classes on acting to members of several labor unions, including the Longshoremen, Cooks and Stewards, and Bus Drivers unions. Hay and Tarcai taught the Stanislavski method, of which Tarcai was an early though uncredited advocate. In their classes, people often re-enacted actual confrontations with their bosses, living out the idea of shops learning from one another's struggles. So Harry joined the clan of theater teachers, from whose distinctive bag of communications tricks he would draw heavily in his future activism. One of his secrets as an acting teacher came from hours of cruising. "There was much in Stanislavski's art I used to improve the self-preservation improvisations I occasionally needed in cruising the Park or evading the demure football player types who promenaded the skating rink at Rockefeller Plaza at lunch time. When they suddenly reversed their hauteur and came on *too* strongly, or just plain smelled wrong, I had to invent a scene to escape." Sometimes, an agitprop circumstance could overlap with a pick-up. "'Join the Union! Join the Union! The truth shall make you free!' And with the employment of a not-universally-noted eye-lock, I could connect without speaking. 'Join me in another kind of Union! This way lies another freedom!'"

In the summer of 1941, Bill Alexander won a contract to design and build a house in New Hope, Pennsylvania. The house was to be built on the famous Main Line Highway for a wealthy male couple. Bill hired Harry to assist, especially in planning and locating the building materials. Harry learned to read blueprints and manage materials on this job, which he would turn into an employment mainstay in later years.

Back in New York, the Hays felt increasingly discontent, vaguely homesick, and restless for the West. Their quandary over whether to leave vanished in early December with the bombing of Pearl Harbor. At the moment they heard the news, they happened to be in a partitioned restroom at a gas station in Mystic, Connecticut, returning from a visit to relatives of Anita. A radio was playing and the announcement came through. "We weren't sure it was real when we first heard the news. It was like another Orson Welles stunt." As he realized the seriousness of the situation, Harry grew worried for his brother, Jack, stationed in Hawaii with the Air Force. By the time they got through to Margaret, who had learned that Jack was all right, Harry had decided to return home. Head-lines immediately proclaimed that Japanese submarines threatened the California coast, and if there were an invasion, Harry dreamed of organiz-ing a guerrilla resistance group which he could easily teach to appear and vanish in the mountains he knew from childhood.

He dropped in unexpectedly to say good-bye to Bill Alexander. A young man had been pursuing the architect, but nonetheless Harry was perturbed to find the fellow seated, having lunch. Bill seemed embarrassed and finally said, "Well, you told me you were leaving."

Harry later said that reasons deeper than fear of Japanese invasion made him want to leave the East. "My gay consciousness was beginning to stir. I sensed it would do better in the West. I felt no room in New York, no company to daydream. And daydreaming is important to gay consciousness."

Top left: *Shown here as a college senior, "Big Harry" was a wealthy mining engineer by the turn of the century. At forty-two, while working for Cecil Rhodes in Johannesburg, South Africa, he married Margaret Neall, shown* **above** *in her wedding portrait.*

Left: *"Little Harry" in his linen suit at age two.*

Ancestors and influences.
Clockwise from top left: *Harry's paternal grandparents, William Hay and Helen MacDonald, emigrated from Scotland to New Zealand to California. Harry's maternal grandfather, Captain John Mitchell Neall. Harry's great-aunt Kate, who was closer to Harry than were either of his parents. Harry's uncle, Jack Neall, the dandy Harry suspected was gay.*

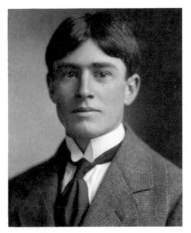 

Left: Big Harry is carried ashore to a job in the Gold Coast in 1911 — a striking image of what Harry rebelled against.

Bottom left: Colwell, the English house where Harry was born.
Bottom right: Little Harry on a burro in Chuquicamata, Chile, where Big Harry had another mining job, 1915.

*Harry at nine, leading a
mountaineering expedition.*

*Harry, Peggy, Jack, and Margaret,
1924.*

*Harry with his parents in front of
the Windsor Avenue house, 1926.*

*As a captain in L.A. High's ROTC,
1929.*

*Right: Harry as a "temperamental" actor in 1933, and later, **at lower left,** in one of his many character roles.
Lower right: Harry's friend Helen Johnson Gorog, whom he knew from the Hollywood Filth and Famine League.*

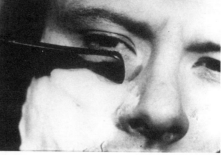

Right: Two stills from the surrealist film spoof Even — As You and I *with LeRoy Robbins and Roger Barlow.*

Below: Harry's woodcut for his holiday card; his progressive sympathies are clearly apparent.

1937 HAY

*Actor, activist, and mentor
Will Geer*

*A clipping of poet Smith Dawless,
Harry's lover from Stanford days.*

*Stanley Haggart,
interior decorator.*

Architect Bill Alexander.

*Harry's wife, Anita,
before they met.*

photo by Roger Barlow

*The model Communist
couple during their
honeymoon in 1938.
Their faces here portend
a relationship that was
amiable but, for Harry,
had bleak undertones.*

Fatherhood.
Left: *Katie, on Harry's shoulders, was the beauty; Hannah was a gifted, fiery dancer. This picture was taken in 1948, the same year Harry founded Bachelors for Wallace, the beginning of the Mattachine Society.*

Below: *Anita and Hannah on vacation at Echo Lake the next year. The marriage was already tense.*

Mattachine men.
Above left: *Rudi Gernreich was a catalyst for change in Harry's life and, later, in modern fashion.*
Above right: *Paul Bernard, an actor, brought in supporters.*

Left: *Clockwise from top are Konrad Stevens, an unidentified man, Bob Hull, Jim Gruber, and Chuck Rowland.*

photo by Jim Gruber

Above: *The Mattachine founders were so afraid that it was illegal for homosexuals to organize that they spoke in hushed tones and avoided pictures. In this rare shot, Harry Hay sits with the group at his feet: (l-r) Dale Jennings, Rudi Gernreich, Stan Witt, Bob Hull, Chuck Rowland (with glasses), and Paul Bernard.*
Below left: *Martin Block camps it up after a Mattachine meeting.*
Below right: *Dale Jennings, whose successful defense of an entrapment arrest was a watershed for the gay movement.*

photo courtesy of Martin Block

photo courtesy of Chuck Rowland

Left: John Burnside in the
mid-sixties, by then Harry's
loving companion.
Below: A youthful John Burnside
in a kaleidoscopic pattern.

*Harry and
Margaret on
Mother's Day,
1964.*

Harry and John found renewal and adventure in New Mexico. **Above left:** *Pat Gutierrez and John Ciddio, the other half of the "joto junta."*
Above right: *Harry speaking at the first gay pride parade in Albuquerque, 1977.*
Below: *John and Harry with their friend Sue-Ellen Jacobs in front of the ruin at Puye, 1972.*

Calling the faeries of folklore into modern existence under the name the Radical Faeries found Harry in the thick of the modern gay movement. **Above:** James Broughton and Harry were reunited after fifty years at the 1980 Denver Faerie gathering. At the far right in this trio is Broughton's lover, artist Joel Singer.
Left: John Burnside after the mud ritual at the first gathering in 1979.
Below: The ancient faerie circle reconvenes.

photo above and below by Mark Thompson

photo by Walter "Butterfly" Blumolf

"The Duchess," still vital and vocal. **Left:** Harry wears the sacred Faerie shawl.
Below: The sign Harry tried to wear in the 1986 L.A. Gay Pride Parade. He was determined to stand up for yet another unpopular cause in the face of opposition, this time from the gay establishment.

VALERIE TERRIGNO WALKS WITH ME

NAMBLA WALKS WITH ME

photos by Sandy Dwyer

Above: *with friend William Moritz in a moment of communion.* **Left:** *The contemporary Harry Hay.*

Changing worlds

It may well be that the impossible at a given moment can become possible only by being stated at a time when it is impossible.
— Leszek Kolakoski

The war years stretched into a decade of tensions for the nation, for the Party, and for Harry. He perfected the mask of a heterosexual and lived for thirteen years in what he later called "an exile world." He fell out of touch with the temperamental life, and consequently with his peace of mind. In those respects, he regarded the decade as lost. He once reflected, "I missed the forties, because I was being married and a Communist."

Harry and Anita's return to Los Angeles at the start of 1942 involved a full schedule of logistics, finding a place to live, and getting work. They settled in the district around Silver Lake and Echo Park, a charming, hilly area where Chaplin and Sennett had made their movies. The home they found was on Lake Shore Avenue, a winding street that cuts through a sandstone canyon still lush and green today, yet close to the surrounding city. That rented cottage, set on a steep hillside, was so tiny that the tall couple had to stoop most of the time, but it was home, and it was nestled into a ready community of friends. The Hays' landlords, a German emigré couple named Fritz and Alma Meier, rented several other units in the area to progressive tenants; the canyon was such a haven for Leftists that it was known as "the Red Hills," and well-worn paths connected the houses scattered over the ridge of hilltops. On many nights Harry and Anita walked to nearby meetings or fund-raisers.

Harry immediately found a job with Russian War Relief, for which he had previously worked in New York. He organized fund-raising events in Long Beach and Santa Ana, and ticket sales to a major concert at the Hollywood Bowl. But that job paid poorly, so through Charles Maddox, an artist friend, he got a true proletarian job as a puddler, pouring molten brass and aluminum at a foundry. Peggy Hay Breyak said she never really knew what her brother did for a living, and for a Communist, making money was always secondary to making social change. But Harry had a steady stream of jobs, no less than eight during this period, and his employment finally stabilized in 1948 when he became a production engineer in a manufacturing plant.

To all the world, the Hays were a happily married pair. "I remember them as a lovely couple who adopted two kids," recalled one of Harry's superiors in the Party. "They were extroverted and well liked." For more than a decade, straight couples were his comrades, and, characteristic of all he did, Harry and his wife became a model Communist couple. They kept a heavy schedule of meetings and activities and when they entertained, as they did frequently, it was almost always within their progressive circles. During this decade Harry and Anita started a family, and with other Leftist parents they formed a cooperative nursery school. They even joined a church. "Kay and John McTernan and Anita and I got sprinkled [baptized] on the same day in Steve Fritchman's First Unitarian Church on 8th Street, though we only went to two sermons in five years." The progressive pastor wasn't counting and was offering large meeting rooms to Leftists.

Though most of the Hays' friends were sympathetic to progressive causes, not all were in the Party; in fact, particular political alliances were not discussed casually. "There was a lot of careful discretion in those days," one close friend recalled. "People didn't talk about what they were involved in except for certain fund-raisers. Harry and Anita had lots of friends, and they themselves were involved in a million things. Almost everybody we knew was involved in some liberal issue, but I don't think anyone knew who was a member of the Communist Party or not."

Harry went to meetings of his Party club, took classes, and participated in dozens of regional campaigns, from walking precincts for progressives in local elections to serving as the only man on the L.A. Communist Party Women's Commission in 1945. There were always commissions, committees, and campaigns, as well as regular meetings and classes. The Party's "meetingitis" was legendary, and Harry and Anita attended as many as nine C.P. events a week. His Party colleagues uniformly recall Harry as intelligent, sincere, and hardworking. "I knew I could always rely on him," said

Miriam Sherman, his section organizer. "Whether it was to give a report or do fund-raising or anything else, Harry was reliable."

Harry's youthful protests were now solidified by the disciplined, purposeful structure of the Party. All of his C.P. activities were useful training for unforeseen political challenges. Many formulas of Marxist theory, such as the program for "bringing a new idea into the world," have obvious implications for the challenges he faced in conjuring a gay movement out of nothing. His fascination with Marxist theory consumed his mental energies; he was captivated by the Marxist approach of studying and understanding humanity as a whole, and in bringing previously obscured aspects of history into that understanding. Many Marxists, particularly Europeans, published extensively in the fields of history and anthropology in the thirties and forties, and Harry read their books avidly. His "lost" decade served as a valuable period of preparation.

The foundry where Harry worked was closed by a government program, and Margaret, ever ready with the *L.A. Times,* spotted an ad for a materials planner at a new company called Interstate Aircraft. The work involved reading blueprints and calculating supplies, jobs Harry had already done on the Main Line house. He was hired there as part of a team to develop a pilotless airplane, and as was common during the war, he exhausted himself with sixteen-hour workdays.

At the ends of those feverish days, he rediscovered an old haunt. "Echo Park Lake became important to me again. I started cruising there on my way home at midnight." The idyllic water park, its benches crowded with old men and children by day, seethed erotically at night, and the war infused it with lusty servicemen. Accordingly, the police frequently shut it down. "There were periodic raids during the war. It was easy to be trapped," he recalled. Harry noticed at Echo Park Lake that "I would pass certain people and get butterflies and leave fast. Ten minutes later there were lights and cops." Aside from this "radar," Hay also maintained that he could distinguish heterosexuals from homosexuals by smell, and that compared to gays, he found straight men distinctly unpleasant.

At work, Harry sometimes became so enthusiastic about solving a problem in the complex blueprints that he waved his hands excitedly. "What are you?" his straight male colleagues reproved him, "a goddamn fairy?" But it was trade union politics, not arm-waving, that ultimately cost him his job. He and a co-worker recruited about fifteen others to form a chapter of the Federation of Architects, Engineers, Chemists, and Technicians at the company. They had no salary demands and wished only to organize, but management refused to negotiate. Harry and the other picketers were fired.

Another aircraft firm quickly hired him. Avion Aircraft was the largest and most impersonal company he had ever worked for, and there he created a card system to pinpoint the location of tools and supplies, including millions of pounds of scarce aluminum. He regarded that as his contribution to the war effort, and indeed, when Harry's number came up for military service, he was given a special deferment because of his war-related employment. His immediate supervisor, impressed with Harry's ability, tried for years to get him into the new discipline of systems engineering at Cal Tech, but a security clearance problem, stemming from Harry's radical politics, barred him from the profession.

Their marriage at the five-year mark and Harry's earnings steady, Anita began talking about a family. They'd already attempted to have a child; the marriage was physically passionate for the first several years (though Harry admitted to increasing reliance on male fantasies), but they were unable to conceive. A friend of Anita's, connected with the Children's Home Society, helped them explore adoption. The couple's radical politics were not a concern but their mixed religions were and the Hays had to wait through months of investigations.

In the second week of September, 1943, a baby was finally brought to them. They named the five-week-old red-headed girl Hannah Margaret for both her grandmothers. The Lake Shore Avenue cottage instantly felt squeezed and they found a larger house in the same neighborhood. The Hay family's new home was an old three-story house beneath a spreading pine on a cul-de-sac named Cove Avenue. The house was split-level, with kitchen and dining room below and more rooms above. There was even a study for Harry. The centerpiece was a huge, high-ceilinged living room with a picture window overlooking the reservoir for which the Silver Lake district was named. "That view was our pride and joy," Harry said, and the gentle hills reflected in the lake as if it were indeed polished silver. The acreage was generous, extending far down the hill, which was landfill and could support no more building. Harry kept Sundays free of meetings to maintain the huge yard. The rent was forty dollars a month.

They turned it into a home, and saved for a set of Winfield china, a California ceramic decorated with spiral patterns of burgundy, gray, and slate blue. Within a few years they furnished the cavernous living room with a grand piano Harry got for a song because the case was scratched. Its tone was so beautiful that a professional musician friend used it for recitals, and Harry occasionally composed protest songs on it, but over the next few years, Harry's friends kidded him that he was too busy with politics ever to play it.

The house at 2328 Cove Avenue hosted an endless cycle of meetings, classes, and parties. Pete Seeger was a guest there during some of his early West Coast concert appearances. Mostly married couples passed through the door, but within seven years the first Mattachine meeting would be clandestinely held there. It was always a house of mixed elements. In 1944, Anita's sister moved to an apartment in San Francisco too small to house the jade mosaics and screens she had bought in Macao years before, so amidst Harry's collection of American books and records, the exotic furnishings somehow were fit in.

The neighborhood around the cul-de-sac was peaceful. Down the hill spilled several bungalows of Craftsman or Japanese style, accessible from landings off a long stretch of concrete stairs. In the 1980s the neighbors still recalled in hushed voices that the large house at the end of Cove Avenue had once been a Communist cell.

▽

Education was central to the American Communist Party, and it was there that Harry found his niche, both as eternal student and as a popular Marxist teacher. His prowess as an educator earned him a job offer as Communist Party educational director for Los Angeles County, but he declined; he knew he was best in the classroom. There he could follow and synthesize the severe changes that beset the Party during the war years, and communicate these to people ranging from factory workers to white-collar professionals, most of whom, he observed, had an equal distaste for study. "Party line" changes were often abrupt and extreme, and were tied to shifting events in the world and within the Soviet Party. In a central C.P. change of this time, CPUSA chief Earl Browder forbade union strikes during the war emergency, an action later repudiated as a compromise with capitalism — heresy to the fundamentals of Marxism. "Browder's Revisionism" fomented discord within the Party for years to come. Additionally, even before the end of America's war alliance with the Soviet Union, some federal agencies planned a campaign of repressive legislation to harass "subversives," particularly American Communist Party members. The most notable of these laws was the Smith Act, which required Communists to register as agents of a foreign power. This culminated in imprisonment of many American C.P. officials and more than a decade of UnAmerican Activities Committee hearings and blacklisting in the private sector. The stresses from within and without were so great that in 1944, the Party was officially dissolved and replaced by the Communist Political Association.

Depending on which Communists from that time one talks to, the old Left was either "breaking down" or "tightening up." By 1946, Earl Browder, the man who dissolved the Party, was officially expelled and his "experimental Marxism" was reversed. The rank and file were often confused about how to assimilate changes in Party policy, and urgent back-to-basics classes were regularly required to keep Party members current. Harry was particularly well equipped for such classes because he loved the puzzlements of theory and had studied the fine points of Marxism in high-level courses.

"There were various levels of comprehension of theory," he said, "which can be compared to elementary school, high school, and college." The Marxism classes he had taken in New York were "college-level," but Harry had to develop a unique method of his own. He asked personal questions to draw out the everyday experience of his students and apply it to complex political principles. This was partially influenced, he said, by the Stanislavski acting technique of getting players to relate their "lines" — in this case theories of Marxism — to their own experience so that they could become convincing. As respect for his teaching grew, Hay began to feel what he called "finally, in my life, a feeling of control."

In Los Angeles, he taught first at Party Headquarters downtown and was also assigned to teach "fraction" classes for Party members who needed private tutoring because they were unable to keep up. He also taught at the People's Educational Center on Vine Street in Hollywood. The P.E.C. called itself "a bridge between labor and learning" and offered nuts-and-bolts courses such as "How To Run a Meeting," and many cultural classes. The school also had a heavy concentration of motion picture production classes; director Frank Tuttle taught "Motion Picture Direction," and John Howard Lawson (later of the Hollywood Ten) also taught a class.

"Harry was a guy who knew his subject," recalled his friend Irv Niemy. "He always put a lot of time into being prepared. And Harry didn't use clichés, which a lot of Party people did." Niemy observed Harry as an opinionated and powerful persuader. "He'd aggressively declare how he felt about something when an issue came up, say at a meeting. He'd be forceful in making his position prevail. Sometimes a bit of arrogance would flow into that. There was almost the feeling he was saying 'I'm the teacher, why do you question me?' He never said that, but it was implied sometimes." Earl Robinson, who taught Marxist music classes with Harry, agreed. "I hesitate to use the word 'elder statesman' because he wasn't much older, but there was something of that feeling about him," Robinson said. Hay's courses distinguished themselves as he expanded and interpreted theories. In studying political economy, for example, he identified five kinds of imperialism and was encouraged to teach a course on the subject. He was sent to teach all over the Los Angeles basin — Maywood, Hawthorne, El Segundo, Redondo.

Harry's teaching put him in contact with information that later influenced his gay thinking. While digging through books about the historical development of economics in Europe, he amassed data about pagan religion, the oppressive campaigns of Christianity, and roles seemingly assigned to gay men in certain former societies. (The latter subject was, of course, a secret study.) He rediscovered Edward Carpenter in *The Making of Man*, by V.F. Calverton, an anthology of anthropological articles. Carpenter and Edward Westermark discussed these roles. Hay also credited George Thompson and Christopher Cauldwell, British Marxist writers who had a mystic aspect, as important to him. The metaphysical, while never tolerated within the theory of the Communist Party, often tinged Hay's passionate, effective communications style and his personal view of politics as a matter of vision and dreams.

Up the hill from Cove Avenue lived a pretty young war widow named Martha Rinaldo, who became friends with the Hays and made them her second family. She spent many hours with them, and nearly every holiday. "Harry and Christmas trees were something to be avoided at all costs," she recalled with a laugh. "After they separated, Anita said that never in her life was she going to have another Christmas tree, because Harry was such a *fanatic* about the way it was decorated. There was no such thing as anybody throwing tinsel at the tree and hoping it would stick; every single strand had to be carefully draped just so. All of us were on pins and needles about the issue, and we were all engaged in a sort of conspiracy to keep Harry from blowing up over it." Rinaldo, a lifelong friend of Anita's, speculated that the tree may have been the object of inner identity conflicts she learned about later. His obsession with holiday decoration, however, may also be traced to his folk-culture research. The Yule log and the tree of St. Brigit, he found, were actually disguised holdovers from pre-Christian times, ceremonially carried out to insure an end to winter and a bountiful spring. Harry's trees were always decorated with ornamental fruit, nuts, and birds as well as the lead tinsel. He tried to explain to his two-year-old the "relational and symbolic significance" of all of the decorations. She didn't understand; it was Harry's private pagan ceremony.

The pressure of the overtime hours in both job and Party took its toll. Near the end of the war, in the spring of 1945, Harry fainted at work and was diagnosed with hypoglycemia. In retrospect, he realized the collapse was a by-product of his campaign of self-repression: "I was keeping myself so busy I didn't have time to think deeply." While being treated for low blood sugar he told his doctor, Yanny Nedelman, that the idea of being conscripted also preyed on him. The problem was not political — America was allied with the Soviet Union at that time, and many Party members eagerly enlisted in the service — but Harry was "terrified of falling uncontrollably back into homosexuality" if he went into the Army. He did not declare himself homosexual to the draft board, as some gay men did just a decade later, because during that period such an admission seemed an invitation to legal harassment. His deferment came as a great relief.

All this time, Harry passed for straight to many of his married friends and even to his brother. One incident that reveals the extent of his masquerade as a straight man dealt with cars, in this case several European models that Roger Barlow (Harry's co-star in *Even — As You and I*) had brought back to the United States after the war. These early samples of post-war luxury, Armstrong Healeys, Renaults, and Jaguars, were parked for months in the Hays' driveway on top of the Cove Avenue hill. Harry got to drive one of the cars to work, and the sleek Talbot-Durac racer, with its customized gearbox, was the envy of his co-workers at his Avion job in Maywood, where he spent every coffee break showing how it raced up to 120 miles an hour. From them he heard no remarks about "goddamn fairies."

But while Harry believed that Anita saw his homosexual past as a closed and forgotten issue, it seems to have held unspoken tension. Irv Niemy and his wife Sue, who were close with the Hays, stopped by the house one day when the English automobiles were in the driveway. Recalled Niemy, "There were some male friends of Harry's around, some of whom were obviously gay. Harry and Anita were usually such warm and gracious hosts, but the other visitors seemed to unsettle them, so our visit was stilted and short. When Sue and I got home we talked about that." Sue Niemy, a therapist, had already wondered about their friends. "She'd say, 'I have the feeling Anita wants to talk to me about something — she raises the fact she wants to talk, then seems blocked about actually saying anything.' She guessed it was about Harry's sexuality."

Anita's vexation might have been partly related to Harry's deep-seated emotional anguish. Long after the divorce, Anita told Hannah that violent nightmares continued to torment Harry throughout their marriage. Harry's eldest daughter recalled, "In one he was holding onto the edge of a cliff, and knew he was going to fall a long, long way. He was just holding on by his fingernails. It would be painful and very frightening, and he would wake up feeling terrible." Harry continued to sleepwalk, and one night Anita found him searching through the freezer, his fingers numb, convinced that the family cat was inside.

The Hays sought their second child, this time through a nurse who assisted unwed mothers. The arrangement was made and the baby, another girl, was delivered within forty-eight hours of her birth. After two tender weeks, the new bond was abruptly severed. The parents of the mother arrived from the Midwest and objected, insisting their daughter take back the child and (as a moral punishment) raise it. Legally powerless, the Hays returned the child they had started to love. Again they waited through the long application to the Children's Home Society. A blonde, blue-eyed baby girl born December 7, 1945, was brought to them within days of her birth. They named her Kate for Harry's favorite aunt, and her fair coloring drew her constant compliments and the recollection of Martha Rinaldo that "Katie was the beauty."

But outgoing Hannah was her father's favorite. "Lithe as a faun and chattery as a chipmunk," he described her in a short story, "a child who thought all grown-ups were made to love children just because she loved them." On Victory-in-Europe Day, the family went to Hollywood Boulevard to celebrate, and dozens of servicemen picked up the brown-eyed, strawberry-blonde Hannah and kissed her. Pretty, precocious, and talkative, she was in many ways close to what Harry's biological child might have been. He was ecstatic at the early affinity she showed for music. At the age of two, she heard Prokofiev's Seventh Piano Sonata, one of Harry's favorites, on the radio. She pointed to it and gurgled to Anita, "Daddy play piano," a feat of cognition he crowed about for years. Harry encouraged her musical interests, and started her with a small phonograph mounted on an orange crate and a collection of records.

Hannah's greatest flair was in dance. Harry enrolled her in classes with Lester Horton, the premier dancer of Los Angeles since the thirties. He and Harry had had a brief fling in the mid-thirties and since then had known each other in Party circles. Horton was prominent both as an inventive choreographer — Rudi Gernreich, one of his dancers, called him the Martha Graham of the West Coast — and for including progressive themes in his dances. His multiethnic company performed shows about war, women's, and racial issues. For years, Horton had offered children's classes. His children's program was designed, in the progressive tradition, to impart "mastery of the body as an instrument of social expression."

With parental pride, Harry described Hannah as "a little flame once she stepped onstage. She distinguished herself from the others and naturally held the attention of the audience." Horton agreed that she had exceptional potential and awarded her a scholarship with his company that lasted until his death. She devoted herself to dance through her teens and took classes from Bella Lewitsky and Carmen Delavallade, Horton protégées who became celebrities in the dance world. At home, Hannah remembered dancing for Woody Guthrie and Pete Seeger when they visited Cove Avenue.

Harry was careful to observe the rituals of fatherhood, and friends noted his closeness to the children. Every summer, he filled an old wooden, canvas-lined swimming pool for the girls. Joan Mocine, the girls' constant playmate, recalled that Harry loved to help them with theatrical games, and when they put on circuses, he showed them how to put on makeup from their Max Factor Junior Makeup Kits. Like his father before him, he packed the family car "with everything we needed and a lot we didn't," as Kate recalled, for their camping trips. He undertook to pass on all that he knew, and both Hannah and Kate recalled that he "lectured for hours in terms we could *not* understand."

They were a family both happy and troubled. Hannah ceased communications with her father in the 1970s over what she called his "tormenting gay chauvinism," but many of her memories of him were tender. He took her hiking and showed her the most beautiful spots he had known as a child, as well as the wonders of the backyard. "He used to carry me out at nighttime and set me on the white barrier at the top of Cove Avenue and tell me all about the stars and what was going on in the sky — the relations in the universe. He made the moon very special to me, and animals. He could be very spiritual." He instilled a respect for nature and its ways. "Any creature that died — bird, rat, cat — we would bury it and sing a special song. That was a spiritual thing too." Family photos show Anita always smiling and the children bright-eyed, but in most pictures, Harry looks sadly burdened.

▽

Harry's mother Margaret remained a fixture in their lives. She made sure that birthdays and holidays were always observed with cards, gifts, and occasionally, meals in fancy restaurants. So that the children would read something other than the *People's World*, she paid for the *L.A. Times* to come to Cove Avenue. One night Harry and Anita tried to broaden her horizons by taking her to a public rally against Gerald L.K. Smith. A white supremacist, anti-Semite, and anti-Communist, Smith was campaigning to establish a beachhead of his fascist ideology in Los Angeles, among other American cities. The Mobilization for Democracy, a coalition of popular political and public figures, sponsored the rally at one of L.A.'s largest auditoriums, the Olympic.

"This particular event was jammed, with 11,000 inside and twice as many outside," Harry recalled. "Poor Mother — we were trying to help her understand how wrong all of her political information was (taken, all of it, of course, from the *L.A. Times*)." A number of celebrities, including Gregory Peck, Orson Welles, and Burgess Meredith, were visible in expensive first-floor box seats and took turns at the microphone denouncing Smith's credo of bigotry. The band leader Harry James was among those who pledged a sum of money, and he introduced his wife, Ava Gardner, who sang the still little-known Kentucky folksong "I Wonder As I Wander." "She sang it a capella, and in the middle of this political demo, it starkly touched the listening throng, and the many outside for whom loudspeakers had been set up that night." In the subsequent edition of the *Times*, Margaret was shocked to read that only a few thousand people milled in the otherwise empty Olympic. With her unshakable faith in the status quo, she insisted, "The reporter must have gone on the wrong night."

Harry recalled a more intimate protest in the fall of 1945, when Josephine Baker brought her glittering show to the Biltmore Theater in downtown Los Angeles. "A large fund-raising dinner in her honor was planned at Silver Lake's Thistle Inn, for the late afternoon," he wrote in a letter. "Among the first fifty to sixty guests to arrive were a number of local celebrities from L.A.'s Black community. To the utter shock and consternation of the planners, the Thistle Inn management adamantly refused to seat or serve them because of their race. These formally dressed and coiffed celebrities and socialites threw a picket line around the entire premises and out onto Glendale Boulevard at the height of late afternoon homecoming traffic. When Miss Baker and her entourage arrived, she joined it with gleeful hilarity."

As the CPUSA continually adapted its Party line, Harry maintained his faith in the Party and its principles, even though some members were beginning to drop away. "I remember him as very determined that we should follow the fundamental line of changing society," wrote Pete Seeger, who had regular contact with Harry during the forties. This clannish loyalty, the stuff of political commitment, was in Harry's blood. Helen Johnson, Harry's friend for more than twenty years, observed that from ballroom dancing to walking picket lines, "whatever Harry did, he did it two hundred and ten percent. That rigidity was like a motor, driving him forward." His allegiance to the Party raised conflicts, and Harry could make savage comments to friends or relatives he considered unenlightened. Just after the war, there was a strike at Warner Brothers by the Conference of Studio Workers. Johnson, by now married to screenwriter Lacie Gorog and a secretary at Warners, was one of the picketers. Jack Warner called in armed police, and Gorog was hit in the eye with a tear gas bomb. Her own doctor was not immediately available, so she went straight to the Hays. "I, who was so rarely political, expected to be embraced as a wounded comrade by Harry," she said. "But the C.P. line was 'no strikes till the war is over,' so he snubbed me." (Upon hearing the story forty years later, Harry winced and offered amends.)

This tendency to rigidness, combined with his temper, could make the simplest disputes explosive. "Harry stormed out" is the exact phrase used by many friends and associates to describe the end of his short fuse. On one such occasion, progressive lawyer John McTernan and his wife, Kay, were visiting the Hays. "Harry and I were arguing a point," Kay recounted. "I can't recall over what, but it got heated, and Harry said, 'I'm going to go check,' and went up to his study. It was a name or a quote in a book, something he could look up. He never came down. We waited, and finally just went home." Anita did her best to keep things in check. Once when they and the Gorogs were playing charades, Harry acted out something and his partner couldn't get it. When the game was over and the term was revealed, they disagreed about the definition and, insisting he was right, Harry left angrily. "Anita brought him over early the next morning and made him apologize," Helen remembered. "That was just Harry. It didn't affect our friendship. Later, when our daughter ran away and we stayed up all night worrying, it was Harry and Anita who held our hands."

By 1946, Harry's sister-in-law, Mina, would escape her San Francisco job for regular week-long visits in Southern California. She, Anita, and the girls often took a motel in South Pasadena, or in Avalon on Catalina Island. Harry joined them on weekends, but during the work week he stayed home alone. On some of these occasions he brought home men he met while out cruising. One such night, he chanced to meet an old flame named Clyde Rossman. In 1935, Harry had introduced Clyde to poetry and Clyde had introduced Harry to marijuana. Their intense flirtation was not consummated then, and when it finally was, eleven years later, the changes in Harry's life were sharply underscored.

After years of quick, furtive intimacy, even the luxury of an entire night could not fulfill his reawakening need for gay company. "Occasionally we were invited to an art opening, or some Hollywood-type fund-raiser. I'd be there with Anita, but I was aware of men talking together on the other side of the room. And I'd so much want to cross the room and rejoin the fold. But I knew I couldn't." Such lonely flashes of insight pointed to a bleak future. "Other married men I knew were looking forward to their retirement, to time with their wives," he realized. "I didn't have those dreams. I had made a dreadful mistake and I felt I must simply play it out, getting through every day."

It got worse. The five years that began in 1946 with the adoption of the second child and ended with his divorce were Harry's "period of terror," a sort of stifled breakdown. "I was quite struck, during the late stages of the marriage, at the amount of tension Harry showed," recalled John McTernan. "He was a very somber, very tense human being." Harry's bad dreams worsened. "While Anita and the kids were away at Catalina with Mina once, I had dreams of blacking out and hurting them," he recalled at one point. It was a nightmare that disturbed him deeply. "I was confronted by the horror of my own existence. I didn't know what to do."

▽

The last years of Harry's married life were taken up by a Leftist mass organization called People's Songs. This early wave of the folk music movement was established during the spring of 1946. Hay recalled, "We first caught fire as a couple of folk-song round-robins held at Otto K. Oleson's building on Vine Street in November, 1945. At the second one, we discussed working out songs for demonstrations, to replace the usual chants. We continued to have sing-alongs, and, taking a hint from Woody Guthrie's activities, we called these 'Hootenannies.'" A New York chapter of People's Songs was run by Pete Seeger, and by the fifties, every major American city had a chapter. Seeger's friend Mario "Boots" Cassetta, a Left-leaning disc jockey who had served in the Army with Seeger, joined a West Coast branch along with progressive composer Earl Robinson, who wrote the classics "Joe Hill" and "That's America To Me." Harry, with his interest in performance and his passion for music, threw himself into the new movement.

The effort quickly divided into a performance group, People's Chorus, and at the request of the People's Education Center, a music history class.

"Earl and Billy Wolfe were too busy," Harry recalled, "so they said to me, 'You do it.' So I did it. By then I was working at Alfred Leonard's Gateway to Music, a major music store in town, so it seemed perfect." According to Robinson, "Harry became the theoretician of People's Songs," in keeping with the Marxist practice of creating a theory for everything. "Harry took it seriously, so people had to go along with it. And he was able to inspire them. Harry was an enthusiast." Fifty to seventy-five people gathered at Cove Avenue for monthly meetings, which sometimes had Left celebrities, like Pete Seeger and Malvina Reynolds.

People's Songs helped popularize progressive ideas years before they became mass movements. Its messages were catchy, current, and meaningful. Poet Ray Glazer and musician Bill Wolfe wrote songs along with Harry. "Atomic Energy" called for control of nuclear weapons proliferation: "It's up to the people to crusade, / To see that no more bombs are made." Another offering from the *People's Song-Bag* (the forerunner to the national journal *Sing Out)* was "Put It on the Ground," a blunt assessment of government excuses for social ills. To the endless stream of bureaucratic doubletalk, the song exhorted, "Dig it with a hoe, it'll make your flowers grow!"

By the fall of 1947, Harry had outlined and begun to teach his music class, "The Historical Development of Folk Music," which he referred to in later years as "a survey of historical materialism in 3/4 time." His typical, exhaustive research drew heavily on the work of musicologists Evelyn Welles, Sigmund Spaeth, John Jacob Niles, and many Marxist historians; more than 500 reference readings and musical examples are cited in his course outline. Harry also brought his personal insights into this novel and original counter-history of music. His guiding principle was that music was a people's method of communication, a language, and that it always sprang from the grass roots, the "folk," to become the official culture. He viewed it as a valuable tool of rebellion and social progress. One example in his class was the Negro spiritual, which was used in the underground railroad during the slave days. "This language beyond the spoken word had the power to communicate ideas, plans, and issues through the form of songs and dances under the noses of the authorities — as a weapon of struggle against oppression. The people's collective language of music always had the power to inspire revolt and revolution."

The class got longer each time he taught it. From ten weeks to two months, then finally to two years. A syllabus for the course, which Harry copyrighted in 1948, was by then titled "Music, Barometer of the Class Struggle." Individual lessons were at once scholarly and familiar, with such titles as "Feudal Formalism and the Guerilla Warfare of the Carol," and "The Counter-Reformation of the Baroque and How It Dug Its Own Grave." Those who took the classes always found the theory buffered by fascinating musical selections Harry played from his extensive 78-rpm record collection, including folk music from around the world. (Harry delighted in flabbergasting people with his esoteric musical knowledge; a friend once asked to hear bagpipe music, and Hay asked which of a dozen countries he meant.) His entertaining musical lecture technique so enchanted his students that many repeated the course, which he taught through the mid-fifties, even after leaving the Party. By the late forties he became a popular culture act at fund-raisers and similar gatherings. Phonograph at his side, he presented a diverting sampler of his class, and using innovative techniques such as sing-alongs of ballades and medieval part songs, he invariably held the audience in the palm of his hand.

It was in his research about music that Harry first encountered the term "Mattachine Society," and recognized it as an ancestor of modern homosexuals. The ancient Romans celebrated the New Year time with a lavish week-long festival, Saturnalia, during which all laws were relaxed, so that slaves and women enjoyed equal rights to participate in festivities where masked revelers could freely satirize their superiors, and sexual orgies proliferated. This pagan custom survived into the Christian Middle Ages as the "Feast of Fools," celebrated in churches everywhere from spring Equinox until April 1 — All Fools' Day. In those days, "fool" meant, as it does in Shakespeare, jester or clown, and during the Feast of Fools, the populace would choose a Lord of Misrule, an Abbot of Unreason — even a Pope of Fools — who, dressed in the jester's motley with mock scepter and crown, would reign for the fortnight of Feast days and could freely ridicule those in control.

During the fifteenth century, when the Holy Roman Empire seemed to be verging on collapse, both Church and state banned the Feast of Fools in an attempt to suppress its biting satires, but secret societies formed to continue the festivities — and the social parody — under private aegis. These "Sociétés Joyeuses" ("Gay Societies") had different names in various towns — for example, the Société Basoche in Paris consisted only of lawyers. The Mattachine Society performed a special dance with staffs that was a parody of lance warfare and warlike posturing, similar to the Morris Dances in England. It proved so popular that it spread to other countries. This all-male society was called Matassins in France, Mattaccino in Italy, and Mattachino in Spain. The dance even spawned jester characters in the Italian commedia dell'arte and Moliere's *comédies françaises,* and it spread to the Spanish colonies in America, where, called "Las Matachinas," it is still performed as a ritual dance by a secret male society among certain Indian tribes at Easter in Mexico and at Christmas in New Mexico.

An alternate French name for the dance, "Bouffons," gave rise to our English words "buffoons," which also preserves the essential characteristics of the Mattachine — the flamboyant costumed jester who ridicules the false pretenses of society by his critical mocking cloaked in comic antics and graceful dances. The famous Mattachine dance, notated in 1588 by the French musicologist Arbeau (though it originated much earlier), had consistent elements of masks, magic, humor, and clownishness. Harry was particularly concerned with the social activism of this society. According to his notes, "the Mattachine troupes conveyed vital information to the oppressed in the countryside of 13th–15th century France, and perhaps I hoped that a such a society of modern homosexual men, living in disguise in 20th century America, could do similarly for us oppressed Queers."

Because his research into folk music, particularly ballads, was so extensive and original, Harry was approached by John Storm, his brother-in-law at Crown Publishing, to update a book on the subject. This too-good-to-be-true opportunity withered under Harry's daily crush of political commitments.

The Hollywood progressive community then was nothing if not eclectic. One night at a People's Songs meeting Harry got a call from Bill Oliver, a reviewer friend. He had met three Peruvian singers at the Wilshire Ebell Theater and would be late to the meeting. He explained that the singers had been promised a solo at intermission, but it had not worked out. Oliver invited them to come to the meeting, commenting, "I don't think they've eaten in a week."

Accordingly, the People's Songs meeting turned into a dash to the deli for cheese sandwiches and a few salads. Harry noted, "American cultural capitalism had failed them, [so] we offered supper and entertainment with American folk songs." Harry translated Spanish to the male of the trio, who in turn spoke Quechua to the two women. "At about two o'clock in the morning, the man suddenly gestured that they would like to show their thanks by singing a song of their country they'd not yet been able to share here. He turned his guitar belly-down to use as a drum. A small, stunningly handsome Indian woman threw back her head and in the most glorious, tremendous voice started 'The Inca Hymn to the Sun.' We were all simply stunned, so unprepared were we for anything of that quality. I was in total tears. I knew I'd heard it before — in the Andes when I was a child — sung almost identically. The singer, of course, was Yma Sumac, eighteen months before she was discovered by Hollywood." Harry's subsequent attempt to secure a quickie recording session for her at Alco, a small record company he knew, failed. Over the years Harry watched, a little sadly, as Sumac developed from a first-rate ethnic folk singer into a Hollywood glamour exotic.

His job at the music store was pleasant, but Harry proved himself to be more of a record enthusiast than a salesman of the more profitable hi-fi equipment. After nine months of friction with his boss, he left. He worked next in a friend's television repair shop, but the business foundered and soon Harry was again looking for work.

At Leahy Manufacturing, an old, somewhat eccentric company at Eighth and Alameda Avenues in an industrial part of downtown Los Angeles, he finally found a job that lasted. Its patriarch, whom Harry always referred to as "Old Man Leahy," manufactured burners for the boilers that heat large buildings. His wife, "a Tennessee biddy who left a whiff of swamp water whenever she passed by," always watched over the old man's shoulder, especially to bowdlerize any unionizing attempts — earning Hay's eternal bile. He again had the job of production engineer, keeping track of plans, tools, and inventory. At Leahy, which had neglected such matters since it opened in 1902, inventory was scattered in thousands of pieces over several locations. Given the dramatic intensity of the other parts of his life, Harry may have found something comforting about the intricate mindlessness of the place; he boasted that his system enabled the company to cut prices and show a profit for the first time in its history.

This lower-end job was the best Harry could get in his field; the security clearance problem prevented better. His suspicions of this were confirmed shortly after starting at Leahy when Deb Watt, a friend he and Anita had known for a decade, called to say he needed to talk to Harry.

"The FBI came and talked to me," he told Harry when they met. "They knew all about you anyway."

"Anyway?"

"When they said all the things they knew about you, I said yeah, I knew that too." Harry thanked Watt for telling him and never saw him again. This was not the only time the FBI came making inquiries; once an agent rang the door of the Cove Avenue house, and Anita automatically invited him in before she realized who he was and that she could say nothing to him. The Federal Bureau of Investigation has acknowledged that it has files relating to Harry in Los Angeles and New York, though it has not, as of this writing, complied with Hay's Freedom of Information Act requests for their release.

FBI harassment and infiltration of the Party was an increasing problem. By the late forties, many organizers had the comfort of paid positions, and according to Harry, began enjoying extramarital affairs as part of their newly plush lives. When, after several distressed C.P. wives saw psychiatrists who turned out to be FBI informers, the Party directed "no psychiatry." This spurred Harry to begin seriously re-evaluating his own marriage, based, as it had been, on a psychiatrist's advice. At this same time arose another form of government intimidation known as Executive Order 9835, the loyalty oath, known more simply as "The Oath." This demanded that people swear, among other things, that they were non-Communist, and it became a prerequisite for teaching and civil service jobs. The oath caused bitter debates over the nature of intellectual freedom at U.C.L.A., where it was first introduced in Los Angeles, and some teachers resigned over it.*

Harry saw the oath as an attack on freedom that induced "psychological terror in the workplace, especially the arts and the schools — and all industries involved with government contracts." There were signs of even worse measures afoot, specifically the appearance of stories in Los Angeles newspapers about putting known Leftists in the concentration camps that had unconstitutionally but effectively held Japanese-Americans during the war. And a new scapegoat was emerging at the federal level: homosexuals.

The clerk–typist at Leahy's was an attractive young man named Bill Lewis, who became friends with Harry and was always interested in his ideas about organizing homosexuals. "One day Billy brought a friend to have lunch with me. The guy worked in the State Department in Washington, and told me that kids were already getting kicked out of the Department because they'd all slept with someone named Andrew. This was in the summer of 'forty-eight. Billy had told him that I was interested in organizing people, and he had sought me out to tell me about what was happening in Washington, to warn me."

▽

On August 10, 1948, Harry Hay first formulated what later became the Mattachine Society. The day began as important for other reasons. It was Margaret's birthday, and more importantly, Harry had been invited to sign

---

* Hay's section organizer, Miriam Sherman, turns out to be the only person fired at U.C.L.A. for actually having been a Communist. Sherman, who left the Party in 1958, never *spoke* to students since her job was as pianist for dance classes. Still, she was blacklisted for "playing with too heavy a left hand!"

the state candidacy petition of Henry Wallace, who was running for president on the Progressive Party ticket. Ray Glazer, who wrote for People's Songs when he was not writing for the popular radio show *Duffy's Tavern,* had invited Harry to the occasion. He considered that invitation an honor and an indication of his rising recognition in progressive circles. He finished drafting a cost-breakdown analysis for Old Man Leahy and left work early to meet Glazer and the others at a municipal building downtown.

The Wallace campaign was a high point of People's Songs, and in some respects of the preceding twenty years of the American Left. Henry Agard Wallace had been secretary of commerce under Herbert Hoover and secretary of agriculture for Franklin Roosevelt. He later served as F.D.R.'s vice president, and was considered his spiritual heir. Wallace was committed to continuing the social welfare policies of the New Deal. Handsome and plain-spoken, he had been a successful horticulturist, and his slogan was faith in "the quietness and strength of grass" — the grass roots. Hoping to overwhelm the main parties, many progressive constituencies lined up instantly; in Los Angeles, U.C.L.A. Students for Wallace marched against racially segregated barber shops near the Westwood campus. The campaign was a wild card and, for many, a grandly hopeful play.

Business (including most major newspapers) uniformly dreaded the implications of a Wallace adminstration. They Red-baited and ridiculed him. Claire Booth Luce, author of *The Women* and wife of Time–Life publisher Henry Luce, summed up the establishment's aggressive dismissal when she called Wallace "Joe Stalin's Mortimer Snerd," referring to the country-bumpkin dummy of popular ventriloquist Edgar Bergen. Many people were afraid Wallace's candidacy would act as a spoiler, taking votes from incumbent Democrat Harry Truman and putting conservative Thomas Dewey into the White House. The drama only fired up the Left, including Harry, to work overtime on the campaign. There was hope for major political change in America, they thought, if they could demonstrate that there was a choice other than the Tweedledee and Tweedledum of the Republican and Democratic Parties.

The signing of Wallace's candidacy petition exhilarated Harry. Most of the ninety people present (fifty signatures were needed, but there were reserves in case some were disqualified) were Democrats who had changed their registration to Progressive. Several Hollywood personalities added to the thrill, including actress Gale Sondergaard, her husband, director Herbert Bieberman, Writer's Guild president John Howard Lawson, and director Frank Tuttle. Viola Brothers Shore, whom Harry had known from the thirties, and Reverend Fritchman were also there.

Over dinner that evening, Harry excitedly described the signing to Anita, to slight response. She was already well into her disenchantment with the Party; she would break from it completely the following year. When he added that he was going out to a meeting, she merely nodded.

But he was not actually going to a meeting; he was going to a party to which a handsome man had invited him. The man was named Paul Falconer, and the two had met while cruising Westlake Park, and later at the music store where Harry worked. Falconer, whose name came from his interest in falconry, had beautiful coloring and a premature world-weariness. Paul had never given his address, and the party he invited Harry to was at the apartment of a friend, also interested in music, who lived on St. James Park near the University of Southern California.

What Harry later described as a "beer bust" was actually a sedate gathering of seminarians and music students in a Victorian-style apartment. He found to his delight that all the two dozen guests chatting and sipping beer on the plush sofas were male and seemed to be "of the persuasion." The first he spoke to, a seminary student from France, asked if Harry had heard of the recently published *Kinsey Report*. Its first volume, *Sexual Behavior in the Human Male,* was the season's most talked-about book, especially among homosexuals, with its claim that thirty-seven percent of adult men had experienced homosexual relations. To Harry, that newly revealed number suggested the dimensions of an organizable minority. He voiced the idea. When his friend protested that organizing homosexuals was impossible, Harry rebutted him. There could be millions of people who might fall into a group that would find great benefit in organizing. Certainly it would be difficult, but it was not impossible.

Others were listening and added their objections. There was too much hatred of homosexuals. Any individual who went public could be entrapped and discredited. There were too many different kinds of homosexuals; they'd never get along. And anyway, people belonging to such an organization would lose their jobs. Hay countered each objection enthusiastically, further convincing himself of the viability of organizing homosexuals. Since the Wallace campaign symbolized a new era in U.S. politics, an era full of possibilities, he leaped to the notion that this minority might even be able to somehow be represented at the Democratic Convention. No one got excited.

He spun forth ideas anyway. One was to pool funds to provide fast bail money and legal help for victims of police entrapment. This he referred to as "a fraternal Civil Insurance and Mutual Protection League." Since lewd conduct arrests — or the fear of them — threatened most homosexuals with severe debts to corrupt lawyers and officials, this insurance fund was a high priority. Another was education; hygiene classes in high schools could discuss homosexuality as a way of life.

They might speak to even more of society through a person of respected social standing. Returning to the idea of homosexual representation at the upcoming Democratic convention, Hay proposed that such a person might represent the volunteer work and the votes of homosexuals, and could press to secure a plank in the Progressive Party platform supporting the right to privacy. This aroused considerable response, and Hay spun it out logically. With the right literature and enough volunteers, he argued, some form of political recognition might be possible. Some men responded with serious interest, though they suggested campy names like "Fruits for Wallace" or "Queers for Wallace." Hay seized upon the discreet yet obvious "Bachelors for Wallace." Both scepticism and seriousness faded with the beer, but Harry forged ahead. On a large sheet of butcher paper, he wrote out a homosexual agenda. One inebriated party-goer started to run out the door with the list, waving it like a banner to show the world. Harry stayed with the idea for five hours that night, buttonholing every party guest to extol its merits.

On the drive back to Cove Avenue, he talked with himself about the idea, and later noted his train of thought: "The post-war reaction, the shutting down of open communication, was already of concern to many of us progressives. I knew the government was going to look for a new enemy, a new scapegoat. It was predictable. But Blacks were beginning to organize and the horror of the holocaust was too recent to put the Jews in this position. The natural scapegoat would be us, the Queers. They were the one group of disenfranchised people who did not even know they were a group because they had never formed as a group. They — we — had to get started. It was high time."

This inspiration changed him. In a letter he wrote years later, he characterized himself as "so pregnant with aspirations ... that it was too late for me to ever return to pre-Bachelors-for-Wallace innocence." On another occasion, he described the details of that day as being "somewhat overexposed in my memory. I was leaving that world in such a rush that I couldn't look over my shoulder to see what it was." Once home, in his study, he wrote two papers. "One was the plank for the Progressive Party, and the other was the structure for an organization to go on after the convention was over."

This second, much more elaborate paper, based in a Marxist perspective, forged a principle that Hay had struggled years to formulate: that homosexuals were a minority, which he temporarily dubbed "the Androgynous Minority."* Since 1941, Harry had taught Stalin's four principles of a minority; these were a common language, a common territory, a common economy, and a common psychology and culture. "I felt we had two of the four, the language and the culture, so clearly we were a social minority." This concept of homosexuals as a minority would be the contribution of which Hay was proudest — and one of his greatest struggles was to convince others of its validity.

As a political strategy, he aligned the "Androgynes" with the Left and set both against "encroaching American Fascism." He suggested a comparison of the political manipulation and murder of homosexuals in Nazi Germany to recent firings of gays by the State Department. This especially alarmed him; could what happened in Germany happen here? Hay modeled the organization and membership structure along the lines of a fraternal order, and so named the organization, using the capital letters that would always mark his customized, emphatic writing style. He called it "INTERNATIONAL BACHELORS FRATERNAL ORDER FOR PEACE & SOCIAL DIGNITY sometimes referred to as BACHELORS FOR WALLACE (A service and welfare organization devoted to the protection and improvement of Society's Androgynous Minority)."

Hay addressed the dominant heterosexual community, equating the civil rights of the homosexual with civil rights for the entire society. Specifically, Hay wrote that "guilt of androgynity [sic] BY ASSOCIATION, equally with guilt of Communist sympathy by association, can be employed as a threat against any and every man and woman in our country as a whip to insure thought control and political regimentation." He further appealed to higher levels of law than the laws of the state, invoking the Atlantic Charter declared by Roosevelt and Churchill in 1941, and the Charter of the United Nations, founded in 1945. "The laws we had in this country were archaic and motivated by fundamentalist religion," Harry

---

* Though he continued to use that term for the next five years, till his expulsion from the Mattachine Society, Hay had reservations about it. "I wasn't happy with *androgyne* since it connotes a combination of men and women, and I didn't believe that about us. I had read Ulrichs's idea, that we were women trapped in men's bodies, and discarded it. I was looking not for that, nor for straight men who would consent to be serviced, which John Addington Symonds proposed, but for other people like me."

explained later. "The idea of reassessing ourselves by a more modern and humane standard of law was the logical approach." He got no sleep that night, and when he finished the five-page document in the morning, he signed it "respectfully submitted to whom it may concern, Eann Mac-Donald." The name was from his own Scottish family, and Harry had used it for acting, ghostwriting, and for some political activity.

The writing of "the Call," as Hay referred to the organizational prospectus ever afterwards, marked the dedication of his life to gay activism. The original was lost during the 1950s, but a revised version he wrote two years later survives. By its next draft the organization was called "Bachelors Anonymous," in reference to Alcoholics Anonymous, the new organization that relied on a grass-roots, self-help model. But the structure and most of the text remained essentially the same. At the end of the first page, he proclaimed a formal incorporation:

WE, THE ANDROGYNES OF THE WORLD, HAVE FORMED THIS RESPONSIBLE CORPORATE BODY TO DEMONSTRATE BY OUR EFFORTS THAT OUR PHYSIOLOGICAL AND PSYCHOLOGICAL HANDICAPS NEED BE NO DETERRENT IN INTEGRATING 10% OF THE WORLD'S POPULATION TOWARDS THE CON-STRUCTIVE SOCIAL PROGRESS OF MANKIND.

Some of this would change radically; the term "handicap" soon vanished from his language. Still, the keystones of the Mattachine Society and of Hay's lifework were laid down that night: to bring homosexuals together for the purpose of self-understanding and, even more unheard-of, to recognize their contribution to humanity.

"The bubble soared to burst promptly in the dawn's early light," he wrote. The next morning at Leahy's he got the phone numbers of everyone who had shown enthusiasm the night before. But they had lost all interest in the light of a sober day. "Many gasped in fear, as if I were trying to tear away their Divinity degrees. Others simply sneered, 'Honey! That was the *beer!*' I heard that over and over again." He even heard it from the host. "The handsome Falconer roasted the very idea with his self-destructive and withering cynicism," Hay recorded. No one gave him a shred of encouragement. He turned for support to several progressives who were well established as social workers, teachers, and ministers, but their response was politely evasive. "Several said, 'Tell you what you do. You get a discussion group on your ideas going, and we'll come. If we think it is promising, we'll loan our names as sponsors.' And the progressive-minded gays I spoke to said, 'Now, tell you what you do. You get a couple of prominent people who'd be willing to lend their support to such an endeavor, and we'll look over their names. If it looks like we've got good allies and good protection, maybe we'll come and bring friends.' So — there it was! I couldn't get a list of sponsors until I got a discussion group going, and I couldn't get a discussion group going until I had a committee of sponsors."

He looked for both constantly, and without success. It took Harry Hay two years to find even one person who was interested in his unlikely dream.

·8·

Mattachine

No mortal eye hath seen, No mortal ear hath heard
Such wond'rous things
　　　　　— J.S. Bach, *Sleepers, Wake!,* Cantata No. 140

After two years of dead-end pleading Harry found support from an unexpected turn of events — he fell in love. His relationship with the young Rudi Gernreich changed everything. It brought an end to Harry's marriage, terminated his membership in the Party, and most important, lifted his deep psychic distress. The day he met Gernreich, he often said, they created a "society of two" that became the Mattachine.

Gernreich's friends recall him as a dazzling combination of intelligence, looks, and élan. "Rudi was very charismatic and had a presence that could fill a room," said his friend Martin Block. Harry recalled of the lover he never completely relinquished: "Rudi had a gentle command of everything. He was bright, witty, and had the most subtle sense of humor. He had come from Vienna as a sixteen-year-old refugee in 1938, but could make double entendres in English without batting an eye. Everything he touched had a little something extra — that spirit was in his dancing, his speaking voice, the clothes he designed. Even the way he dressed himself every day had that signature."

For years, Gernreich was Mattachine's mystery man. In accordance with the Mattachine oath of secrecy, Harry never revealed his cofounder's identity until after Gernreich's death from lung cancer in 1985. The necessity for this was dramatically underscored when Gernreich achieved world fame as a designer through the sixties and seventies with such fashion breakthroughs as his topless bathing suit, unisex look, and shaved heads. Harry referred to him by his initials or as "X" in interviews in the 1970s, but since his death, Harry has frequently credited Rudi Gernreich with cutting the pattern for the gay movement. Gernreich never commented publicly on Mattachine or the gay rights movement, explaining privately that the rules of the fashion industry prohibited his taking a public stand. His public "coming out" was posthumous: The American Civil Liberties Union announced that the estate of Gernreich, along with his surviving life partner, Dr. Oreste Pucciani, had endowed a charitable trust to provide for litigation and education in the area of lesbian and gay rights.

Harry met this remarkable new friend on Saturday, July 8, 1950, at Lester Horton's Dance Theatre on Melrose Avenue. The company had a markedly progressive membership; Eleanor Brooks, its prima ballerina for a time, was the sister of Miriam Sherman, Harry's C.P. section organizer. As Harry sat in the audience that afternoon observing seven-year-old Hannah, he became aware of being watched. Harry recognized the observer, Gernreich, from several Horton Troupe productions. Rudi had recently quit dancing to pursue a fashion career; some of his first designs, in fact, were costumes for Horton's company.

As the children practiced, the two men found themselves sitting near one another and chatting intensely, mostly about the war that had been declared in Korea less than two weeks before. Gernreich ran in Leftist circles and agreed with Harry's scepticism of the official justification for the war. But politics aside, the handsome Viennese set all Harry's romantic bells to ringing. After nearly a decade of denying his emotions, he was overcome. "Almost from the moment of our meeting," he wrote after Gernreich's death, "we were in love with each other and with each other's ideas." They made a date for dinner the following Monday.

The 28-year-old Gernreich had the gracefully developed body of a dancer and large, dark, expressive eyes. He wore a standard uniform of black pants and turtlenecks, which made his pale, clear complexion stand out, Harry thought, like a cameo. Thunderstruck, Harry spent the rest of that Saturday wondering "how such a beautiful creature had wandered into my life." But he also worried. "What were we going to have in common? I was determined we were going to have something in common, and it was going to be profound." He remembered too well his relationships with arty boys that had failed because of political differences. "At age thirty-nine," he said, "I wasn't going to repeat those mistakes." Over the weekend, he feverishly revised his prospectus calling the "Androgynous Minority" to unite. This is the version that survives, complete with a few typographical errors, including the misdate of July 7 instead of the actual date, July 9. It was Harry's third draft since the Bachelors for Wallace prospectus, and it had grown to six typed pages.

When Monday came, he took Rudi to the Chuckwagon, a new restaurant just west of the Sunset Strip. He passed the prospectus over the table. Rudi was intrigued. "It's the most dangerous thing I've ever seen, and I'm with you one hundred per cent," Hay recalled him responding. While he encouraged Harry's undertaking, Gernreich counseled extreme caution and discretion, both for the sake of individuals and for the stability and potential of such an American movement. He explained that before leaving Europe, he had been aware of the homosexual movement lead by Magnus Hirschfeld, whose publicly known Institute for Sexual Research had been easily smashed by the Nazis: its records sent homosexuals to death camps. They talked about many aspects of "our kind of love." The vastness of the subject and the prospect of an organization excited both men. "We sat there, by law unable even to hold hands, but looking warmly at one another, a sort of glowing through tears across the table."

After the restaurant closed, they parked on a hill overlooking the glittering nighttime cityscape and talked between kisses about their various interests, but mostly about this new goal of organizing. The affair that developed was emotionally intense for both. Before meeting Harry, Gernreich's relationships had rarely lasted more than a few months.

Since Gernreich lived with his mother and aunt, and neither Rudi nor Harry had money for a hotel room, the lovers had to cast about for privacy. Bill Lewis, the gay typist at Leahy's, offered the afternoon use of his rented room in a clocktower of the First Presbyterian Church, but the loud bells clanging on the quarter hour disturbed their secluded trysts. Bill Alexander, then alternating between jobs in Los Angeles and New York, offered the use of his apartment at 313 Alta Vista Drive in Hollywood. They met there twice a week for a year. Harry still lived with his family and never told Anita of his new relationship. He did buy one of Rudi's samples for her, a simply cut dress of an oversize hound's-tooth check. "It was one of those dresses she wore forever because it never went out of style," remembered her daughter Kate. Rudi painted Easter eggs for the girls that spring, but they never met their daddy's talented friend.

Harry explained to Rudi the frustrations he had experienced since writing the first prospectus the night of the beer bust. After the rejection of the initial plan for meetings, he had devised a facade: He would announce a public meeting to "objectively" discuss the *Kinsey Report,* a cautious and security-minded approach to organizing. But even with such a buffer, he found himself caught in the maddening impasse of paralyzed homosexuals and noncommital sponsors. "I had talked to hundreds of people between Bachelors for Wallace and Mattachine, and people on both sides were afraid to take the first step. It was like being told you had to have a harp to get into heaven and that you had to go to heaven to get a harp." So the organization remained unborn.

Cautious but enthusiastic, the well-networked Gernreich asked for sixty copies of Harry's treatise. "Rudi immediately had a whole program of activities we might undertake — but with more potentially viable people," Harry noted. The sociable Gernreich had already come to know many such individuals. In the film industry, he had worked as a sketch artist for Edith Head, and around the studios the handsome young designer had been befriended by such celebrities as Marlene Dietrich and Dorothy Dandridge, who were charmed by his gentle glamour. Dancing with Horton set him at the center of L.A.'s most socially conscious audiences and avant-garde artists. He took Harry to various social events and introduced him to "the bright young people." To some of these he showed the daring proposal.

Gernreich provided a steady supply of high-end contacts, including several prominent film industry people, such as MGM director George Cukor. All such discussions, of course, were marked with the same careful discretion Rudi had demanded the night they first talked. "Since we would both decide whether or not to approach somebody," Harry recalled, "Rudi would show me a photo or mention a first name to get my OK. Then, when they said no, as they usually did, he'd sternly ask me to forget he'd mentioned them." ·

Within a month of their meeting, the two set out on a field trip to drum up a discussion group on homosexuality. As an icebreaker they armed themselves with copies of the Stockholm Peace Petition, a Leftist initiative to recall the early troops that had been sent to Korea.* With his gay agenda in mind, Harry took the petitions to a strategic spot. "We set about discovering new adherents on the two slices of beach Gays had quietly made their own," he wrote later. "The section of beach below the Palisades just west of Marion Davies's huge waterfront estate, and that slice of Malibu

---

* This in itself was a daringly radical act. W.E.B. DuBois, the 82-year-old founder of the National Association for the Advancement of Colored People, was arrested and handcuffed for circulating the same petition without registering as a foreign agent under the Smith Act. The case against him was ultimately dismissed.

between the pier and the spit — which would be taken over by the surfers in the 1960s."

Nearly five hundred sunbathers signed the petition, and while chatting, Hay and Gernreich asked each if he or she would be interested in attending a discussion on new findings about social deviancy. Not one was: "They were willing enough to designate themselves Peaceniks by signing our petitions in the teeth of the Korean War and its accompanying patriot-mongering ... but were *not* willing to commit themselves to participating in easily disguised semipublic forums, oh-so-diffidently fingering the newly published *Kinsey Report*." Altogether, the canvassing only repeated the disappointment Harry had gone through during the previous two years. All he managed to glean was a mailing list of extremely tentative supporters.

Even if the beachgoers had eagerly joined up, however, the roster would have fallen far short of the solid organization and "movement" Harry envisioned. Rudi counseled perseverance. By November, after more unproductive weeks of outreach, Rudi proposed that Harry take a chance on Bob Hull, a man who had come to his music classes. Very blond, small, and boyishly handsome, he was one of those who had repeated the course often. Harry thought Hull was homosexual, but he was not sure he would join a homosexual organization. He nervously gave Hull a copy of the prospectus at the next Thursday evening class. Chuck Rowland, who lived with Hull, recalled how that night, "Bob came home and told me about this delightful and brilliant teacher who had approached him about this."

On November 11, 1950, late autumn's strong winds blew up Cove Avenue. Around noon, Bob Hull called Harry and asked if he and a couple of friends could come over to discuss the paper he had received two days earlier. He gave no indication of his reaction, but said he'd be over at about three o'clock. Anita and the girls were away that day, so Harry called Rudi over and together they waited pensively outside to steer the visitors to a quiet spot on the oak-studded hillside overlooking Silver Lake. A thrill broke over Harry when he saw Rowland "running up the hill, waving the thing like a flag, saying 'We could have written this ourselves! When do we get started?'" Rowland's later recollection was similar. "We were enchanted with it. I did say, 'My God, I could have written this myself.' I don't remember actually waving the thing in the air and running up that steep hill with it, but I might have." The five sat on the hill overlooking the restless water that windy Armistice Day, talking and basking in each others' excitement. "We sat there," Hay wrote, "with fire in our eyes and far-away dreams, *being* Gays."

As a result of that fateful meeting, Robert Hull and Charles Dennison Rowland became two founding members of the Mattachine Society. They had become lovers in 1940 in Minnesota; in 1950 they were best friends who shared a house in Norwalk, near Los Angeles. Rowland was a thoughtful, cordial man with glasses, a crewcut, and tattoos thickly covering his chest and arms. He held a production-control job similar to Hay's in a furniture factory downtown, but his real interest was in theater. Hull was also culturally inclined, but had given up an unsteady living as a pianist for a job as a chemist. Hull's large eyes and narrow face prompted Harry to compare his looks to those of the boy Tutankhamen.

Though Rowland and Hull were roommates and best friends, they had other lovers, and Hull was having an affair with a man named Dale Jennings that winter. They had shown Jennings the prospectus and brought him along. Opinionated, intelligent, and aggressively virile, Jennings had worked as a carnival roustabout and was developing a career as a writer and publicist. He was highly sensitive and in spite of his curmudgeonly persona, he could write with clarity and slashing wit. In fact, he wrote for the homophile press under a broad spectrum of names, including one as a lesbian. Though Jennings was not a Party member, Harry knew his sister and their mother, "Ma Jennings," from Party circles of the thirties, and Hay and Rowland both regarded Dale Jennings as "one hell of a fellow traveler."

Both Hull and Rowland had been Party members. Only a few years younger than Hay, they had been caught up in the ferment of the thirties; by the late forties, Rowland was heading an organization called American Youth for Democracy, which, he explained, "wasn't officially Communist, but it was." Neither Hull nor Rowland had encountered trouble with the Party because of their homosexuality. "All the kids I worked with in A.Y.D. knew I was gay," Rowland said. "It was not an issue you discussed, but they knew. Leaders of the Party in Minnesota knew. But I don't recall the issue arising in the two years I was active. I didn't even discuss it with Bob or another gay friend who was in the Party."

Harry called Rowland "the great organizer." Less extroverted than Harry but just as learned and determined, he shared much of Hay's outlook and organizing know-how; the other Mattachine founders described them as an effective team. (Rowland stayed active in the gay movement for many years and eventually founded Celebration Theater in 1982, still the only openly gay theater in Los Angeles.) Jennings, never shy about confrontation, served as a counterweight to Harry's forceful nature. Hull easily followed their flights of strategic theory and was able to translate that political language for others, a talent that earned him the nickname "Viceroy of Mattachine."

The idea of a homosexual organization was not completely unknown, but in the America of 1950 it seemed like a new and dangerous invention. Role models were nonexistent; the often-cited conspiracy of silence regarding homosexuality was overwhelmingly effective. The Chicago Society for Human Rights, an organization for homosexuals, had been started in 1924 by one Henry Gerber, who had been in Germany in World War I. Gerber had registered his society with the state of Illinois and had turned to socialism as a model for homosexual liberation. His group, however, was shut down after a few months, and Gerber and his ideas remained obscure. Champ Simmons, the man who brought Harry out in 1929, had told him of Gerber's group, but only in terms of dire warning, and did not discuss Gerber's political intentions. Back in Minnesota, Rowland and Hull had discussed the idea of forming some advocacy group for homosexuals, and Martin Block, a New Yorker who later became involved in Mattachine leadership, recalled that "you always heard that there should be a gay organization." He heard it in New York, mostly from older refugees who remembered Hirschfeld, though there was little printed information available about that movement. Officially, there was a wall of silence.

In the United States, that silence was giving way to a growing chorus of new voices. Not only had *Kinsey* been published in 1948, but a slew of novels from critically praised young writers drew public awareness to homosexuality. These books included Gore Vidal's *The City and the Pillar,* Truman Capote's *Other Voices, Other Rooms,* and James Baldwin's *Giovanni's Room.* James Barr's *Quatrefoil,* one of the first gay novels to end on a hopeful note, was published in 1950. Few publishers in this period would consider a play or novel for publication unless a gay protagonist came to a bad end — was killed, committed suicide, or was branded as fallen and outcast for life. The five men who sat on the hill overlooking Silver Lake that windy afternoon in the year of *Quatrefoil's* publication were more than a little afraid. But the prospect of creating a movement by, of, and for homosexuals overshadowed worries of danger.

▽

The five met weekly over the next season, trying out formats for a discussion group on homosexuality. They told their life stories and pooled scraps of gay knowledge to, as Jennings later wrote, "make a little sense out of much nonsense."* They were frequently amazed by how much they had in common but had never before expressed, and a heady intimacy bonded them. On Hay's cue, the founders sometimes referred to the group as "Parsifal," after his beloved operatic knights in search of the Holy Grail, but officially they were known as the Steering Committee, or, more commonly, as the Fifth Order. Harry continued to live as a married man, keeping his straight world and his new gay world carefully separated. His success at this prompted Rowland to remark in 1987, "By the time Mattachine got started, Harry was already divorced and the wife was out of the picture," though this was not the actual circumstance until the following autumn.

The very real possibility of a police raid and legal persecution required that their meetings always be held in secret. When the occasional guest was invited, it was a standard security process for him to meet a Mattachine member at some public landmark, then to be driven around for a few blocks before being taken to the meeting place. "We did not want to lead the police to our meetings, so we did not give guests the address," said Rowland, and they tried not to use the same location too many times. Blinds were always drawn. ("All those *men* — people would be very curious!") Because they had read that telephones could be used to bug a room, Rowland always put the phone in a dresser drawer and put a pillow over it. When people left the meetings, they kept their voices down.

One Fifth Order member explained the need for these cloak-and-dagger affectations. "It was dramatic because anyone in the early fifties who was gay had a strange feeling of fear. Everyone had experienced something. For instance, picture walking into a bar you'd been going to for some time, not a gay bar but one where gay people had been welcome to drink. Drinks were a quarter there, but one day the bartender says, 'That'll be a dollar to you.' You'd realize with a shock that he didn't want you there. That's a minor example."

The laws and customs of the era were stringently anti-homosexual; in California, as in most states, any sexual act except the missionary position between a heterosexual couple was a crime punishable by up to twenty

---

* An article entitled "The Mattachine Movement" was printed in an early edition of *ONE* magazine under the name of Hieronymous K., and in 1956 was republished in the homophile compendium *Homosexuals Today* as having been written by one of Mattachine's founders. Though pseudonyms were regularly shuffled, that one was especially associated with Jennings, and the other founders recently agreed that Jennings must be the author.

years in prison. Anyone caught doing anything else could be made to register as a sex offender. Repeat offenders and those whose partners were minors were often sent to Atascadero state prison and given electroshock "therapy," or even subjected to castration. Since any public mention of homosexuality was equated with scandal, few workplaces would retain an employee whose involvement with such an organization became public. Harry knew his own job at Leahy's was on the line, but by this time he had completely reset his priorities. By the fall of 1951, as he later told historian Jonathan Katz, he decided that organizing the Mattachine was "a call to me deeper than the innermost reaches of spirit, a vision-quest more important than life."

It is hard to imagine today what a new and exciting prospect this was in 1950. For homosexuals to meet and share with each other in a non-sexual environment was rare, and for most, being identified as homosexual bore a distinctly negative connotation. Jim Gruber, who joined the Fifth Order that winter, emphasized that "the population in general tended to be sedate in sexual matters, not only in behavior but even what they said, how they phrased things. Talking about gay sex was something you just didn't do." Those early meetings, which continued through the winter and into the spring of 1951, probed topics such as the homosexual personality and society as well as sex. Chief among their challenges was overcoming the negative, cynical mentality about gay life — epitomized by the cutting-ly bitchy language of bar talk — so prevalent in homosexual gathering places. Hay and Rowland thus stressed the development of an "ethical homosexual culture" as a steady theme of their work. This sort of social context, where homosexuals were supportive of one another instead of being sexually competitive and acid-tongued, was rare. Harry described it as a "glorious shock" simply to sit in a room with other gay men "and suddenly find one another good, and find ourselves so at home and 'in family,' perhaps for the first time in our lives."

This new bond began to edge into Harry's other life. On Christmas Eve, 1950, Harry and Anita threw one of the holiday parties they had become known for. Anita cooked large amounts of food while Harry, as always, meticulously trimmed the tree. The guest list included John and Kay McTernan and Steve and Frances Fritchman among the married couples, along with "several of the fellows in my music class" — Harry's friends Chuck, Bob, Dale, and Rudi. The men from Mattachine played it straight and low-key, but they were still single and long past youth, sore thumbs in a heterosexual environment. Fritchman, the Unitarian minister who had married Harry and Anita and whom Harry had unsuccessfully approached about sponsoring the organization, was clearly uncomfortable. So was Anita, who must have sensed that Harry's affections lay elsewhere; only days before, to commemorate their first Christmas together, Harry had played Rudi the Gaelic folk song "I Live Not Where I Love."

As the guests sipped Harry's traditional mulled wine, Bob Hull made his way to the grand piano and played carols. Harry joined him, first alternating accompaniment, then falling easily into four-handed harmony. Hull suggested they sing "Now Let Every Tongue Adore Thee," an excerpt from the Bach cantata *Sleepers, Wake!,* which both had sung in high school. Hull sang the tenor part, Harry took the bass descant, then Rowland joined, carrying the melody: "Now let every tongue adore Thee! Let men with angels sing before Thee! Let harps and cymbals now unite! With angels round Thy throne of light!"

The harmony of their voices was laden with emotion, symbolizing — perhaps even betraying — the developing feeling among their secret society. "No mortal eye hath seen/No mortal ear hath heard/Such wond'rous things/Therefore with joy our song shall soar." As the last notes faded, Harry suddenly noticed that Anita and the married couples were on one side of the room, listening, while on the other side, he and the single men took up a new song.

$$\triangledown$$

The new group's endless talk sessions often sought to give an articulate voice to "the love that dare not speak its name." Common parlance was deliberately evasive to protect homosexuals from persecution — terms like "nervous," "sensitive," "musical," and Harry's favored "temperamentàl" were politically useless, and other terms — like "deviant" and "invert" — were defensive at best. This problem was shared by other organizers of that time. Del Martin and Phyllis Lyon, pioneers of the Daughters of Bilitis, the first American lesbian organization, recalled how during the early days they used the subtly homophobic phrase, "the problems of children with mothers who were lesbians," before the term "lesbian mothers" evolved. "If you weren't living in that era," Jim Gruber stressed, "you would have a hard time understanding this. There was a prevalent attitude that there wasn't a middle ground. You were either straight or a screaming faggot and mentally unstable. A healthy acceptance of oneself as a gay man was just an unheard-of idea."

This void in homosexual semantics was to become a major concern of Harry's. The term "homosexual" itself was invented by Austrian Karl

Maria Kertbeny in 1869 in a tract pleading for social tolerance, and other contemporary attempts to define gays were created and lost, including "contrary sexual sensitivity" and "spiritual hermaphrodism." The first consistent advocate of legal reform for such people, the German lawyer Karl Heinrich Ulrichs, dubbed them "Urnings" ("Uranians" in the English translation), a term denoting heavenly love, which was adopted by Edward Carpenter and other English writers. By the mid-twentieth century, the predominant term, "homosexual," had developed such clinical and pathological connotations that Harry and some of his friends were determined to find a new word. Those interested in the task spent hours poring over dictionaries, listing the Greek and Latin prefixes *homeo* or *homo,* meaning "same," with suffixes. (Hay's handwritten notes on this survive.) "Homeoamative" (lover of same), "homeo-entropic" (drawn to the same), and "homeoprosphoros" (naturally fitted to like) were among the contestants, but the word they finally settled on was "homophile." This term was derived from the New Latin *philia,* meaning friendship, which was in turn from the Greek *philos,* which means loving. The word stuck, and the pre-Stonewall gay movement is still called the homophile movement. This same term had also been used by the European gay movement since the turn of the century, but those in Los Angeles were unaware of this. "I really thought we had invented something new," recalled Harry. "I was astonished when Rudi told me that he remembered the same word from the Hirschfeld movement."

By the end of the year, the group was holding small, semipublic meetings, as Harry had envisioned, to discuss "the homosexual question." They contacted the people who had signed the Stockholm Peace Petition on the gay beaches the previous summer, and Rowland, Hull, Jennings, and Hay invited likely candidates. Harry recalled that their first open discussion group took place about December 11, 1950. "Rudi brought Flo, a model he knew who was lesbian. She was blonde and very pessimistic. A couple of other women and half a dozen men were there, including one young black man. In all there were about eighteen of us. The questions raised were pretty superficial because we knew so little. We were discussing 'a point' but not ourselves. We liked being together. The conversation flagged, but no one wanted to go." They planned another meeting for January.

Rowland recalled, "The five of us said we were going to keep meeting every week forever. We kept holding meetings, but no one ever came and stayed. Not until Steve and Jim, these beautiful young people who were everybody's dream couple."

Konrad Stevens and James Gruber, the handsome young lovers, became the final founding members of the Fifth Order in April of the new year, 1951. "It was like magic when they joined," said Rowland. "Suddenly everything started to happen." This included replacing the interim name, Society of Fools, with Mattachine Society.* The new pair lived near Occidental College, where Gruber, twenty-four and just out of the military, was studying for his teaching credential. His lover, known as Steve, was two years older and was establishing a career as a photographer. Upon hearing from a friend that a new homosexual society existed, Stevens proclaimed, "That's for me," and he and Gruber were quickly invited to join the Fifth Order. Stevens enjoyed a good relationship with his family, which had always accepted his homosexuality, but Gruber's Christian fundamentalist background left him shy and quiet. Their opinions were so often in accord that Steve and Jim were referred to with the contracted nickname "Stim."

Neither had had much exposure to Marxism, and they were not at first aware of the Marxist background of the five Mattachine founders. It was not broached during several months of meetings. Gruber recalled, "We would meet in various homes, and once, when we met at Chuck and Bob's, I was sitting on the couch and innocently picked up a newspaper. It was the *Daily Worker*. I thought it was a gag and made some sort of funny reference to it. Bob just took the paper. He didn't find it funny." The incident, nevertheless, raised the topic, and as it became apparent that neither Stevens nor Gruber was particularly anti-Communist, the others opened up about their backgrounds. The group experience of the ex-C.P. members provided a vital blueprint for the shape that Mattachine was to take. The young couple (and, to a degree, Gernreich) sometimes felt like "the kids," more wide-eyed apprentices than full-fledged participants, but their very youth played a greater part than they knew in the Society's healthy start.

What were later called, with great sensationalism, the "Communist origins" of the Mattachine became its most explosive issue. But in reality, only one central concept was heavily influenced by Marxism: Harry's

---

* Memories vary as to whether Konrad Stevens or Bob Hull suggested the name, taken from the masked dancers in Harry's music class, but shortly after the new couple joined, the name fell into place.

application of the term "cultural minority" to homosexuals. "That was a new idea," Chuck Rowland said. "Harry is the first person I know who said that gays are a minority — an oppressed minority. This was a profound contribution, and really the heart and core of the Mattachine movement and all subsequent gay movements." This started, Rowland recalled, "once we decided we were going to organize. With my Communist background, I knew I could not work in a group without a theory. I said, 'All right, Harry, what is our theory?' And he said, 'We are an oppressed minority culture.' I agreed instantly."

Harry extrapolated that as such a minority, homosexuals had to rely on a change of consciousness, an active evaluation of their identity and relationship to society, to obtain future power. Harry's inspiration had been Marxist dicussions of minorities and what constitutes them.* As the Mattachine grew to include more people, many resisted the minority model. "They said I was making 'niggers' out of them," Harry recounted. "They thought this identity was merely 'predilections.'" Konrad Stevens remembered another argument — that identifying as a minority diminished individuality. "They steadfastly said, 'We're *not* a minority.' I think they didn't want to be. To admit that meant you were in an inferior position."

Though the structure of the Mattachine Society has been compared to Communist Party cells, its real model came from an older prototype, secret fraternal orders. "Of course those of us who had been in the Party drew on the techniques we'd learned there, such as democratic centralism," Rowland explained. "But the groups were much more like the Masons." As Harry had meticulously laid out in his 1948 prospectus, the "International Bachelors Fraternal Order for Peace and Social Dignity" was to be composed of members "anonymous to the community at large, and to each other if they so choose ... Membership and inter-Order activity shall be Masonic in character; shall be understood to be sworn to secrecy..." This plan also allowed for various degrees of involvement, a system that the Society ultimately used.

---

* In fact, the idea of homosexuals as a viable minority was in the air. Edward Sagarin, who under the name Donald Webster Cory wrote *The Homosexual in America,* published in 1951, called the first chapter "The Unrecognized Minority," playing on the growing national consciousness of minority problems. Cory had been in correspondence with Hay and Rowland prior to the publication of his book but most likely reached his conclusion independently. By the following year, *The Homosexual in America* was stacked in bookstore windows on Hollywood Boulevard.

A page out of Rudi Gernreich's notebook of Mattachine minutes illustrates the pyramid form they agreed on: Public discussion groups on the bottom provided entry into the first order of the Society, the secret cells known as guilds; the second order was made up of representatives (or councilors) from those guilds; third and fourth orders of increasing exclusivity and responsibility were planned but never actualized; and at the top was the fifth order, the inner circle of founders. Harry followed the Masonic model so carefully that he designed a series of lapel pins, again reflecting degrees of achievement. As a discreet code, an IBFO pin could be worn upside down as a symbol of distress.*

Harry had found his model, the Freemasons of the eighteenth century, in his music research. The Masons had been illegal and underground at that time, though leading musical figures, such as Mozart and Haydn, belonged. Chief among the tenets of the Freemasons was the promotion of fraternity among the membership and, on a larger scale, of universal brotherhood. That word "brotherhood" was key to the early Mattachine. More than any complex statement of purpose, Harry called the organization "a brotherhood of like-minded people." Just as Harry felt that joining the Party was like the taking of holy orders, he imbued a similar sense of spiritual mission and devotion into the foundation of the Mattachine. In the larger context of the gay movement, this first phase most closely resembled an underground resistance.

These early talks could "soar off into fantasies of what could be achieved, and at other times were lead-footed," Harry recalled. Most participants were frustrated at "having to put up with a lot of dreary, time-consuming drivel ... the drone of getting an organization going and functioning and being effective," as Jim Gruber put it. Some of that slowness arose from the group's dedication to the principle of unanimity, that no decisions be made by the group unless everyone agreed. This method, along with the protective anonymity, was accepted as the formula to safeguard the group from internal and external harm. Stevens recalled that, despite the inertia, "you got a shot of adrenalin every once in a while when you realized what you were doing." Gruber referred to organizing

---

* The insignias for the various degrees were to be: for initiate, IFBO; for first degree, "Androgyne" in Greek; for the second, "berdache" in Hopi; for the third, "Order of Saint Medarus" (a figure Harry had discovered in the thirties whom he believed to be a patron of homosexuals); for the fourth and highest degree, "Order of the Pharaoh," which Harry called, "the historic personification of the Androgynous Ideal." The pins, alas, were never made.

at that time as "a dare" — with serious possible consequences. "I give Harry credit for that. I think part of his whole existence is the excitement of being at the center of something daring."

Not all was euphoric, unanimous harmony, however. The legal dangers added to personal tensions. Some members censored their private misgivings out of a sense of obligation for the general good. "There was a group enthusiasm that we were doing something socially constructive, and in that sense I can remember hearing Harry say we had to suppress any negative feelings or any dissension," Gruber said. "There was so much to do and so many things to decide and we were united against a common enemy and so on — we didn't feel like we could afford to sit around and bicker." Even though they went unvoiced, his uncertainties elicited no small amount of guilt, and Gruber sometimes felt like "the gargoyle on the cathedral of Mattachine." Dale Jennings, who later became a virulent antagonist of Harry, felt that within the consensus process, Harry would wear down the others with a "ceaseless stream of gray logic" when pressing his point. The C.P. practice of "democracy by exhaustion," as observed by Communist writer Lester Cole, was Harry's long suit.

His temper, however, remained his shortcoming. Most often, he fought with Jennings, who had a similar disposition; one of Harry's letters mentions "my ridiculous knock-down-drag-out with Dale" at a Fifth Order meeting. With his dominant personality and founder's status, Harry was regularly in the spotlight, but he struggled to be flexible. "He would listen to other input," remembered Gruber, "but if you confronted him on any major point, he would just erupt and prove how wrong you were. If you didn't see it, he would simply go on and figure that you'd straighten out eventually." Gruber remembered a particularly volatile meeting at the tiny house he shared with Stevens. "Harry stormed out and slammed the door. After ten minutes he came back and took his rightful place of leadership. It was like a lovers' quarrel; no one dared say anything. Finally Chuck, I think, said, 'Are you all right now?' and he answered, 'Yeah, I just went out and ran down an old lady and I feel much better.' After that we all loosened up a little." Though displays like this created a vivid impression of Harry as an authoritarian, it was more a matter of his strong personality and fiery temper than his political tactics; Harry was usually scrupulous in obeying the wishes of whatever group he was in, even when the programs he most favored failed to be adopted, as often happened. Konrad Stevens assessed Harry's political style by saying, "Harry would be domineering whenever he could get away with it, but he wasn't out of control, and the rest of us weren't so passive."

By the spring of 1951, new people were taking interest in the group. Phil Jones, a former Broadway actor who worked at the Pasadena Playhouse and at a radio and television school, brought a faculty member to a guild meeting that spring. She was Ruth Bernhard, a handsome woman with silver hair combed into a pompadour. Bernhard had a photographer's detached studiousness of everyone around her, and indeed became well known for her camera work. She volunteered to work with the Fifth Order, becoming member number eight and the most active woman in Mattachine. She in turn brought Paul Bernard, who also became involved, as did Howard Senn, a friend of Jennings and Rowland.

Senn suggested that the ideals of the new organization be set in writing. Begun in late March and ratified in July, the Mattachine "Missions and Purposes" was arrived at after countless hours of discussion. The document identified homosexuals as "one of the largest minorities in America today." Using Harry's emphatic capital letters, it stated the group's threefold purposes: "TO UNIFY" homosexuals "isolated from their own kind and unable to adjust to the dominant culture ... [to] a consensus of principle around which all of our people can rally and from which they can derive a feeling of 'belonging'"; "TO EDUCATE" and improve the "woefully meager and inconclusive" information about homosexuality, and to further research in various academic disciplines "for the purpose of informing all interested homosexuals, and for the purpose of informing and enlightening the public at large"; and "TO LEAD ... the whole mass of social deviates" to achieve the missions of unification and education.

The document called political action on a legislative basis "imperative." The founders also insisted on the emergence of "a highly ethical homosexual culture" as a result of their work. Citing Negroes, Jews, and Mexicans as "our fellow minorities," they proclaimed that "homosexuals can lead well-adjusted, wholesome and socially productive lives once ignorance and prejudice against them are successfully combatted, and once homosexuals themselves feel they have a dignified and useful role to play in society." In an era where the outer world threatened anti-gay imprisonment, electroshock, and castration, and guilt, alcoholism, and suicide plagued gays internally, these ideals were astounding.

A set of inner purposes simultaneously tugged at Harry. This was a simple but heretofore unanswered set of questions that obsessed him. "Who are gay people? Where have we been in history? And most important, What might we be for?" These questions had been discussed by visionaries such as Edward Carpenter fifty years before, but to Harry they were still compelling mysteries. "He found [those questions] very important," remembered Jim Gruber. "I think the central group thought that was all very nice, but that there was so much more that was pressing. Those issues got lost in the shuffle because of the legal persecution." Harry grumblingly deferred to the group priorities but later returned to the inquiry, which took up years of his life.

The Society's powerful initiation ceremony was developed by Harry, with his sense of spiritual drama. It filled an important need. As Dale Jennings wrote: "To many a homosexual, who may have lived out years of loneliness or bitterness, believing that his lot in society was a miserable one and without hope, the whole proceedings, the sense of group fellowship, the joining of hands in solemn oath, bespoke something so new, and of such dazzling implications as to be well-nigh unbelievable." In a room lit only by candles, the members stood in a circle with hands joined. To the accompaniment of music carefully chosen by Harry for its emotional effect and its revolutionary historical context, they pledged:

> Our interlocking, sustaining and protecting hands guarantee a reborn social force of immense and simple purpose. We are resolved that our people shall find equality of security and production in tomorrow's world. We are sworn that no boy or girl, approaching the maelstrom of deviation, need make that crossing alone, afraid and in the dark, ever again. In these moments we dedicate ourselves once again to each other in the immense significance of such allegiance, with dignity and respect, proud and free.

Entry into the Society was by attendance at a discussion group. Ideally these held about twenty, though as the groups sprang up with increasing frequency, numbers could rise toward one hundred or more. Jim Kepner, who first went to one toward the end of 1952, remembered nearly 150 people there. "It was at a large home belonging to a doctor and his wife; they were one of the couples who seemed to be sympathetic straights, though a lot of those types eventually came out. Their large living room was full; and a circular staircase coming down into it was also packed. More people listened from the balcony and the foyer."

An air of polite formality ruled most of these groups. The Fifth Order produced a simple guide called "How to Lead a Discussion Group." Suggested topics ranged from "Camping, Pro and Con" to "The Case for Homosexual Marriage," which produced earnest conversations. Often personal emergencies would overtake the agenda, and these were the liveliest, most meaningful sessions. Men wore a suit and tie or at least a sports coat and often brought a woman they claimed was a wife. The occasional outré dandy slipped in; Dorr Legg recalled seeing Hollywood bohemian Samson DeBrier posing in an elaborate outfit, but "after the coffee break I saw Samson in a completely different suit of clothes, complete with different jewelry."* The formality could be stiff, depending on who was running the discussion. Kepner saw "two guys sitting in each other's laps, being somewhat lovey-dovey, which upset a number of people." Nevertheless, he said, "there was really the feeling that for thousands of years we'd been secret and hiding and alone. Now we were on the march and were convinced of the idea, 'We'll solve this problem — within a few years!'"

The most enthusiastic participants were privately told about the secret Society, and were invited to participate. Dorr Legg, who became a First Order member (and later became a homophile movement mainstay), at once suspected that there was something behind the discussion group. "It didn't take long to see that this thing was more organized than it pretended to be," he said. "It was too well run. After a meeting one night, Dale Jennings said, 'Can I walk with you?' He said, 'You may have noticed that the group is more than it appears to be. It's patterned after a medieval guild. Would you be into that?' We met at someone's house and I was duly inducted into the First Order. Once you were in, you were given a discussion group. That was your baby; you had to keep that going ... that's how they grew."

Within the First Order guilds, many of the same topics were discussed, though with less formality and more personal depth. Another benefit of the Society was social events. Following the tradition of the original Mattachines, the Fifth Order discussed (but, as fate demanded, never held) a "Feast of Fools," the spirited medieval festival where roles were reversed. They held occasional dances, to which Harry gave a historical twist by teaching eighteenth-century dances, including the rustic French gavotte. Instead of swing or the new rock, they preferred to waltz. Harry remembered, "The Society's first community dance was at Dale and Paul Bernard's house in Echo Park on a hot July night. We threw aside the furniture in the large living room, and about twenty male couples were waltzing. I remember Billy Lewis, the typist from Leahy's, standing in the door just gaping with tears running down his cheeks. Rudi and I waltzed over to greet him, and Billy said, 'I've never seen so many guys dancing together and looking so beautiful.'"

---

* DeBrier confirmed his early participation with Mattachine in a phone call with the author. He stopped going, he said, because "the personal jealousies of those involved ruined things," though such a social crowd was not exactly his style, anyway.

As Mattachine blazed into being, Harry's marriage was turning to ashes. Old questions had a new urgency for him. Since at least the mid-forties, he had agonized over the right course of action concerning his politics, his family, and himself. Years of nightmares and anxiety attacks hammered at his awareness that "something was *radically wrong*" yet he had nowhere to turn for help; no sympathetic family or friends, and, because of C.P. taboos, no psychotherapy. The political bond between him and Anita had diminished since her leaving the Party. Now she sought counseling.

By April of 1951, the steady growth of Mattachine and his relationship with Rudi pushed Harry to clear the air. He started cautiously, informing Anita about his organizing. The homosexual world, he explained, could never be rooted out of him; it had taken him years to prove this to himself. "I told her that what the psychiatrist had said wasn't true, that the book would not close." He tried also to explain in political terms that his group was a scapegoated minority — and that it *had* to be organized.

Her first reaction was shock. "She was appalled and forbade use of the house for any meetings or visits whatsoever from one of those people." She hurled terms like "physical addiction" and "character weakness" at Harry, and after some consideration, suggested that her therapist, an Adlerian, might be able to help cure him of this "socially and politically irresponsible behavior." Harry declined to see the therapist, but, mindful of the tremendous adjustment he was calling on her to make, he made little reply. He had decided that "I would not propose that I move out until Anita felt secure enough with her own decisions and new concepts of how she would conduct her life to feel safe in asking me to move." The situation remained static.

In July, Harry finagled a weekend so he could be alone with Rudi, at a house in the San Fernando Valley that Bill Alexander had just finished but had not yet moved into. It was the anniversary of their first year together. The relationship had become serious; they had even looked at property in Laurel Canyon with the idea of building a house together. On the beveled bed that Alexander had designed for his modern home, Hay recalled Rudi toasting, "May this be my and your *last* first anniversary ever!"

At the same time he was involved with Harry, the ambitious young designer was restless to proceed with his career. Through Margaret, Harry tried to raise $50,000 to start a showroom for Rudi in Los Angeles, but such funds were unavailable. Only a small group of maverick designers lived in California; conventional wisdom held that Seventh Avenue in New York was the only place for Fashion. In August, 1951, Gernreich received a sudden job offer from New York, and took it. Harry and Rudi behaved as if this were only a brief interruption to their relationship, but neither was really certain how long a hiatus it might be. If Gernreich was lucky in business, it could be permanent.

Harry felt suddenly lost without his partner, which opened his eyes to how quickly his marriage had deteriorated. Despite a vacation the family took that month to Fallen Leaf Lake, the situation worsened. Photos from the trip show an edgy Anita and a doleful Harry framed by magnificent wilderness. A near-tragedy occurred during that trip when Harry took Hannah on a long hike. Heedless of the hour, they found themselves at sunset with a six-mile return trail to camp, so Harry took a shortcut he had found nineteen years before, when he worked there as a college student. As they descended, it became iced over and gravelly, petering out in a barely passable cliff. Tying Hannah to his shoulders with his rolled shirt, Harry perilously descended the crumbling sixty-degree slope, once almost falling off the cliff. He recorded the scare in a story he called "The Other Trail," noting that, "for the first time in a life peppered with hiking escapades, I was afraid." It was his first written story in fifteen years, and, viewed symbolically, it describes his compulsion to take a challenging fork in the road of life, despite its terrors.

Not long after the family's return, Anita informed Harry that his organizing work could easily get into the newspapers and that the resulting publicity could "destroy the children" and harm her. (She did not seem to have known of Harry's relationship with Gernreich.) On September 23, 1951, at a ten-minute trial, a divorce was granted on grounds of "Extreme Cruelty." Anita was awarded the community property and a weekly alimony. Hannah remembered her father bending down, looking in her eight-year-old eyes, and saying, "I won't be living with you anymore." Katie, only five, kept no memories of the divorce. Harry took only his personal belongings, his phonograph records, and the DeSoto. Their former landlords and friends of ten years, the Meiers, happened to stop by, and watched in silent shock as Harry sadly crated his records, carried them out to his car, and drove away from Cove Avenue. He stayed with Joe Webster, a primary-school teacher he knew from Mattachine discussion groups. Webster's apartment at Eighth and Western was small and already crowded, so Harry's records stayed crated in the car for months.

The next breakup Harry faced was his relationship with virtually all of the friends he and Anita had known together. The end of this 'perfect marriage' was, to most, a complete surprise. Martha Rinaldo, who counted the Hays among her closest friends, was amazed. "At the time she and Harry separated, Anita told me that she had had thirteen wonderful years of marriage and she didn't regret any of it," Rinaldo recalled. Some weeks later Harry visited her. "He explained why this had happened and that he hoped it wouldn't make any difference in the way I felt about him. Because of the witch hunts that were starting up on Leftists, I remember saying something to the effect of 'Harry, are you sure you aren't trying to jump out of that fire — and that you're not jumping into a bigger fire?' None of us who weren't gay knew anything about the intensity of feeling that must involve. Looking back, I don't see how I could have said something like that."

His farewell to the Party was toughest. At that time the Party was calling upon each member in one of its periodic re-registration campaigns. This was a project of the County Verification Committee of the Party, to make sure there was nothing politically vulnerable about the membership and to protect against a growing number of infiltrators and informers. Hay took this opportunity to present his situation, in a considered, formal, and political manner, to his district section organizer, Miriam Sherman. Sherman had been a friend since 1934, when Harry met her as an accompanist for Lester Horton's dance company. Harry handed her a full report he had written on his case. "It was two or three typed pages that outlined my service to the Party and my current involvement in the Mattachine," he remembered. His continuation in the Party, he concluded, even under the best of circumstances, would be a liability to the organization, so he recommended his own expulsion as a security risk because of his homosexuality.

The ever-dutiful Harry had special reasons for this. "Since homosexuals were forbidden membership in the Party, according to its own constitution, I felt that those members in California who knew my Party work would know I had never endangered Party security. But, were this matter to be aired in the *People's World* or the *Daily Worker,* members in other states might feel the Party had been lax about safeguarding the membership. I felt that a proposal for my expulsion would exonerate the California Party in *their* eyes, and that was the important thing."

For almost four hours, they sat at her kitchen table and talked. "I said that I felt that this was an important conversation she and I were having politically," Hay recalled, "and that one of these fine days, when it had been made clear that my people were socially responsible, maybe we could all come back together again. But at that moment we couldn't."

Sherman was distressed by his report. "It was traumatic for me. I felt this guy was such an original thinker and hard worker and asset to the Party." He was also, according to policy, a security threat. Dedicated both to her lifelong political ideals (Sherman had been active in the Left since her early teens) and to her friends, she probed uncomfortably to see if there were other, as she put it, "AC/DC" Party members that Hay knew; they too were threats. This posed a dilemma. In the thirties, when he had joined the Party, new members pledged to be faithful to all Party requirements and tenets over every other allegiance in life — "even those of your wife and family," Hay explained. This pledge had fallen out of use during the war, but with McCarthyism, it was coming back.

Hay recounted to Sherman "the ancient and traditional pact faithfully adhered to in the Homosexual Brotherhood wherein one never reveals the identity of another without his permission — under *any* circumstances — even in the face of Party membership requirements. I suddenly realized what that could mean, and so did she, and we both got involuntarily teary-eyed. Like so many other Party people in those Loyalty Oath and McCarthy-ridden times, we had both experienced *best* friends who turned out to be FBI spies. We all had friends and relatives whose Jewish cousins in Poland or Germany had their hiding places and identities revealed to the Nazis by friends, neighbors, and even family members. After looking at each other for that long, blurry moment, Miriam blurted out, 'Could that be why the Party always insisted that homosexuals shouldn't become Party members or shouldn't be allowed to come close to inner Party life?' If I had gotten involved with a guy who had been an FBI snitch, this reason would have been very legitimate as regards Party security." This, Harry decided, was one of the clearest explanations of the tension over Party policy on homosexuality — not the modern idea of homophobia.

Miriam Sherman termed Harry's revelation that he was gay "less a shock than an eye-opener" because it was the first time she had thought of the issue in political terms. She added that the manner in which he handled it posed a challenge to the Party. For a respected, valued Party member to make such a declaration was "something new," she said; "nobody knew how to handle it." The paperwork took a year and a half to travel to the county, state, and national levels of the CPUSA, and according to Sherman, Harry was given the Party equivalent of an honorable discharge. For his years of service as a Marxist teacher, Hay was called "a lifelong friend of the people."

But while the matter was handled cordially on an official level, personal reactions of C.P. comrades were distant except when directly abusive. At one Lester Horton recital where Hannah was performing, a man whose daughter was also in the recital and who himself had been close friends with Anita and Harry made the loud, withering comment, "It's amazing how at events like this you can see people like me and queers like Harry Hay." Anita heard the worst attack — a rumor that he had been expelled from the Party for being "caught in the act" with a man — from its source, a hairdresser, who also spread the rumor to many wives of Party officials. Anita told Harry that she knew this not to be true, and that he had to find a way to counter it. There was no way to do that, however, and the slurs continued for years. "I would go to various events around town, meetings at the Embassy Auditorium," Harry recalled, "and people would cross the street to avoid speaking to me. I'd find myself going to speak to someone I hadn't spoken to in years and get this cold, closed-down, almost 'how dare you' look. I'd feel like such a leper." The wrenching feeling was doubled by the fact that bonds within the Party were based on a deep, idealistic companionship that Harry had enjoyed for a decade and a half. Already wounded, he felt his erstwhile comrades were deliberately rubbing in the salt.

Harry found little sympathy among his old friends. Even artists he had known from the Filth and Famine League were embarrassed. Divorce itself was regarded as a personal failure and cause for shame in 1951, and adding homosexuality made the mix explosive. To ease the transition as much as possible, Harry made quick good-byes and left their circle of mutual friends intact around his wife, thus losing whatever understanding there might have been.

Anita was cordial to Harry on the surface, but privately she struggled with feelings of betrayal. Divorced at age thirty-eight, she never remarried. Hannah, the eldest daughter, described the dissolution as "a scandal" and "an abrupt jilting," not only for her mother but for the entire family.

The hostility occasionally got high-pitched. Martin Block, a Mattachine member, once mentioned Harry Hay's name in front of Anita's brother, John Storm, and was shocked when Storm loudly threatened to kill Harry. Such reactions convinced Harry to cut off his old circle so quickly and completely, though with severe pain. Earl Robinson, his friend from People's Songs, recalled, "That Harry would recommend his own expulsion is fantastic. He was consciously cutting himself off from a lot of his closest friends." It was not until Anita's funeral in 1983 that he saw many of them again.

Every month for the next dozen years, Harry sent half of his paycheck to Cove Avenue. To supplement that income, Anita took a job as a meatpacker, stuffing bacon into packages. She chose the company because it was near the Clifford Street School where the girls were enrolled, and they could wait on the factory steps till her shift was over. In 1959, she took the job at Valley Cities Jewish Community Center, where she worked until retirement. Through the years, Anita maintained a devoted familial relationship with Margaret and stayed in touch with Harry by telephone. She showed great ambivalence about Harry's actions, defending to the children his right to be gay but complaining to confidantes about his "selfish decision." His sorrow over having hurt someone he loved by attempting to "go straight," Harry often remarked, firmly convinced him that gays should not marry.

▽

Rudi's job in New York came to naught, and in November he returned to resume his relationship with Harry and Mattachine. He found the Society had a major new project, turning the "concerned citizens" front group into a state-registered, nonprofit corporation called the Mattachine Foundation. Harry's mother agreed to be president of the board of directors and Konrad Stevens's sister, Romayne Cox, and his mother, Mrs. D. T. Campbell, also served. Behind these figureheads, the Society could control things; thus the gay people had a channel for dealing with the public and with officials, but at reduced risk. State incorporation papers were filed, but they were so slow in working their way through the state bureaucracy that the Foundation was never officially incorporated. The impartial Foundation broke no laws in its solicitous concern for "the welfare of the homosexual."

Margaret Neall Hay stood beside her son and earned herself an FBI file. Not only did her address become perhaps the first publicly registered gay address in California, her name was identified with the budding movement in the newspapers. She opened the account for the Mattachine dues at her own bank, Security First National at Hollywood and Highland, and she observed board meetings, pouring tea, though her influence was so nominal that several Mattachine members don't even remember her presence. Harry never pretended that his mother completely understood or endorsed a gay organization, but he always honored her participation. Margaret seems to have regarded the Mattachine members as personal friends of her son (who in her eyes could do no wrong), and as such they were "fine boys." Even when Harry was not there, members of various Mattachine guilds would sometimes stop by the Oakcrest Drive house and pour out their love problems. In a polite, intuitive manner, Margaret simply listened.

To bolster its image, the Fifth Order wanted professional and prestigious people on the Foundation board. Several were approached, and there was even an attempt to arrange a tea with Dr. Alfred Kinsey during his 1953 trip to Los Angeles, though he canceled at the last minute. In the spring of 1952, they did secure two such visitors, Dr. Evelyn Hooker, a psychologist, and her friend Christopher Isherwood, the English novelist and screenwriter; Isherwood had been the lover of Konrad Stevens when both worked at MGM, and it was Stevens who secured the audience. Despite great excitement over their attendance at the meeting, neither of the professionals agreed to serve on the Foundation board. Hooker, who was just starting her pioneering research in this controversial field of homosexuality, worried that membership in the Foundation might compromise her image of professional objectivity. Isherwood, who described himself as "not a joiner," contributed money but not his name. Rudi Gernreich recalled in 1980 that Isherwood was "not too helpful."

Harry took the lack of helpfulness personally. At every opportunity, he referred to Isherwood's behavior to the Mattachine as "rude and sneering," and spoke disdainfully of the novelist. "Isherwood made no bones about his contempt for our socialist mass-organization approach," Harry explained. "He told us we were recruiting the wrong people — we should aim for the important people among the film colony, the queens with money and influence, not the workers, not the ribbon clerks. At the rate we were going, we'd never get anywhere and we were wasting our time." Rowland fully agreed with this memory; Stevens and Gruber, who were also present, disagreed, however, suspecting that Communist-partisan and ego frictions were at work. "Chris never committed himself from the time he was a child, he just recorded everything he saw," said Stevens. "He was a known homosexual, but he was never a committed one. I didn't think he was rude."

The Mattachines themselves soon provided their own "prestigious person" by creating a hero of Dale Jennings, the salty writer whose entrapment case for "lewd and dissolute conduct" was a turning point for the Mattachine and is a little-remembered milestone of gay history. In Rudi Gernreich's blocky printing in the Mattachine minutes notebook for 1952 are the bare details of its beginning:

March 28. Attendance 12.
Swearing in 2 new guild members, Cliff, Tommy.
Second Order report: Entrapment case. Decision to fight on basis of 5th Amendment — politically, not morally. Test case — willing to fight from lowest courts to highest. Try to get support from ACLU and other civic

groups. Wire sent to [Donald Webster] Cory. Every minority in danger on entrapment basis. George Shibley being approached to defend. Suggestion by Second Order to cancel Saturday night party. Motion unanimously accepted.

What started as a commonplace arrest diverted to its unusual course when Dale Jennings, in jail and needing fifty dollars bail money, called Harry at two a.m. Harry had just enough cash on hand, and by six-thirty Dale was released. Over a cheer-up breakfast at the Brown Derby, Harry learned what had happened. He recalled, "Dale had just broken off with Bob Hull and was not, I know, feeling very great. He told me that he had met someone in the can at Westlake Park. The man had his hand on his crotch, but Dale wasn't interested. He said the man insisted on following him home, and almost pushed his way through the door. He asked for coffee, and when Dale went to get it, he saw the man moving the window blind, as if signaling to someone else. He got scared and started to say something, when there was a sudden pounding on the door, and Dale was arrested."

The practice of entrapment, which still lingers today, was a grim standard in the fifties. It amounted to a financial and emotional lynching, in which an officer accused a gay man of making a sexual advance. Often the officer had engaged in no more than a glance; sometimes he encouraged advances to the point of full participation. (A joke from the time went, "It's been wonderful, but you're under arrest.") These arrests created a victim in a victimless situation and served as a controlling threat to all male homosexuals. Harry knew dozens of men whose lives had been marred by this, and some went into a permanent decline following an entrapment arrest. Most respectable lawyers would not touch such cases.

Two lawyers in Los Angeles did defend these cases, a middle-aged woman named Gladys Towle Root and a man still practicing today. Many gay men considered these two more an injury than a remedy, as they invariably instructed those accused to plead guilty and then charged a fee ranging from $300 to $3,000, depending on the person's ability to pay. Often, men convicted of "vag-lewd" (vagrancy and lewdness) charges paid large fines rather than spend time in jail, where they would be singled out for beatings and rape. The dilemma, Harry recalled, made "everyone plead guilty, and plea bargaining was a tactic not yet in practice. So to the average ribbon clerk this could mean years of debt."

That morning while Harry listened to Dale, a light came on. "I said, 'Look, we're going to make an issue of this thing. We'll say you are homosexual but neither lewd nor dissolute. And that cop is lying.'"

An emergency meeting was called for eight o'clock that night. Aware that this untried strategy might sound foolhardy, Harry prepared "a firebrand harangue on how this is the perfect opportunity to press the issue of oppression," which he delivered at Jennings's apartment on Lemoyne Avenue in Echo Park. There was surprisingly little opposition to this proposal, but the air was still thick with tension. Next, Rowland stood up in support. As Harry recalled, "His eyes dark and blazing, Chuck said passionately, *'The Hinger of Fistory points!'* There was a pause while everyone stared at each other. Rudi gasped and dissolved into uncontrollable laughter, and the rest of the group followed." That mirthful moment sealed the decision to take on the Jennings case. "We seized on it as a rallying point," Gruber recalled. "There wasn't much arm-twisting at all. Inasmuch as I was often a dissenter, I was aware that any of the dissenters would have spoken up at that point."

Anyone in the group could have been in Dale's shoes. In fact, Gernreich had been entrapped several years before. He too had done nothing, insisted on pleading innocent, and demanded a jury trial. "Rudi was stunned when a guilty verdict was returned," said his life partner, Oreste Pucciani. "He told me that he looked in the face of every jury member, and one woman, who had been pleasant earlier, turned to the wall to avoid his eyes."

Fred Snider, the attorney who had handled the Mattachine Foundation's incorporation, was unavailable to take Jennings's case, so Harry approached George Shibley in Long Beach. A confident, handsome Arab-American, Shibley had become known as a political firebrand and a brilliant trial lawyer by defending the Latinos accused in the racism-tinged Sleepy Lagoon case a decade before. In the thirties and forties, he represented many labor unions, and in the 1960s, though a Kennedy supporter, he defended Sirhan Sirhan. Always on the side of the underdog, Shibley agreed to represent Jennings. He explained to the group that he knew almost nothing about homosexuality, however, and needed to be educated about it. Thus, for several weeks, the Fifth Order carpooled to Long Beach after work, had supper somewhere, then met with Shibley to educate him with the only means at their disposal: their own experiences. Harry recalled that at these intense meetings, the Fifth Order probably learned as much about homosexuality as did the lawyer.

The Citizen's Committee to Outlaw Entrapment was set up by the Mattachine Foundation to defend Jennings. This was an ideal use of the Foundation facade; if the Mattachine Society itself had organized it, the Committee could have been quickly discredited as made of "partisan" homosexuals, and its members might face harassment and arrest. The Foundation, however, could raise funds and command public awareness through a series of fliers addressed to "the community of Los Angeles" and spread through gay beach areas, bus stops, and selected men's rooms. One, discreetly titled "Are You Left-Handed?," compared homosexuality to any other inborn trait. Another, with cautious militancy, was headed "An Anonymous Call to Arms."

This second leaflet hammered home the "guilt by association" idea in Harry's original prospectus. It began with the declaration, "We, the CITIZEN'S COMMITTEE AGAINST ENTRAPMENT, an anonymous body of angry voters in full sympathy with the spirit of rebellion in our community concerning police brutality against Minorities in general, ARE CONVINCED THAT NOW, ALSO, IS THE TIME TO REVEAL IN THE CLEAREST POSSIBLE MANNER THE FULL THREAT TO THE ENTIRE COMMUNITY OF THE SPECIAL POLICE BRUTALITY AGAINST THE HOMOSEXUAL MINORITY." The "Call to Arms" leaflet detailed the bitter harvest of entrapment. It recounted "the man who parted with his valuable art collection ... piece by piece ... his savings account ... and when he was wrung dry was turned in anyway; the professional man who paid $3,000 to get a trumped-up charge reduced to 'disturbance of the peace'; the West Los Angeles businessmen who pay for protection against false witnessing every week; the dozens of youngsters who are offered rides by 'lonely or maudlin' decoys in wolf's clothing and stampeded into milking the family's savings or turning over the names and addresses of acquaintances who might make likely entrapment candidates." To break this cycle, the Committee promised to fight to the Supreme Court if necessary. Members hit up everyone they could think of for donations, including the owners of decorator shops on Robertson Boulevard. Some of these slipped the fliers into the shopping bags of clients and associates they thought might be sympathetic.

The Fifth Order held more frequent meetings, paying scrupulous attention to every aspect of this major campaign. The well-liked and politically sophisticated Martin Block often chaired. Block, a charming, chubby, Jewish man, donned a fur piece, white gloves, and pearls to provide comic relief in the guise of a Garden Club–type matron. "He called it the 'Helen Hokinson Lady' after the famous cartoonist at the *New Yorker*," Harry recalled. "He would pause in the middle of the most serious business and sort of fluff his hair and check his imaginary lipstick in an imaginary compact. I don't remember that Chuck thought it *appropriate,* but it broke a lot of tension." (Block recalled doing his performances only after "the so-called business was over." He was motivated to leaven them with his humor, for as he wearily recalled nearly four decades later, "God those meetings could be boring!")

Legal representation posed an expensive challenge. Shibley's services would cost $750, and the Mattachines wanted to raise an additional $3,000 to send copies of trial transcripts to at least forty lawyers around the country who might undertake similar cases. Two fund-raising events were scheduled. The most lucrative, raising more than $1,000, was a dance and raffle at the house of Jack Dye, a Mattachine member who lived with his wealthy mother at a secluded canyon estate in Trancas, on the coast north of Los Angeles. This private beach party had a phenomenal response, Harry recalled — almost five hundred attended. Mattachine members brought everyone they knew; one invited Jimmy Shields, lover of former MGM star William Haines, who in turn brought a large entourage Harry described as "a bevy of, let's say, beauties in various stages of decay." The other event, while less lucrative, was culturally noteworthy: Lester Horton offered an evening's take from his current dance program. One of his own dancers had been entrapped that year, and Horton was in full sympathy with the daring campaign. Though the May 23 peformance of three of his popular pieces was not advertised as a Mattachine benefit, most of those attending knew that it was, and the house was nearly sold out. Harry always credited Horton with sponsoring what was likely the first fund-raiser for a gay civil rights cause. In the end, about $1,500 was raised, which paid for Shibley and ten copies of the trial transcript.

The trial began on June 23, 1952, and after Shibley caught the arresting officer in a lie on the witness stand, the jury deadlocked and the judge dismissed the charges. Jennings later described it in *One* magazine:

> The trial was a surprise. The attorney, engaged by the Mattachine Foundation, made a brilliant opening statement to the jury in which he pointed out that homosexuality and lasciviousness are not identical after stating that his client was admittedly homosexual, that no fine line separates the variations of sexual inclinations and the only true pervert in the courtroom was the arresting officer. He asked, however, that the jury feel no prejudice merely because I'd been arrested: these two officers weren't necessarily guilty of the charges of beating another prisoner merely because they were so accused ... the jury deliberated for forty hours and asked to be dismissed when one of their members said he'd hold out for guilty till hell froze over. The rest voted straight acquittal.

The Mattachine Society called the result a victory and cited it as the first time in California history that an admitted homosexual was freed on a "vag-lewd" charge.* But the story went unreported in the newspapers. "We informed every paper in Southern California, every journal, radio, and television station, on every hearing date and on the date of the judge's decision not to renew — *to no avail!*" Hay recalled bitterly. "This was a deliberate conspiracy of silence." The triumph could only be celebrated as it was rallied — by leaflet.

▽

With this success came a turning point for the Mattachine Society. But just as hitherto inconceivable political elation was at hand, so was personal heartache. At the high point of the fund-raising, the Trancas Beach party, Harry was aware that "Rudi was going off into other rooms and other corners with other people." The following Monday, over their weekly dinner, Gernreich broached the subject, saying that he needed to "explore other compartments" of his life. Harry sensed that his children were one specific obstacle. His strong will to have a partner constantly at his side through consuming political work may have been another obstacle, for Gernreich was already being approached by fashion magazines in whose pages his own demanding career would soon begin to flourish.

"I don't remember how that night ended," Harry said, but its clear message of parting with Rudi hit him violently. "The next morning when I started downtown to Leahy's, I got to about Vermont Avenue before I was so choked up and blinded by tears that I couldn't see the road. I just turned around and went home. I sat in my bedroom and started to cry. I must have cried for two hours. I wrote him a long letter and said, among other things, that I didn't want to divide myself up into a 'compartment.'" Harry slipped the letter under the door of the apartment Gernreich shared with his mother and aunt at the foot of the Hollywood Hills, then drove up to Mulholland Drive on the razorback dividing Los Angeles from the San Fernando Valley. He parked his car and, for the rest of the afternoon, wandered the heights.

As June turned to July, Harry numbly attended the meetings of his guild, his discussion group, and the Fifth Order, not sitting as close to Rudi

---

* Jim Kepner was told that similar cases were succesfully fought around the same time, but the Jennings case was unique as a deliberately cooperative gay civil rights effort.

as before. His was not the only discontent; Dale Jennings was too inde-pendent and feisty to serve as the homophile poster-boy the trial had made him. As Jennings chafed and grew distant from the group, Harry worried that the very thing he had warned of was taking place — the problems of individuals were impeding group process. Falling back on the C.P. practice of self-criticism, which the founders had already used among themselves, Harry delivered one on himself, castigating his part in the "internecine resentments" and "factionalisms" threatening the work of the Fifth Order. He further denounced his own tendency to "steam-roller by autocratic action," to "impose by overbearing blasts of rhetoric," and to "bluster on the basis of dubious seniority." He concluded, "If you, my brothers, will agree to tear to shreds any postulates I may present that do not withstand the test of your collective logic, perhaps I can begin to learn a little humility, and ... contribute to our will to grow." He hoped Jennings would follow his example, and either join in the criticism and blow off steam or at least refocus on the importance of the organization. But Harry's dramatic self-rebuke elicited no response from the feisty Jennings, whose resent-ments remained as hairline cracks within the foundation of the Mattachine.

▽

By midsummer Harry had a new lover. "One night I was coming home from my music class and I saw this cute blond on the corner of Hollywood and Vine. I picked him up and brought him home," Hay recounted. "I liked him. It wasn't love at first sight, but he was a comfort." The blond was half his age, a Danish immigrant named Jorn Kamgren. Slender, with large, pale blue eyes set in an open face, Kamgren became Harry's other half for the next eleven years. His childhood, marked by his father's suicide and the war, left him troubled. His family immigrated to Ogden, Utah, in a Mormon recruitment drive. Already an apprentice hat designer, Jorn found nothing but boredom in Ogden and so came to the excitement — and poverty — of Hollywood. For the first dinner he made for Harry, he served a can of pineapple, a delicacy in Denmark, as the entire meal. Harry was overcome with concern and took Jorn on as a rehabilitation project as well as a lover. Jorn soon moved into the San Marino Drive duplex that Harry had taken with Joe Webster and Phil Jones, and shortly afterward, Harry got him a job with Leslie James, an established downtown milliner.

On the surface, Harry's new lover bore distinct similarities to Rudi — boyish, European, refugee, designer — but Jorn proved a poor substitute, all material and no spirit. Still, Harry was determined to establish a relationship and a hat salon. To the latter end he borrowed money from his mother, who liked Jorn instantly and poured a stream of financial assistance in his direction. By December, Harry had secured Jorn a license and a logo and had registered the name "Jorn, Hat Maker."

It was all part of their experiment in homosexual marriage, an instititution Harry had propounded throughout his Mattachine work to refute the prevailing cynicism among homosexuals that they could find no stability or happiness in couples. (Hay's idea of homosexual marriage was inevitably complex; he felt that homosexuals should be able to establish an "ethical relationship," different from heterosexual marriage, but still a supportive commitment. He refined this theme in various papers over the next several decades.) In Denmark, male marriages were common, though not legally valid until 1989, so Harry went along with Jorn's specifications for what such a marriage should be. But those specifications were far too petit bourgeois and hetero-imitative, to use two of Harry's favorite putdowns, for his liking. For the remainder of the Mattachine meetings, Jorn sat close at hand, commenting little. At first Harry thought that it was because of Jorn's shaky English; he found later that Jorn cared nothing for politics.

▽

The greatest product of the Jennings case was an explosion of interest in Mattachine, marked by the steady growth of its discussion groups and guilds. During the waning summer of 1952, word of the victory spread like wildfire. In circles of friends, among "ribbon clerk" professionals like costumers and clerks, in the gay crowds at bars like the Golden Carp on Melrose Avenue and the Pink Poodle on Pico Boulevard, people talked of little else. Dorr Legg heard it in the office where he worked as a city planner. "A guy asked me, 'Have you heard about the guy here who has fought the police and won?' I said no. 'Well he has, and there's an organization about it.'"

The impression that Mattachine was a savior from police entrapment caused a sudden flood of requests from areas wanting to be instantly organized. Chuck Rowland recalled that the crowds at these meetings were enormous. "In Long Beach I had maybe a hundred kids at one meeting. Bob Hull told us about a meeting in the Valley with nearly two hundred people." This began to throw off the original plan of a tight-knit, secret organization. By the time Jim Kepner heard about Mattachine, the fervent secrecy had largely evaporated. With almost two dozen guilds and what Hay termed "a sphere of influence" of thousands, mostly in California, the frustrations of former years, when no one would dare to attend a meeting, was completely reversed. Groups sprang up in Whittier, Laguna, Capistrano, San Diego, Bakersfield, Fresno, Monterey, and the San Francisco Bay Area.* The dream of organizing homosexuals had succeeded beyond their wildest hopes.

* Foundation records indicate that more than 2,000 participated in the movement, though Hay's figure, based on the wider geographical field, was closer to 5,000; both were estimates, since no central membership lists were compiled.

·9·

Collapse

The most incomprehensible thing about the world is that it is comprehensible.
— Albert Einstein

A s the discussion groups proliferated, so did new strategies. Many ideas emerged, but a proposal to produce a magazine soon predominated. During the Jennings case, several members kicked around the idea of a Mattachine newsletter to keep guilds in Southern and Northern California informed — Rudi Gernreich, with typical wit, suggested it be called "The Gaily Homo Journal" — but the Mattachine men had their hands full. Instead, a homophile magazine of exceptional quality and popularity emerged from a Mattachine discussion group in late 1952. Martin Block chaired that meeting, held at an apartment on Westmount Drive in the quiet village of West Hollywood, and Chuck Rowland was among those in attendance.

"That was at the home of Al Novick and Johnny Button," Block recalled. "Johnny was an exuberant young man who said whatever spilled out of his mind. During one long talk we were having about gays, he said, 'I've heard all this before. Why don't we do anything? Why don't we publish a magazine?'" This provoked such excited response that Block had to chastise the group for abandoning the Mattachine discussion agenda. He instructed those unable to drop the talk of a magazine to go brainstorm in the kitchen. "Then I turned over the chair of the discussion group and joined them, because I was just as excited about it as everybody else."

The resulting publication, *ONE Magazine: The Homosexual View-point,* became the first widely distributed gay publication in America and is the forebear of the modern gay press. By the mid-fifties, thousands of copies of each issue were in circulation, often passed from friend to friend; in the film *Before Stonewall,* Allen Ginsberg mentions reading it during the Beat period. Its original board of directors were mostly Mattachine members: Martin Block, who edited the first two issues; Dale Jennings, who oversaw the next ten; Dorr Legg; and new members Don Slater and his lover Tony Reyes, a much-photographed Spanish dancer from El Paso.

The simple, monolithic title was a reference to Victorian essayist Thomas Carlyle's quote, "A mystic bond of brotherhood makes all men one," which extended the mythic fraternity of the Mattachine Society. The Foundation provided the magazine with its substantial mailing list, and, buying *ONE's* first ten subscriptions, supplied one hundred dollars in seed money. After brief stints by Block and Jennings, Don Slater settled in as editor, but Legg became the backbone of ONE, Inc., as the parent group that grew from the magazine came to be known, and worked there full-time for more than thirty-eight years.*

ONE was a remarkable little publication. The 4" x 5½" magazine sported elegant layout, strong, modern graphics — often depicting small silhouettes lost in geometric mazes — and fiction, articles, and essays. Articles were often printed under pseudonyms, but from the beginning, many writers took a deep breath and printed their true names. Letters were published with vague signatures, like "A California Minister," or "Mr. W., Boston." Another use for pseudonyms was to make the staff look larger when one writer contributed several stories. Jim Kepner was Lyn Pederson and Dal McIntire, whose column "Tangents" was a regular feature; Dale Jennings was Hieronymous K. and Elizabeth Lalo; and Chuck Rowland wrote under the name David Freeman. These names were not, however, exclusive; "We swapped pseudonyms all the time," said Don Slater, who also wrote as Dal McIntire.

---

* There is some debate as to details of the beginnings of *ONE* magazine; Dorr Legg has stated that he started *ONE* independently of Mattachine, though neither Block nor Rowland recalled his attendance at the initial meeting. And in keeping with his C.P. background, Harry proposed "that we set up a second homophile corporation around the journal project so that the two organizations could begin a dialogue and reach a wider public." But Legg recalled that the founders of *ONE,* especially Dale Jennings, were determined not to work "under" Hay, and insisted on operating separately.

As a forum for the homosexual mind instead of merely the libido, *ONE* was hungrily devoured. The magazine printed intellectual and cultural articles, but also reprinted details of entrapment arrests or harassment of bars, and documented other measures of oppression against homosexuals. After the Miami city commission ruled that alcoholic beverages could not be served to homosexuals, and that two or more gays could not congregate in a business establishment, *ONE* reprinted one gay bar's spoof of the law. This included the dictum, "Male customers may NOT wave at friends or relatives passing by in the street because we'll have none of those gestures in here, my dear!"

As the year progressed, events began to widen the cracks in the Mattachine. In February, 1953, Harry Hay was named in a Los Angeles daily paper as a Marxist teacher. As the authorized link to the outside world, the Foundation quickly published an "Official Statement of Policy on Political Questions and Related Matters," dissociating itself from any other organization and from any political, religious, or cultural ideology or "ism." With an irony that would continue to haunt Harry, the Fifth Order agreed unanimously that since he had been specifically singled out, he must retire from public association with the Mattachine Society and Foundation. Kicked upstairs, he deferred all speaking engagements to Stevens, Rowland, and the others, and published only under his long-standing pen name, Eann MacDonald.

Partly as a response to criticism of its isolation from grass-roots activism, the Mattachine Foundation sent a letter to the candidates for the Los Angeles City Council. It impressively cited five committees of the Foundation, and cordially anticipated "a great future of socially responsible and productive activities." Almost as an afterthought, a questionnaire about the rights of homophiles was enclosed, to be filled out and returned. Few were, but the mailing set off a disastrous chain of events. One letter was forwarded to Paul Coates, a syndicated columnist at the *Los Angeles Daily Mirror*. Coates, who enjoyed the offbeat and was devoted to the status quo, introduced to the world "a strange new pressure group," the Mattachine Foundation, in his column of March 12, 1953. Coates cleverly straddled both sides of the issue. On the one hand, he explained the origin of the Mattachine name and pointed out that "one of the largest minorities in the country" had a potential voting bloc of 150,000 to 200,000 in the L.A. area alone. He cited the Foundation's demand for protective legislation against police harassment and acknowledged that this "scorned part of the community" could prove to be "a group of responsible citizens seriously concerned with a tragic social problem."

But at the same time, the columnist listed several aspects of the organization that could alarm both its gay members and the general public. State and local government offices, he said, had no records of the Foundation, which billed itself as incorporated. (The incorporation papers had, in fact, been filed, but had been delayed.) And to provoke anxiety about financial accountability, he wrote of trying to locate Foundation treasurer Romayne Cox (Konrad Stevens's sister), without success, and ran the item under the campy subhead, "WHERE IS ROMAYNE?" Because of its seemingly phantom treasurer, he chided, "If I belonged to that club, I'd worry." His real worry was that Fred Snider, the Mattachine attorney, had been an unfriendly witness before HUAC. Such a "well-trained subversive," the columnist speculated, could make Mattachine a "dangerous" organization. Still, Coates concluded with apparent neutrality, "To damn this organization, before its aims and directions are more clearly established, would be vicious and irresponsible. Maybe the people who founded it are sincere. It will be interesting to see."

This publicity, in spite of the Red-baiting, seemed remarkably positive. In 1953, it was a major triumph for the word "homosexual" to see print outside the most lurid tabloid context. The Fifth Order duplicated and distributed thousands of copies. But Coates had handed them a Trojan Horse. In their delight over his qualified acceptance, they had underestimated the effectiveness of his Red-baiting. As Joseph McCarthy's House UnAmerican Activities Committee saturated headlines and television screens with anti-Communist hysteria, the public was increasingly wary of anything remotely Red. The average Mattachine member — unlike group leaders — perceived the publicity as calamitous. The words "unfriendly" and "subversive," common fifties code words for Communist, blared like Red trumpets.

Accordingly, an immediate letter from the Foundation to Coates explained that the incorporation papers were filed but were in limbo; that their financial records were open for inspection; and that while Snider might be considered somewhat problematic, he was the only lawyer that would represent their controversial group. "It is the purpose of the Foundation to turn as much light on the homosexual as possible. If his intentions are criminal, let that be exposed," they wrote. "But if the possibility exists that society's treatment of him is criminal, let that be known also." Coates, however, had finished writing about homosexuals. The reply was never printed.

▽

The Fifth Order was deluged with demands for change. The foremost concern was about secrecy. Coates's accusations of "subversion" made the rank and file uneasy with the anonymous structure. Even before the Coates piece, many guild members reacted to the city council letter by saying, as Konrad Stevens recalled, "They'll think we're *activists!* We'll all get into trouble." He further remembered that a growing faction was "scared to death that Mattachine was being run by the Communist Party and was part of a plot to overthrow the U.S. government!" One guild even called for a loyalty oath denouncing Communism as a condition for Mattachine membership. Harry termed this attitude "the middle-class mentality more concerned with respectability than self-respect." In his view, the organization was growing with the wrong people.

Within the Fifth Order, Harry himself was criticized as out of touch with his own organization. His theatrical yet guarded style, exacerbated by his agreement to keep a safe distance, had put him in precisely that position. "Harry was the theoretician and the consultant, but he was not present at these enormous gatherings," said Rowland. "It became evident to Steve, Bob, Dale, and me that there simply were more people than we could handle." But Harry, fearful of government reprisals, opposed any change in Mattachine's closed-system organization. Others urged a reversal of this policy for fear of losing the extraordinary moment. Rowland pushed for a democratic restructuring and even wrote to Harry pleading this case. But the plea fell on deaf ears. "I knew that Senator Estes Kefauver's committee to investigate nonprofit groups was due to come west, and I was sure the Paul Coates blast would turn Kefauver's scent-hounds onto us. We had made a mutual pledge in the Fifth Order to invoke the Fifth Amendment if questioned, which, I felt, was the best protection for us *and* for the membership of the society." Harry may also have feared losing the intimacy of Parsifal were the group restructured.

Some felt that Harry's political strategy was obsolete; to increase its viability as a movement, they argued, the Mattachine Society should go completely public. The once acute fear of exposure did seem less apparent among many of those now joining. One guild councilor, Marilyn Reiger (known as Boopsie), protested that she was already an open lesbian at work and argued that such openness was a vital strategy. As pressure mounted through the spring of 1953, the Fifth Order took action and called a democratic convention to create a constitution for Mattachine. It would become an aboveground organization. Immediately, the Fifth Order flew into action to write the most democratic constitution possible, hoping to continue the original spirit of the group yet free it from the covert model.

This convention, held over two weekends that April and May of 1953, was an extraordinary event. Two councilors from every guild in California were invited to the First Universalist Church in Los Angeles, which had been offered by pastor Wallace de Ortega Maxey, a member of the Foundation board of directors. (One of the "sympathetic heteros," Reverend Maxey, Harry recalled, was a bachelor with a handsome Chicano male friend.) On the opening weekend, the convergence of such a large number of gay people in one room was emotionally overpowering. Harry insisted that close to 500 were there, though Jim Kepner, who saved voting tallies, counted fewer than 150. But Kepner and Hay agreed on the exhilaration of the occasion. Harry recalled, "This wasn't the period when you hugged much yet, but there was nevertheless an awful lot of hugging going on during that first weekend."

The initial rush of high spirits quickly gave way to intense political polarization. Chuck Rowland made the keynote speech, predicting with amazing accuracy that "the time will come when we will march down Hollywood Boulevard arm in arm, proclaiming our pride in our homosexuality." A well-trained, somewhat formal speaker, Rowland gave an uncharacteristically emotional and touching delivery. Some of his militant language, however, inflamed the McCarthyite sentiments of those present. No more conciliatory, Harry followed him with a speech titled "Are You Now or Have You Ever Been a Homosexual?," in which he addressed the attacks against attorney Snider and the Fifth Amendment stance, and noted that if "political suspects" were going to be punished on a loyalty-oath bandwagon, homosexuals would be there right alongside the Reds. With careful logic, he explained that if opposition existed between the tastes of conservatives and the interests of homosexuals, "the securities and protections of the homosexual minorities must come first."

Many convention delegates responded positively to these arguments. Kepner, still new to Mattachine, remembered thinking that whoever spoke last held greatest sway. Aware of this, key dissenters redoubled their antagonism. Hal Call, a member of the San Francisco Mattachine, became the spokesman for the conservatives. A displaced Midwesterner with an abrasive and often vulgar manner, Call was determined to get rid of "the Communist," who he suspected was Chuck Rowland. (Ironically, Call never knew that Hay and Hull were also Reds — albeit lapsed — a tribute to the protection afforded by Harry's anonymous structure.) Call proposed to replace Mattachine's Red menace with "experts" who knew all about homosexuality — heterosexual professionals. "At that time, Hal Call was young, handsome, and persuasive. He should have been a sales manager,"

Rowland recalled. "Hal spoke blithely about all the connections he had with church people and educators — which turned out to be a crock of shit."

Call had brought his friend David Finn, better known as "Nellie," who was recruited to do the dirty work. Hal Call, Nellie Finn, and Boopsie Reiger joined forces to whip up a dissenting front, though ultimately Call's proposed anti-Communist statement was defeated and most of the agenda items introduced by the founders were passed. But in a surprise move, the provocateurs offered their own constitution, written specifically to eradicate the founders and their most visionary language and ideas. Jim Kepner remembered seeing Call, "redder in the face than usual, screaming at Chuck, 'The Society is not big enough for the two of us — there's no room for Russian agents.'" This Red-baiting reached a horrifying apex at a follow-up convention in November when Nellie Finn, as moderator, threatened to turn over Mattachine membership lists to the FBI if the convention did not exclude the statement about developing a "highly ethical homosexual culture" from the preamble of the diluted constitution. Years later, Dorr Legg summed up the across-the-board outrage with the pronouncement, "We should simply have broken his bones!" But only the feeling of trust was broken.

As the pressure increased, those in the Fifth Order began to realize that "life as we knew it was over for Mattachine." On the morning of the last day of the May convention, the founders met for what was to be the last time. Bob Hull, the Viceroy, expressed his concern over the Kefauver committee; he also was certain that the Mattachine could not withstand an investigation. He confronted Harry with the bottom line: "We can't hold this thing." He joined Rowland in urging restructuring, arguing that the Fifth Order should replace the unanimity process with majority-rules voting. Jennings, for his part, was opposed to anything Hay favored. Harry saw — he would always speak of being "hit" by the realization as if it were a physical blow — that "the unanimity was over, the dream was gone." He felt betrayed by his comrades, and even accused them of being opportunistic, running with the crowd instead of sticking with their original ideals.

"Harry was the most reluctant of the group to accept what we decided on — to resign," said Rowland. But that was the decision: The original board would dissolve itself, hand over the Mattachine name, and present themselves to the convention. There was little other course. If the founders fought, the Mattachine could go under completely; if they let go, a reconstituted organization might carry enough vision to continue. When all seven heretofore-anonymous founders appeared on the stage, a buzz of astonishment went through the audience. Rowland recalled, "When we announced that we were resigning, a lot of people yelled, 'Oh, no, no.' But the Hal Call faction was delighted." This marked the end of what Harry called "First Mattachine" and the inception of the "Second Mattachine," which was to spread throughout the country as the largest gay organization of the next two decades.

The impatient new regime was not even certain it wanted to retain the Mattachine name — though it had gained such popular identification that it seemed an invaluable asset. The new constitution, drafted at a second weekend of the extended convention, was top-heavy and administratively clumsy. Rowland, who stayed with the reconstituted Mattachine for a time, said, "These people wanted a gay organization but they didn't want to be hurt. They didn't want to be secret, but they also didn't want to be open. It was a ridiculous contradiction." While trying to eradicate all traces of its radical founders, the group did continue to use the name, and the new Mattachine Society eventually hosted several national conferences and helped prepare the ground for the gay revolution of the 1970s.

But its idealism and grass-roots activism rapidly declined. Within a few years of the convention, Hal Call had made San Francisco the new center of all things Mattachine, and started Pan Graphic Press, a printing company that published the newsletter *Mattachine Review*. During his tenure, the idealistic, self-help brotherhood degenerated into a San Francisco blue-movie club called "Cinemattachine." The new Mattachine shied away from promoting a self-aware, self-supporting homosexual culture in favor of working for the endorsements of professionals from mainstream society, thus launching the timid "white-glove" assimilationist attitude that characterized the homophile movement until Stonewall.*

From the beginning, Hay had prophesied this turn of events. "Harry said that we were the kind of people who would start this organization," Stevens recalled, "but there would come a time when we would be thrown out and it'd be taken over by less revolutionary people. It was strange how within three years it did happen. I suspect he thought it would be more like six years." Rudi Gernreich left the group at the end of the convention; within a year he was featured in *Life* magazine and was lost to gay politics. Ruth Bernhard, when asked recently about the Mattachine Society, said,

---

* John D'Emilio's *Sexual Politics, Sexual Communities* contains the definitive political history of the Mattachine Society and its gay movement offshoots.

"Time has passed and I hardly remember anything of those years." Stevens, who worked with Rowland on the new Mattachine for a while, found it "very menial. We weren't really doing anything." For Hay and Rowland, the disenchantment was especially sorrowful — marking the end of a utopian dream to which they had dedicated their lives. Many years later, Rowland sadly observed, "When the Mattachine was over, it broke our hearts." He added, a bit darkly, "And it damn near ruined our lives."

▽

After the convention, Harry was indeed devastated. He dropped out of sight, avoiding both the meanderings of the Los Angeles homophile movement and the circle of people with whom he had worked so closely. It would be more than a decade before he again became prominent in gay activities. Many friends wondered what had happened.

Having lived Mattachine every day for three years, Harry went into an emotional tailspin once that connection was severed. His friends felt they were witnessing a sort of breakdown. The Mattachine reversal was some-thing he took "very personally," Jim Gruber emphasized. "Here were the people he was trying to help, and they had turned on him and renounced him. He was — crushed. He felt betrayed by his own people." Harry himself described this as part of a long string of terrible blows. "The break from the Party was a blow; moving away from Anita and the kids was an excruciating wrench; the failure of my relationship with Rudi was a dreadful heartbreak which took me years to get over." He also took political setbacks to mean the death of ideals; Harry regarded the expul-sion of the Left by the Congress of Industrial Organizations and its merging with the American Federation of Labor as a "devastating shock."

A serious dilemma marked the new landscape of his life: As a practic-ing "homophile," he could not be a Communist; unwilling to renounce his Left values, he was, as historian John D'Emilio observed, "hamstrung by his political past" — and barred from both its worlds. On some level, Harry "the example" must have considered the demise of the original Mattachine to be a personal failure. Despite his innate hardiness and optimism, he suffered frequent low ebbs over the next decade, making him almost suicidal with despair. Sometimes he spoke as if the ensuing gay movement had gone tragically wrong. "My grief was not so much that First Mattachine had failed as that Second Mattachine and ONE were failing the dream," the dream of personal trust and of social purpose.

Meanwhile, his daily life was tightly circumscribed by the motions of his job at Leahy's, supporting Anita and their children, and more than anything, by his relationship with his slowly maturing Danish lover, Jorn Kamgren. Throughout the decade, they formed a snug (if prickly) nest, and at some important inner level, the relationship must have been healing. But it was outwardly confounding, since forceful Harry Hay's most frequent excuse for his absence from the movement he had helped launch became, "Jorn wouldn't let me go."

In later years, Harry was adamant that gays avoid what he termed "hetero-imitative" behavior. He had long witnessed gays chafing under the butch–femme model of straight society, and this period, when he was the very model of a fifties henpecked husband, clinched his conviction that it was wrong. His relationship with Jorn lasted almost as long as his marriage to Anita but was by his own admission far less pleasant. In fact it was downright miserable. His gay comrades commented on the jealousy of Harry's new lover as they were blocked out. As Chuck Rowland recalled, "When we tried to visit Harry, there was this idiot-boy shutting the door in our faces." Harry described Jorn's values as the typical lower-middle-class European obsession with status and titles. "He thought that, as my partner, he should be treated as 'Mrs. Founder-of-the-Movement.'" In different terms, Kamgren confirmed that he resented Harry's political colleagues, who, he felt, did not show him proper respect.

Publicly, Harry demonstrated solidarity with Jorn, but private discontent set in almost immediately. Margaret, in whom he confided, urged perseverance: "Your good influence on Jorn is just beginning to take effect," she kept telling him. In reality, she found Jorn a good influence on Harry and a good friend for herself. Twice a week, she had the couple to dinner, a ritual she would practice with all her son's significant others. Long after Harry had gone on to a new relationship, she remained friends with Jorn, as she still did with Anita. Margaret and Jorn were both politically conservative and status-conscious — Harry called them "petit bourgeois." They liked to discuss details of Britain's royal family, and after dinner on Sunday nights, Margaret and Jorn happily watched Liberace's popular new television show while Harry, hating the combination of vulgarized music and homosexual bad faith, scowled and fidgeted.

By 1954 he had decided to leave Jorn, but Margaret argued persistently against it and convinced Harry to at least finish setting up the young man's hat business. In a gesture both generous and controlling, she invested heavily, covering rent and other expenses when the couple's combined resources failed. Ultimately she put up $25,000 — money that Harry would otherwise have inherited. "My inheritance went into Jorn's business," he lamented. "I never got it back."

He tried hard at the relationship. Putting all his energy into making Jorn a hit in the hat trade, Harry managed to work numerous wonders. He moved their domicile from Fargo Avenue in rustic Echo Park to a Beverly Hills address, 920½ North La Cienega Avenue, where he created a stylish atelier in an inexpensive second-floor apartment. Jorn's chief competition, a man known solely as Rex, serviced film stars and L.A. society. Since Rex favored a lavish Louis XIV decor, Harry counter-designed a Bauhaus salon with dark maroon walls, pale blue-gray drapes, and modern furniture. To maximize the illusion of space, the couple decided to forgo a bedroom and slept instead in a cramped, cordoned-off part of the kitchen.

Harry's dedication to Jorn's career stood in astonishing contrast to the sweep of his earlier vision. He seemed to approach the little hat business as he once campaigned for the Left, employing literature, strategy, and endless determination. With long, chatty letters, he petitioned well-placed friends, including John Darrow, the actor now turned agent, whom he had last seen twenty years earlier at Fallen Leaf Lake — and of course Rudi Gernreich. Since the singer Yma Sumac, whom Harry had met years before, was now a much-photographed fashion plate, he wrote to her husband Moises Vivanco, with whom he had often discussed music. At the end of each letter, Harry mentioned his "very talented friend" and enclosed a few of the cards he had designed with Bauhaus ribbons and the name "Jorn, Hat Maker." To his increasingly famous ex-lover, Rudi Gernreich, he pleaded, "You might be engenious [*sic*] enough to figure out how I can get him circulating in those several mixed 'cocktail circles' where the men patronize the designers and the women buy from them."

Bill Alexander came through with a publicist friend who helped popularize their fashion shows at a Sunset Boulevard patio café. Usually at such shows, the best-looking women from the audience would be asked to model the products. Harry, however, deliberately picked the dowdiest matrons, which put Jorn's talent to the ultimate challenge: If a hat was flattering on a plain woman, it would be stunning on anyone halfway attractive. Sure enough, the ploy sold hats and increased invitations from women's clubs to hold similar shows. Jorn's stock soon rose from the little café on Sunset Boulevard to L.A.'s most glamorous hotels — the Huntington, the Miramar, the Ambassador.

Though he was never a serious threat to Rex, Jorn did get a brief crack at the movies. A colleague of Harry's was the lover of a screenwriter working on the film *Jeanne Eagels* at Columbia Studios. The picture, starring Kim Novak as the thirties torch singer, called for a lot of hats. Jorn submitted sketches to Jean-Louis, the famous Hollywood costumer, who hired him. Miss Novak liked Jorn's hats, but they never got onscreen and a Hollywood career did not take off for Jorn, Hat Maker. Harry continued to hold down his job at Leahy's as well as managing Jorn's supplies, purchases, billing, and books — the "manly" tasks in which the Dane professed utter helplessness. Margaret, observing all, reassured Harry that he was doing the right thing.

Three years into this odd domestic brew of depression and frivolity, the ultimate bogeyman of the post-war era intruded. In May of 1955, Harry was summoned to appear before the House UnAmerican Activities Committee, thus beginning the most painful chapter in his life, and one that would dog him for more than thirty years.

A HUAC subcommittee investigating Communist activities in Southern California, including Marxist teachers, summoned dozens of witnesses; their names and those of many others were dragged into the headlines of the L.A. papers when government informers spoke, all with the goal of exposing and driving underground the Southern California Communist network. In the late forties, Harry's music class and his name had been prominently visible on a schedule of classes for the Labor School. But ten years later, when American attitudes toward Leftist causes had come full circle from the wartime alliance between Stalin, Roosevelt, and Churchill to widespread hysteria, such an association became damning "evidence."

Since the Leahy family, who refused even to hire Jews, would surely fire from their employ any known radical, the possibility of Harry's public exposure as a Communist was threatening enough. But Harry also worried that he would be asked about his more recent "subversive activities" of homosexual organizing. His name had already been dropped in *Confidential* magazine, the most lurid scandal sheet of the decade, which trashed social deviation and political dissent with equal glee. In May of 1954, *Confidential* had labeled Hay a "pinko" under the lurid headline "America on Guard — Homosexuals Inc.!" His loyalties, which Harry took with grave seriousness, were completely at odds: He could taint each of these beloved causes with the social stigma of the other. He was more concerned, at that time, about the lavender brush tarring the Communist Party.

One heterosexual Party contact of that time characterized Harry as "a decent guy," and, true to form, Harry decided that the decent thing to do was to remove himself from the organized defense of those associated with the Party and find his own counsel. This proved difficult, since only a few lawyers were willing to work for any Communist suspects at all. By withdrawing from the Party and claiming a homosexual identity, Harry had isolated himself. Even those few lawyers who would help protect an unfriendly witness shied away from him. Fund-raising parties gave other defendants some sense of moral support, but Harry faced a row of turned backs.

▽

Harry needed a good lawyer. Someone who was trustworthy, a fighter, and sympathetic to the Left. John McTernan, his friend from Cove Avenue days, seemed to fill all requirements. He had provided competent legal advice to the district office of the Communist Party starting with the 1948 federal campaign against Leftists. Though another lawyer in McTernan's office had handled the Hays' divorce, and Harry had not seen McTernan since 1951, he still regarded the lawyer as someone he could trust. When they had been family friends, Harry recalled, he had been called upon to offer advice and keep confidences for McTernan.

In great detail, Hay later recounted for historian Jonathan Katz that he called McTernan as soon as he got the summons; they met the next day at Clifton's Cafeteria, near the lawyer's office at Ninth and Main. Hay "told him what the situation was, what I was afraid would be the questions. He looked at me very coldly and he said, 'We're not going to condone queers, you know.' So I said, 'Thanks, John, thanks very much. Who do you suggest I go and see?' He said, 'Well, that's not my business. You find your own lawyer.'"

"I can't recall that encounter taking place at all," countered McTernan to this author in 1986. The first he heard of it, he said, was when someone called his attention to the story in Katz's book, *Gay American History*. McTernan contacted the publisher of the book, Thomas Y. Crowell, and successfully demanded the removal of that portion of Hay's account from subsequent editions, a circumstance of which Harry was apprised only in 1988. Without witnesses, it is impossible to prove either version. Statements by Harry's gay friends and by the attorney who finally did take his case strongly indicate, however, that Harry faced legal rejection and was left hanging — in horrible distress — as his precious preparation time leaked away.

The story illustrates the deep conflicts between the Red and the Lavender. Questions Harry had wrestled with during his "marriage to the Party" resurfaced. Was the Left — and specifically the Communist Party — negligent in its treatment of homosexuals? Was there any excuse for its exclusion of homosexuals as an oppressed minority in general, and its unwillingness to help individuals in need, as in Harry's case?

Leftists of that period have sharply clashing answers. Dorothy Healey, the "Red Queen" of Southern California and a Party functionary during Harry's tenure there, insisted that the Party was not homophobic, and that its policy barring homosexuals from membership was formulated to "help those comrades" who were already stigmatized. Frank Pestana, the lawyer who ultimately represented Harry before HUAC, recalled, "The Party was told they should not deal with these people, not because of homophobia but because these people were too vulnerable to police and FBI penetration." In other words, they were automatic security risks. "They had the same policy about alcoholics and people discovered to have been in psychotherapy ... the police and the FBI sought those people out and would lean on them. They were vulnerable and made the Party vulnerable."* Pestana concurred with Healey that the Party's policy toward homosexuals was benign. "If you would find tolerance anywhere, you would find it in this group."

"Bullshit," countered Ben Dobbs, an activist peer of Harry's who worked with him in the Southern California C.P. "It wasn't until gays began to organize with the gay movement that anyone started to get any political understanding of them. We [in the Party] really had no contact with homosexuality as an issue. We took no position on it; that was homophobic in itself. Homophobia was there without ever being expressed. Who the hell ever came to the support of gays? No one."

This divergence can be understood by looking at the issue as shaped by various factors. One was geography. As a counselor in Minneapolis for the American Youth for Democracy (the reconstitution of the Young Communist League), Chuck Rowland witnessed tolerance of homosexual affairs among his charges, and he was certain that Party officials knew that he himself was homosexual but chose to look the other way. Another variable is indicated by Jim Kepner's observation that a predominance of lesbians existed in the Party, as they did in the U.S. military. In the end, the unmentionability of the subject left individual officials to deal with each case of homosexual Communists as a judgment call; reactions of the functionaries ran from overt bigotry to quiet tolerance.

The overriding social hysteria about homosexuals made for unlikely political bedfellows. In his biography of Roy Cohn, Nicholas von Hoffman

---

* Several former Party members recalled incidents where precisely this happened, and said that gay Party members who were entrapped on morals charges had no choice but to leave the Party.

observed, "The only thing the State Department and the Communist Party agreed on was that homosexuals were security risks." (Cohn, Senator McCarthy's chief counsel, never admitted his homosexuality during his lifetime, despite substantial documentation of his exclusively male–male sexual life. There were popular suspicions that Cohn, Joseph McCarthy, and J. Edgar Hoover were all three homosexual.) Just as the Committee used allegations of homosexuality as a blackmail tool, the Party sometimes used accusations of homosexuality against Party members who were falling out of favor politically. According to Jim Kepner, charges of lesbianism and alcoholism were leveled against writer Ruth McKenney to bolster the argument for her expulsion during the post-Browder period for more overtly political reasons.

In later years, Harry's own stand on the Party's policy baffled many of his friends, for he argued strongly that despite his own misery in it, the Party was not homophobic. His conversation with his section organizer upon resigning — in which they agreed that homosexuals and Communists both had loyalties that were separately paramount and therefore conflicting — figured strongly in his thinking. So did his fierce Scottish sense of loyalty; the Reds had been his clan and shared his highest idealism. In the early sixties, Jim Kepner was appalled to hear Harry defend Fidel Castro's oppression of gays. "Harry said that those were just running-dog homosexuals who were Batista's puppets."

Still bereft of legal counsel, Harry made appointments with two other lawyers but each told him that they were too busy. For five of the six weeks before his hearing, he followed one slim lead after another, seeing lawyer after lawyer, but none would take his case. The financial resources of the Left had been seriously drained by this time, and with the widespread imprisonment, job loss, and suicide that had already resulted from the HUAC campaign, most Leftists were emotionally wiped out. Harry's search for a lawyer proceeded with mounting anxiety, and he felt increasingly convinced that he was being snubbed and excluded out of prejudice. Desperate, he fought his feelings of panic and anger and continued to search for legal help.

At the last moment, he found Frank Pestana, a lawyer who usually handled labor cases. "I knew Harry Hay had been through a harrowing situation," he said, "and had been on the hook for an extended time and needed help." Pestana had had homosexual clients before and felt no prejudice about that issue. He recalled his meeting with Harry: "It was about a week, maybe two weeks before the hearing. He was anxious to get a lawyer. He was a very concerned guy, obviously feeling deserted and terribly anxious." Harry's description of himself during the last two weeks of his search was more severe: "I was almost catatonic with fear."

The HUAC hearings are widely regarded as a modern American inquisition, an exercise in conformity and control. "We understood that all this committee was interested in was names," explained Pestana. "Since they couldn't shoot you or jail you for having these beliefs, they wanted to harass and blacklist people. They wanted to *identify* them." The government had repeatedly tried to criminalize Communist affiliation; now it seemed to be jousting behind congressional acts and loyalty oaths in a low-intensity blitz to break the spirit of the Left. These government-sanctioned harassments would stoop to anything. Pestana recalled discussing the potential of the Mattachine background being used as a spear in the side of the pilloried Party: "Harry knew ... that they would want to tar any organization with the brush of the homosexual charge. This would be a terrific way to appeal to the phobia of the time."

After testing many possibilities, lawyers had determined that the best defense against admitting Communist affiliation was to invoke the constitutional rights of free speech and freedom from testifying against oneself, and that became the standard defense in the HUAC hearings. Still, Harry insisted on putting his own touches on the defense. "He was a good client," Pestana recalled. "He had ideas about how to deal with this. Some of his elaborations of the defense were pure Harry Hay."

The night before the hearing, Harry approached the one person he thought could empathize with his dilemma as a Leftist and as a homosexual — Chuck Rowland. Unfortunately, Rowland had been named the new social director of ONE, Inc., and the night Harry needed him he was beset with a crisis of his own. A substantial bequest was being dangled before him by a benefactor who hoped to seduce Rowland personally as a trade-off. This unwanted advance was especially disconcerting to Rowland because he had recently moved in with a lover, a jealous young man from Mexico named Rudy Renteria. When Harry arrived, Rowland was on the phone with the benefactor. The conversation lasted more than an hour while Harry chatted laboriously in Spanish with the inflamed Renteria. It was a maddening conclusion to his already-severe alienation, and Harry finally left in frustration, never having learned of Rowland's own frustrations and pressures. He thought he had been snubbed, and the incident rankled him for years.

Harry's hearing followed three days of testimony by two government agents, Los Angeles Police Lieutenant William Ward Kimple and FBI agent Stephen Wereb, against Harry and other Southern California Leftists. Both agents had infiltrated the Southern California Communist Party. Kimple had gained a position of high trust over two decades until he was discovered and expelled. Wereb, known as "the typewriter man of Hawthorne" because of his repair business, had attended many classes and meetings — in fact, Harry regarded him as "one of my more devoted if stupider students, who always asked for everything to be explained at least three times." Harry was obliged to sit silently through this testimony while his integrity and nerves were pummeled. The two informants identified dozens of Angelenos as Reds, invariably painting them as Soviet agents bent on violence. The names of everyone accused of Communist affiliations by Kimple and Wereb were printed in the local papers, often on the front page, and whenever possible, with pictures.

Spies (or, in forties vernacular, stool pigeons) appeared prominently in the HUAC investigations. In an earlier hearing, Harry heard about a woman who testified against his friends and realized that some years earlier, she had been a baby-sitter for the children of many Leftists and had taken those occasions to go through their private papers. Yet the newspapers only pointed their fingers at the activists, never mentioning such lowbrow tactics as deploying baby-sitter spies.

Stephen Wereb, who in the forties had attended Hay's classes under the name Steven Webber, identified Hay and ninety other Southern Californians as Communists. He specifically called Hay a Marxist–Leninist teacher who advocated the overthrow of the American voting system. Harry realized with shock that Wereb had played dumb in class and asked certain terms and policies to be explained repeatedly. Now he heard his six-year-old words shrewdly distorted for the public record. Harry was completely alone through these nerve-racking sessions since Pestana's busy schedule allowed for his presence only during Harry's actual testimony. After sitting through two full days and a morning, on Saturday, July 2, Harry was finally called to testify.

As Harry recalled his interrogation, Frank Tavenner, chief counsel of the subcommittee, grilled him about his family, nationality, education, and occupation. Though Pestana advised clients to keep answers brief so as not to expose themselves to more than a minimum of questioning, the spotlight inevitably brought out the ham in Harry; he was dangerously loquacious. His interlaced hands resting on the table before him, he let loose an elaborate answer when asked his place of birth. "I told them about my parents being Americans who were abroad at the time of my birth, about having left England on the last American transport, and so on. By the time I got through describing my education and job experience, I had gone into enormously chatty detail." He was interrupted by Tavenner, who, Hay recalled, suddenly seemed to recall that there was a more important question he needed to ask: "Are you now a member of the Communist Party?"

"No," he answered, truthfully. Indeed, he had not been a member for four years.

Next, as Harry told Katz, "That's when the shit hit the fan. This committee member [Tavenner] — he wasn't a big man, but he was a very chunky sort of man — he got apoplectic-looking and he stood up — he was holding on to the edge of his desk, and stood up in such a way that he pushed this huge oak desk over on its face — *clunk.*" Hay added later that "the court reporter's transcript, a series of tight paper rolls, sailed into the air, uncoiling into a jumble on the floor. Tavenner's face turned purple, his neck was swollen at his collar — looking like the commandante from *Don Giovanni* rising out of the floor — as he yelled, 'When did you quit, out in the hall before you came in?'

"I cracked, 'I'm not in the habit of confiding in stool pigeons or their buddies on this committee.'

"Pestana was horrified and said that he could never get me out of this mess. By this time, several of the stenotyped transcript rolls had unrolled and were jumbled on the floor as the bailiff joined the now-distraught court stenographer in frantically looking through the billowing paper ribbons of typescript. The people in the court were beginning to laugh. Finally Chairman Doyle of the committee said, 'I think we know what the witness meant and I suggest that we dismiss him.'"

Hay thought that his remark about stool pigeons could easily have landed him in jail on a contempt charge. What saved him, he suspected, was what he later identified as "gay consciousness" underlying his glib chatter. "My garrulity disarmed Tavenner enough that he made the error of simply asking — quite chattily, I must say — 'Are you a member?' I suspect that he was hoping to provoke something by catching me off-guard. Instead, I answered him back just as airily." Hay guessed that the committee dismissed him in order to restore their control, since the gallery of the courtroom was laughing harder and harder. The stool pigeon remark, Hay explained, escaped as a result of his rage at Wereb's lying and distortion of facts. When, at the noon break, he saw several of the committee members embrace Wereb and slap him on the back as they exited the courtroom for lunch, Harry was further infuriated.

Another version of Hay's interrogation, however, is recorded in the subcommittee transcript. While it verifies many of Harry's memories, including the one about "stool pigeons and their buddies," Harry strongly refutes its accuracy. He bases this partly on the transcript's showing him addressing Tavenner, the counsel, as "Mr. Chairman" (though Senator Doyle was chairman), and that it contains First and Fifth Amendment replies to queries about whether Hay was a Party member in 1954 and 1955 (years after he had already quit his membership) to which Harry clearly recalled answering "no."

Could the record have been altered? Harry recalled seeing another version of the transcript in the fifties that indicated that the hearing stopped abruptly. He surmised that due to the interruption of the stenotape, his testimony was reconstituted from committee notes. An "altercation" not accounted for in the rest of the text is mentioned in the transcript, and there may have been exchanges that were glossed over as consultations between client and attorney. Attorney Pestana does not himself recall any details of the hearing other than that it was "short and sweet" — without incident. The *People's World* article on those hearings also made no mention of any unusual incident. However, Donald Wheeldin, the author of that article, considered such a reconstitution highly likely. So did James Burford, who was also a HUAC witness that summer. He suspected that his own transcript had been "tampered with" because of a similar shouting match between himself and Tavenner.

Once off the witness stand, Harry was so paralyzed with tension that he could not unlock his still interwoven hands. "The bailiff had to help me get them apart and put the pen in my hand so I could sign myself out," he recalled. Though his name appeared in several Los Angeles newspapers on July 7, 1955, and his picture appeared in one, Old Man Leahy and his wife somehow did not see it. And once or twice, when salesmen over the next few weeks started to ask Harry, "Wasn't that you in the—" Harry would cut them off with a quick, urgent smile.

The real damage, ironically, seemed to have been greater among his homophile confreres. Just a month before the HUAC summons had arrived, Harry approached ONE with ideas regarding fund-raising, outreach, and study activities, intent upon re-involving himself in the movement. But because of the stigma of the House committee association, he said, "I wasn't even *notified* about anything more ONE did after that, let alone invited. My speaking at the next ONE Mid-Winter Institute was at my initiative, not theirs."

·10·

Between the lines

There is a law in life: when one door closes, another opens.
— Goethe

After the drama of the HUAC hearing, Harry settled into a domestic life that left him more housebound than ever. Jorn insisted that because Harry had been snubbed by the Communists as well as the gays, he should reject both. In compliant despair, Harry allowed twenty years of collective companionships — an outlook as well as many individual friendships — to cease. He noted to a friend that Jorn's domestic alternative was "uninhibited sex, a pleasant lodging well-dusted, and even the possible future of a comfortable mutual income." Jorn let him sleep late on weekends and gave him first one night a week to study, then expanded it to three. But as years passed, the cute blond from the corner of Hollywood and Vine became less "a comfort."

Harry remained morose and at times felt completely lost. "I was cut off from people. From progressives. From the gay movement. I remember going through one birthday after another, and the only people who'd be there were Jorn's family." They were accepting but insular, and Harry never felt comfortable with them. Even Christmas, which he normally savored enthusiastically, felt staid with its tables of heavy Danish delicacies more suited to icy latitudes than to Southern California. Harry felt even more put off by their equally bland conversation. Jorn himself in no way matched the like-mindedness and companionability Harry had felt with Anita, nor the breathless passion he had enjoyed with Rudi. This incompatibility with his new spouse brought up Harry's old lament: "I'd long for another gay person."

Although he vocally defended Jorn to the rest of the world, Harry suffered privately as their differences became more fundamental. Jorn simply did not fit Harry's definition of "gay" as a homosexual seeking more than secretive sex. Their differences — and tensions — were fundamental. In a letter to Gernreich, Harry described a problem child:

> Jorn is to all intents and purposes a manic depressive; almost vulgar in his bouyancy one minute, he is violently depressed the next, and this depression can take the form of asthma as well as that of a mild migraine. What with ulcers he must have incipiently acquired in Denmark, psycho-genic heart-attacks, and diverse ailments extending from his war-time malnutrition, he has cost me more at Community-Medical than both the children did in nine years.

The problem child kept their life on a shrewdly regimented schedule, which Harry accepted passively. In the same letter, he sketched its tight parameters:

> I may go nowhere without him except to work and back. If I'm five minutes late, the rest of the evening is unpleasant ... Even my mail is opened, and if the missive is other than commercial, I am duly chastised. My phone calls at the office or home are subjected to the same examination. My personal papers have been carefully sorted, and most of the Mattachine stuff, Anita's picture, all your letters and pictures, have been thrown out without my previous knowledge or consent. (The reason given here, as for all the stringencies, is that this is always the second wife's prerogative.) ... Worst is his hate of dancing, which he won't learn, and of my dancing with anyone other than himself. (Guess how much dancing I do, and remember how I loved it.)

The stresses piled up throughout their relationship, which came to resemble a soap opera parody of a heterosexual marriage. One spring, Jorn used Harry's collection of rare American coins as bus fare for downtown shopping trips. If Harry objected or criticized, Jorn flew into a rage; more than one of Harry's shirts were torn from his back when Jorn got angry.

Part of this may have resulted from Jorn's early perception that he had to fight for first place in his lover's affections. At one of the last holiday dinners held for Parsifal — the Mattachine founders — Harry noticed the others staring at him in horror during the after-dinner conversation. He suddenly realized he had just made a series of references to "Rudi and I" while describing current plans. Jorn, "his cheeks flaming against that pale skin," left the table in a silent rage and stood at the front door.

For his part, Jorn complained that Harry often insulted his intelligence. "'You're so dumb,' Harry would tell me. I couldn't stand that. One day I told him, 'If you tell me that again, I'm going to hit you.' He said it again, so I hit him. Gave him a black eye. We had to go visit his mother that night, who was in the hospital recovering from a cancer operation. She took one look at Harry and one look at me, and she didn't say a word about it to either of us."

Though outwardly inscrutable, the relationship had its underlying meaning. In contrast to his politics, Harry's social instinct was for propriety, which made him reluctant to admit failure in this "second marriage." In fact, he had cultivated a bit of a reputation as a homosexual moralist in his efforts to distinguish homophilia from the "degenerate" stereotype of promiscuity. He even mockingly referred to himself in one of his letters as "the Priscilla Alden of the Homophile movement."*

He was also aware that as a middle-aged man in the homosexual world, his chances of having any lover at all seemed diminished. "Jorn would remind me of that constantly," he recalled. "I was to be grateful that I had him." Cruel jockeying was a common underside of intergenerational relationships between men; often the older person paid emotionally as well as financially. For Harry, the debts were compounded by his mortgaged inheritance and his mission to change Jorn from a desperate, dependent refugee into an independent businessman. The term "duty-driven," which one Mattachine founder applied to Harry's movement politics, also describes his liaison with Jorn.

Harry's weekly allotment of three study nights carried him through this melancholy for eight years. He was so intellectually voracious that he made an art of surreptitiously extending his studies many hours more, mostly by denying himself sleep. He processed as many as thirty books a week in the fields of history, anthropology, and mythology, constantly scanning texts for traces of gay people and gay culture. Gay history, he realized, was "between the lines" of straight history, and would take enormous labor to reconstruct. With his attention to detail and discreet suggestion, Harry searched "between the words and the word-shadows" in the work

---

* Harry speculated endlessly on the cause of "compulsive cruising" but later rejected the application of heterosexual morality as inappropriate to gay impulses. He concluded that all respectful relations were positive and regarded "our lovely sexuality" as "the gateway to spirit."

of scholars who, through personal prejudice or professional intimidation, rarely mentioned any aspect of homosexuality. The terms "immoral," "lewd," and "too vulgar to merit discussion," which he found frequently in standard reference works, became red flags for further investigation. Harry also noticed that "if something got juicy — and dealt with our sexuality — it would usually be printed in Latin. If it was extremely steamy, it would be in Greek, or even Hebrew."

Like many before and after him, Harry was fascinated by the mystery of homosexuality. Unraveling the subterfuge of society's "conspiracy of silence," an intelligent gay mind almost inevitably wondered about where the homosexuals had fit in. Had they lived underground or in the light? In other eras, under different conditions, how might life have been different? Harry reapplied the questions he had proposed in Mattachine: Who are gay people; where have they been; and what might they be for? And an unstated question seemed to shape his obsession: *Why* has the oppression against gay people been so fierce?

At his office, Harry sneaked in more spare moments of study, and many of the thousands of pages of notes he made during this period of research were written on half sheets of office memorandum paper. This research formed his interior world — a world much richer than his outer one — until the early 1960s. Jorn later agreed that study was Harry's escape from depression.

Harry had taken on an enormous investigative project. His earliest document was a six-page typewritten outline titled "The Homophile in History: A Provocation to Research," sketched out from 1953 to 1955. Divided into fourteen periodic sections, it traces homosexual prototypes from the Stone Age through the European Middle Ages up to the "Berdache and the American Scene," where Hay cited Johnny Appleseed as one example of an "American Fool Hero." Much of the study for this was expanded from the syllabus of his music classes at the Labor School.

The model Harry used for his study was the *berdache*. A French term applied to cross-dressing Indians found by the European colonists in the New World, berdache sometimes referred simply to an Indian who committed "the abominable vice" of homosexuality. But to Harry, it meant a cultural role. He became aware of the term from V.F. Calverton's *The Making of Man,* an anthropology compendium published in 1931. Harry found this book in 1948 and in it rediscovered Edward Carpenter's writings, which discussed the intermediary roles gays filled that could be found in many nontechnological cultures, both ancient and modern. Harry further researched these writings, as well as those of Edward

Westermarck and Ruth Benedict, who were represented in the same volume.

Extending his view of such medieval European figures as the Mattachines, glee-men, jongleurs, and many others to this model, Harry became convinced that social roles for gay people had existed throughout history. He hoped to trace these roles over thousands of years in almost every culture, to collect "the total corpus of what gay consciousness had discovered and so contributed to human growth in the ancient and modern worlds."

Harry believed that, especially in ancient times, some homosexuals were devoted to specific roles by the community at large. According to Will Roscoe, who has conserved and studied Hay's notes, "Harry attempted to make a historical materialist study of the emergence and development of gay roles. He saw, for example, that these men who did women's work were the first craft-specialists." To those specially trained homosexuals, Harry applied the general term "berdache." These he further divided into the "folk berdache" and the "state berdache," following the division of social roles in rural villages and cities.

The completion of this research into gay anthropology became Hay's lifelong ambition, and his fascination with the subject extended well into the 1980s. It was one of the backhanded benefits of life with Jorn — Harry's sense of intellectual desolation, his isolation from his former causes (which the apolitical Jorn shut firmly out of their house), and Harry's drive to escape the henpecking encouraged his persistent reading and note taking. The "Jorn period," restricted as it was, fostered a tremendous accomplishment of personal work. It saw both the deepening of Harry's original research and his fashioning of an overview of history that was free from the blinders of heterosexual ideology.

Many of Hay's writings from the fifties reflected a strikingly evolved feminism, especially in his concentration on the religion of the Great Goddess, popular in many parts of the ancient world, and the ways in which its values offered harmony to civilization. More specifically, Hay's references to a cultural unity of Druids, fairies, and other queer historical types in his 1955 paper "The Homophile in History" anticipated the work of such writers as Arthur Evans, Judy Grahn, and Starhawk by two decades. Harry was literally ahead of his time; in the fifties, the official dismissal of homosexuality stunted most serious attempts at publication, and Hay's work had almost no exposure. Recently, however, Harry's place in gay studies has gained some recognition: In a 1988 interview, Australian professor and writer Dennis Altman referred to "the Harry Hay/Judy Grahn approach to gay history." (Like some other modern gay academics, Altman actually derided Hay's ideas, but in doing so acknowledged their popularity.)*

Some of Hay's research did see publication. In a paper called "The Hammond Report," published in 1963 in *ONE Institute Quarterly,* the serious homophile journal of the time, Harry unearthed a forgotten document written in 1882 by a former United States Surgeon General. Dr. William A. Hammond, while in the field, observed Indians called *mujerados,* a Spanish term meaning "made women." This tantalized Harry as a possible type of berdache. Hammond described the *mujerados* he had found among Pueblo Indians in Northern New Mexico, who were the "chief passive agent in the pederastic ceremonies." Hay offered a lengthy commentary, and roundly protested this paper's "burial by omission" for nearly one hundred years.

Though limited in distribution, Harry's article was significant for the time as a rare scholarly treatment of the berdache, a subject that has become popular in recent years. Years later, several scholars researching the berdache, including Walter Williams and Will Roscoe, found the article and sought Hay out for further consultations. Williams, author of *The Spirit and the Flesh,* the definitive study of the berdache thus far, called Hay "the inspirer" to many current berdache scholars, and Roscoe, biographer of the famous berdache We'Wha, credits Harry with doing more than any other single individual to promote research into the subject during a long period of academic neglect.

Harry's long search for the report was not an easy one. He had read references to Hammond's paper in several turn-of-the-century books. But in 1962, when he decided to look up the original text, he ran into trouble. He started at the U.C.L.A. Research Library, which listed in its holdings Volume I of the *American Journal of Neurology and Psychiatry,* the first publication to print Hammond's findings. But when Harry requested a copy, he found, to his and the librarian's surprise, that the Hammond article had been cut out.

---

* This painful irony echoed other slights Harry suffered for being ahead of his time. Until the 1970s, writers and scholars sympathetic to homosexuals were forced to do their ground-breaking work independently, on the margins of academia. In recent years, as homosexual studies have become assimilated into university research departments and curricula, Hay and other pioneering gay scholars have suffered derision for lacking credentials and being out of step with prevailing theories.

Four more copies of the journal that Harry ordered from other libraries had been similarly mutilated. He surmised that Hammond's findings may have been repudiated by some governemnt official and censored. After many months, Harry found a copy of the report in a later text by Hammond titled *Sexual Impotence in the Male and Female,* published in 1887. Over the years, Hay continued to find many other such cases of obliteration of historical references to homosexuality.

Once or twice a year Jorn "allowed" Harry to present papers at ONE's Mid-Winter Institutes, small educational symposia held at respectable hotels, and several of these papers were also published in *ONE Quarterly* and *ONE Confidential.* The story of David and Jonathan stimulated Harry to research the Biblical era for a gay subtext. The resulting paper, "The Moral Climate of Canaan in the Time of Judges," grew so extensive that it had to be published in two separate twelve-page installments. (In 1972, he expanded some of the same ideas in an unpublished paper called "Christianity's First Closet Case.")

Harry's scope continually broadened as he found that many writers whom he otherwise admired would minimize or omit evidence about gays in whatever field they studied. Harry especially scrutinized Marxist anthropologists Gordon Childe and George Thompson as well as mythology specialists Jane Ellen Harrison, Sir James Frazer, Karl Kerenyi, and Robert Graves. At the U.C.L.A. and U.S.C. libraries, Hay spent endless hours looking up their sources, "always hunting for *us.*" In the process, he created thousands of note cards, all headed "berdache," with countless subheadings. Frequently, Harry stumbled upon related areas of study, such as the political impact of the changes in calendrical forms on peasant religions. These detours consumed further attention and resulted in reams of additional notes.

In trying to express himself, however, he faced a familiar frustration — "the lack of words, the lack of language, and the lack of idea-forms to describe who we had been throughout the ages." Harry spoke of assessing gay history as decoding a language from a different universe, or as trying to build a temple out of splinters. Another obstacle was his own dense writing style, often laden with esoteric vocabulary and lengthy asides. To Harry's great frustration, many of his friends were unable to follow his writings, and Harry himself often attempted many drafts of ideas he could never express to his own satisfaction. Konrad Stevens remarked that during the Mattachine meetings, "It took a while to understand what Harry meant with some of his very unusual ideas, but once we did, everything was fine." But when he had only the page to work with, Harry's very unusual ideas often seemed incomprehensible.

What he lacked in clear writing skills, he more than made up for with dramatic intensity while speaking. Sometimes the papers seem to have been written as scripts, with his signature jumble of capitalizations, italics, underlinings, and every possible combination thereof. This allowed his voice to pound out urgency for a plan of action, or to caress a tender new idea, and he always made an emotional connection with his listeners. That charismatic delivery often clarified his Marxist-tinged anthropological discourse. Even when it couldn't, he at best made a memorable appearance. Dorr Legg recalled, "Harry made a very impressive entrance and impression, then went off into the clouds, like Joshua lifted to heaven. He was like that — he manifested and he disappeared. He was a *star,* with a star kind of approach." Martin Block added that the intense persona could obfuscate as well as illuminate. "Most of my memories of Harry are in a haze," he said. "Sometimes I had the impression it was a haze he was deliberately creating."

The haze could overtake those interested in gay organizing. When Del Martin and Phyllis Lyon attended an event at ONE's Mid-Winter Institute in 1957, they listened as Harry read a paper that was allotted forty-five minutes but ran through lunch and took up two and a half hours. Martin and Lyon were all worked up by the Hay charisma, but lost by his terminology. "Isn't he marvelous!" Dorr Legg recalled them exclaiming at the lunch break. Then they turned to Legg and asked, "What was he saying?"

Harry was better understood in the scholarly realm. In 1961, he wrote to Robert Graves, the British poet and scholar known for his historical novel *I, Claudius* and for his studies of myth. In *The White Goddess* (1948), an important study of the historical patterns underlying mythology, Graves implicitly repudiated homosexual love, skirting the importance of androgynous mythical figures in his scholarship. He concluded in his afterword that a man can achieve true creativity only in heterosexual union, by "the love and wisdom of a woman" and by "the experience of a woman." In 1955, in *The Greek Myths,* Graves dismissed most of the famous male–male relationships in classical mythology and legend as late, "decadent" additions to the true heroic tradition.

Harry's long letter to Graves was filled with scholarly questions and observations, in part because he respected much of Graves's work and wished to congratulate his meticulous, highly original scholarship. He also cordially chided the great writer's "hate" and "blindness" regarding homophilia. Harry's secret hope was to provoke a comparing of notes, as one scholar to another, on historic homosexuality. He suspected Graves had surely gained vast amounts of original information about the subject but had maintained a prudent silence. Harry recalled pointedly, "I wanted to find out what he knew."

Graves's brief reply, dated only six weeks after the date on Hay's own letter, is postmarked Majorca, Spain, the site of his retreat. He graciously thanked Harry for "a very kind and decent letter," adding, "I'm glad you don't consider me an enemy." The poet offered his position that "Homophilia as a *natural* phenomenon is respected in most societies — and by me ... Homophilic careerism, and Homophilia indulged in for *kicks* are what I hate." (Emphasis his. Graves's capitalization of "homophile" apparently follows Harry's lead.) The letter further confirmed Harry's belief that homophiles had been traditional advocates of the Goddess. Graves closed with a challenge: "An alliance of Goddess worshipping Heterophiles with natural Homophiles makes sense to me. The literary and art world is so full of irreligious and perverted messiness. You should purge your ranks! Yours v. s. Robert Graves."

Whenever Harry visited ONE, his friends there would inquire after his mammoth study. But after a few years went by and no book was forthcoming, they eventually stopped asking. His deep concern with "the contribution of gay consciousness" to humankind did not turn up in his writings for many years. His masses of notes ended up in boxes that he hauled from household to household over the next twenty years, but the questions and memories of the data on them became the underground stream to nourish his future work.

▽

His mental travel down the sideroads of history lured Harry to travel the physical world of 1956. Starting that year, with Jorn at his side, he took off on a series of excursions over the next half dozen years. For these vacation retreats from Los Angeles, Harry customized his two-door Studebaker sedan so that the back seat could be replaced with a foam rubber and plywood bed he designed. The bed, when not in use, was carried on top of the vehicle in a locking container, also of his own design.

Harry and Jorn visited Mexico and San Francisco, but most often they traveled in the American Southwest, where Harry found the fulfillment of his academic interests and of his heart. He was looking for surviving remnants of the *mujerados* or of other queer traces and tradition he had read about. It had become obvious to him that if they did survive, such things would not be reported with accuracy by contemporary anthropologists. The Pueblo Indians of Northern New Mexico were a stable

– 199–

society with their own languages, economy, and culture. From a Marxist historical perspective, they were a nontechnological "peasant" culture — an ideal laboratory for Harry's studies and theories.

Combining vacations with field research led to adventures and occasional humorous mishaps. On one trip to Northern Mexico, Harry noticed an Indian man in a loincloth working in a field. "He was the most breathtakingly handsome man I'd ever seen in my life. We stopped and I asked if I could take his picture. He agreed, and signaled for us to wait a moment, whereupon he carefully donned his pants, shirt, hat, serape, and string tie, adjusting each carefully. Having covered up every bit of the handsome physical attributes which had caught my eye in the first place, he was then ready to pose. All I could do was smile and take the photograph."

On these trips Harry and Jorn saw performances of many Native American dances Harry had researched (including the Mattachine dance, which he saw performed by masked dancers in Sandia, New Mexico, in 1962) and met same-sex oriented Indians who would become friends and, in anthropological parlance, informants. Harry and Jorn made friends with so many Indians that after they split up, an entire Tewa family took up their earlier invitation to visit out west and camped at Jorn's for months. Jorn remembered spending hours of every vacation in libraries and church archives associated with towns where Indians lived. Occasionally they were offered friendship and hospitality by men they were certain were homosexual — though rarely was this verbally acknowledged.

By and large, Harry was disappointed in his hope of finding berdaches functioning on reservations or in other Indian populations. The Bureau of Indian Affairs, he came to realize, had systematically educated Indians throughout the nation to abandon their original language and culture, especially those cultural practices found "vulgar" or "abominable." He did, however, find references to a few Indians who were "like the berdache," and his fascination grew. It was piqued even higher one summer while talking with Ann Smith, a librarian at the Laboratory of Anthropology in Santa Fe. They were discussing the suggestion of an anthropology professor (Omer Stewart of the University of Colorado at Boulder) that an "observer–participant" relationship, a traditional technique in anthropological study, could be highly intimate and highly informative between a gay subject and a gay investigator. Smith said that she had heard of a homosexual Tewa man at San Juan Pueblo, just to the north. Harry went up to try to find him, and confirmed his existence, but the man himself was gone — vacationing in Mexico that summer.

The first Indian with whom Harry did form a close relationship was a heterosexual man. He lived in northern New Mexico, at San Ildefonso Pueblo, part of the same cluster of pueblos as San Juan, where Harry would live in the seventies. Enki, as he was known, had a tribal role as the head *K'ossa,* or sacred Winter Clown, and was Harry's first "contact" inside a pueblo. They met through a salesman Harry had befriended at work in Los Angeles; the salesman retired early to northern New Mexico and for several years invited Harry to visit.

When he finally did, in 1957, Harry met this "very strange, very interesting little man," who took care of his friend's garden. He had braids at either side of his head and sharp, dark eyes that seemed to observe everything. "Every morning Enki started work at ten, but at nine-thirty it was time to have coffee. The first morning we were visiting, he took one look at me and shook my hand and said, 'Saturday we will go to Zia.'" Indeed, that Saturday the small Indian took the tall Anglo on his first visit "inside" an Indian pueblo to witness dances. After this experience, Harry couldn't wait to visit New Mexico again, and whenever he did, he usually saw Enki. Their friendship lasted fifteen years. Enki talked about Indians called *kwidó,* who had lived their lives as spiritually responsible people, who had been trained for a set role. The *kwidó,* he informed Harry, were "your people."[*]

Harry figured Enki must have been born at about the turn of the century, and it was through Enki that Hay observed what he called "the ceremonial mind," which had an ordered understanding of how things were to be prepared and accomplished for any undertaking. The name Enki was a diminutive for his baptismal name, Encarnación. Under his Tewa name, Soh-kwa-wi (or Soqueen), he was famous as a painter of ceremonial images. Harry learned that he was known by other names too. "Were I to telephone him at his house at eight o'clock in the morning, I would have to ask for 'Dough-maker.' Enki would not be there. At sunset, he was 'Grandfather Teller of Tales.'"

At times Enki acted in ways Harry could only describe as psychic. On a visit in 1959, Enki showed Harry and Jorn an unexcavated ruin northwest

---

[*] Harry seems to have been the first contemporary scholar to recover this term, a contraction of the Tewa words for "old woman" (*kwio*) and "old man" (*sedo*). Hay's transliteration of it, *kwih-doh,* appeared in several publications, though has since been superseded by the preferred *kwidó.* Hay insists that he transliterated it as Enki and Harry's Tewa friend Tony Garcia told him was required for proper pronunciation.

of San Juan, on the Rio Oso. At one place, he stopped and announced that there was something nearby. He began digging and soon unearthed several ceremonial objects known as paint sticks, which Harry later had dated at between four and six hundred years old. He showed them another ruin called Tsankwe, where San Ildefonso Indians had lived in former times. "Tsankwe had a section set off from the Pueblo proper, which, curiously, had its own urn-field, where the pottery of a person was broken when he or she died. Enki pointed at this place and said, 'This is where your people lived.'" This meant, in Hay's mind, where the berdache lived. More than a decade later, when Harry was living in the area and helped organize its nascent gay movement, he would take special groups and individual friends to the place at the edge of Tsankwe, to show them where "our people" had lived a thousand years before.

▽

The cares of his own white man's world did not go away. Tension with Jorn increased, alimony for Anita remained a steady outflow, and the girls required new fatherly responsibilities. Harry as a dad was conscientious; a raft of cards attest his presence at recitals, performances, and graduations. He continually sent gifts and letters of advice. And Dad regularly provided money. He financed vacations, auto insurance, and many "extras" not covered by the child support, a payment, Jorn recalled, which was always prompt. "If it was a day late, Anita would call and say 'Where the hell is the check?' Harry never missed." Harry remained close with his daughter Hannah, and he often wrote, encouraging her to stay in school and to pursue her dancing; she was now a graceful adolescent who had been training for a decade.

Their father's relationship, however, distressed the girls. Though Jorn tried to be friendly and made hats for her to play in, Hannah complained that he was cruel to her and in turn she was hostile to him. So was Kate, on occasion, suggesting that the "second spouse" syndrome applies to homosexual as well as heterosexual divorced parents. The most serious hostility came from Anita: In 1958, she forbade Harry to bring Jorn along during visits to the children, partly because the men had exchanged rings, which she did not want the children to see. In his response, written in May of that year, Harry's blast of rhetoric masks his anguish over this attempt to split apart relationships he had struggled for six years to integrate: "It was with a deep sense of shock that I heard you parrot that neat little petit-bourgeoise cliche of reactionary Freudian cant, 'that's not my problem.' What a long ways from collective sympathy and wisdom has your cozy little path into country-clubbish Babbitry taken you."

He continued to protest Anita's condemnation of his relationship and expressed anger at apparent judgments of erstwhile friends from the Left. He continued,

> Since WE are not welcome in your house, I cannot see that it is my problem to explain this to the children. You should have no trouble finding clever little brain-washing platitudes to handle it. "Dear children — since your Father continues to contain the same incurable condition he had before our marriage, and since he now seems unable to leave it outside when he comes to visit, we mustn't let him in, must we?" ... Incurable did I say? Yes, I did. Only your precious little coterie of die-hard sectarians clings to the fetish that it isn't — even though they have never been able to validate a genuine "cure" for all their blather ... My people constitute the second largest minority in the nation, and signs are already beginning to appear to confirm that we shall require to be socially and civilly accepted as a valid social minority — not merely tolerated or patronized or diffidently negated as at present.

$$\triangledown$$

Despite his protestations to outsiders about Jorn's traumas and privations, Harry's eleven-year homophile marriage to the strait-laced Kamgren was coming to an end. What mutual support had earlier balanced the relationship was long gone, and Harry felt a growing despondency over its restrictions.

In the fall of 1962, they happened to visit Harry James, leader of the Trailfinders boys' group in the 1920s. The two Harrys had stayed in touch over the years but had long stopped visiting until that November afternoon, when Hay accepted an invitation to the beautiful handmade house on a vast plot where James had retired in the San Jacinto mountains, southeast of Los Angeles. Other Trailfinders alumni were there, among them a college instructor who was using James's extensive collections to research the language and culture of his Indian ancestors. As the afternoon wore on, they swapped memories and songs. Hay was transported. "To be sitting at Harry James's bonfire once again and to hear this man sing 'The Water Is Wide And I Can't Get Over,' that lovely, lilting old Scotch song I'd known as a child, was a tremendously moving experience."

But, inevitably, the visit was marred by Jorn. "We were supposed to stay for supper," Hay recalled, "but Jorn took offense at something — as he so often did — and put me in the terrible position of having to side with him against Harry James. Back home that night, I realized that I'd have to get out if I didn't want to see myself cut off at his whim from everyone I'd ever loved." He informed Kamgren he would leave as soon as possible.

At that declaration, the relationship effectively ended, and Harry counted each day of the next few months until he could move out. Even then it took years to extricate himself fully; Harry continued to fill out Jorn's tax forms and balance his books until 1966, when Harry's new lover, John Burnside, insisted he had done enough. Kamgren thereupon abandoned the business Hay had labored to set up and became a private clothes-shopping consultant for rich women.

Some months before leaving, Hay began a relationship with Jim Kepner, a friend from the tail end of First Mattachine and through most of ONE, Inc., who over the years involved himself in almost every activist campaign available. A compulsive reader and inveterate pack rat, Kepner eventually amassed the largest collection of gay and lesbian material in the world, known today as the International Gay and Lesbian Archives. Like Hay, he was self-educated and had an intuitive approach to researching and analyzing gay culture. At the time they met, Kepner drove a taxicab, one of many trades he plied to subsidize his studies and activism. As an editor for *ONE* magazine, he had worked on several pieces Harry submitted and found them "full of bad typing, worse handwriting and very interesting ideas; for me, it was an enormously pleasant job." It was also the basis of their lifelong friendship.

When Kepner quit ONE in 1960 over a falling out with Dorr Legg, his friendship with Harry began to deepen. Kepner was also an ex-C.P. member, and he combined deep shyness with an opinionated intellect that could spar with Harry's. He was also slender and wistful, with large, soulful eyes. By 1962, Harry and Jim had regular lunches in Kepner's cab, parked on Leahy's small lot. They talked about everything from gay historical theories to their personal problems, but mostly they lamented the lack of a viable gay group within reach. "Mattachine was dead in Los Angeles and I couldn't become a Daughter of Bilitis," Kepner said. "Harry and I became one another's father confessor."

They carried on an enormous dialogue, much of it in correspondence. Harry often spun off thousand-word letters, many of them typed on quarter-page strips of paper to look like Leahy estimate summaries. (The better to throw off the watchful eyes of the boss, Hay often opened these billets doux with the word "Gentlemen," conspicuously at the top of the page.) Along with romantic personal plans, Harry pitched many activism proposals, from researching actual child abuse statistics (in response to a homophobic series in the *Hollywood Citizen News)* to fighting for gay rights on constitutional grounds. He even laid out an elaborate schema for a "Mattachine III," all in an attempt to revitalize the homophile movement from its doldrums.

Occasionally, Kepner managed polite, cautious visits to the Hay–Kamgren domicile. At these times, he witnessed his normally deep-minded friend consumed by superficial concerns. "Harry was very tense," Kepner recalled. "He paid inordinate attention to food and how it was prepared and served." Like most of Harry's friends, Kepner was mystified by this odd coupling. "Jorn was the most unpleasant person I think I'd ever met," Kepner said bluntly. Kepner lived alone and was smarting over a recent bad relationship; Hay sought to bail out of his. They secretly discussed moving in together and used an elopement reference from Dickens's *David Copperfield*, "Barkis is willing," as they gathered the strength to make the move.

Though Hay had prepared him for months, Kamgren took the departure as an ambush. He threw all Harry's clothes in the street, drank an entire bottle of Pernod, and woke up two days later, "my head on the floor, my feet still in bed." Harry recovered his clothes and possessions, which left Kamgren feeling typically aggrieved. "Harry had three or four thousand records at the time we split up," he said. "He left me six of them. I never even played them, but he only left me six!" The jilted party, however, recovered swiftly. Within weeks Kamgren took a taxi to the first gay bar he'd visited alone in a dozen years and left with a new lover, with whom he stayed for the next dozen, until the man's death.

Harry moved into Kepner's cottage on the steep hill of Baxter Street, just a block from Fargo, where he had first lived with Jorn. Immediately, the romance became tentative instead of intense. The two spent much of their time discussing a magazine they envisioned as a gay version of the *New Yorker* crossed with *Playboy*— they were boycotting *ONE,* as would many others. Not until 1966 were two issues published by Kepner, under the name *Pursuit and Symposium,* to reflect the erotic and cerebral poles of the gay life cycle.

At such close range, Kepner felt overwhelmed by the strong personality of his new housemate. They clashed on everything from decorating styles to ideas about where to go on trips. Once, rather than take a rugged camping trip Harry had planned over his protests, Kepner found his only escape was to cancel his vacation entirely. Frequent late-night phone calls from Jorn, complete with threats of suicide, capped the craziness of that summer. The insurmountable problems, Kepner said, "sent our relationship to hell pretty quickly." When Kepner accidentally ran over the Siamese cat that Kamgren had awarded Hay from their eleven-year union, it seemed almost to symbolize the ill-fatedness of the new relationship. Still, Harry persisted in their intellectual bond and what he called his "spiritual passion" for Kepner.

Their mutual devotion to the ephemeral gay culture around them prolonged the affair. The most extraordinary such event they attended was a series of private seminars on homophilic studies conducted by the British savant Gerald Heard. Then seventy-three, Heard had developed a quiet legend in both Britain and the United States as a historian, anthropologist, philosopher, and mystic. He was a BBC correspondent on science and current affairs in the thirties, and a sought-after speaker, with a delicate but rich voice. Christopher Isherwood had known Heard before they separately came to America in 1937, and together they edited two books. Heard was also an intimate of Aldous and Julian Huxley, H.G. Wells, George Bernard Shaw, and Igor Stravinsky.

Kepner had already heard the Englishman discuss his ideas of possible goals for the homophile movement back in 1953. Heard's provocative theories included the belief that homosexuals, whom he called "isophyls," had a prolonged youthful nature. He also believed gays were the next step in the evolution of humanity. His lectures continued, some at ONE, some in private residences, for ten years. Jorn had prevented Harry from attending these talks, but another chance came in 1963, when Heard invited a group from ONE into his home for what turned out to be his last seminars. In attendance, along with Jim Kepner and Harry, were Dorr Legg, Don Slater, and two U.C.L.A. students. Also there that day was John Burnside, a heterosexually married engineer who manufactured kaleidoscopes for a living. Partly to tease him personally, Harry was sure, Dorr Legg referred to the engineer as "our capitalist."

Kepner recalled (though Harry did not) that the soon-to-be life partners were already chatting away during these lectures in the book-lined room, which was illuminated only by a small fire. Heard, his red hair graying and wispy, kept his large blue eyes closed most of the time he spoke. The effect of darkness, flickering fire, and the brilliant mind expressed in a solemn British accent was captivating. Over four evenings several weeks apart, he spun out an overview that Harry called "enticing, appealing, and mysterious."

Kepner likened Heard's speaking style to "a shower of ideas" that he found mesmerizing, but he had trouble following a central thread. The main thrust, Harry recalled, was a Masonic-style secret gay brotherhood that had existed throughout history, influencing kingdoms and regimes.

"Heard kept hinting at a sort of hidden 'Illuminati,' or secret, Sufi-type brotherhood with initiates in each generation down through the centuries. At our fourth session, he asked if our group was willing to make a commitment to study this brotherhood and hinted at our joining it." Harry was fascinated with the idea of studying with the great scholar, but felt extremely reluctant to reinvolve himself in a secret gay group. "I did not think it was historically correct to go back underground. What Heard wanted were adepts" — the initiate covert alchemists of mystical orders of the past. Harry argued strongly against the idea. When the ONE group adjourned to the Gold Cup Coffee Shop in Westwood to rehash the discussions, Harry made sure his view was known.

In contrast to Harry, Jim Kepner recalled rather that Heard had proposed "some group yoga-like exercise" involving gay consciousness and sexuality. Moreover, he felt, Heard had spoken mostly of a general brotherhood that gay organizations such as ONE must actively consider; he did not believe Heard was proposing a specific power-oriented lineage. Kepner recalled Heard's annoyance that several members of the group were distracted by the historical points and concepts he threw out as peripheral detail, ignoring his main thesis. After an unfocused response to his fifth discussion, the Englishman angrily terminated the sessions.

The friction between Heard and Hay may have also resulted from their similarities. Kepner, who had edited manuscripts of both, found them alike in several respects. Both were armed with vastly esoteric homophile knowledge, and both were personally driven to formulate a unified theory of gay existence. Though Heard had published many books, he never wrote more than a few obscure articles about the "isophyl." Within five years, he lapsed into a coma from which he had not emerged at the time of his death in 1971.

By the end of that strange summer, Hay and Kepner knew that a relationship between them was not going to work out. Harry was "back on the cruise again, and at fifty-one, I knew I was a full twenty years over the hill." With low expectations, he visited a few gay bars he had known in the past, the House of Ivy and the Vieux Carre, both on Las Palmas on either side of Hollywood Boulevard.

After several dismal experiences, he decided he was "past the end" of that sort of hunting. He was lean, but had acquired a craggy, middle-aged look. Love was, after all, a young man's game in gay life. How little did he know.

·11·

Loving companions

Live *the questions now. Perhaps then, someday far in the future, you will gradually, without even noticing it, live your way into the answer.*
— Rainer Maria Rilke, *Letters to a Young Poet*

Harry's "final coming out," as he called it, was marked by his relationship with John Burnside. Hay began wearing his longer hair, brighter clothing, and a necklace or earring muted in tone but bold in shape. "I decided I never again wanted to be mistaken for a hetero," he explained. "Ever."

His daughter Kate noticed the startling change one day in the early sixties when her father came to meet her for lunch. She had just started a job in a conservative company, and, anxiously anticipating Harry's nonconformist attire, she asked a fellow employee to alert her of his arrival so she could shepherd him out quickly. "But," she remembered, "in walks Harry with his logging shirt and long hair and a long earring. At the same moment, the president of the company walked in. I think they greeted each other while my girlfriend called me. It seems cute now, this meeting of opposites, but it wasn't cute to me then." She added, "I saw him twenty years later at my mother's memorial service and he hadn't changed one iota."

Harry came into this pivotal romance quite by chance. After a few weeks of wasting his time and his heart in the bars, he characteristically rebelled against that system and set about designing another, a new venue where gay men might form relationships. An old inspiration resurfaced — square dancing. He had included square dancing in his 1950 prospectus for Bachelors Anonymous, partly because it had served as a favorite form of recreation for married C.P. couples. To make it gay, Harry drew on the journals of Bret Harte, which describe men dancing together. In Hay's scheme, as in Harte's, "the butches would wear red hankies in their pockets, and the femmes would wear blue. Of course, they'd swap every so often."

He retooled the idea and, in mid-September, 1963, took it to Dorr Legg at ONE. As Harry expounded on his visions of gay square dance leagues, gay square dance competitions, and even statewide square dance matches with mixed gay and straight couples, he heard what he later called "a cascade of silvery laughter" coming from an adjoining office. He insisted on meeting its source, who was a middle-aged man with youthful, cherubic features and deep dimples — just Harry's type. As he subsequently manuevered around the man with the silvery laugh, it dawned on Harry that "just maybe I was coming to know a five-foot-eight version of the man of my dreams... (and I always thought he'd be tall!)" They mentioned meeting again the next day at ONE, and did so nonchalantly — Hay dressed in a tight yellow cashmere sweater he had not worn in years, and Burnside wearing scarlet shorts and a matching t-shirt. Then they made a date for a future evening.

John Lyon Burnside III had already met Harry at Gerald Heard's house, but the lightning struck at this second meeting. Burnside's background was respectable; he'd studied physics and mathematics at U.C.L.A., graduated in 1945, and pursued work as an engineer in the aircraft industry, winding up as a staff scientist at Lockheed. His current business, manufacturing his own optical invention, represented his dropping out of the system. The device worked like a kaleidoscope, but without the traditional glass chips to color the view; instead it turned whatever was in front of its telescopic viewfinder into a symmetrical mandala. Burnside named it the Teleidoscope, and in 1959 he launched an independent business called California Kaleidoscopes, Cal Kal for short.* The offbeat business reflected John's personality, which was liberal and aesthetic; he had recently studied modern dance with Bella Lewitzky. Inquisitive and precise — Jim Kepner described him as a "small town skeptic" — Burnside was at once an attentive listener and as discursive as Harry, the perfect partner for Harry's ongoing dialogues about gays.

---

* The Teleidoscope caused a minor sensation, getting write-ups in many papers, including the *Village Voice* and an inquiry from the *New Yorker*. The lucrative business was his economic mainstay for more than a decade, and was at its height when he met Harry.

Though John arrived a nerve-racking three hours late to their first date, they postponed the chef's salad Harry had prepared for another five hours, which they spent in bed. They fell for each other at every level, as they found out how much they had in common. Burnside was also a westerner, from Seattle. Both were lapsed Catholics, were close in age (Burnside was forty-seven; Harry fifty-one), and had weathered long heterosexual marriages. Next to Harry's bravado, however, Burnside was timid in nature. He had realized by age fourteen that he was homosexual, but after one unfulfilling experience and a distaste for the limitations of gay life as he saw it then, he repressed those urges. Fate had taught him such caution; John's mother, out of economic necessity, had left him in an orphanage for periods of his early childhood. His marriage at age twenty-three to Edith Sinclair, a German immigrant, precluded any exploration of the gay world. He described their childless union as "not unhappy," but his inner life he considered "cursed" until 1962, the year he first visited ONE, which he had heard about from some gay employees at the kaleidoscope factory. Within two weeks of meeting Harry — they date their anniversary as October 6 — their relationship was "fixed." But there was a hitch: John's wife Edith.

Not only was he still married, but Edith was his business partner. For two months John attempted to will an impossible harmony between his straight marriage and his gay passion. Harry found this painfully tense, as epitomized by an "incredibly strained" Thanksgiving dinner, during which John and Edith shared a table with Harry and Margaret.

Obstacle or no, Harry's sights were set. In keeping with his pattern of determined wooing, he knew he had to leave Baxter Street. Because of Burnside's domestic situation, the courtship had moved there, and Kepner, though relieved at the end of his own tense affair with Harry, smarted at the sight of "Harry and Johnny spooning in my living room." Harry brought up the need for an apartment of his own, but the implied question — whether he should rent a bachelor flat or something larger — was dodged by Burnside, who was still summoning strength for his leap into gay life.

He began inviting Harry over for weekends at the expensive house in the Hollywood Hills he shared with Edith. She liked Harry instantly and was happy that her husband had acquired such a cultured, intelligent friend. The Burnsides' large home on elegant Outpost Drive had a swimming pool, which served as a pretext for weekend invitations. Harry could sleep in the guest room, across the hall from the master bedroom. One night, after Edith had gone to bed, the two men stayed up late talking, and ultimately made love in the living room. When Harry went to the guest bedroom, John joined him, leaving the door open in an odd gesture of goodwill. For Harry, who had already endured the stress of a disintegrating marriage, the tension became unbearable. He left in the middle of the night, got all the way back to his apartment, but then, terrified that he had alienated John, returned to Outpost Drive. Once there he was unable to so much as knock on the door; all he could do was to stand in the driveway.

He did not hear from Burnside for days and was certain he had destroyed their relationship. But on December 9, John showed up at Harry's tiny bachelor flat and moved in. Falling in love again at fifty-one was, to Hay, a phenomenon of healing. He wrote of the experience, "The pain is lost in an amazement of love and friendship and intimacy. I can remember when John and I first felt that amazement." The affair was even more of an emotional milestone for Burnside, who came to this first love with a preserved innocence. They began a never-ending dialogue about their backgrounds, reading, and ideas, starting on Friday night and continuing till Monday morning, when each had to return to work.

They continued attempting a three-way truce with Edith. John even hired Harry as office and production manager for Cal Kal. This was less strange at the time than it sounds today. Until the 1970s, a popular model for dealing with homosexuality was for a gay man to marry, repress his emotional needs from the mainstream of his life, and have homosexual affairs on the side. Donald Webster Cory, author of *The Homosexual in America,* and a pioneer of the homophile era, insisted that for homosexuals *not* to marry was "maladjusted." This idea of having a foot in both worlds made Harry distinctly uncomfortable, but for Burnside's sake, he tried.

Hay's first duty as production manager was to find a larger work site to meet the growth in the business. He found an ideal building on Washington Boulevard near Western Avenue. Having thus established himself, he gave his thirty-day notice at Leahy's, where, he said, "the employees were expected to die at their desks — and several already had. Old Mr. Leahy was furious." For Harry, freedom suddenly flowered in all directions.

Outsiders sometimes assumed that Harry's masculine demeanor and their relative stature (Harry was half a foot taller than John) reflected butch–femme roles in their relationship, but Harry had consciously abandoned that model. At parties they attended, most male couples were attired one in a suit and the other in a flowered shirt; Harry and John both wore flowered shirts. They took a honeymoon, of sorts, to Baja, California, camping in places Harry already knew and discovering new spots of their own. Their car was caught in a sandstorm and they were stranded for a few days while the engine was cleaned, but they didn't much care. Such gypsyish trips became a never-ending motif of their relationship. They homed in on New Mexico for more trips, and Harry was delighted to find that John already owned land there.

Over the Christmas holidays, Harry and John went to New Mexico and visted Richard Tapia, an old friend of Harry's who had come out in the Army during the Korean War and gone in the closet again and who was now governor of Pojoaque, one of the pueblos north of Santa Fe. Excited by the optics products and the jobs the business offered, he proposed that Harry and John move the factory to the reservation. "We were instantly intrigued and we met with the tribal council. They agreed to provide a building with living quarters attached," Harry recalled.

As events turned out, that never came to pass, but when they applied for a business license, Harry made an important new friend. The State Employment Office specialist in Native American employment was a Tewa Indian man named Antonio Garcia. Almost immediately, Harry realized that "this rather vividly handsome — though no longer young — Tewa was the gay man I had tried in vain to make contact with on earlier summer trips." Harry mentioned the names of the mutual friends who had told him about the gay Tewa, and dropped a few hairpins about the gay movement as well. "Tony, as he was to be thereafter known, invited us to supper the next night," Harry recalled, "and thus began a deep and unflagging bond of friendship and brotherhood" that lasted until Tony's death in 1983. They would see him many times in the intervening twenty years.

When Harry and John returned to Los Angeles, the factory had begun the annual hiatus during which its officers balanced the books, prepared tax records, and conducted the annual meeting of the board of directors. This year, however, Harry witnessed a shocking change: "John came running into the front office where I was working one evening. He was upset and was saying, 'They're throwing me out! They're throwing me out! I don't understand!'" "They" were Burnside's wife, his mother, and a lawyer, who were the other members of the board of directors of Cal Kal. Seemingly in response to Harry's presence, they had secretly met, planned, and voted Burnside out of his own company. In retaliation, Harry and John barricaded themselves in the office. Edith Burnside barred them from the factory premises and allied herself with most of the workers, including, to Harry's shock, two gays. After her apparent success, Mrs. Burnside dramatically warned everyone against dealing with Harry, commanding, "Don't look in his eyes!"

The reversal of the couple's fortunes was total: Burnside, his assets frozen, was penniless. The newly unemployed Hay was forced to cash some life insurance policies he'd carried during his long tenure at Leahy's. Any thought of moving the factory vanished. Throughout most of 1965 the pair lived on little more than love. Their great indulgences were the flamboyant matching outfits in bright sixties styles and colors that Harry found on sale at Ohrbach's. So dressed, they did their best to scandalize the dinners that ONE held, where the other homophiles wore gray suits and ties.

Though John was paralyzed to inaction, Harry swiftly realized that the Teleidoscope patent was in the name of the inventor — John Burnside. An effective strategy, he calculated, was to announce that the patent was being sold to Edith Burnside's worst perceived enemy — himself. John sold the patent to Harry for one dollar, and within a year an agreement had been negotiated and Burnside was then able to purchase control of the factory.

The couple's social life continued to center around ONE. After chilly exchanges at the group's official functions, Harry and Dorr Legg found opera a safe topic to discuss. "One of the finest amateur performers I know in the ancient and honorable ART of High Camp is Dorr Legg," he once noted in a letter. "When we weren't clawing each other's eyes out from opposite sides of the political fence, we would get going on famous 'blips' we had either seen, had been a party to, or had heard of, in Theater, Opera, or Ballet... The two of us, topping each other off, could keep a roomful in stitches for quite a stretch." These get-togethers were often hosted by a pair of chubby lovers dubbed the Heavily Twins, who opened their china-dog-and-porcelain-cherub-packed home to the ONE crowd. (The Heavily Twins were at first called the Heavenly Twins, because of their storybook romance — one had waited ten years for the other to come out and leave a marriage — and when they finally got together, they each gained more than one hundred pounds.) A six-foot-plus transvestite named Sherrie who came to ONE found an especially sympathetic ear in Harry and John and visited them regularly. Even Margaret, now wheelchair-bound from arthritis, visited ONE in 1965. "They honored her public participation in the Mattachine Foundation," he said. "We were both very touched."

His feelings were not so warm toward the slowly growing national homophile movement. He was in fact "appalled" by its increasingly assimilationist direction. The yearly conventions of nationwide Mattachine chapters did "nothing but rewrite their own constitutions," he complained.

Harry's founding vision of a "loving-sharing brotherhood" had long vanished, but to see it replaced by a gray-suited respectability that might as well have been the Elks or the Kiwanis distressed him deeply. He may also have felt increasing annoyance at the disappearance of the radical vision of the movement. In 1975, he wrote a nettled letter to the national gay newspaper *The Advocate,* blasting its timid battle cry, "Gay is Okay!" Harry retorted, "Is *that* all? Big Deal — for 1954!!" Referring to the so-called missing link known as Java Man, he signed his letter "Harry Hay, Pithecanthropus Erectus of the Gay Movement."

Domestic life, however, kept him too satisfied to make much trouble. The couple moved into a charming old house with a garden on Edgeware Road, in a quiet section of downtown Los Angeles. In 1965, Harry founded the Circle of Loving Companions, a gay collective that was to remain a part of their lives for decades to come. The Circle was often politically active, and Harry stressed that the name symbolized how all gay relationships could be conducted on the Whitmanesque ideal of the inclusive love of comrades. The Circle's membership specifications were based on affinity, and it seemed to be Harry's effort to re-establish the subjective intimacy of Parsifal, the Fifth Order of the Mattachine Society. Over the years, the Circle included a number of close friends, including Stella Rush and Helen Sandoz, Lawndale lesbians who, under the names Sten Russell and Sandy Saunders, edited *The Ladder.* For long stretches, though, it included only Harry and John, which prompted some ribbing about how the ever-ingenious Harry Hay had managed to construct a circle composed of two points.

From their new residence, they would walk to Main Street and spend hours at Harold's bar, one of the city's older and seedier gay spots. There Harry gave John private seminars in homosexual mores and bar rituals. On Fridays, this continued at Joly's, a bar for older men on Western Avenue, which offered dinner. Sundays they went to the Red Raven on Melrose, which featured movies and a buffet. The middle-aged couple sat at the back of the bar, holding hands (under the tablecloth since displays of affection were still grounds for closing a gay bar). They watched the leather men and the pretty boys pose and circulate, and Harry liked to predict — often with high accuracy — which ones would get together as closing time approached.

▽

In the spring of 1965, the homophile establishment of Los Angeles was shaken to its rather brittle core by a bitter struggle for control of ONE, Inc., its legendary magazine, and the ownership of the group's physical assets. The incident has been called an audacious political maneuver, a theft, and even a bitch-fight, but was most often referred to as "The Heist." It happened the weekend that Don Slater, a disgruntled ONE member, surreptitiously packed and moved the thousand-volume-plus ONE library to his own premises.

The offbeat drama that held Harry and others spellbound was well cast, and provides a precious glimpse inside the Southland's homophile society, a society that, despite his long absences from it, remained Harry's chief social outlet. Longtime editor Slater and longtime administrator Dorr Legg were as committed and determined as Hay. Though their styles were dissimilar, all three were firmly opinionated, strong-willed, and so passionately devoted to the homophile cause as to forsake traditional career and income.

Harry was on the opposite end of the political spectrum from both. Slater was a peppery World War II veteran, though Harry found him impishly charming. Dorr Legg was a well-educated, iron-willed man with ultrarefined East Coast manners. In an unguarded moment, Harry once confessed that "I could never look at Dorr without thinking of the carved wooden handle of my grandmother's umbrella." Indeed, Legg's icy dignity lent him a stern, proper facade which he sought to extend to ONE by gravely boosting the importance of every aspect of the organization. ONE, he insisted, was the omniscient pinnacle of homosexual culture. He worked devotedly as its business manager; on paper his salary, forever deferred, accrued until it reached six figures, a debt some cited as an instance of the hold that Legg had on the organization.

Legg's entrenchment posed serious limits as well as provided support. In Slater's words, "Here it was, 1964. We'd been going along since '52 and ONE was still talking about what it had done back then. But we as editors of the magazine were looking ahead. We had to. New organizations were forming out there. But when we brought up new issues, Bill Lambert [Legg's other name] would not deem them appropriate." Many members of ONE agreed that while Legg single-handedly kept ONE going longer than any other gay organization, his unbending conservatism locked many new people and ideas outside.

Internally, Legg wanted to expand the activities of the organization. He had launched the conferences and the classes in homophile studies, and now he was making further plans — to the dismay of other members, who felt that putting out the magazine was all they could handle. As these interests polarized, Slater and his lover, Tony Reyes, led one faction, and

Legg led the other. Eventually the board of directors split evenly down the middle. Even Harry and John, who largely avoided political entanglements, got ensnared at a ONE board meeting in 1964. Slater nominated the two men to the board, but before the vote, he instructed them to vote for the candidate who would tip the impasse in his direction. Harry quickly withdrew his and Burnside's names from nomination as a sign that he would not follow orders. This signal given, he suggested that they be renominated, but the renomination was not forthcoming. "Which was fine, with us," said Hay. This was but one of the bureaucratic power plays leading up to the split.

"To Don Slater," Slater himself wrote in a subsequent newsletter,

> the situation appeared increasingly alarming. Nor was he the only Member or Friend of ONE to feel this way. Many other alert and forward-looking Members shared his conviction that action would have to be taken to stop the downward spiral. The Chairman of the Board, however, arbitrarily blocked any and all attempts at free discussion and arbitration. His dictatorial frame of mind was nowhere more evident than in his unilateral attempt to gain complete control over *ONE Magazine* and its editorial format functions. This resulted in the resignation of the editors of *ONE*, some of whom had been with the magazine ... for periods of up to eight years.

Slater, galled and incensed, recalled that "I festered and festered. But one night I woke up, and said to Tony, 'I have a solution.'"

Slater's solution, arrived at after legal consultation, was to assume that the board was at least evenly split on the question of control of the corporation's assets, and to invoke a legal measure known as "self-help." In this case, he decided to relocate the corporation. He hired a truck for the weekend of April 17 and 18, 1965, contacted his sympathizers, and emptied out the contents of that large second floor at 2256 Venice Boulevard.

Dorr Legg, of course, saw things in quite a different light: "Don Slater got a group of people together and, from our point of view, stole everything. The library, plus all documents and furniture. We had offices taking up an entire floor of a building. One day it was just empty." Slater agreed that "we didn't leave them so much as a return address label." He had called a board of directors meeting for the Monday to follow the Heist. "So when they came to the office, they didn't come to an empty room. I was there."

Harry recalled how, earlier that Monday, Slater called him and Burnside to a large, sloping-floored garage at 3473½ Cahuenga Boulevard

West, not far from his mother's house. "We didn't know what had happened, and when we found out we were absolutely astonished," said Burnside. By June, the story broke in the *Los Angeles Free Press*. Evoking the image of a queer amoeba, the *Freep* headlined, "ONE Becomes Two; Homosexuals Split." Immediately, Slater's faction began referring to their garage full of appropriations as ONE and advertised a forthcoming issue of *ONE* magazine. Legg's group, still on Venice Boulevard, did likewise. For several months, there were two organizations called ONE, Inc., two *ONE* magazines, and unlimited snickering over "the strange case of ONE vs. ONE," which wags referred to as ONE vs. NONE.

Harry, already inclined to retire the term "homophile" and many of its associations, was wagging his own tongue that "this was a matter of two dinosaurs spitting at each other and not realizing that dinosaurs had become obsolete." The spitting got increasingly sulfurous, with hints of blackmail tactics. Slater was said to have either threatened or joked (which was taken as a threat) that any of the several teachers on ONE's board would lose their jobs if they tried to stop him.

The spoils, however, did seem worth the fight. Since the fifties, ONE had published three periodicals; its flagship, *ONE* magazine, had been in existence for eleven years, and inspired a Canadian counterpart called *TWO*. *ONE* had run original articles by the likes of Norman Mailer ("The Homosexual As Villain") and Albert Ellis ("Are Homosexuals Neurotic?") and had accumulated vast correspondence, the stories of hundreds of average gay men and lesbians struggling for sanity under oppression, as well as the letters and manuscripts of its celebrity authors. Along the way, many admirers of the homophile cause had donated their personal libraries, often containing rare and valuable books, to ONE. All of this got heisted.

Dauntless, Dorr Legg filed suit against Slater, who countersued — an expensive process for all concerned, the membership especially, which was constantly pumped for legal-fund contributions from both sides. Legg's ONE was represented by a lawyer named Hillel Chodos; Slater's ONE was given preliminary advice by Herb Selwyn (who, according to Slater and Kepner, had long been one of the few area lawyers to help with gay entrapment cases). In court, Slater was ably represented by attorney Ed Raiden, and despite his legally tenuous maneuver, Slater made out fabulously. Part of his success was due to Legg's imperious statements in the courtroom. "Your Honor," Jim Kepner remembered Legg reprimanding the judge, "you must not treat us as equals. This is clearly a case between a banker and a bank-robber." According to Slater, Raiden cannily appealed to the judge's bigotry. "Ed said, 'You know, Your Honor, this is a bitch-fight. They're suing themselves in a way, because legal title to the name has not been established by either party." The judge's final pronouncement, Harry recalled, was repeated all over the gay grapevine: "You two old aunties go out in the hall and fight this out."

The agreement, arrived at through arbitration, was to split the library down the middle. Some multivolume sets were even split every other volume. Slater agreed to make copies of documents on a rented IBM copier, but on Raiden's advice copied only documents that Legg could request by name. Since Slater had been the librarian, he knew the collection far better and thus kept many of the treasures of ONE's library and most of the valuable magazine files. Slater agreed to give up the name ONE and called his group Tangents — ironically, a name Jim Kepner created for his column in *ONE* magazine. Though part of the agreement was that neither side would lay claim to winning the case, Legg defiantly issued a victory statement. In a tribute to their tenacity, both Legg's and Slater's groups (the latter eventually became known as the Homosexual Information Center) survived into the 1990s.

Despite comic undertones, the event really was a tragedy for the burgeoning gay movement. The books and papers that made up the treasury of the homophile movement were never reunited. The brimstone fury between the litigants, both valiant servants to the cause of homosexuals, took decades to cool. Worse, the Heist came to symbolize how members of that now-older generation could not even work with one another, let alone with a broader gay constituency. In this, those involved were not much different from other minority leaders seized by righteousness and driven by oppression.* Kepner commented of the affair, "Those not involved frequently underestimate the tremendous differences between those struggling to set up a movement." Despite their mutual animosity, the principals in the case of ONE vs. ONE never broke ranks and discussed the matter outside the gay community, and spoke little of it even within that community.

In light of such goings-on, Harry Hay was content to move ever further from traditional forms of organizational power. He concentrated instead on his Circle of Loving Companions, adding its voice to the wider gay

---

* See Taylor Branch's *Parting the Waters: America in the King Years* for a parallel discussion of agonizing intraracial political fights that were kept tightly within the African-American community for decades.

circles that would convene for progressive campaigns. His private life with John, which flourished, became his central focus.

The other founders of the Mattachine went in various directions. "For Konrad, Harry, and me, this was a life work," said Chuck Rowland, who continued to work with ONE. He started a new organization, the Church of One Brotherhood, similar to Mattachine but under religious auspices, but it was short-lived. Rowland resigned his job at the furniture factory and, unable to get work in Los Angeles, returned to Minnesota, where he taught college-level drama until his retirement in the late seventies.

Jim Gruber and Konrad Stevens, the sweethearts who had tipped the balance and gotten Mattachine going, left activism and joined the Satyrs, a motorcycle club.* Eventually, after a decade-long relationship, they split up. Gruber remained a schoolteacher but took up writing fiction; Stevens gave up photography to work in a lab.

After his landmark trial, Dale Jennings worked on *ONE* magazine for its first year, writing under a variety of names and styles, and even penned the "Feminine Viewpoint" column when no lesbian was available. He turned his talents toward commercial ventures, and worked as a promoter for the Ice Capades to supplement his residuals from writing. Eventually he became wealthy enough to buy a ranch outside of Los Angeles.

The most visible success, of course, was Rudi Gernreich. After a string of accolades in the late fifties for his breakthroughs in fashion and fabric design, he skyrocketed to fame in 1964 for his creation of the topless bathing suit. Known as both boy wonder and bad boy of fashion, he was its reigning innovator and showman throughout the sixties. His great wit and progressive politics continued to show up in such ground-breaking concepts as unisex and anti-fashion, and in the professional heresy of his declarations that "fashion is dead" and that "the only relevant issue is freedom." When he died of lung cancer in 1985, Jacques Faure, art director of the French *Vogue,* summed up Gernreich's career as that of a "fashion activist."

The saddest story, by contrast, was that of Bob Hull. The "Viceroy of Mattachine," known for his capacity to communicate with everyone on every level, continued to work as a chemist and participated minimally in ONE, but never again pursued activism. Several friends noticed that as the boyish Hull entered early middle age, he had great difficulty adjusting. His

---

* The Satyrs, founded in 1955, is the oldest gay motorcycle club and is still active today.

love affairs became increasingly brief and unhappy, and he slid into alcoholism. "Part of his problem was that he had difficulty letting go of his boyishness and his youth," sighed his friend Jim Gruber. "Back then you were either cute or over the hill. If you reach that mid-life crisis and pour alcohol over it — and Bob, as a chemist, had knowledge and access to lethal materials — it adds up to disaster."

The disaster happened in June of 1963. "He set it up one night with things he brought home from work," Gruber recounted. "Turned on the TV and started getting drunk until he could face taking the chemicals." Hull knew exactly what chemicals to mix and in what doses, and he downed an effective concoction. The gifted, idealistic, and humorous Hull was mourned by many, and Harry wrote a eulogy for him that was printed in *ONE*. Evelyn Hooker, who had been a close friend, observed, "I know everyone has a right to end his life. But why Bob?"

▽

The crumbling of the homophile movement, as symbolized by the ONE fiasco, had long been coming. Dino De Simone, a member of the original Mattachine West Side Discussion Group in New York, quickly decided its members were "Sissy-Mary-Nit-Pickers, the most bureaucratic old ladies I'd ever met." The homophiles' strategies were executed through white gloves: to educate instead of to confront; to use "experts" to explain (and sometimes even condemn) homosexuality; even to refuse to identify as a homosexual group.

But changes were coming. New organizations were forming with younger, more flexible personalities at the helm. The civil rights and counterculture movements sent out strong messages about oppression and militancy and many gay people were active in these movements. When new gay organizations began to coalesce throughout the country, many of the organizers were veterans of freedom struggles, and they advocated a new militancy.

The struggle of reforming the homophile movement was shared by such people as Franklin Kameny, who in 1961 had founded a Mattachine Society in Washington, D.C., and Guy Straight, who started the League for Civil Education in San Francisco that same year. Meanwhile Harry was actively organizing in Los Angeles. One particularly daring campaign he worked on was the first gay pride parade in Los Angeles and perhaps in the nation. This effort was guided by Don Slater and the Tangents group, whose Committee to Fight Exclusion of Homosexuals from the Armed Forces had already fought a number of draft cases involving homosexuals.

In February of 1966, at the first meeting of the North American Conference of Homophile Organizations (NACHO) in Kansas City, a nationwide day of protest was planned with events scheduled for San Francisco, Philadelphia, and Washington, D.C. The group planned to bring public attention to the discriminatory policies of the Defense Department, setting a pattern that would become widespread in the 1970s and '80s as dozens of court cases challenged the military's exclusion of homosexuals. May 21, 1966 — Armed Services Day — was chosen for the nationwide demonstrations.

Harry became chairman of the Los Angeles committee, which met twice weekly for two months to plan the protest. Though his politics were not exactly in favor of military service (indeed, within a dozen years Harry would establish a Gay Draft Counseling Network in his living room), he supported this action. Since at that time an oath compelled inductees to pledge they were not homosexual, he thought that a campaign to illegalize the oath as an invasion of private conscience would be progressive; he argued that the resulting confusion and suspicion about who was and wasn't gay would paralyze the generals. In brief, he explained, "You can't say 'Shaft the Draft' if you're excluded."

The Los Angeles group conceived of a picket line on wheels; automobiles would take protest placards all over the city. News releases advertised the gay motorcade as a first, and reporters from *Newsweek* and *Time* made inquiries, whipping up the already excited planning. Harry made dozens of sketches of John Burnside's designs to secure four-foot-high boxes on the tops of cars. On the sides were painted eye-catching slogans: "10% of All GI's Are Homosexual!" "Homosexuals Are the Most Moral People in the Service — They *Have* to Be!" The succession continued, "Sex Belongs to Private Conscience," "Write LBJ Today!"

They leafleted gay bars for three weeks with maps of the motorcade route and pleas for support, but Harry hesitated to predict a revolution. His doubts were quoted in Slater's *Tangents* article.

> If this comes off, it will be something our city has never seen before. *If* it comes off. Imagine a motorcade of fifteen cars on about a twenty-mile route through Los Angeles. Ideally we should have had the support of the entire community; then we could have really staged a grand demonstration. But most homosexuals are still hiding. With the work we have put into this thing, [most of which had fallen, by default, to him and Burnside] and with the thousands of homosexuals in the area, it is fantastic to realize we will be lucky to have forty persons show up for the motorcade tomorrow — and at least twenty per cent of those who do will not be gay.

A handful of clerics attended, along with "at least one actor, two engineers, two teachers, a couple of beatniks, and others," making up a total of thirteen cars. "Before amazed neighbors and passing motorists," reported *Tangents,*

> the placards were boldly attached, and with riders visibly tense, the cars pulled into formation down Cahuenga Boulevard, past the Hollywood Bowl, to head east on Sunset Blvd. in the direction of the Plaza and downtown ... In front of Central Market, Mexican women with bulging shopping bags and wayward youngsters barely noticed or understood the signs. Servicemen gawked and shrugged; a few clenched their fists at their sides helplessly. At Pershing Square crackpots interrupted in their harangues shouted louder.

Though the homophile motorcade felt vividly historic to its participants, the previous year's Watts riots had changed what most of the media now regarded as newsworthy, and the city editor of the *L.A. Times* said he would be interested in the gay motorcade only if someone was hurt. In what they felt was a small consolation, the parade was featured at six and eleven on the CBS News. Said Hay, gratified by the experience if not by the coverage, "I can honestly say that I did not expect to see such a public demonstration on behalf of homosexuals in my lifetime."

The next day, he appeared with John on a television show hosted by Melvin Belli. There, and at every media opportunity, Harry stressed his message that gays should reject society's negative stereotypes and insist on defining themselves. On April 24, he squared his account with Paul Coates, the columnist who had deviled the Mattachine thirteen years before. Now he was with the *Los Angeles Times,* which printed Harry's response when Coates rose to the bait about the funny word Harry kept using.

> "Homophile ... why do you prefer that to being called a homosexual?"
>
> "Because it's a word that expresses much more," [Hay] explained. "It has an implication of spiritual love, while homosexual is a legal term relating to people who commit specific sexual acts."

Such media activism swiftly became an important tool for the gay movement, but it was still rare; few people were willing to identify publicly as homosexual. Another occasion came in 1967 when Hay and Burnside were invited to appear on "The Joe Pine Show," hosted by a well-known television muckraker. They plotted their appearance as an openly gay couple, wearing identical outfits, blue yachting tops with vermilion pullovers, which Harry bought on sale at Ah Men!, a gay-ish boutique in West

Hollywood. To combat the notoriously aggressive host on an equal footing, Harry brusquely began many of his sentences, "Look, Pine," as he jabbed his finger. To an inane question about "How could you guys control yourselves in the Army?" Harry made his frequent point that homosexuals "*had* to learn to control ourselves so we could get through high school with a full set of teeth." The exchange was so lively that they were asked to do a second taping.

By August of 1966, the newly formed North American Conference of Homophile Organizations, convened in San Francisco. The Circle of Loving Companions, with its vote of two, attended, and Harry became acutely aware at that conference of the division of temperament between movements on the East and West coasts. Easterners, he sensed, were overridingly conservative and assimilationist, while activists in the West seemed more radical. (Harry felt their politics were more "truly gay.") A resolution passed at another conference recommended that street people (the voluntary dropouts of a more generous economic era) be included in the liberation efforts — a contentious issue then, and one thus far frowned upon by the white-glove homophiles. The resolution, proposed by Jim Kepner, began, "Since the homosexual has no image to lose..." and Harry quoted it frequently in his exhortations for gay people to develop the unique identities still latent within them.

The Council on Religion and the Homophile (CRH) was another subject of Harry and John's attentions. An interfaith body of clergy and openly gay people, CRH initiated discussions to "bridge the gap" between those groups at a time of growing social activism in religion. Del Martin and Phyllis Lyon, founders of the Daughters of Bilitis, were active in its northern branch, the Council on Religion and the Homosexual. The CRH had many statewide conferences and meetings, which John and Harry attended faithfully. At a theology convention in San Francisco in 1966, several CRH participants were struck by Harry and John's tenacity as a couple. All couples who arrived together were asked to split up, a technique organizers felt would open up dialogue. The Circle of Loving Companions refused. With amused annoyance Lyon recalled, "With all of us against them, those two won."

For several years in the late sixties, the Circle took its message to the Renaissance Faire; John sold piles of kaleidoscopes and Harry, dressed in authentic costume with the sign "Sodoma" hanging from his neck, passed out thousands of leaflets. He continued working with various organizations, traveling to conferences, writing letters to other active gays. He lived every day as a gay activist, earring and gay perspectives swinging in the breeze. Sometimes, just doing the laundry was gay activism, especially if he and John dared to snuggle up next to each another while driving home. Every bit of action promoted the social and political climate from which the Gay Liberation movement would take off at the turn of the decade.

The kaleidoscope factory paid the rent. The flower-petal vision of its products seemed tailor-made for the psychedelic motifs of the counter-culture. It grew popular in the mainstream as well, and orders poured in from museums, department stores, and head shops. After regaining control of the factory from Edith, Harry and John began hiring anyone they liked, including more gay people, the new "long-hairs," and other non-conformists. (In fact, when Dorothy Healey was let go as secretary of the Southern California Communist Party in 1968 and applied for unemployment benefits, Harry extended a job offer at the factory. She declined but was touched by the gesture for years afterwards.) The proprietors cultivated an anything-goes atmosphere, and young people enjoyed the work and brought constant discussions about the sexual revolution, consciousness-expansion through drugs, and the tactics of flower-power activism. The large old building became a free-flowing community center. "We had long, high tables at the factory," Harry recalled, "and the kids were always bringing in their pounds of marijuana and separating out the seeds and weighing it. This amid Gay Liberation posters being silk-screened and in various states of color registration, hanging over the tables to dry; meetings being conducted; and even a few kaleidoscopes being made."

Open to anything, these graying free spirits even attended some of the mass love rites of the sixties. One be-in, held in Elysian Park, a canyon adjacent to Dodger Stadium, made an indelible impression. "As we entered the park, we could see this great river of young people — perhaps 25,000 were there," Harry recalled. A utopian, sharing essence seemed to rule the day, and as their contribution, they brought a box of twenty-five teleidoscopes which they passed out among the crowd. After many hours and thousands of hands, every single teleidoscope was returned in perfect condition. They were amazed. "Whether it was the excellent quality of the pot that was being passed around — which John and I did occasionally sample — or simply the spirit of the day, it was a mind-blower, watching this mass of people relating to one another with what I would later call subject–subject consciousness. Whatever it was, we felt it just blowing through us, and it made a big difference in our thinking."

Those winds of change reached deep into his inner life as well; the political dogmatism and the tense homophile facade were falling away. Others noticed the change. Del Martin observed that "this was a different type of Harry Hay than we had seen before — one who was filled with the joy of life and love and spirituality. And one who could speak our language. He was a different character than we knew in the fifties."

Harry's last progressive odyssey of the decade was not a gay one but combined many of the fascinations of his life. A main flagship of the American Indian movement of the sixties, the Committee for Traditional Indian Land and Life (CTILL), rekindled his long-standing concern with Native Americans, this time in explicitly political terms. It started in early 1967, after local radio personality Peter Bergman of KPFK broadcast Hopi prophesies that had been printed in the San Francisco *Oracle,* an organ of the counterculture.* A resulting colloquium between traditionally minded Indians and interested non-Indian youth gave birth to the Committee, which became an active support group. All this caught Harry at a deep level and held him for almost three years.

When he attended the colloquium, Harry felt an "instant connection" with the 130-member group. This connection must have been amplified by his lifelong associations with Indian people and by family stories ranging from that of his great uncle in the Battle of Wounded Knee to his own encounter with Wovoka. CTILL adopted consensus decision making when Harry related its effectiveness as a nonparliamentary method. John Burnside volunteered the kaleidoscope factory as a meeting place, and they became immersed in the movement. Among the close friends Harry and John made through CTILL were Silvia Richards, a non-Indian woman, and Craig Carpenter, a part-Mohawk man. Carpenter was intelligent, radical, and with his dark skin and green eyes, he was also extremely handsome. From the time he was a teenager in the late forties, Carpenter explained, he had made a life mission of discovering and communicating with the few Indians still practicing traditional cultural roles throughout the country. Almost two decades of this work had developed a unique communications network integral to the formation of the Traditional Indian movement. Carpenter made fast friends with Harry, calling him "Chief Long-hair."

Harry's work with CTILL involved fund-raising, research, and handling the travel logistics for a series of national conferences. He applied his vast organizing knowledge to dozens of different aspects of the committee, mediated disputes, and was happily in his element. In one

---

* Though traditional Hopi do hold prophecies sacred, much of the material that was printed in the *Oracle* turned out to be exaggeration.

time-consuming project he helped American Indians to beat the draft by uncovering in the U.C.L.A. library an old treaty that forbade Shoshone Indians to bear firearms for any reason. He took several trips to the Hopi country in Arizona, where he met some of the same people Harry James had known forty years earlier.

That summer of 1967, the first North American Traditional Indian conference was held at Tonawanda, an Indian ground in upstate New York. Harry and John attended, taking along several participants who had no transportation of their own. Early one morning there, Harry was cleaning up the campground, as he had learned to do in the Trailfinders. An old man approached him and said, "I see you are a Snake Brother." He explained that members of the Snake Clan always tended the campground, adding that a person could only be a Snake Brother after being bitten by a rattlesnake but not killing the snake. Astonished, Harry confirmed that thirty summers before, in 1937, this indeed had happened, but the old man gave no indication of how he knew that.

He introduced himself as Clifton Sundown, an elder of the Seneca tribe, and Harry recognized the man's name and remembered that he had a message to give him. At a party at Morris Kight's house that summer before leaving, Harry had met a young Seneca Indian who was in the process of having a sex-change operation. When Harry mentioned that he was going to the meeting at Tonawanda, the young Indian said that his grandfather, Clifton Sundown, would be there. He knew that after his operation he could no longer visit his homeland, and he asked Harry to deliver a farewell message. "He spoke to me in Los Angeles," Harry relayed, "and he sends you his love."

Though little open tolerance of gay people was exhibited by the Indians they met in CTILL, Harry and John remained inseparable as a couple and always felt accepted on a personal basis. (Their friend Craig Carpenter told Harry that though he "had no use for queers, maybe Scotch queers were okay.") Group homophobia, however, persisted. CTILL had provided their mailing list of more than 6,000 names to a Mohawk Indian named Jerry Gamble, whose traditional name was Rarihokwats. With it, he began a national Indian newsletter called *Akwesasne Notes*. In 1979, under new editorship, *Akwesasne Notes* began returning exchange magazines sent by gay publishers such as *RFD*, the periodical for rural gay men. They complained that they did not want such "European behavior," which they equated with Christianity and alcoholism, encouraged among their people. Their elders, they said, considered homosexuality "not normal and a detriment to our way of life." This raised a storm of protest from gay periodicals, gay supporters of CTILL, and as-yet-unorganized gay Indians themselves.

Harry soon parted with CTILL. His conclusion was that there was "no such thing as a traditional Indian — only Indians trying to find their way back to a traditional way." This influenced him to give up city activism and changed his thinking about the gay movement and community. Harry did not, he said, equate the transitions of Indian culture with the transitions of gay people's culture, but he acknowledged a strong parallel between CTILL and the Radical Faerie movement of the following decades, mostly in redefining cultural identity, assimilation, and relationship to environment and society.

Harry's involvement with CTILL ended after he helped organize the third colloquium of Native American Traditional Leaders in March of 1969. The event was successful, but other events, such as the Indian occupation of Alcatraz and a physical attack on his friend Craig Carpenter, disturbed him.

As the sixties drew to a close, Harry felt adrift in the wake of the fragmenting counterculture. He was particularly disillusioned by the growing discussion of violence as a means for changing society, which displaced his hopes for a revolution of enlightened consciousness. The new decade offered him no sure direction.

But a summer riot called Stonewall would soon change everything.

·12·

Change of scene

The pedigree of honey
Does not concern the bee;
A clover, any time to him
Is aristocracy.

— Emily Dickinson

The riot that transformed every gay American's life began when Inspector Seymour Pine led a routine raid on a Greenwich Village gay bar during a mayoral campaign. But on the night of June 27, 1969, at the Stonewall Inn — an otherwise unextraordinary bar that featured go-go boys and catered to transvestites — gay people fought back. Costumer Jack Buehler was at the scene that night, and remembered hearing a black drag queen say, "We ain't taking this shit no more," as she hurled a trash can through a window. The ensuing civil disturbance, which lasted several nights, involved an estimated two thousand gays and lesbians protesting openly and fiercely in the streets. Years of frustration over bar raids, entrapment, and other forms of harassment were suddenly vented and rose like a great smoke signal across the country.

The Stonewall riot acquired the aura of a mythic battle and tended to eclipse all previous gay activism. It marked a new public consciousness about gay people and has been annually commemorated as the anniversary of the gay movement. Harry commented on how suddenly "the individual gay identity we had first postulated in Mattachine in 1950 had become a collective gay identity; the gay movement had moved from 'I' to 'we.'" Dozens of organizations sprang up in the riot's wake, and many still bear the bar's name. The demonstration's historic place was set as the gay movement's Boston Tea Party.

It also became the nation's first large-scale gay media event. By October of that year, *Time* magazine ran a cover story entitled "The Homosexual, Newly Visible, Newly Understood." Beneath its titular sympathy, *Time* didn't really understand much about gay people, whom it portrayed as promiscuous, unstable, and inherently miserable. It prominently quoted the most loathing line in Mart Crowley's camp-drama *The Boys in the Band:* "Show me a happy homosexual and I'll show you a gay corpse." *Time* even suggested that a "homosexual conspiracy [was] afoot to dominate the arts and other fields." Their hopeful closing note was that this distasteful condition, "most experts agree," could be cured.

Harry had his own, very different reasons for dismissing the new gay wave. "I wasn't impressed by Stonewall, because of all the open gay projects we had done throughout the sixties in Los Angeles. As far as we were concerned, Stonewall meant that the East Coast was finally catching up." But the growing incorporation of the gay movement into the mass movements of the sixties was of inescapable importance. Among the passionate responses to its story, *Time* even printed a letter from Harry, in which he denounced male chauvinism as the true enemy of "the Free Generation," gay, straight, female, or male. He wrote, "Chauvinism, in all its social and racial aspects, is the real enemy of all men and women who seek the one security that is viable — community — and the one freedom that is transcendent — individuation." Harry and John renewed their activism in what was now known as "Gay Liberation." This was an entirely new order, bringing in people who were experienced in other social justice movements and the counterculture.

One of these was a white-haired, fast-talking Texan named Morris Kight, primarily known for his Dow Action Committee, an anti-Vietnam protest campaign aimed at the manufacturers of napalm. Quite openly radical on such issues, Kight had until 1969 identified himself only as an "underground gay liberationist";* Harry recalled with amusement that

---

* Kight came to Los Angeles via New Mexico in 1958 and settled in Bunker Hill, still a gay neighborhood since the days of Clarabelle, the queen who saved Harry from the police in 1933. Kight regularly bailed gay people out of jail, found lawyers for them, provided counseling and other support services, and generally served as a one-man gay crisis center. He even had an underground V.D. clinic. "I had a ring of gay nurses who purloined antibiotics for people who were afraid to face straight doctors," he reports.

Kight invited him and John as token gay people to cookouts he hosted for peace activists. But around the time of Stonewall, Kight came above-ground in a big way, displaying the high-powered organizing techniques and media savvy that would shape the gay movement in Los Angeles for the next decade. Kight's grantsmanship alone carved out the landscape of Los Angeles's gay social services, and he seemed well connected in City Hall. Ultimately, Kight succeeded Harry as the town's grand old man of gay politics and attained almost the status of a gay godfather. Morris and Harry were sometimes not on friendly terms during the ensuing decades, but almost any time they got together they chatted at length and with relish.

In December of 1969, the Southern California Gay Liberation Front was formed, one of many regional counterparts to the militant New York organization that had formed after Stonewall. The earliest meetings were held at Don Slater's Tangents office, though GLF wandered through dozens of facilities — including the Cal Kal kaleidoscope factory and a heterosexual disco known as Satan's (complete with pentagrams in the decor), on Sunset Boulevard. Free, freaky, and vital, the GLF suddenly overshadowed ONE. Gay hippies and college students were at the fore-front of the new organization, and many of the homophile generation followed in fascination. The following June, Gay Liberation Fronts nation-wide led parades to commemorate Stonewall; in L.A., Tinkerbell on a crucifix was carried down Hollywood Boulevard.

Harry and John participated in the founding meetings of the Southern California GLF and Harry was its first elected chair. Hay was instrumental in planning one of GLF's first and most visible events, a picket of Barney's Beanery, a West Hollywood restaurant, over its notorious (and misspelled) sign "Fagots Stay Out!" (The sign was not actually removed until the mid-1980s, as one of the first acts of the newly elected West Hollywood City Council.) The spirit of that radical time saw spontaneous, anarchistic actions everywhere. In sixties style, it was popular to pass marijuana joints and ampules of poppers down the picket lines of Gay Lib events. Same-sex dancing was of tenuous legality in Los Angeles then, and as a challenge, GLF held regular gay "funky dances" at Troupers Hall, an old Hollywood theater. And in Griffith Park, they held a one-day "Gay-In" in defiance of police warnings against any public gathering of homosexuals. Pickets against businesses intolerant of gays were increasingly frequent, and Harry and John were at most of them.

The following May, however, they decided to leave all that excitement behind them. The couple had long discussed moving to northern New

Mexico; both were familiar with San Juan Pueblo and had friends there. Now, Harry and John opted to make it their permanent home. They threw out their old suits and overcoats that dated from the thirties, packed everything else, including Harry's vibrating-belt spot-reducing machine, in a U-Haul trailer, and left.

There were several reasons Harry uprooted from his nearly lifelong home of Los Angeles, not least among them financial pressures; life in the city was growing more expensive, and, since many of their accounts were mail-order, the kaleidoscope business could relocate. He also wanted to pursue his study of homosexual roles among Indian societies, and to put something back into the Indian community in the form of jobs. His strongest desire was to bring gay liberation to the rural northern part of New Mexico, where its arrival seemed otherwise decades away. Some observers sensed that seeing a new wave of gay organizing firmly in the hands of newcomers — most notably Morris Kight — made him feel shut out. Underlying everything else, Harry was beginning to feel mortal. For nearly forty of his fifty-nine years he had been a smoker, and he worried about developing emphysema. He did not expect to grow very old.

The "Land of Enchantment," as New Mexico's license plates proclaim it, is mountainous in the north, with the occasional rise of high stone mesas and fall of majestic canyons and gorges. Its powdery earth ranges from pastel tones of orange to gray to chocolate adobe, and structures made of the sun-baked bricks, some new, some hundreds of years old, seem almost to grow from the earth. The northern region of the state has particularly pure light that has lured artists to settle there for nearly a century. Though the climate is arid, most of its small cities and towns survive by farming. Fields of chilies, tomatoes, and squash dot the landscape, along with orchards of apple, apricot, and plum trees. The weather can be harsh, with scorching summers and subfreezing winters, but its citizens, Chicano, Indian, or Anglo, treasure the land's natural purity and beauty. "Spiritually," said one of Harry's friends, "it's a hot place."

Residents recall that gurus, hippies, artistic superstars, and cocaine dealers began to accumulate in once-sleepy Santa Fe, but John and Harry's home for the seventies was a short eternity away, on a fenced-in refuge near the village of San Juan Pueblo. The largest of eight Indian pueblos clustered between Santa Fe and Taos, San Juan was already old when the Spanish arrived in 1598. The Jemez Mountains and the Sangre de Cristo Mountains frame the pastoral Española Valley, which is divided by the Rio Grande. From their front door they could hear the hiss of its convergence with the Chama River. That river confluence makes the Española Valley a point of intersecting weather patterns; storm fronts often abut blue skies over San Juan. Like glinting, reflective ribbons by muddy roadsides, old ditches crisscross the area. These are the *acequias,* an aquaduct system dug by Indians four hundred years earlier and faithfully maintained. Together with the high water table, the *acequias* ensure productive farms and earn the area's nickname, "the womb of New Mexico." Still, the residents of San Juan Pueblo and neighboring towns struggle against poverty and a high mortality rate.

The property where Harry and John lived lies within the boundaries of the San Juan Indian lands, but for generations it had been privately owned. A New York socialite and artist named Dorothy Kent (sister of the famous illustrator and Leftist Rockwell Kent) bought it in the late 1920s and built an adobe hacienda on the property. Behind a high wall of woven willow branches she planted roses, peonies, and lawns for croquet. By the time she stopped building there were five adobe cottages (one with a grand piano), and Kent offered frequent hospitality to artistic friends. She was in her eighties and still the landlady when Harry and John occupied the house so far at the end of the compound that one friend characterized it as "immune to twentieth-century interferences." If they were remote, they were still comfortable — their bathroom was so large Harry called it an "entertainment center," and he offered showers to local friends who had no plumbing facilities. Neighbors collected in their large kitchen for hours at a time, and in the guest room, a steady stream of out-of-state visitors would stay for long periods.

Established friends lived nearby, including Enki, the Indian *K'ossa,* or Sacred Clown of San Ildefonso, and Richard Tapia of Pojoaque. Tony Garcia, the handsome middle-aged gay man they'd met in 1964, became their closest friend. One of the most educated people at San Juan, Garcia was valued by Indians for his county job as "the magician of Social Security." The transplanted couple met Santa Fe's gentry, including Monica Collier, granddaughter of John Collier, the distinguished commissioner of Indian affairs under Franklin Roosevelt.

Harry and John set up shop in the mercantile building of San Juan Pueblo. It was offered to them by Dr. Manuel Pijoan, a wealthy local who had befriended them early on. He owned the old U-shaped building and thought the kaleidoscope factory could provide an economic boost to the Pueblo. Pijoan's building already housed a café and a store; they could use the open-air wing of the building where hides had been dried in earlier years. The deal was sweetened by a very reasonable rent if they agreed to put up a bond for reconstruction of the wing. They did and soon occupied the manufacturing warehouse and a separate gallery-shop for kaleidoscope sales. With their open, outgoing temperaments and the constant strains of classical and folk music that flowed from their quarters, Harry and John quickly became accepted.

Once settled into village life, Harry received daily visits from Isabel Cata, an elderly widow skilled as a potter. She was so rotund and well-swathed in serapes and deerskin boots that people called her "the bundle." Upon meeting Harry, she announced to her friends that she would marry him, and every day she stopped at the trading post to teach him a few new words of Tewa, as would befit an incoming bridegroom. Before she could accomplish her mission, however, she died.

With its timeless feeling and dusty stability, San Juan Pueblo held particular promise for Harry to pursue his studies of the berdache role in Indian culture. The area of the *mujerados* mentioned by Hammond in his report a century before was within a few hundred miles, and Tony Garcia was a remarkably well-placed contact. Harry had searched libraries extensively for even brief suggestions of homosexuality among Pueblo Indians, but found nothing. On his previous short trips, he had heard of a few men who did have spiritual and mixed gender qualities, but their relationships with their tribes and even with any ceremonial roles appeared highly diminished. It was not surprising that they would be, as the cultural bulldozers of assimilation had effectively destroyed any open tolerance of the merest implication of homosexuality. But Harry hoped that continuing gay-related tribal roles were still secretly alive.

To his great disappointment, however, Harry made virtually no new gay contacts at San Juan or at any of the nearby pueblos, partly because he was in a high-profile couple. He may also have grown too old to attain the "observer–participant" relationship he had hoped to establish among gay Indians. Harry sensed that a generational change in the values of gay Indians of the Rio Grande valley increased his difficulty. He explained this change through the scenario of San Juan Pueblo. "Tony's house, for years, had been the place where the affluent white artists and aesthetes from Taos to Santa Fe would come for Feast Days to meet Indian studs who were willing to be 'trade.' Tony was adamant that gay men *never* were supposed to have sex with each other. He would say, 'That's like sisters having sex with each other. Yecchh!'" Garcia laughed openly at Harry and John's sexual relationship.

Though Garcia enjoyed certain distinctions — he was one of the few at San Juan who could speak ceremonial Tewa, and his house had the most beautiful garden of anyone's — he repeatedly told Harry that he was not a *kwidó* (a Tewa berdache). "In the sixties, Tony would say that the *kwidó* society and tradition — terms he used interchangeably — had died out at San Juan before he was born. But in the later seventies, after it was known that a young Tewa boy was being trained into the tradition, Tony didn't seem surprised, and simply said that it wasn't active when he was growing up.

"All of Tony's men were at least thirty-five, married, with three or four kids, and made it clear that they played around sexually *only* with women, but came to Tony's house because of his financial generosity and liquid hospitality. This was well known in the village. But the young gay Tewa at San Juan who came out in the Army or while away at college would have nothing to do with this old-fashioned hetero-stud domination. And would have nothing to do with Tony — so obviously they gave us a wide berth too. We were convinced of this when we met some of them at the gay dances we threw later; these kids made us swear we'd pretend not to know them if we saw them with their families or friends."

One of the few areas of disharmony between Harry and Tony involved Harry's firm ideas about the advocacy roles of gay men — that all gay men should be defenders of the Mother, wherever she appeared. Tony, however, ridiculed the wives of the married lovers he took; when Harry and John gave him a Polaroid camera one Christmas, he took compromising portraits of his lovers and showed them to the women he had cuckolded.

Harry worried particularly over B.Q., the wife of Tony's favorite lover.* She was in unusually poor health, though only in her forties, and, because of Tony, was often abandoned by her husband. Harry decided that it was his responsibility as a gay man to befriend her. He did so with frequent visits through 1970 and 1971, and when her health became delicate Harry arranged for her to do light craft work at home, which he sold at the trading post. His friendships with women were unusually strong; Sue-Ellen Jacobs, an anthropologist Harry met later, commented on his exceptional ability to communicate with the Tewa women. Mrs. Q. recalled that when other Tewa women saw Harry at her house, they at first asked why a white man was there, but soon relaxed and treated him as "one of the girls."

---

* The Q. family were a couple in their late sixties with middle-aged children. Harry and John became particularly close with them. Out of respect for their privacy, their names and those of other Indians still living are not disclosed.

Despite Harry's frustrations with his berdache investigation at San Juan, he suspected that a berdache tradition — at least in part — remained beyond the observation of whites. This suspicion was bolstered one afternoon as he watched San Juan schoolchildren debarking from their bus in front of the trading post. "A small boy of about eight was weeping and hiding behind a girl of the same age. I heard her shout at some other boys who were taunting this poor scared kid, 'Leave him alone! He has every right to act however he wants to, and you know it!' It was clear she was defending a little sissy." Harry never got the chance to catch a clearer glimpse of this possibility, but felt that any such tradition would be carefully guarded from outsiders.

Not long after he and John settled into their new home, Harry volunteered to work on *El Grito (The Cry)*, a radical newspaper aimed at *la Raza*, the Chicano and Indian communities. He distributed it in the mercantile building, and was featured in one of its long profiles as a Communist and as a founder of the gay movement. This was an indication of his swift acceptance in this rural, somewhat rough area; Harry's age, authority, and cordial manners could always smooth his path. Harry and John listed the Circle of Loving Companions as a public organization and became the first openly gay address in the northern part of the state. This brought many new friends into their lives, including Alejandro Lopez, a young artist who was shocked to find a gay listing so near his hometown. He drank in their knowledge, ideas, and enthusiastic friendship. "Many were the evenings that we shared in their cool patio or kitchen around a pot of coffee discussing issues ranging from instinctual behavior to ritual dances and gay consciousness," Lopez recalled. "It was the exploration of gay consciousness or the 'gay window' on the world that concerned Harry most. As he and John kept a constant dialogue going, already many years in progress, they would make new discoveries which excited them greatly."

Not content to let the world come to them, the couple sought gay community where they could and traveled the hundred miles to Albuquerque when a group called Lambda formed at the university there. Like many gay students' groups, that community seemed unfocused, wavering between politics, cruising, and midterms. Some close friends from Lambda, however, came for regular weekend retreats with the Circle of Loving Companions in the Kent compound.

Harry's innate restlessness was forced to settle into the measured schedule of the chilly winter, the spring floods, and the summer harvest. He managed, however, to keep tabs on his outside passions. In the summer of 1970, he sent a donation to sponsor a sign to be carried amid the jubilant mass of protesters in the first gay pride parade in New York City. Among hundreds of other placards, it read, "San Juan Pueblo."

▽

In spite of his isolation, new friends came to Harry as if by serendipity. His first summer at San Juan, a young associate professor of anthropology from California State University at Sacramento had car trouble while passing through the town. "My personal and professional life changed when my van broke down and I met Harry Hay," said the stranded driver, Sue-Ellen Jacobs. In 1965, while a graduate student at the University of Colorado at Boulder, she had been assigned by anthropologist Omer Stewart to do research on the berdache. He handed her Harry's paper on the Hammond report about the "made women."* Like Harry, she became endeared to San Juan Pueblo. It became an ongoing part of her personal life, and eventually she carried out long-term anthropological studies on women's roles there.

When Jacobs's camper overheated, she recalled, "we had hoped we could take it to a gas station, but there was none — just an old pump that hadn't been used since World War II. There was a mercantile store with a sort of café, though, and we stopped there. Harry, being the gregarious person that he is, came over to our table and started talking to us. He kept saying, 'You girls this' and 'You girls that.' I was beginning to chafe quite a bit at this, and finally said that I didn't appreciate his application of that term to us. Harry paused a moment and said, 'You have California license plates and you've mentioned leading a study group in women's history... Is it possible you're *feminists?*' When I said, 'Yes!' he waved his arms and called a local woman over from the counter to join us. We talked till the place closed, about four in the afternoon. Harry and John invited us over to dinner, where we talked more — till 4:00 a.m."

Ever the fixer, Hay found someone to repair the camper, and Jacobs returned to Sacramento but stayed in touch. That fall, Harry called to suggest that she study the changing status of women at San Juan Pueblo. Jacobs liked the idea; two years later, she went to New Mexico and stayed with Harry and John. Harry arranged for her to meet the family of B.Q., who had died unexpectedly of a heart defect at Christmas of 1971. The

---

* Jacobs's paper, "The Berdache: A Review of the Literature," was published in the *Colorado Anthropologist* in 1968.

aged Mr. and Mrs. Q., he realized, needed a new daughter. "By the end of that first summer of getting to know one another," Jacobs explained, "I was invited to stay. The relationship that started so tight with Harry and John changed to a close relationship with the Pueblo. Harry provided an entrée that dramatically altered my entire life." Jacobs eventually became a professor of anthropology and the director of Women's Studies at the University of Washington.

Harry got to know every Indian dance, every festival time, and the best route to every Catholic cathedral and windowless church of the *Penitente* Catholics. He baked his own recipe of high-nutrition bread for the gay waifs who came for showers, dried apple chips when there was a bumper crop, and made wine from currants, pears, and plums. His vigor revived, and in August of 1972, while visiting a Hopi mesa, surrounded by several howling dogs, he wrestled all night with smoker's cough and decided to quit cigarettes. He wrote to Jim Kepner, "After 42 years of diligent exercise in the opposite direction, I gave up smoking *cold turkey*." Life grew serene in the land of enchantment.

But the following summer, on July 7, 1973, tragedy struck. After two years of good business by mail order, the factory and all its inventory were destroyed by fire. The blaze was started accidentally by several young men who habitually slept on the trading post's stone porch. On this night, the fire they lit to ward off the chill was laid too close to the building's wooden doors. Before dawn, Harry and John were awakened and rushed to the site, only to watch helplessly as the entire complex burned to the ground in a fire so hot it fused the colored bits of kaleidoscope glass. The cardboard tubes, the brightly patterned papers that covered them, and all other supplies went up in flames along with business records and personal possessions they had stored there (including the flag Harry's great-great-uncle had carried at Wounded Knee). "Harry almost died that day — literally," recalled Sue-Ellen Jacobs, who was at the Pueblo that summer. "He was moving things out of the wreckage, and I looked at him and realized that the kind of sweat on his face was the kind you get when you're in serious shock. He collapsed and, with help, I got him into his truck and drove him to the Q.s' house, where Mrs. Q. made some medicinal tea that was used for heart problems."

They salvaged a truckload of charred tools, but in practical terms, they were wiped out. To compound the disaster, they were told that their insurance was invalid because the business was on an Indian reservation and consequently outside the jurisdiction of state law. They lived for almost a year on less than thirteen hundred dollars, too poor to travel even a short distance. Only their dozens of paid subscriptions to newspapers, journals, and gay magazines kept them sane. Outwardly, they shrugged off the misfortune, but their livelihood had vanished, and with it their daily link to Pueblo life. They still managed, with the help of lesbian friends named Lily and Hawk, to drum up a gay discussion group (probably Santa Fe's first), through which they met several new friends, though the group itself did not catch on in the conservative community and lasted only about six weeks.

Old friends like Jim Kepner and Morris Kight sent regular news of the L.A. scene. Kight, who by now was shaping the rise of the Gay Community Services Center, wrote irregular but warm and witty letters informing Harry and John that while many things were changing, others — like ONE, Inc. — were not. Picking up on a reference that Harry was drying fruit to survive his financial pinch, Kight responded, "I recently visited the spacious parlors of the world's oldest, largest, fastest-growing and most responsible homophile organization ... and I can't look another dried fruit in the face for a whole year."

They never rebuilt the kaleidoscope factory — sales were beginning to drop off anyway — but another optical invention of John's took up his attention and some of Harry's. This was the Symmetricon, a device which allowed the image of the kaleidoscope to be projected. In the mid-sixties, John had hit upon an arrangement of lenses which perfected what he and others had attempted before, but with limited success. He patented his "instrument," as he always referred to the Symmetricon, and its slowly moving colored designs, which resembled an ever-changing rose window, eventually proved of great interest to the fine arts and entertainment worlds. For the time being, however, the soothing, meditative state that a Symmetricon show induced was often a sublime 'dessert' to the speeches and workshops Harry carried out; it became almost a visual counterpart to the inspiring, idealistic spell he cast when he spoke.

During the bleak period after the fire, an especially important letter arrived from historian Jonathan Ned Katz, who sought to interview Harry about the origins of Mattachine. Harry knew the work of Katz's father, Bernard Katz, who had written a book on Negro spirituals. The younger Katz, through a series of telephone interviews and letters, included Hay's stories of the founding of the Mattachine Society and of his HUAC hearing in his ground-breaking *Gay American History*. Katz, who became Hay's first modern chronicler, was thrilled at making contact with Harry. "I couldn't believe that I had found him," said Katz. "As a gay Leftist myself, it was exciting and very moving." When Harry learned in December of 1976 that Katz had dedicated *Gay American History* to him and to Jeannette Howard Foster, author of *Sex Variant Women in Literature,* he was breathless with surprise and pride at the honor. The young author and the old activist did not meet face to face until 1983.

Another historian also visited Harry in New Mexico. Jim Kepner brought out John D'Emilio, who was researching the homophile movement and would later publish a complete account of its history in his book *Sexual Politics, Sexual Communities: The Making of a Homosexual Minority in the United States, 1940–1970.* Harry found D'Emilio to be as fascinated as Katz with the radical roots of the gay movement. (At one point in their interviews, Harry stopped just short of the radical climax in his dramatically rendered saga of the Mattachine and said, "Oh dear. I've been going on and you haven't had any supper yet," at which point the historian implored him to ignore such trivialities as food and continue talking — a response Harry must have savored if not planned for.) When the Mattachine chapter of D'Emilio's book was previewed in three parts in the Canadian gay newspaper *Body Politic,* Harry's legend was further launched for the Gay Lib generation.

The most dramatic episode of his life in San Juan involved a political struggle over water rights in the area. This unexpected campaign became the largest-scale activism Harry ever attempted. Although the campaign succeeded as a result of hundreds of New Mexicans' efforts, Harry played the central role of strategist. He seldom spoke of this event, partially because it was such a detour from his lifelong commitment to gay liberation, but it is one of his finest credits, since Harry Hay helped save the Rio Grande from being dammed by the federal government.

It all began in 1962, when the Federal Bureau of Reclamation, which had partial jurisdiction over the Rio Grande, received congressional authorization to consider construction of a dam on the Rio Grande just north of San Juan Pueblo. Popularly known as the El Llano Canal project, this scheme would divert a thirteen-mile stretch of the river into a concrete canal so that the water could be used for private land. By law, the diverted water would be earmarked for irrigation. The land it was destined for, however, was unfarmable — in fact it was a dry wash subject to annual flooding. The owner of that land was Richard Cook, a wealthy New Mexico developer who had contributed heavily to the coffers of state representatives. Cook also owned the construction company that had won the bid to build the canal. It was rumored that Cook bought the property for seven dollars an acre, but, once the canal was approved, had priced it at

$32,000 for an acre and a half. There could be no more classic political pork barrel.*

In March of 1975, thirteen years after the first legislation, the Bureau began to lay survey stakes and make construction contracts for the project. An alarm was sounded among the area residents. Such a dam, they soon realized, would benefit none of those dwelling in the area; it would, in fact, devastate hundreds of farms, ranches, and even entire villages. It was inevitable that during low rainfall years, that part of the Rio Grande would dry up.

Upon hearing of the matter, Harry was the first to notice that something was missing from the paperwork in violation of federal requirements. "At a meeting on April 6, I asked for a copy of the environmental impact statement and threw New Mexico State engineers into a tizzy," he recalled. It was obvious to him that "the goddam Bureau," as he would often refer to the Federal Bureau of Reclamation, was determined to ignore the citizens of the Española Valley, some of the poorest farmers in the nation.

Though the arrangement was of doubtful legality, little action was taken by the community council that oversaw the *acequia* ditch system. Meetings to discuss the canal were dispirited, pessimistic, and rough: At an early meeting, a voice from the dark reaches of the hall suggested killing a couple of the surveyors to scare away the rest of the workers. John Ciddio, who got involved with the campaign, summed up the community's gloom: "We weren't sure how we could stand up to the government on an issue like this, or if we could at all."

Harry had exact ideas about how they could. He attended the *acequia* council meetings, and his earthy persona and astute questions about various points of law gained him official status on the council. He produced arresting but sensible literature; the first flier listed sixteen questions anyone living in the area "ought to begin asking himself." And Harry quietly bolstered and focused the meetings toward tangible progress. He proposed a bilingual newspaper, *La Voz Del Rio/The Voice of the River,* and an umbrella group, the Association of Communities United to Protect the Rio Grande, both of which promptly became vital parts of the campaign.

---

* The situation was not unlike the diversion of water to Southern California from the Owens Valley in the 1920s, which turned the San Fernando Valley from a desert to a developed suburb of Los Angeles. Santa Fe was filling up fast, and a new city would have been attractive to both transplanted outsiders and to displaced locals.

Harry realized, however, that to defeat the entrenched power structure of rural New Mexico, they needed outside support. He conceived a secret weapon, a national environmental organization, which he created at his living room typewriter. The Nation-Wide Friends of the Rio Grande constituted his grandest flowchart ever. Like the Mattachine Foundation, it was an effective false front; gay and progressive organizations from around the country made up its ranks. A Jewish New Yorker named Esta Diamond Gutierrez (married to a local Chicano farmer) helped. She was involved with the co-counseling movement, another extensive network which provided sympathetic contacts. Hay and Gutierrez got many of their friends to quickly register as "chapters" and through this ersatz federation they launched a sizable mailing campaign to congressional leaders across the country. For good measure, Harry wrote public advocacy figures, including Jack Anderson and Ralph Nader. Harry's paper tiger was developing a mighty roar.

One surviving outreach letter is a classic example of Hay's personable and effective style of agitation. Reflecting his determination to give a lavender tint to an essentially nongay project, it is prophetically headed, "NATION-WIDE FRIENDS OF THE RIO GRANDE — faerie divison." It accompanied the first edition of *La Voz Del Rio* and reads:

> Please find enclosed our first Newsletter giving some idea of what we have been about this Spring, and since we returned from our trip west ten days ago.... We'd love it very much if one or two of you would write the Bureau of Reclamation in Amarillo ... and request a copy of their Environmental Impact Statement... If for some reason you could think of a good reason to ask for it in Spanish it would be a real gas. Your actions will help to assure the goddam Bureau of Reclamation that we are not just an isolated little gaggle of helpless Colonials ... [and] will help us demonstrate that many eyes are watching over our beloved river. Big hugs all around, Harry and John

Within a few weeks of local organizing and nationwide agitation, Harry stumbled across another secret weapon. A friend volunteered to contact a powerful Eastern senator with whom he had a personal friendship. This became a vital channel; Harry realized that the canal bill had already been passed by Congress and that the only chance to stop it was in the Appropriations Committee. The senator, once contacted, critically increased the pressure from within Congress to take a second look at what they had allowed. Despite his grass-roots orientation, Harry did not refuse a backroom opportunity if it would help.

The fight dragged on for months on the grass-roots level. More than two dozen sympathetic professionals donated legal and research assistance to the campaign. Charged community meetings of Indians, Anglos, and Chicanos consumed most of Harry's energy, though more people from each community took on increasing responsibility as the options became clearer. At one of these meetings Harry was intrigued by two Chicano men. Monica Collier had told him that another gay couple lived in the valley, but she had never gotten around to introducing them. "I went up to these guys and mentioned that I thought we might have more in common than concern over the water situation," Harry recalled. "We agreed to meet for breakfast the next day."

His intuition was on target: John Ciddio and Pat Gutierrez were indeed a couple, and from that day on they visited almost every day. Ciddio was in his early thirties, of Italian and Chicano heritage, and was piercingly handsome. Gutierrez was shy, very cute, and not quite eighteen. Both were from the area, though Ciddio had lived in Denver, and had been in the Denver Mattachine Society in the mid-sixties. In San Francisco, he was a member of the Diggers, a radical Haight-Ashbury commune, and had been involved in the anti–Vietnam War movement. Ciddio credited the Mattachine Society with pulling his life together at a critical time, and he was honored and somewhat awestruck to meet its founder. The two couples became fast friends, and Ciddio and Hay formed a particularly strong bond. The Chicano couple ultimately became members of the Circle of Loving Companions, and, together with Harry and John, made a faltering start at a collective farm; they still own tools in common.

Ciddio, whose family had a farm in Velarde, just north of San Juan, became deeply involved in fighting the canal. Harry trained him to head the legal committee, and these two rural agitators cut such a strong — yet daringly queer — public presence that people began to refer to them as the "joto junta" ("joto" is Spanish for "fag"). Ciddio spoke for many when he acclaimed Harry's importance as a vital organizer and catalyst: "He was an instructor in how to bring power to bear, how to force an issue. He brought an awful lot of raw power to bear on the federal government."

In May, a married couple who were friends of Dorothy Kent came to help the elderly painter maintain the acreage. Phillip E. Blood and his wife, Joan, known to all as JB, were from the the blue-blood town of Groton, Massachusetts. Almost as soon as they stepped off the plane, the head of the joto junta inducted them into fighting the feds. Phillip Blood recalled that "Harry introduced himself and explained the situation, and told us that we were on the legal committee. Bam! That night we found ourselves on our way to a meeting." This sort of welcome seemed absurdly appropriate. "As we were following this truckload of gay guys on a dusty road under a full moon," said Phillip, "JB and I found ourselves laughing uncontrollably. We were realizing what our bridge-playing friends in Groton would think of us now."

In 1975, an unexpected twist of fate brought a crucial ally who was hired by the Bureau of Reclamation to write the social impact assessment of the environmental impact statement. This was their friend Sue-Ellen Jacobs, who several years earlier had been offered a consulting job with the Army Corps of Engineers. As a feminist and progressive, she wanted nothing to do with the military, but Harry advised her to reconsider. "He said, 'Well, let's take a look at this thing, because you may be able to find out what's happening on the inside,'" Jacobs recalled. "The next thing he said was 'We're going to have water problems here someday. We need to prepare.' As soon as I heard that, I decided to take the job." When that experience brought her the social impact assessment job, she did her most serious and detailed professional work, since the evaluation would have to stand the scrutiny of the locals, the feds, and possibly the courts.

A sad bell tolled in the midst of this political flurry. Harry's mother, bedridden with arthritis, suddenly died in Southern California. Harry was unable because of campaign commitments to leave for her memorial service, but the following month he dedicated to her memory the publication of a paper in *RFD* called "The Gays — Who Are We? Where Do We Come from? What Are We for?" Margaret, a genteel pioneer who had traveled around the world, died two weeks before her nintieth birthday.

When the crucial research on environmental and social impact began, Jacobs coordinated that large task. She was given only twenty days to conduct library, field, and community research, the last category of which involved almost three hundred interviews. Harry arranged and scheduled interviews in advance to maximize her efficiency. Still, she remembered the process as "nightmarish." Three nearly sleepless days were spent analyzing the statistics and writing the final report. "The night before it was over, I was still typing the draft. It would be copy-edited by Harry and someone else, and then typos were corrected. JB then typed the final draft. It was a real cooperative assembly line.

"At four in the morning, I finished writing the report and I crashed. Harry and John and the others compiled the final typed version and had a copy made at the university. Then I drove it ninety miles per hour to the Albuquerque airport. It had to make the deadline, otherwise I wouldn't get paid, and more importantly, it wouldn't qualify." Jacobs's report was sent to Senators Ted Kennedy and Scoop Jackson to prompt a congressional investigation into the way that government agencies had mis-handled the entire project.

The Bloods, the two gay couples, and Jacobs (following the completion of her report) now formed the core of the campaign. By this time, scores of articles had been written about El Llano in the state paper, the *New Mexican,* and Jacobs recalled that Harry used his legendary speaking powers throughout the mobilization, regularly addressing conservative farmers and getting them fired up to take on the government. "This was Harry, the bull-Harry, as a matter of fact. This was no 'Faerie' tripping the light fantastic. There was nothing that would identify Harry as anything less than the most masculine macho man." Hay insisted, however, on maintaining his gay identity, even when it confounded the area's macho local social structure. His favorite example of this arose when the straight Chicano community held a formal dance at the country club as a fund-raiser. As key campaigners, Harry and John were invited. "They told us we'd have a great time, and that they'd even get us some girls to dance with. 'But we want to dance with each other,' I told them. They shook their heads with great, confused reluctance and said, 'Well — maybe you can come next year.'"

In mid-January of 1976, New Mexico congressman Manuel Lujan, Jr. (later secretary of the interior under President George Bush), wrote to Harry that legislation was pending to prevent water diversion as called for in the original plan. "For all practical purposes," he wrote, "the canal is dead." The people had won the battle, and local hearings in subsequent months guaranteed the free flow of the Rio Grande. The results were more far-reaching than just saving the land in the immediate area. Recalled Jacobs, "A lot of people lost their jobs on a state and federal level. The investigation exposed a lot of lawbreaking. We caught them at it."

$$\triangledown$$

It didn't take long for Harry and John's attention to shift back to Gay Liberation. Harry was asked to serve on the newly forming National Gay Task Force, though he declined over an argument about the definition of the term *gay.* So instead, the Circle of Loving Companions kept their attentions local, returning to the concerns that had originally sent them there. They had already investigated a short-lived gay services center in Albuquerque and attended several gay events at the University of New Mexico, but found little organized activity in the early seventies. Hay and Burnside encountered numerous young men from the rural reaches who informed them that the gay bar scene was "so dismal they'd thought of throwing in the towel."

New Mexico, however, already had a reserved but established tradition of bohemians. Mabel Dodge, D.H. Lawrence, and Georgia O'Keefe had fostered artists' colonies in Taos and Santa Fe, and for several generations, wealthy gay men and lesbians were among those who settled in northern New Mexico and found the freedom to be more open than before. Coupled with tourism, this produced a rich local arts community. Annual visitors from New York, Chicago, and other large cities added to the discreet gay parlor society, though Harry often took exception to these people, who were, in his words, "following the advice of their psychiatrists and trying to 'get comfortable' with their gayness — which made me freeze!" (To Harry, "comfort" was an appalling compromise.) At the lower end of the social strata, violence against gays was commonplace; one night, John Ciddio was forced to watch at gunpoint as local rednecks beat up his lover Pat. Gay organizing in such an environment thus proved a severe challenge — one Harry could not resist.

Anti-gay beatings were the flashpoint that brought about Lambdas de Santa Fe, an early gay organization in northern New Mexico, in 1976. Santa Fe's straight-owned gay bar, the Senate, "incensed" the quiet gay locals, Harry said, when despite repeated gay-bashings in its parking lot, the bar owners refused to provide security. Lambdas de Santa Fe was formed to fight such problems and to provide a sense of community for lesbians and gay men in the area. The Circle of Loving Companions took on many duties in Lambdas, and in return John and Harry made many new friends. One was a tough-talking lesbian named Tibby, whose favorite expression was "Piss, crap, balls, and corruption!" Of Harry's unheard-of brand of confrontational activism, she succinctly declared, "Oh, is Harry balls!"

Another friend was Katherine Davenport, a lesbian feminist and Leftist who lived in the next Pueblo, Tesuque. Davenport worked in the media and later served as press coordinator for the first national Gay and Lesbian March on Washington in 1979. An imposing woman with a strong chin and long, parted hair, she recalled of meeting Harry that "it was the first time I had met somebody who was both gay and Leftist, which I considered myself. It was intriguing to be able to talk with someone who was so articulate about those issues, who had given their resolution some thought." Davenport wore a flat-brimmed hat low on her forehead, and Harry was one of the few people who could get the stern feminist to smile by dubbing her "Smokey Bear."

Lambdas de Santa Fe did its part to shake up the complacency of both the gay and the nongay communities of northern New Mexico. Lambdas had its own short-lived gay services center and sponsored Santa Fe's first gay ball at the La Fonda Hotel. Katherine Davenport and John Ciddio went on Santa Fe's "Joe Question" radio program with Harry, who described its host as "Joe Pine with a Mexican accent." They put up with gay-baiting to publicize the dance, which was "hugely successful," Hay noted. "People came from Las Cruces, 400 miles to the south; from Durango, Colorado, 300 miles to the north; from Roswell, 300 miles to the east on the Texas border." A Lambdas security team served to preclude any incidents, and Harry recalled that the feeling of fulfillment was so extraordinary that "nobody wanted to go home." In June of 1977, Lambdas held the first gay pride parade in Albuquerque. Because of threats of violence, Ciddio rode shotgun in his truck alongside the walkers. Harry, oblivious to this, spoke rousingly in a public park.

Lambdas's strongest public impression was made by its participation in the Santa Fe Fiesta, a massive annual arts fair. The group sponsored a booth which sold green chile tacos prepared by Ciddio, who was known for his cooking. Both the food and the decorations — hooped poles topped by streamers of colorful ribbons, which Harry researched as locally authentic — proved popular. They did great business, partly because the general public did not know the implication of the word "lambda," a term that became a popular gay symbol in the seventies. In fact, Santa Fe gays who did know the term made a point of staying several yards from the booth, for fear of guilt by association. At the end of the fair, winners of various prizes were announced over loudspeakers to the crowd of thousands, and certificates were given out from the stage. "Our booth won first prize," Katherine Davenport recalled. "It was for having the best food in combination with the best architecture. I went up and, right into the microphone, accepted the award on behalf of Santa Fe's gay and lesbian community. The mouths just dropped!" And some stomachs may have turned; John Ciddio recalled how "this hush fell — all these straight people realized they'd been eating tacos from gays!"

Though Harry proudly claimed success at bringing gay liberation to northern New Mexico, some residents felt otherwise. "I think he was twenty years ahead of his time in Santa Fe," suggested Tom Dickerson, a gay native New Mexican. "Harry and John stood out with their passionate views and active life, [though] Harry's radical views and confrontation stance just didn't go over. But he did kick up some shit." Their artist friend Alejandro Lopez agreed: "Most of the gay people who attended the meetings where Harry was present perceived him much like a bolt of lightning. He was a powerful, illuminating figure, but he seemed to appear from a realm quite different from theirs." This is not to say that his work was without impact; any gay liberationist helps enhance the climate of openness, and Harry was a great inspiration to many who met or heard him. Joan Blood, who remained Harry's close friend, sensed that as much as he brought ideas and missions to New Mexico, part of his purpose there was to absorb the restorative qualities of the region. "I always felt that Harry needed to be here for that time," she said.

Through the next two years, Harry and John began to draw Social Security. They eased into retirement and redoubled their reading, dialogue, and camaraderie within the Circle of Loving Companions. They occasionally visited Los Angeles, and in 1976, went with Ciddio and Gutierrez to investigate joining the gay collective at Wolf Creek in southern Oregon.

But they returned to New Mexico, and Harry continued to make music tapes, work on his studies, and tend to his "friendship responsibilities." After dinners and discussions with visitors, he'd offer the apple and pear wines he had made from Dorothy Kent's orchards. It was during this mellow and pastoral period that two young filmmakers named Peter and Nancy Adair filmed him and John for their ground-breaking documentary *Word Is Out,* which featured interviews with a carefully balanced group of gay men and lesbians, and received wide distribution. After Harry talked of his early memories of being different, and told of the beginning of the Mattachine Society, the camera cut away to the two white-haired lovers walking near the ditches, picking berries. "At one point I reached out and caught John's hand," Harry recalled. "I didn't think anything of it, because I do it all the time, but many people came up to us and said that was their favorite moment in the whole movie."

·13·

Radical Faerie

Remember, the serpent is still living in the Garden of Eden — only the heterosexual couple was expelled.
— Edward Carpenter, *Civilization: Its Cause and Cure*

In the Faerie circle, each man's story matched down to the subtlest details. The green meadow, the blue sky, and their very bodies seemed to glow as each shared early memories of feeling different. They had always been called sissies, but they always knew that they were somehow strong. And however many years they had been out of the closet — succeeding in business, in organizing, or in the bars — they felt that until they found the Faeries, something had been missing.

A carved talisman was passed around the circle, and where it stopped the group's undivided attention focused. A delicate black man wearing only a sparkling scarf and hiking boots took the talisman into the circle, and while walking slowly, addressed the ring of two hundred. "We Faeries need to stop saying, 'My consciousness is better than your consciousness.' That's heterosexist. No one person, no one group, no one ideology has the answer. You need a spirit."

It was the search for such a spirit that had led them all there, including Harry. A short time after he had gone into retirement, he was out again, and was part of the circle — in fact he had worked hard to call it into being. Privately, he regarded the Radical Faeries, as this new phenomenon of gay identity came to be known, to be a flowering of the Circle of Loving Companions, a joint quest for an adhesive gay comradeship. The Radical Faeries responded to the emptiness of both the straight establishment and assimilated gay society. Those who flocked to the Faerie gatherings had found little distinction between the two — to them, both were oppressive, shallow, and mired in such macho values as male competitiveness and dominance. Don Kilhefner, who with Hay helped found the Faeries, wrote that "gay activism has given us a little breathing space" from the stifling decades of oppression. It was the aim of the Faeries to find out what could grow in that new atmosphere.

The spirit seemed to flow through the circle. A heavy-set, gray-haired man wearing a floppy hat stepped into its midst and told of his career as a lawyer. "I deal every day with people who fight with each other — and they're all he-men. Policemen who abuse power. Judges. And because I am a Faerie, I feel great pain in that world." He struggled momentarily with his emotion, then continued. "All of those people are he-men. I come to my fellow Faeries because I need the love that I get here. And so many times in the gay world, I do not get that. I get the same kind of alienation that I get in the world of he-men."

A young, hardened street person from San Diego spoke. A long strand of bells stretching from his neck to his left sandal strap tinkled in the still mountain air when he walked. He offered the circle a verse from Jean Genet: "Faeries are a pale and motley race that flowers in the minds of decent folk. Never will they be entitled to broad daylight, to real sun. But remote in these limbos, they cause curious disasters which are harbingers of new beauty."

The crowd whooped and applauded. A voice called out, "Right on, Madame Genet!"

When the circle closed, the men came together, arm in arm, body to body, and a deep *om* began to sound, vibrating through the huddle of men, each more completely a living part of the circle. Male voices rose in humming harmony, and the sound gained momentum, like dozens of fingers on wineglasses. As they dispersed, flute music played as if from a sylvan sound track. Voices accompanying it sang: "Dear friends, queer friends, let me tell you how I'm feeling / You have given me such pleasure, I love you so."

▽

The Radical Faeries, like their mythological antecedents, cannot be easily defined or pinned down. A mixture of a political alternative, a counter-culture, and a spirituality movement, the Faeries became Harry's "second wind" as a major figure in gay culture and found him enmeshed in a new kind of organizing — a networking of gentle men devoted to the principles of ecology, spiritual truth, and, in New Age terms, "gay-centeredness."

The term "movement" could not contain what the Faeries were all about; in fact Harry carefully avoided that term at first. He saw the Faeries rather as a process or way of life. Just as he took to describing gays as "not-men," the Radical Faeries could be called a "not-movement." One early participant, David Liner, attempted to explain the phenomenon thus: "What Harry Hay did was give thousands of gay men the space to get over the most painful wounds that this society could possibly inflict on them." However they may be called, the affiliation of Faeries provided a deep-seated resolution to Harry's tenacious search for genuine gay community.

The new movement uprooted Harry's life and propelled it forward. He and John moved back to Los Angeles and traded old friendships for new ones, only to experience dramatic changes in the new as well. Harry's growing exposure as a political presence — thanks to the film *Word Is Out* and the book *Gay American History* — gave substance to his airy dream of a revolution of Faeries.

With a few key exceptions, the history of the Faerie movement follows lines strikingly parallel to the history of the Mattachine. As in the fifties, Harry entered the eighties on a high of defining, planning, and organizing with a close inner circle of intense individuals. In both periods, ideological and personal struggles posed severe, painful obstacles. Many of the issues, however, had changed — and so had Harry himself. He still maintains his involvement with the new movement and is regarded as its elder statesman.

The ethereal network of Radical Faeries is more than a decade old at this writing and has become international, with Radical Faeries gathering in Italy, Great Britain, Canada, and Australia. On a grass-roots level, it is at the forefront of the contemporary gay movement, a bright fringe with increasing news coverage and popular interest. The Faeries' positive, aerial aesthetic of bells and skirts seemed a predestined complement to the leather jackets of AIDS activists.

It was Harry's idea to couple the words *Radical* and *Faerie,* and the combination was carefully chosen. "Radical," in this case, meant "root" or "essence" as well as "politically extreme." The term "faerie" also had two meanings, one modern and one ancient. In recent times, "fairy" was a scornful epithet, but one that many gay men were now re-evaluating. (Parallels of this in other minorities include "Chicano" and "black," which both began as pejorative terms.) The ancient fairy, on the other hand, was an immortal, luminous nature spirit who danced in circles in the moonlight and did good deeds at whim. By combining these meanings, the Radical Faeries expressed one of their basic tenets, the oft-bandied notion that gays are a spiritual tribe.* Harry always used the antique spelling in what seemed an effective visual reminder that this was a new — or at least resurrected — meaning for the word. The potency of the image came partly from its mythic heritage. In selecting fairies as a role model for gays, he combined logic with inspiration to surpass the medieval Mattachines — to a pre-Christian time and beyond human limits.

Harry's thinking on this had evolved over several years, and reflected an obsession with homosexual semantics that had concerned him since the Mattachine days. In 1969, in a speech commemorating the 150th birthday of Walt Whitman, he had wrestled with the old problem of a lack of language to describe who gays *were* instead of who they were not. He wrote, "What had bedeviled Gays and Lesbians in particular was that, from the very first days of the re-invention of 'Gay Identity,' we kept trying to explain in STRAIGHT language ... and it kept coming out all wrong .. which is the Butch and which is the Femme? ... Which one does the dishes? ... Our explanations seemed to raise more questions than they answered." Over many years he considered a basic question: Since gays had always organized in reaction to the brutish forces of oppression, could not a newer, greater wave of the movement base itself on an essential nature of gay people?**

The following year, in his keynote address to the Western Homophile Conference on February 14, 1970, Harry coined a new phrase to explain gay people in new terms. "We are a minority of a common spirituality," he said, "[and] this shared commonality of outlook is a world-view totally unfamiliar to the accrued experience of our parent society. It is a view of the life experience *through a DIFFERENT WINDOW!*" The term he soon

---

* The anthropologist and mythographer W.Y. Evans Wentz collected essential information on fairies in his *Fairy-faith in Celtic Countries*, published in 1911. Hay found the book in the thirties and was particularly interested in the author's discussion of the pygmy theory of fairies, which posited that a race of small people known as the Faerie tribe had inhabited the British Isles, where the fairy faith persisted.

** It was this concern with the "gay essence" that brought his work great popular interest as well as earning him no small antagonism as a leader of the so-called "California essentialists" in the period when academia largely favored the model known as social constructionism for the gay identity, which asserted that gayness was societally produced rather than inborn. This was unfortunate, since Hay himself favored the social constructionist argument in many instances, especially his insistence that homosexual identity evolved in response to changing social conditions.

settled on — and with which he liberally sprinkled his discourse — was "Gay Window." At the end of that address, he slipped in the word "faerie" as a positive description of gay people. "Let the Spirit be betrayed, let coercion or opportunism bind us against our will, and PRESTO, like the Faeries of Folk-lore, suddenly we are no longer there." He sensed that this quality of quicksilver elusiveness explained why a gay movement had gone unorganized for so long, noting, "Our Faerie characteristic is our Homosexual Minority's central weakness." But, he added, "paradoxically, [it is] also the keystone to our enduring strength... We Homosexuals are moved to act ONLY when the call — as heard in our hearts — is a spirit call to freedom."

By the time he moved to New Mexico, Harry freely promoted the term "Faerie" as well as "Gay Window" and "Gay Consciousness," all with related theories. He pondered, researched, and started paper after paper about these ideas; often he was unable to get beyond the first page. But determined as always, he struggled to formulate some workable ideas and sent these attempts to dozens of correspondents.

Meanwhile, the gay public, from which Harry had retreated, was evolving. The counterculture wave of the sixties, with its open-minded spirit, hit gay people in the seventies, and the emerging gay community became a bubbling laboratory of names and identities. Long-familiar words such as "queer" and "queen" were tried out, along with newer ones like "groovy guy." The most enduring proved to be "gay," although in some regions, the militant "faggot" was a close second. Sometimes there was an air of competition; in San Francisco, gays known as the Sissies professed disdain for those they called STIFs — straight-identified faggots. Genderfuck, an outrageous form of costume combining exaggerated signals from male and female — such as a beard, bouffant hairdo, and glittering kabuki eye makeup all on one person — was employed as a cultural guerrilla attack on rigid sex roles. As the decade turned, genderfuck groups like the Cockettes and the Angels of Light spoofed political events with camp, consciousness-raising spectaculars in both San Francisco and New York.

At the same time, popular interest in non-Western spirituality was growing, as epitomized by the Beatles' pilgrimage to the Maharishi. This cultural drift affected gays too, and in 1976, writer Arthur Evans mingled radical politics and pagan models to begin "the faery circle" in his Haight Street apartment in San Francisco, where a dozen men explored the Dionysian tradition of "the magic of nature and the creative sexuality of gay men." The faery circle was part of Evans's research into the spiritual history of gay men, which he published as several articles in the gay journals *Out* and *Fag Rag* and in the book *Witchcraft and the Gay Counterculture* (1978).*

As the seventies wore on, "gay ghettos" sprouted in cities across America. These rapidly expanding gay neighborhoods were quickly seized upon by an army of entrepreneurs; both gay-owned and straight-owned ventures sought to exploit the new territory. The gay community became the gay market. So many gay businesses eventually formed that gay business councils formed around them.

The new-style resident of the gay ghetto was the "clone," a close descendant of the straight-identified faggot. In the sexually active age-bracket, the clone was athletic, square-jawed, and swinging. His trum-peted masculinity was almost caricatured: Muscles, mustache, mirrored "cop" sunglasses, bomber jacket, and boots became a veritable uniform for the scores of gay men so identified. (The gay painter Buddha John Parker christened this rampant new breed as "male impersonators.") Fashions, urban hot-spots, and, in that pre-AIDS decade, sex itself were steadily packaged by ever-creative marketers. Because their gay identities had been delayed, clones were perfect consumers, ever living out long-suppressed fantasies. This emphasized such a restless materialist outlook that many gay men complained that the chase from object to object tainted their ability to achieve intimacy in relationships. The dubious ideal of the clone was, in reality, only a high-profile minority of homosexuals; never-theless it was widely emulated.

Some clone-weary gays retreated from ghetto life. Big cities, the tradi-tional "end of the rainbow" for gay men, had for years offered anonymity and opportunity to those fleeing small towns and stifling straight society. But as the seventies progressed, a few began to leave the cities, some carried by the hippie back-to-the-land movement, some just burned out from urban excess. Though they hardly constituted an organized group, rural gays had established several collectives by the mid-1970s.

One of the most long-lasting was the RFD collective, founded in Iowa in 1974. When the countercultural *Mother Earth News* refused to run an ad with a gay reference, this seven-member group began a homespun publi-cation that sold for fifty cents: *RFD: A Magazine for Country Faggots*. While protesting the "adamant heterosexuality" of existing rural magazines, *RFD*

---

* Evans and Hay have never met, though both have acknowledged parallels and synchronicity in their independent work.

also provided recipes, poetry, farming information, and pictures for isolated gay people living on the land. *RFD* took its name from the postal designation Rural Free Delivery, but extended it every issue to "Really Feeling Divine," "Raving Flamer's Diary," "Rabbits, Faggots and Dragonflies," and further amusing titles. The contributors and readers of *RFD* overlapped substantially with those gays who would soon call themselves Faeries; gatherings of rural gay men were already advertised in its pages during the seventies. However, the favored term at *RFD* was "faggot."

The piece Harry sent to *RFD* in 1975, which he dedicated to his mother, was the first of many of his writings that *RFD* would publish. Poetically written, it discussed gayness as a genetic mutation difficult for the individual but ultimately beneficial to the group. "To be a true homosexual," he proposed, "is to be ... put at odds with home, school, and society ... We are so *other* that we have to learn early how to protect our very survival." He finally called for "Gay love, Gay life, Gay vision, and Gay creative self-fulfillment." His conclusion that gayness lay in "our stubbornly perverse genes" elicited a lively commentary from the publishing collective. One member, Carl Wittman, provided the most supportive response. Revealing the depth of Harry's challenge, he wrote, "I yearn for such words. I am embarrassed to use them. Who talks of vision, light, splendor and strength? It certainly would not do, not on Castro Street or in the pages of *Fag Rag* ... The notion of foundling, growing up a foreigner in family and culture, and returning to the larger whole — this notion I put on gently, like a new robe, wondering if it becomes me." He found that the concepts in Harry's essay "fit," though Wittman still expressed some doubts. "But politically, is it misleading? Where are my hard-won ideas about separatism, confrontation, group consciousness? Isn't it a bit spiritual, ignoring the real needs to unite politically? I reread it and decide not... Yes, brothers from New Mexico; Thank you."

Harry held the affirmation from Wittman especially dear. Carl Wittman was a Red Diaper baby who had grown up to be national secretary of Students for a Democratic Society in the sixties, and was highly visible and effective in the anti–Vietnam War and civil rights movements. Wittman became a Gay Liberation celebrity for his *Gay Manifesto,* which he wrote a year before the Stonewall riot and which was widely published and read. Hay and Wittman's interest in a political analysis of the gay movement were close, and they later developed a friendship and correspondence.

The following year, 1976, Harry refined these ideas even further in a position paper called "Gay Liberation: Chapter Two," which he regarded as his most important piece of writing and as a central catalyst of the Radical

Faerie movement. This self-described "position paper" was inspired by a bitter exchange of letters he read in the alternative press between a young gay Leftist and his straight comrades in the Pacific Northwest. Distressed that struggles between gays and the Left continued twenty-five years after his own separation from the C.P., Harry wrote a letter to Faygele Singer, the embattled gay Leftist, hoping to comfort him with "newer levels of Marxist perceptions which were emerging in me as gay values." Harry used personal experiences to illustrate his points, and halfway through, recalled his peers in high school manipulating their opposite-sex dates like objects in order to "score." This he contrasted to his secret fantasy of finding a lover who was "a wondrous being with whom I would always share as I shared with myself, not subject to object, but subject to subject." As he wrote this, he realized he had made a breakthrough. "I was just beside myself with excitement," he recalled. "I ripped the letter out of the typewriter and began to write the position paper."

"Chapter Two" presents a new theory about gay people and politics. As background, Hay traced the development of models of modern thought, from the Cartesian–Newtonian model of a limited universe that man could control, to the twentieth-century view, which, though modified, still survives in most social sciences and refuses to allow for the existence of gay people. "Add or subtract, GO or NO-GO, (if you're not a man you're a substitute woman— what else is there?)" was Hay's characterization of the dominant mode of thinking, which he called binary, or subject–object, thinking. But the style Hay promoted, which he called analog thinking, factors in relativity and other expansive dimensions of comprehending the universe. He proposed that it had an attendant "subject–subject relationship" that was similarly more dimensional. He also posited that this was inherent to all gay people, arising from the egalitarian bond of love and sex between two similars, but it went on to pervade all the relationships of a gay person — even relationships with things not human, such as nature, craftsmanship, or ideals. "Humanity must expand its experience of thinking of another *not as object*— to be used, to be manipulated, to be mastered, to be CONSUMED— *but as subject*— as another like himher self, another self to be respected, to be appreciated, to be cherished."

With Einstein's famous warning in mind, that "the unleashed power of the atom has changed everything save for our modes of thinking, and we thus drift toward unparalleled catastrophes," Hay then called for mass change in thinking. He proposed that the qualities of noncompetitiveness and creativity, characteristics often observed in gay people, made gays naturally suited to guide this change in thinking:

Natural selection, early on in human evolution, set into the evolving whirl a small percentage of beings who appeared to counter-balance a number of prevalent characteristics of the emerging human conformity. Humanity, thus, would be wise to finally give consideration to these deviants in their ranks ... to begin to grant the GAYS the peace and growing space they will need to display and to further develop in communicable words and in models of activity, the "gift" — the singular mutation we GAYS have been carrying so unfalteringly and preserving so passionately, even over the not infrequent centuries of despair and persecution.

To Harry, this "Gay gift" was a difference in consciousness that could introduce new ideas necessary for human survival. In the fifties, he had argued that in the ancient world, it was the gays who passed on certain craft skills with greater devotion than heterosexual family lineages, whose blood devotions surpassed all other; this sort of role in favor of cultural evolution, always shifting with changing social needs, was, he suggested, the biosocial reason for gays — and could be used as their political justification. Hay concluded his essay by calling on "Gay Liberation Faeries" to "reassemble" and help society at large "learn to respect us precisely for our behavioral and perceptual differences ... [then] the laws and customs favoring us with Space and Freedom ... will take care of themselves."

This paper served as more than one milestone for Harry. Aside from achieving a theory for gay identity — a goal toward which he had long worked — it showed a rare distancing from his past political ideas. By moving beyond the "binary" basis of Marxist dialectical thinking (where opposites of thesis and antithesis produce a new truth), Harry was able to release some of his loyalty to Marxist formulas. His paper bemoaned that Marx and Engels, who he said were of "exemplar integrity," had been born too soon to reorient their theories in the light of twentieth-century discoveries — an oblique and polite bow away from his idols who, like so much of the rest of the world, had shut out gays.*

---

* Hay claimed for the record that his only influences for this work were Konrad Lorenz's books dealing with ethology, particularly the development from individual consciousness to group consciousness, as well as various of his readings in archeology and anthropology. An early New Age book called *The Morning of the Magicians,* published in 1960 by French authors Louis Pauwels and Jacques Bergier, also, he admitted, influenced his thinking. Hay insisted that despite similar terminology, his thinking was not related to that of Martin Buber or Simone de Beauvoir.

Harry's ideas caught the imagination of many who found in the concept of subject–subject consciousness a deeply felt yet unspoken truth. The argument that there existed a gay reservoir of untapped potential was refreshing to those for whom ghetto liberation had grown hollow. Continuing his tendency to take up the baton of such thinkers as Walt Whitman and Edward Carpenter, Harry posed that homosexuals carried an intermediary consciousness and that once this was made clear, a new era would begin.

Hay submitted his paper for publication to *RFD*. "They rejected it as gobbledygook," he shrugged to a friend in a letter, and indeed, his eccentric use of mixed type faces with italics and capital letters could be visually wearying, as was his insistence on writing "subject–SUBJECT" to emphasize his new idea. Carl Wittman, again the dissenter, was fascinated with these ideas and talked with Harry about developing them together. He hoped to set more clearly on paper what he once expressed as seeing "that language reflected in Harry's sharp eyes." Though they never got around to rewriting "Chapter Two," Harry continued to send copies to friends and colleagues, and promoted its ideas at every opportunity.

▽

Harry's most receptive listeners were two Californians, Don Kilhefner of Los Angeles and Mitch Walker of Berkeley. By 1978, along with Harry, they formed the cabal that would conjure the Radical Faerie movement. Since Hay was then sixty-six, Kilhefner thirty-nine, and Walker twenty-five, they spanned the generations. Their personalities held strong parallels but also striking differences.

Kilhefner was known for shouting down anti-gay bigots at public events but when it came to friends, he mildly addressed everyone as "Toots." He had grown up in an Amish-Mennonite community in Pennsylvania, left at seventeen, and went to Howard University, where he studied cultural history. He came out at Howard and also became active in anti–Vietnam War campaigns and in the Student Nonviolent Coordinating Committee of the civil rights movement. Following graduation came a stint in Ethiopia with the Peace Corps, then a move west to U.C.L.A. By the late sixties he was involved in the Peace and Freedom Party and carried Mao Tse-tung's *Little Red Book*. With Morris Kight (also in the Peace and Freedom Party), Don led the main activities of the Gay Liberation Front, which lasted from late 1969 to 1971.

Dedicated, righteous, and introverted, Kilhefner preferred to work behind the scenes and leave the spotlight to Kight. In time, GLF's anti-establishment anarchical tenets gave way to the practical concerns of nonprofit organizational service for the disenfranchised, and GLF evolved into the L.A. Gay Community Services Center, which became a prototype for such institutions. Kilhefner was its first executive director. He also founded Van Ness House, an alcohol recovery facility for gay men and lesbians. His earthy persona and hippie apparel of jeans, bushy beard, and wire-frame glasses masked his managerial prowess, but within a few years, Kilhefner was administering millions of dollars in grants when the Center moved from its ramshackle Victorian residence of 1614 Wilshire Boulevard to a building it now owns on Highland Avenue in Hollywood.

As it matured, the Center (renamed, after a contentious struggle, the Gay and Lesbian Community Services Center), sought the support and involvement of rich gays; many felt that it abandoned activism for a slick hybrid of social work, public relations, and bureaucracy. Disheartened by this rapid assimilation, Kilhefner took a leave of absence from his post as executive director in 1976. A connoisseur of various human-potential movements, he spent a year in retreat with Baba Ram Dass (author of *Be Here Now*), the psychedelic guru incarnation of American psychologist Richard Alpert.

Kilhefner wanted time to reassess the movement. "I was concerned that the gay movement had become all about assimilation into the mainstream culture," he told *The Advocate* in 1987. "The idea was, you come out and the journey ends. The growth stops. For me that didn't make sense. I didn't know what it meant to be gay. Something that was missing from this gay identity was a consciousness, a sense of spirit."

The third of the Radical Faerie triad was Mitch Walker. From a middle-class Jewish family in Hawthorne, a suburb of Los Angeles, Walker studied psychology at U.C.L.A. in the late sixties but did not integrate his studies with his coming out until a 1971 transfer to U.C. Berkeley. There he focused on Jungian psychology, but as well as academia, Walker was influenced by the turned-on-and-tuned-in gay scene in the Bay Area, and his persona became long-haired, Leftist, and quintessentially Berkeley. Walker's proposed Master's thesis at Lone Mountain College was a gay sex guide balanced with historical anecdotes and psychological reassurance. This was approved, then rejected by his faculty committee* but was published by Gay Sunshine Press in 1977 as *Men Loving Men: A Gay Sex Guide and*

---

* Walker's replacement thesis was a Jungian treatise called "Gay Depth Psychology."

Consciousness Book. In his book, he expressed frustrations similar to Harry's regarding the Gay Liberation movement. "Anybody who feels they're gay," he wrote, "has a hell of a time ... with little encouragement and much resistance — even active hostility — within our so-called gay community."

If Harry Hay was the homophile Father and Don Kilhefner the Stonewall Son of the Faerie trinity, Mitch Walker was inescapably the New Age Holy Ghost. Following his studies, he applied himself to become a shaman, a modern embodiment of the traditional role about which Edward Carpenter had written. Walker described his initiation into shamanism as landing him in "a bizarre psychotic realm ... a shadow, a gleam of light, the kitchen, might all suddenly ... become evil."* He also regarded himself as being "forced into my vision," and he persevered with his protracted ordeal, but it rendered him barely able to sustain himself — he worked in a factory gluing the eyes on beanbag frogs and rarely socialized.

A regimen of Humbolt brownies and meditations at the underground pool of the Ritch Street Baths intensified Walker's already intense personality. What was left was a stern gay version of Carlos Castaneda who blended magic, psychology, and Gay Liberation. Often silent for hours at a time in group settings, Walker was ceremonious and keen in private conversation. He could be witty and insightful, and some of his readers and friends regarded him as the new gay messiah, a post-Stonewall seer. Others, however, considered him a mind-tripper with an air of psychological supersophistication and mystical superiority.

Walker learned of Harry through a mutual friend named Matthew Rush, who had lived in New Mexico. Rush and Walker met at a slide and lecture series given in 1976 by Arthur Evans. There Rush asked Walker what he did. "I work with the spirit and I'm a gay spirit worker and I'm a gay shaman and that's what I do," Walker answered. To this, Rush replied, "You sound just as kooky as someone else I know. You should meet him. He talks just like you, and he's really old. He lives in New Mexico." For Walker, hearing those words was "like a light going on." He immediately got Hay's address and began a correspondence that lasted almost a year. To his delight he found that they were both "working on the same stuff. When I wrote him and he wrote back, we were already so much in harmony that it was like meeting a brother, a twin."

---

* For more on Walker's account, see his essay "Becoming Gay Shamanism" in *Visionary Love.*

This temperamental compatibility finally compelled Walker to buy a plane ticket to New Mexico. He flew out and stayed for most of February, 1978. The beauty of the Kent Compound and the vicinity charmed him. Harry served as tour guide, taking him, among other places, to the part of Tsankwe Pueblo where Enki told him the queer people had lived. "He took me to this mound of pottery shards that he said was the queer mound, and shoveled around with his hands and pulled out a few little shards and gave them to me. He said I had to promise to bring someone else to this place, and give them a little piece of one of these pots, too ... It was wonderful." Walker understood Harry's rarefied language of Marxist historical theory as applied to gays, and encouraged him to expound. They recorded twelve hours of their discussions on history, mythology, and the meaning of gay consciousness, which Walker proposed to transcribe and edit, possibly for a pamphlet. Harry had heard of women calling retreat conferences in the mountains of New Mexico, and suggested they call a gay male conference based on the ideas they'd been discussing. John Burnside observed a "tremendous excitement and great affection" developing between Harry and Mitch.

Meeting Walker was a critical link in Harry's development of a new kind of gay movement. In some respects, Walker's position was analogous to that of Rudi Gernreich in the Mattachine: Walker and Hay formed the "society of two" that grew into the Radical Faeries. The mythic, hidden aspects of gay identity that they had studied separately suddenly converged, with a greatly increased current. Personal passions may have blended with the political ideals that united them — particularly on Harry's side. Walker commented in 1989, "I wouldn't have put it in those terms, but that's probably the truth. Historically, love is often involved in these things. Certain passions cross, and with us gay people, they are intertwined with our politics." When he boarded the plane back to California, Walker felt a solid connection had been made and that "we were well on the way to starting the Faerie movement."

Don Kilhefner had met Harry twice, once in Los Angeles and once while passing through New Mexico, when they had a long talk. In December of 1973, he wrote to Harry, "The visit was so important to my thinking that I have had an idea buzzing in my head ever since. I would like to do an extensive taped interview with you concerning the Homophile Movement (second priority) and the development of Gay Consciousness (first priority) ... Our gay brothers and sisters need to hear your ideas and share in your observations."

They did not begin a sustained relationship, however, until after a third meeting, in May of 1978 at Lama, Ram Dass's retreat just north of Taos, where John Burnside had been invited to show his Symmetricon. At that encounter Hay gave Kilhefner a copy of his subject–subject position paper. Once Kilhefner returned to Los Angeles, where he lived in a yoga commune, he exchanged a steady flow of letters and phone calls with Harry and John, often addressing them "Beloved Brothers," and surrounding his signature by fluttering hearts. Kilhefner valued "the talking connection" with Harry more than what he got from Harry's writings, but he felt that Hay was the first fellow traveler he had met in a long search for a new perspective on Gay Liberation, and he was deeply excited. He even inquired into the job market in Santa Fe, suggesting that he might move there if Harry and John could not bring themselves to move west again.

In the fall of 1978, Kilhefner was asked by therapist Betty Berzon to participate in the annual conference of the national Gay Academic Union. Berzon, then chair of G.A.U., arranged for Kilhefner, Walker, and Hay to lead a workshop titled "New Breakthroughs in the Nature of How We Perceive Gay Consciousness." Harry and John traveled to Los Angeles for the conference, held at the University of Southern California that November. An overflow of more than fifty gay and lesbian academics from around the country sat in a circle, passed a talisman, and, instead of discussing any academic theory, were invited to drop the academic mask and share personal, subjective concerns. (Mitch Walker, flaunting his rebelliousness and his personal tastes in enlightenment, scandalized Kilhefner by lighting a joint and passing that.) Their debut in the G.A.U. forum was a success, and afterward Hay told Walker that with "this magnificent organizer," Don Kilhefner, they were now a society of three. Their dreamed-of conference could now proceed.

Walker wrote several letters to Harry complaining that the financial demands of the straight world were cramping his gay spirit work, and pleaded with Hay to hurry up with his plans for a retreat where they could all live together. Harry reassured Mitch that he would not have much longer to wait. Indeed, the Circle of Loving Companions, including John Ciddio and Pat Gutierrez, was growing restless in New Mexico, and the promising work with Kilhefner sweetened the prospect of moving. Once Kilhefner joined the Circle, they sealed the decision to move to Los Angeles. Phil and Joan Blood sadly heard the news that Harry and John would be leaving their paradise by the Rio Grande.

Though Walker was in Berkeley, Kilhefner was in L.A., and Harry and John were in San Juan, a group identity congealed via continued calls and letters. The three radicals made a "three-sided square," according to Walker, with John Burnside "hovering around the edges," helping out as needed.

Kilhefner, again working at the Gay and Lesbian Community Services Center as education director, developed a course called "Gay Voices and Visions." A sort of primer on gay consciousness and spirituality, the class was a combination of a traditional seminar (with Walt Whitman, Edward Carpenter, Walker, Hay, and other authors on the syllabus) and a touchie-feelie encounter group with massage, personal sharing, and exercises for retrieval of childhood memory. The phone wires between L.A. and New Mexico buzzed with descriptions of the breakthroughs and excitement the course elicited from its students. This was like gasoline to the flickering hopes of Harry, Don, and Mitch that this new gay consciousness could be organized, that Gay Liberation was indeed approaching a new chapter.

▽

In the early spring, while investigating a site for the conference, Kilhefner came across a prospect in *The Advocate* when he found an ad inviting gays to meditate at the Sri Ram Ashram, a spiritual retreat in the 5000-foot-high desert near Benson, Arizona. It seemed perfect for their needs, so he contacted the owner, an American who went by the name of Swami Bill. Swami Bill sent Don a plane ticket, so Don flew east and Harry and John drove west from San Juan.

When they converged there, forty miles off the main highway, Sri Ram Ashram greeted them like an oasis. The entrance led through a landscaped garden with a fountain to a complex of buildings surrounded by shade trees, beds of flowers, and statuary. By the pool (spring-fed and Olympic size), scenes from the Buddha's life were painted on a low stucco wall. There was a meditation tent carpeted in orange-and-salmon parachute silk. Ponds of carp nestled in beautifully kept emerald lawns.

Harry took a quick distaste for the owner and discouraged the others from using the place. Kilhefner, however, persevered and by the end of the following day he was arranging for Sri Ram Ashram to serve as the site of the conference. Harry finally decided he too felt that this was the perfect place, and momentum for the conference increased.

He and John continued west to Los Angeles to look for a house and to visit as guest lecturers during the "Voices and Visions" class. Walker joined them, and the four incipient Faeries stayed in Kilhefner's one-bedroom apartment in Hollywood. These quarters were already small, and in the cramped space, friction between Walker and Hay, which had briefly surfaced during Walker's visit to San Juan, was aggravated. Much of the tension stemmed from personality differences. Walker had grown up fatherless, and Harry's physical and psychic embodiment of a gay patriarch had a strong effect on him. He regarded Harry as a man of intellectual and spiritual power, and sometimes spoke of himself as the heir to that power.

Walker identified their differences as ideological — based on their differing stance regarding psychologial theory. Jungian analytic psychology was central to Walker's worldview. Harry had a long-standing disdain for the entire subject, and had never factored it into his thinking, but to Walker it provided crucial explanations. He viewed psychological awareness as vital to the political process, and applied it to the gay movement. The younger man also worried that Harry's tendency to dominate decision making threatened the nascent Faerie movement with its ideal of collective process. In Walker's view, the solution was that Harry should convert to psychoanalytic thinking — and change parts of his personality.

The psychologist–shaman attempted to convey this one afternoon when he and Hay strolled to Wattles Park, a quiet garden at the base of the Hollywood Hills, not far from Kilhefner's apartment. Taking the offensive, Walker hammered at Hay for his refusal to make such a conversion and accused him of being incapable of ethical leadership because he "projected his shadow." (In Jungian parlance this refers to seeing in others the qualities suppressed in the conscious self.) Walker saw in Jungianism "a new moral imperative" that everyone must adopt. "Once psychology was invented," he explained later, "you could no longer be neutral. It's ethically true for everyone. You must not project your shadow unconscious anymore, the way humans always have."

From Harry's perspective, the encounter was less a holistic counseling session than a surprise attack. "He wanted to talk to me about my 'leadership complex,'" Hay recalled. "And I didn't understand, because as far as I know I don't have one. He was rather rough and he insisted for about half an hour. He said, 'You have it and you've got to face it.' I felt threatened and frightened." Indeed, Harry's self-image was of a person who "walked with others," and he made a point of correcting anyone who called him a leader. According to Walker, Hay lashed back with dramatic curses and threatened to leave Los Angeles and their work. Harry ran from the park and called Kilhefner, who immediately left his desk at the center to attend to the situation. Only his soothing intervention prevented Harry and John from leaving the new movement right then. But the conflict between psychology and politics was to be a continuing tension.

During that visit, Hay and Kilhefner secured a home that could fit the entire Circle of Loving Companions. It was a 1920s house with three bedrooms located on the fraying eastern edge of Hollywood, on a quiet street called La Cresta Court. There was even a workshop and a garden. After considering it, Walker decided not to move in. Harry and John returned to New Mexico to spend several months packing. Kilhefner moved in, and so did John Ciddio and Pat Gutierrez, but Kilhefner and Ciddio took such a strong dislike to one other that the Chicano couple moved to a separate residence.

By July, Kilhefner joined Harry and John at the Kent compound where they packed a rented moving truck so full that it sank into the soft dirt road. When that truck, driven by Kilhefner, and their own small truck hit the road, they parodied the citizens band radio craze by calling themselves Big Faerie and Li'l Faerie. Barely had they set their boxes onto the porch of the La Cresta Court house when the dizzying demands of producing the Radical Faerie conference overtook them. The boxes stayed there, untouched till that winter.

Each member of this core group took on a specialized role: Harry handled the political duties; John was concerned with logistics and mechanics (though in matters of decision he usually backed Hay); and Walker was the spiritual leader. The manager, Don Kilhefner, was prized for his budgetary and administrative genius. He poured his efforts into the Circle with gusto, and compared the new movement to the high-spirited early days of GLF work.

The organizers were uncertain that the undertaking could break even financially, and their hopes (they needed at least twenty-five enrollees) depended on spreading the word through an effective flier. It was at this point that Harry coined the term "Radical Faerie," and he always referred to this as "the Call" that started the Radical Faerie movement, much as he credited his 1948 and 1950 prospectuses with starting the homophile movement. (A biographical sheet he wrote later said that he "invented the concept and called into being" the first gathering and ensuing movement. Though others would argue that he was one link in the chain, he saw himself as the blacksmith.)

The flier was stunning. Bruce Reifel, who had created fliers for GLF's Gay-Ins and gay dances a decade earlier, created an image of a nude Adonis watching a huge sun rising over a desert rock. "A Call to Gay Brothers" breathed across the masthead in cursive script, and below that bold type announced "A SPIRITUAL CONFERENCE FOR RADICAL FAERIES." Slated for Labor Day weekend, the conference promised a blend of the spiritual, the radical, and the "faerie" — and to further the tease, the reverse side quoted New Age politician Mark Satin, Aleister Crowley, and Harry himself. It suggested a synthesis of spirituality and politics "beyond Left and Right," and assured gays that they had a place in the "paradigm shift" to the New Age. All that was said of the secret location was that it was "Don Juan country near Tucson." The flier was sent to gay and Leftist bookstores, schools, gay community centers, and health food stores, and the three-sided square waited anxiously.

▽

Some 220 men recognized themselves in the flier and showed up at Sri Ram Ashram, which could accommodate at most seventy-five. That space was found for everyone symbolizes the freewheeling magic of that week-end. The gay men who trickled in from all directions had no idea what to expect. As they registered, they were warned of the dangers of midday sun and scorpions. Many were progressives, most were feminists, and, at least for the weekend, all were Radical Faeries. The definition of what that meant seeped in through bits of jargon; no "workshops" were scheduled, for example, only "Faerie circles." Faeries joining in a ring was, after all, a known magic formula. People chatted about times the word "fairy" had been hurled pejoratively at them, or about the secret fascination they'd had with fairies. New friends would huddle excitedly, staring at one another in wonder, as if their eyes had opened for the first time, and repeating the word as the appropriateness of the identity sunk in. "Faeries." When one urbanite searched for an electric outlet to plug in his travel iron — to keep his trouser pleats sharp there amid the sleeping bags and desert — someone cracked, "Now *that's* a Faerie!"

At the first Radical Faerie circle that evening, a spontaneous theme of paganism emerged. Invocations were offered to spirits; blessings and chants rose and fell. Some people shook rattles or clusters of tiny bells. Harry, whom many recognized from the film *Word Is Out,* gave a short welcome and presented his remarks about subject–subject consciousness. He called on the crowd to "throw off the ugly green frogskin of hetero-imitation to find the shining Faerie prince beneath."

For listeners who had felt a lifelong proscription against being truly themselves, this message was profoundly moving. Will Roscoe, who first met Hay that night, recalled, "The scene was dramatic. Harry wore a caftan and appeared statuesque in the twilight. When he made his call, many of us cried." Stu Szidak, who recognized Hay from the GLF days in Los Angeles, agreed. "Harry Hay worked his magic that night."

– 265 –

After a slide presentation called "Erotic Consciousness" by Christopher Larkin,* the strangers in the desert night found places to sleep, mostly on the lawn. Of that first night, one person wrote that "there was much giggling and some lovemaking, and hardly anyone slept because we were excited about the prospect of being together."

The following morning more people arrived to find a new Faerie aesthetic blooming: cosmetic rainbows trailed from eyelids, past mustaches and around nipples; feathers, beads, and bells dangled everywhere; any clothing worn was for shade or to pad a seat. Modesty was quietly banished. Everyone felt a deeper transformation. To Fritz Frurip, "It was lovely to see so many people shedding clothes as they shed anxieties and fears and found themselves among friends who thought as they did. There was no one around except gay men. We were the society. We weren't meeting in a building outside of which were heteros. We were the society, and we were beginning to experience what it was like to be the majority and make the rules." Stories of growing up gay were told with such fervor that the circle did not realize it had gone hours over schedule. Mitch Walker, described by Mark Thompson as "the man with the laugh in his voice," gave an invocation to "turn everything upside down" and invite acceptance of the spirit world.

At a certain point, indefinably but undeniably, the conference "clicked." There are many descriptions of the change that occurred — from a spirit descending to a veil being torn away from the moon. Time and physics had somehow altered, and one partipant noted, "I recognize the symptoms. I'm on a four-day acid trip — without the acid!" Harry later described the phenomenon, which became a regular dynamic of Faerie gatherings, as a "collective gear-shift of consciousness, which galvanized us as a group. That consensus of shared consciousness subject-to-subject was the doorway we went through, and once through it, you knew you had changed irrevocably." Walker, in Jungian language, called it "creating a crucible for the alchemical transformation." The practiced shaman had a somewhat matter-of-fact attitude about the transformation of those at the conference: "I think our plan was to set up a milieu and provide a direction and structure. But you can't make the alchemical process happen, you can only set up an environment and

---

* Larkin was a wealthy gay man who produced the 1974 gay-themed feature film *A Very Natural Thing* and later, under the name Purusha, a coffee-table book on fist-fucking called *The Divine Androgyne.*

hope. It worked. I don't think it was spectacular. We all worked hard to make it work and it worked."

Circles overlapped one another, finely tuned sensitivities harmonized at all levels of interaction, and mealtimes were blissfully thrown off by hours. A blackboard served anyone who wanted to propose a topic for a circle and invite others to join. The tremendous variety of topics soon scrawled on it included a native desert plant walk, politics of gay enspiritment, gay publications, massage, a guided orgy, rape and violence, ritual makeup, Celtic and English country dancing, healing-energy, auto-fellatio, silly sissies, myths of male bonding, and nutrition. The word "conference" was quickly rejected as "too hetero" and replaced by the word "gathering." Impulsive dances frequently broke out, and men confessed that the sullen, macho standards of the gay ghettos had inhibited their dancing impulses for years. Suddenly they were able to dance their true dance.

The idea of faerie circles or faerie rings has mythical precedent, but Hay, Kilhefener, and Walker quickly imbued it with a political ethic. A faerie circle, they explained, had no head, no foot, no hierarchy. The form seemed to harness goodwill, candor, and humor; for many, it proved to be the most egalitarian way they had ever conducted business.

The event that everyone remembered most from that first gathering was a spontaneous ritual involving mud. This came about the second morning, when someone said, "I have this fantasy about taking water out there and making mud — and seeing what happens." About fifty naked Faeries carried gallons of water several hundred yards from the ashram and mixed it with the fine clay dust. Situated in the womblike hollow of a dry river bed, they seemed to be possessed by tribal instincts as they covered themselves and each other with the red mud. Neal Twyford, one of the participants, recalled, "It was centered around a guy who was lying down and had an erection — everyone built it up with mud until they'd created a huge earth-phallus on this earth-covered man, and put laurel leaves around his head." The man was lifted above everyone's heads as an "om" rumbled out of the huddled, mudded circle. A harmony and ecstasy built and seemed to go on and on. Intense dancing broke out, and it, too, seemed endless. Near the ashram, as they hosed each other off in a prolonged sensual baptism, many murmured, "Scraping off the ugly green frogskins."

There was an uncanny feeling of power in the mud ritual. Twyford puzzled, "For years I've been asking myself, 'Why was that little event so powerful?' I remember looking around and saying, 'Holy shit, we're in another world. We're back in time...'" Similarly, John Kyper wrote in *RFD*,

"It evoked a sense of timelessness that I sometimes feel during especially satisfying lovemaking, that I am in touch with something thousands and thousands of years old." Haunting photographs taken by Allen Page and Mark Thompson seem to glimpse just that: a different tribe from another time. Harry, Mitch, and Don were all at another circle, but John Burnside partook of the earthy rapture.

On the last night of the gathering, a more planned ritual also had a powerful effect. Fritz Frurip, a participant who had studied theology at Notre Dame, recalled, "I learned more about ritual that [night] than I had in five years of study." A slowly building procession crescendoed to a cacophony. In the thick of the cathartic howling and drum beating, some people reported that a black bull wandered calmly into the midst of the group and stood with the evening star just over its shoulder. Some saw this as a visitation, a vision straight from some ancient frieze. Others doubted that such an animal could have been in the area at all. Bull or not, everyone reported having undergone a transcendent high, and, as the culmination of an extraordinary sequence, many found themselves seriously moved. As gay people, most had renounced spiritual beliefs because religion had renounced them, but the spiritual jolt of the gathering caused them to undergo a complete internal re-evaluation.

On the last night there was a performance of the Symmetricon. Its glowing mandalas flowered and tumbled like the rare blossoms of ecstatic feeling and expanded consciousness that comprised this shared time. Harry made a few closing remarks as the new comrades spent a last night together. The following morning, Frurip saw "simple brothers, washed clean of the night's faerie glamour, stronger and more serene." Still, no one wanted to return to the world, which demanded their relinquishing the magic they had found. One car loaded with Faeries overheated while still hours of desert highway from the Tucson airport. "We did a fairy circle standing around the open hood," one recalled. "The car started up perfectly and we all made our flights."

▽

"That a movement came out of it was a shock," Harry said a decade later. The outcome of the gathering, he urged at the time, should be a matter of personal and collective re-evaluation of Gay Liberation, a "digging-in to our own lives." But when the La Cresta group returned to Los Angeles, a movement pursued them; everyone wanted to continue whatever it was that had gotten started. "Faeries kept calling us," Harry remembered, "saying, 'We just can't stand not being together.'" Besides the hunger for

Faerie company and the desire to recast the movement, many wanted to discuss the oppression that they had "tuned out" before their visionary experience at the gathering. This problem of reorienting to the straight world at the conclusion of a gathering became so common it was known as "re-entry trauma syndrome."

Most of the newfound Faeries felt wildly enthusiastic about this new vision of gay identity and what it could mean for the entire world. Simultaneously, they hesitated to share it too much, feeling protective of the luminous, newborn idea. Instead of continued outreach, a Faerie circle formed in Los Angeles and met Fridays at the La Cresta house, now known as "Faerie Central." The group decided that half of its time would be devoted to serious work — discussions about gay and Faerie identity — and half to recreation. The English country circle dancing that Carl Wittman had taught at the gathering was seized upon as the perfect recreational activity, and early Faerie circles opened with circle dances. As attendance rose, the group moved to the First Presbyterian Church in West Hollywood, but when the moon was full they met in the olive grove atop the hill at Barnsdall Park.

These urban "gatherettes" faced different problems from the large rural convergences. Some members felt unable to arrive at the new levels of ecstasy they had attained before — just divesting the day's straight-world traumas took most of the time. The self-creation that came so easily in a rural setting was harder to find in the city. For example, though the word "faerie" had at first been used experimentally and tentatively, increasing amounts of time were devoured by defining and exploring the term until it became "Faerie" with a capital "F" — and an object of either fast adherence or suspicious rejection. Some gay seekers began to worry that a seeming contradiction loomed: Faerie conformity.

The biggest issue of contention was whether the Faeries were going to direct their energies outward toward politics, or toward inner reaches of psyche and spirit. To Harry, it seemed that his ideal comrades had, after decades, finally arrived, and his well-honed skills for educating and politicizing kicked in. He excitedly promoted the political possibilities of the Faeries and discussed subject–subject consciousness as a new theory against which everything must be re-evaluated. Bill Fishman compared the circles at Faerie Central to "a Marxist study group with no text except what Harry would dish up." Hoping to fulfill his call in the "Chapter Two" position paper for gay people to make a unique social and political contribution, Harry pressed the Faeries to attend demonstrations, work in coalitions, and write to congressional representatives. In the spring of

1980, when President Jimmy Carter reactivated the draft in response to the Iranian hostage crisis, Harry plunged vigorously into local protest campaigns; this renewal of progressive contacts undoubtedly stimulated his political focus.

Many Faeries, however, rejected all politics as the ultimate product of a straight world. "I always resented Harry bringing in things from the outside world," said Stu Szidak, himself a former activist. "What a lot of us wanted was to shut out the world again and be a tribe and discover who we were." That stratum of discontent simmered for a long time. It should be noted, however, that Hay was not the only one interested in politics. Kilhefner, especially, had advocated a blend of the spiritual and political, and occasionally unanimous interest among the new Faerie circle triggered such political actions as the Radical Faeries' picketing the film *Cruising* in 1980 and protesting Jerry Falwell's Century City appearance in 1981.*

Debate increased over defining what was "Faerie." Some worried that its deeper meanings would be lost if it was used as a surface term. "There's something more to being a Faerie than just the label," explained Walker. "If we had called ourselves the Cocker Spaniel Princess Association and promoted ourselves as enlightened dogs, we could have kept the essence." But most were enchanted by the term and attempted to redefine the world with it. Was there a Faerie way of doing everything? Was alcohol straight and the psilocybin mushroom Faerie? Did a Faerie smoke cigarettes, eat meat, have kinky sex? The desire for consistent, "correct" answers contradicted most Faeries' intolerance of any form of repression.

The question of who was a "real" Faerie — who belonged in this new world — was a growing issue. Harry's standards for a "true homosexual" or of what it meant to be "truly gay" were firmly idealized. When challenged over his subjective standards, Harry regularly said that the exploitive or sadistic people one ran into in gay bars the world over "were simply not really gay." For Faeries, his criteria were even higher, and almost inevitably clashed with the average gays who walked in the door of La Cresta Court. Consequently, though many people felt they'd found "home" amongst the Faeries, others felt almost instantly booted out.

---

* As AIDS and reproductive rights activism swelled in the eighties, spontaneously drawing substantial Radical Faerie support, the argument became moot.

Among the latter was John Callahan, a gay theater director who was taken to the La Cresta Faerie circle in February of 1980, and was disturbed by the venting of hostility against straight people. Callahan had recently left a heterosexual marriage and belonged to Gay Fathers of Los Angeles, so he felt personally nettled. When the talisman came Callahan's way, he knew his remarks would be unpopular, but he also felt that his participation in the group would be hypocritical if he did not speak up against what he called "Faerie chauvinism against heterosexuals." Straight-slamming had been raised as a minor issue at the gathering, but when Callahan raised it here, it was not well received. After the circle, Harry approached him and said he did not have the "correct consciousness" and should not return, which greatly pained Callahan and turned him off to the new movement. (Most in the circle were not aware of Harry's action, and since at that time he did not feel at liberty to discuss his own previous marriage, Callahan may have presented him with a particularly loaded issue. Two years later, Hay and Callahan found themselves working together to organize gay and lesbian constituencies in Jesse Jackson's presidential campaign, which brought a lasting rapprochement.)

On the other hand, the generally prevailing open-armed inclusivity of the Faeries probably brought more trouble. A fundamental determination to be open to all brothers invited the disruptive, the distracting, the emotionally and psychologically way-out, and the politically ambitious to take up hours of circle time and chafe the structure of trust and exploration. Such "problem-child Faeries" — and nearly every gathering had them — made group mastery of a level-headed, fair consensus an essential skill.

Harry caught occasional flak for his tendency to act outside the consensus of the group, and Kilhefner grew bothered by his tendency to proselytize new Faeries on first meeting, and to dominate conversations in and out of meetings. But next to the promise of ecstatic fellowship, these issues seemed minor, and no discord between the founders was apparent. Fritz Frurip, part of that early Faerie circle, observed that "they would check with each other carefully about anything." As spring approached, however, Don Kilhefner withdrew to his room. By the time the second gathering was scheduled, Kilhefner announced that he would go to Oregon to scout land for possible purchase by the Circle of Loving Companions instead of to the much-anticipated Faerie gathering.

▽

Twice as long as the first gathering and almost twice as large, the second spiritual gathering for Radical Faeries, in August, 1980, became known as

Faerie Woodstock. Whatever the first gathering had produced, this one produced more of it. It was held in the alpine meadows above Boulder, Colorado, in Estes National Forest. Mountain streams and piney hills could only enhance the romantic otherworldliness in the hearts of the more than three hundred who registered. Harry and John drove out a week early to help the Denver Faerie Circle plan, order, and transport everything needed — including food for two dozen mass meals, a giant striped tent, and 500 restaurant candles in jars.

To properly prepare the site, Mitch Walker insisted on going up before anyone arrived. In his shaman garb of skirt, vest, bangles, beads, and bells — and undissuaded by the presence of curious straight couples in campers — he communed with the spirits of the land and blessed the areas where the Faeries would gather. This was done with the encouragement of the others; he had done the same at the ashram, and seemed to be fulfilling his role as official mystic. Soon all the supplies, plus toilets, plumbing for hot showers, and generators for power, were carted up the hill and assembled by Faerie hands.

On the first morning, and at regular intervals therafter, three hundred men linked up in a huge circle on a meadow rimmed with dark pines and dotted with small daisies. Just surveying the circle was a mind-altering revelation. There was no hesitation this time; these were Radical Faeries. They wore straw hats, sun bonnets, overalls, body paint, hostess pajamas, plaid flannel shirts, scarves, sneakers, and their male bodies. The vividness of freedom rushed into them faster than in the previous year as they poured out stories of their travels toward being gay, their wonder at the rare occasion of togetherness, their great possibilities as a people who were finally coming together.

The Denver Faeries had compiled a collection of chants and songs. The Seven Goddess chant, by Deena Metzger and Charlie Murphy, was the most popular. The names Isis, Astarte, Diana, Hecate, Demeter, Kali, Inana, a superinvocation of goddesses of Egyptian, Assyrian, Roman, Greek, Hindu, and Babylonian cultures, reverberated into the air in thickly woven harmonies of male voices at morning circles and again at late night campfires. The theme of neopaganism, reflected by the popular books *Witchcraft and the Gay Counterculture,* by Arthur Evans, and *The Spiral Dance,* by Starhawk, was becoming strongly integrated into the new Faerie culture. The Rainbow Family gatherings and women's music festivals were also cited as inspirations.

That was something Harry had to battle for among the Mattachines — the creation of a culture. But here, a gay culture took off like a wild weed, and flowered with numerous, often topsy-turvy innovations. At the first great circle of the Denver gathering, it was proposed that since snakes were sacred to the ancient earth goddess, the hiss should be a sign of approval. Thereafter, happy Faeries hissed.* Faerie names were adopted with increasing frequency. Some came to the gathering with names they had already chosen, such as Crazy Owl (a homeopath) and Kevin Woven (a weaver), but most were acquired at naming circles. Favorite categories emerged, such as astronomical names (Star, Morning Star, and Ultra Violet Nova); meteorological names (Neon Snowflake, Beautiful Day, and Rosy-Fingered Don); and botanical names (Oak Leaf, Flower, and Marvelous Persimmon). Some Faeries, like Toy, Judy Jetson, and Gidget, pilfered pop culture. Ideally, a name would come to a Faerie as a result of deep inner searching or during a moment of openness to the divine. The first Faerie Directory, littered with faerie names, ultimately grew into the Holy Faerie Database, tended by a Faerie named Baba Ram Rom.

An important emblem of Faerie culture was presented at that gathering by Dennis Melba'son, who belonged to a New Orleans collective called Louisiana Sissies in Struggle (LASIS). Inspired by a vision, he crocheted a triangular shawl with an eight-foot hypotenuse. Inside was a precise lace portrait of Cernunnos, the horned god of wildlife who was the Celtic version of the Greek god Pan. His horns and beard reach to the points of the triangle. Over the grinning, bearded face, a stout phallus spewed a garland of leafy vine. The shawl became the favorite talisman of the Faeries, sent from gathering to gathering to be worn by each speaker at every large circle. Over the years it embraced thousands of shoulders as Faeries shared, argued, wept, and wondered with one another.

A circle on Faerie sanctuaries proved to have particularly long-range effects and was attended by about a hundred men. A light rain fell on a warm afternoon as they huddled under a large tent. As nude male figures ran a wet and merry chase in the distance, Harry passed around a two-page outline of his ideas. Reading aloud from it, he dramatically called for the establishment of an "intentional residential community." There gay men could "explore deeply the many new facets of gay spirit, politics, re-inventing ourselves as a people in the process. It would be a place of affirmation, nurturance, and healing; a place for developing new

---

* Not long after that gathering, gay director Martin Worman was bewildered to hear half the audience hiss his San Francisco production of *Dear Love of Comrades*— until he was informed that Faeries were in the audience and that this was how they did things.

models of being with and connecting with each other and with nature; a place where we can re-learn to be stewards of the Earth." Further, he argued, it should be arable rural land, self-sustaining to its residents. Surplus food could be shared with urban brothers who, Hay worried, might soon face catastrophe. With these words, he held the audience's rapt attention.

He cast this vision of utopia on solid political ground. Citing the recent election of Ronald Reagan, he said, "We feel that hard times are coming, and because the gay community has the visibility that it's got, in many situations we will be the last hired and the first fired, the situations which Blacks and Chicanos in previous times enjoyed, but which will now be our 'honor.' We feel this is a time for families, and in this our gay family, we are going to have to take care of ourselves and each other because nobody else is going to ... We must be ready to think in these terms, whether we are in rural situations or in urban situations. We have to think about forming faerie families, groups of people who can nurture and sustain one another, economically as well as spiritually."

This project had been already over a year in the planning at Faerie Central. It involved setting up a nonprofit corporation to purchase property under community land trust tax-exempt status. Referring to it as a haven, a homeland, and most often as simply "the land," the founders discussed it as a way to stabilize the fleeting confederation of men who were identifying themselves as Radical Faeries. With such a sanctuary, Harry's abstract "next step into gay consciousness" could be a step onto tangible ground. This center could also serve as a springboard for other such collectives.

It was a shared fantasy for those in Faerie Central. It tapped into Harry's 1930s vision of a farming team of gay brothers. Similarly, Don Kilhefner's childhood in a religious farm community and his years of living in collective households made the idea attractive to him. Like Walker, all of them suspected that life away from the straight world would unleash energy and fulfillment. Moreover, Hay, Walker, and Kilhefner all had pet areas of gay research for which such a commune, they hoped, might serve as library and laboratory. A self-sufficient, all-gay community seemed perfect for the true gay self-discovery to which Harry thought gays should aspire. Though many Faeries were urban-based and seemingly incapable of tilling the soil, Harry nevertheless researched modern small farming techniques and 'miracle grains,' envisioning a vast change in the national attitude of the gay community once it had broken its dependency on the straight urban complex.

After reporting on Kilhefner's continuing search for land in the Northwest, Harry turned over the floor to a lively discussion. A briefer presentation of this idea at the Arizona gathering had found little interest, but this time the discussion continued for hours. Many expressed alarm about the instability of American cities and about the endangered natural ecology. The idea of a network of sanctuaries found strong support, and urban spaces for "healing and nurturing" were also called for. Various people offered pledges of land, financial support, and work. A member of Short Mountain, a gay collective in rural Tennessee, reminded the group that this was already going on. He described the sense of security that collective living had reclaimed for him, then invited "all you Faeries who flew away from the South because it was the South, come home."

Meanwhile, beyond the gathering Faeries, Mitch Walker had pitched his tent in a high, dry creek bed set apart by signs declaring "off limits."

He was absent from most of the circles, busied instead with a new secret project of extreme urgency that he called the Faerie Fascist Police Force. Walker gleefully described this as a covert agency to prevent power-tripping or "Faerie fascism" within the tender confines of the gathering. His target, however, was specific — Harry Hay. Walker explained, "I decided that if this was the Revolution and Harry was being Stalin, I would be, as second in command, his minister of a secret, CIA-style police force." In person, Walker could sound campy and playful, as if his frequent motifs of demons and fascists were mere rhetoric. But his hyperstylized charm notwithstanding, Walker and his Faerie Fascist Police Force meant business. "I recruited people to spy on Harry and see when he was manipulating people, so we could undo his undermining of the scene," he said. Explaining that Hay was his own worst enemy, Walker said he felt honored to betray Harry for the sake of the movement. These "honorable" intentions, however, were neither stated at meetings nor expressed privately to Harry since the confrontation at Wattles Park the year before. Harry remained unaware of it, but Mitch's whisper campaign would put trouble in his path for months to come, and it was only a first shrewd step in Walker's elaborately choreographed strategy.

Few at the gathering were aware of this. For most, deep personal transformations took place as they had the previous year. Friendships blossomed, lovers paired, souls healed — all on the ineffable Faerie cloud.

Two sweat lodges that Faeries had built stayed in constant use all week. Nightly circles turned into ecstatic dances. One of these was a ceremonial bonfire for Kali, the Hindu Mother Goddess, as well known for her aspect of destruction as for her life-giving. The fire consumed objects imbued with unwanted qualities — oppression, self-hatred, envy. On the last night of the six days, a spontaneous circle began around a fire. "That ritual mushroomed into an intense, orgiastic connection with the spirit world," recalled a Faerie named Aro. "It was much like the mud ritual the year before. But because it was this Eastern death goddess, a few Baptists were freaking out." The hundreds of rejuvenated gay men conjured their purest energies; it seemed an ancient, profound communion with a glorious power of gay men that reached through millenia.

The next morning, convinced that their lives had been unalterably changed and that they had found the magic to change the world, the Faeries scattered.

In the aftermath of this gathering, the land-trust circle took off like a rocket. Kilhefner, ever the efficient manager, had already filed for non-profit corporate status, and now a groundswell of interest was moving the project forward. Will Roscoe offered his help, drawing on his experience in grant writing. Two other Faeries also declared total commitment to the land trust. These were San Francisco residents David Liner, former minister of a psychic church in Georgia, and his friend David Lathrop, a carpenter. Both moved to Los Angeles to work full time on the land trust. Liner, the more extroverted, was a dwarflike man with bright eyes and a tremendous enthusiasm for new projects. At Harry's suggestion, he adopted the name Sai, for "Short And Intense." The core circle, now six members, diligently filled out state forms to grant nonprofit status for what would henceforth be known as the Gay Vision Circle.

In the winter of 1980, they decided to take a land-scouting trip to southern Oregon. Billy Russo, a friend of Kilhefner's from the Center, offered the facilities of his cozy Trillium Farm near Winston, Oregon, to the Gay Vision Circle. They stopped on the way there at a regional gathering of 150 Faeries at Harbin Hot Springs, north of San Francisco in Sonoma County. There, they talked excitedly about a major fund-raiser for the land trust, to be held the following spring in San Francisco, on the occasion of Harry's sixty-ninth birthday.

Immediately upon arrival at Trillium Farm, a problem arose. The group had agreed that only a small, closed board of directors should conduct business, including the land search. This would maintain consensus and, just as important to Harry, with his memories of the infiltration and disruption faced by past radicals, security. But two unknown people joined anyway. Mitch Walker brought Chris Kilbourne, who was twenty-three years old and just out of the closet; Sai brought Eon, an ethereal drifter. Sai and Mitch insisted that these young men were "true Faeries" and belonged on this new frontier from the start. They demanded an instant policy decision. Kilhefner, Hay, and Burnside reluctantly compromised: they allowed the two to stay but not to become involved in business dealings.

Pressure remained to address the issues of who was a "true Faerie" and whether the core group was open or closed. They also had to decide whether the sanctuary itself would be open or closed. Sai, particularly, felt that it should be borderless, that all gay people in need of healing should feel welcome there. Harry argued that was impractical and unmanageable. Furthermore, he pointed out, crops and livestock would require strict responsibilities. None of this pleased the anarchists. During most of these discussions heavy rain trapped the ten of them in a cabin made for six at most. Pressure soon built to an explosion.

The fuse for it was Kilbourne. Tall, lithe, square-jawed, and handsome, Kilbourne was a recent dropout from U.C. Berkeley. His upstairs neighbor, Mitch Walker, encouraged him to explore his gayness and to attend the Denver gathering. There Kilbourne felt "a sense of freedom I'd never experienced before. I was really revved up." Suddenly he was a full-fledged Faerie, one who, under the masterful guidance and counseling of Mitch Walker, knew the inner workings of the circle. "Mitch had told me about the politics of it," Kilbourne recalled many years later. "I knew that he was freaked out. The big issue was that it was a closed circle." Kilbourne remembered some of the power dynamics involved. "Mitch talked about consensus, and his feeling was that consensus could cover dominant power factions. Mitch did not feel he had any power. Every time he'd tried to deal with Harry, he'd been shot down." Harry's reaction to the interlopers was to ignore their presence entirely. That and the innate hauteur of the Duchess — which had strengthened, not faded since the thirties — increased his image as a distant ruler.

Kilbourne knew why he was unwelcome: "They wanted to get the land trust going, they wanted to get it done," he acknowledged. "Anyone else would not facilitate that happening." One full day of exclusion, however, made Kilbourne feel devastated and he was intent upon leaving, but Walker counseled him to "work it through." The young activist decided to challenge Harry.

The next day, those in the core circle went out to look for land. Kilbourne and Eon stayed behind and cooked a meal for everyone. Kilbourne also prepared to confront Harry and John and Don. When they returned, Kilbourne recalled, "Don somehow hung back in the hall, and I asked them [Harry and John] why I couldn't be involved. They just ignored me. It infuriated me. I got even more worked up, and I think I called them hypocritical pigs. What is this subject–subject consciousness? What is this Faerie bullshit?" A green ceramic bowl, full of fresh-fruit-and-yogurt salad that Kilbourne had prepared, was on the counter. He suddenly hurled it at Harry's feet. With harmless but accurate aim, it splattered on the floor and on John Burnside's ankles.

By all accounts hysteria followed. Kilhefner yelled, "I can't take it any more!" and fled the house, running into Mitch Walker, who offered support. Hay and Burnside, in utter shock, retreated to their truck for hours. Kilbourne stayed and wiped the fruity mess up off the floor. It was a splat heard round the Faerie network with lightning speed.

The fruit salad incident served as a turning point for the solidarity of the group. Though he had given up graduate school to pursue the sanctuary, Sai was the first to go. Obsessed with consulting the I Ching against almost everything (he joked that he threw a hexagram before deciding to do laundry), Sai used the Chinese oracle to reflect on his personal discomfort with Harry, whom he saw as "angry and anguished." Sai cast repeated hexagrams and read their lengthy, oblique metaphors during business circles, which insured that little actual business would be accomplished.

Sai and David, still adamant about the open-sanctuary issue, quit the Gay Vision Circle. After leaving Oregon, the remaining members promoted the spring fund-raiser, but in San Francisco, that project was sunk by the defectors who came to the public meetings and denounced Harry. "It became impossible to carry the plans forward," recalled Will Roscoe. Said Sai, "I proceeded to tell a lot of people what I had experienced on that trip. To some degree, I was blamed for sabotaging the fund-raising and recruitment efforts," he acknowledged. Sai's bitter denunciations tied in with the continuing whisper campaign of the Faerie Fascist Police Force, which caused many Faeries who had not even met Harry and John to feel alienated from them. When the dust settled, Sai took most of the heat for derailing the land-trust hopes — summed up by Kilhefner's remark to him: "You, Sai, ended the Faerie Dream." But the key disrupter, Mitch Walker, was still at large.

This discord echoed in Southern California. A breakaway Faerie circle formed at the home of Stu Szidak; it was not exactly a split, since the new circle frequently overlapped and related with the first, but it further eroded the Gay Vision Circle and Harry's reputation.

The "Oregon fiasco," as it was dubbed, generated lively dish among the San Francisco Faeries — and since Northern California had a large community of potential land trust supporters, the gossip was deeply distressing. Will Roscoe anxiously wrote to Harry that fund-raising efforts were stymied by the resulting partisanship, and that "the whole Faerie sanctuary project might go down the tubes, as far as the Bay-Area Faeries were concerned, unless there is some clear communication about what happened in Oregon and what would happen next."

·14·

Above all, audacity

It is a terrible thing for a man to suddenly realize that all of his life he has been telling the truth.

— Oscar Wilde

The fragmenting core circle quickly regrouped, recruiting three new members, all from San Francisco: Mark Thompson, arts editor of *The Advocate,* who was promoting the Radical Faeries in its pages; Will Roscoe, who had already done extensive work on the tax-exemption papers; and Roscoe's lover, a graceful, handsome young man named Bradley Rose.

To clear the air of differences, Harry sent a letter to those who had met in Oregon, restating his own hopes for the Gay Vision Circle and inviting responses. He aired his growing anxiety about Mitch Walker by comparing him to a "classically malfunctioning shaman," and referred to a rumor that Kilbourne had boasted of carrying out Walker's instructions to stage exactly the kind of explosive confrontation that had happened. Then Hay demanded, "Did you indeed introduce Chris into our Oregon situation as your puppet-agent? Under other situations, your interestingly phrased 'round-robin-hood's-barn' excursions in lieu of answers are not only poetic but intriguing; in this situation I should appreciate a simple 'yes' or 'no.'" He never got one. The openness of this blast signaled that his anger had been brewing and would soon come to a head.

Despite these tensions, there was still determination to secure the land trust, and the new group of seven met in April of 1981 at a cabin Don Kilhefner located on Big Bear Lake in the San Bernardino Mountains. The purpose of the meeting, according to Rose's notes, was "to see if we could commit ourselves to working in consensus as an enlarged core circle." No one at that meeting voiced misgivings, though during a private moment Will Roscoe recalled Walker taking him aside and telling him that "weird stuff was going on around Harry." Pushing forward, the group agreed to hold an event in the Bay Area to address the strong Faerie community emerging there. With luck, it might revitalize the image of "our tattered gang of four," as Harry rather glumly quipped. Twenty Faeries attended the pot luck and discussed the sanctuary with enough excitement to induce commitments to raise funds, tithe income, and look for land — immediately.

The luminous new form of the Radical Faerie, free of the shackles of the clone, still held powerful appeal to many gay men. Enthusiasm was so high that they called a larger meeting. Kilhefner, who was particularly anxious to get on with the land trust, took on the logistics and reserved a cabin for July, this time in Sequoia National Forest, then sent an announcement to dozens of interested Faeries. He also sent a letter to his fellow core-circle members making plain his insistence on accomplishing something other than just 'being Faeries' at the upcoming Sequoia meeting. "No more introductions and generalities for me," he explained. "Yeah, I guess I'm going to have to say it — I think I've reached the point in the project where I can no longer suppress my goal-oriented tendencies — sob sob."

But at the same time, Kilhefner began to re-evaluate his allegiances, and a month later the balance tipped. Complaining of stress and anxiety, he flew to Berkeley. The trip was quietly labeled "first aid" for his frayed nerves, and the consulting health provider was Mitch Walker. At an emotional counseling session that lasted all weekend, the laconic, private Kilhefner let out his misgivings, most of which centered around Harry's conduct. He felt the Faeries had become dogmatic under Harry's influence, and that tensions in the La Cresta collective signaled trouble for a larger community. (Harry noted that Kilhefner never attempted to raise these issues to him, despite the commitment they had made to each other.) Kilhefner was no stranger to the tensions of radical dreams and practical compromise and had a reputation as a peacemaker, but these conflicts seemed insoluble.

Walker supported Kilhefner by expressing identical feelings about Harry. The counseling session quickly became a strategy session. Don decided to quit. He pondered sending a resignation letter to the rest of the circle, but instead they kept their discussion quiet until the next meeting of the core circle; that way, they decided, everyone involved could discuss it. Walker said he did not express his own discontent because speaking against Harry would only be perceived as betraying the movement.

The meeting where Don would spring his news was set for June 20, over the summer solstice weekend. The main agenda item was planning for the Sequoia event and the meeting place was Mark Thompson's apartment in San Francisco. Harry and John drove Don up and dropped him off in Berkeley to stay with Walker, then continued to Thompson's charming and slightly vertiginous flat on the top floor of a stone art deco high-rise overlooking Buena Vista Park. There they stayed the night. The solstice weekend had been chosen as a good omen, but the meeting proved so disastrous that it became known as "Bloody Saturday."

When Roscoe and Rose arrived in the morning, they were greeted by Thompson, who hinted that something was afoot concerning Don. The next arrival was Mitch Walker, who riled Roscoe by commenting that his jeans and t-shirt looked straight-identified. Roscoe recalled, "He attacked me for having a clone image — a typical Mitch tactic." Walker (who later favored a crew cut and a black leather jacket) was dressed that day in the Mexican skirt he had worn to bless the land in Colorado. It was stiff muslin with a flounce at the waist, solid black save for its border design of skulls encased by a lightning pattern.

Everyone took a seat. Thompson remembered that "Mitch and Don were on one end of my apartment, which was rather long and narrow, and Harry and John sat at the other end." Mitch, who was designated as chair, recalled his manner as "very businesslike," although others remember his wild shaman affectations in full force. "During all of this [meeting]," recalled Rose in extensive notes, "Mitch was changing his bead necklaces, putting on one, then another, then removing the first. Rummaging in his big medicine purse. Wrapping things and unwrapping them in Cost Plus scarves. Smoking lots of dope, mumbling, snickering, humming."

Walker called the meeting to order and announced that, for emergency reasons, he would give the floor to Don Kilhefner. According to Rose, "Don began complaining of problems he was having with John and Harry. He talked about the accusations of Faerie Fascism, and said he believed Harry and John were power-tripping, especially Harry. He was not specific, but he eventually reached his point, which was that he was resigning, that his 'heart was no longer in the project.' Don removed himself to a corner of Mark's apartment so the rest of us could continue our meeting." (In an open letter he wrote July 26, Kilhefner repeated the sole reason that "I was no longer working on it [the project] from a heart-felt place.")

The shock of Don's resignation was compounded when Mitch followed suit. The reconstituted core was crumbling again. "Brad and Will and I all sat with turning heads, like at a tennis match," recalled Thompson. "It was formal, at first. But I remember saying to Will later that it was like watching a horrible, slow automobile accident." There was more actual arguing over the second resignation than the first, inflamed when the defectors announced that they might call an open meeting in the Bay Area within six weeks. As words grew heated, Walker delivered an especially cruel coup de grace. Though Mitch later denied it, most present vividly recall Mitch's statement to Harry: "How I feel is, you are like a cancer on the gay movement. And what do you do with a cancer? You cut it out!" Harry also remembered Mitch saying something else. "He demanded that I pass on the torch to him, that I was a burned-out cinder and that he was to lead now."

Will, Brad, John, and Harry walked numbly down Haight Street to the Cordon Bleu restaurant, where they ate a Vietnamese dinner. For months, Harry felt devastated and betrayed. He wrote to friends shortly afterward that he felt "other people's projections" had been forced upon him, and that he could not understand much of it. The following day, at Roscoe's insistence, the group had a final meeting in Berkeley's Tilden Park to tie up several loose ends — most importantly the already-publicized meeting in Sequoia National Park, which now had to be canceled. Roscoe hoped that specific issues related to the break would surface, but none were forthcoming. Afterward, while they were returning to their cars, Harry stopped to pick berries along the trail, disturbed a bees' nest, and complained of being "doubly stung." A shaken Harry and John drove Don back to Los Angeles, and they coexisted for four strained months at La Cresta Court before Kilhefner was able to finance a move.

Muted antagonism continued. Walker circulated a mock press release summarizing the meeting to select Faeries. It read: "Harry Hay, founder of the modern Gay Movement and a Gay Vision Circle Director, was shocked and hurt but vowed to go on with His Dream. Meantime, the two resignees say they are presently planning a new corporation — tentatively titled PRIMEVAL SLIME — and they feel the situation is far from a setback." The phrasing mocked Hay's often-quoted definition of spirituality: "The magnificent heritage of consciousness, which is everything from the first cells dividing in the primeval slime to what you and I just thought." For months, the new group offered "Primeval Slime Study Groups."

This defeat was a particularly bitter one. The Faerie sanctuary, where Harry had hoped to make his last years his most meaningful, was a dream that had taken a pounding and now seemed irreparably damaged. Having dismantled their retirement paradise in New Mexico, he and John felt too old to sustain another move. But perhaps the worst of it was the searing familiarity of seeing his hopes of a cooperative gay brotherhood shattered. "I've built up the dream so often," he said once, "only to see it torn down."

▽

There were now two gay spirit organizations. Rank-and-file Faeries pondered the opposing camps. Harry and John wanted to persevere with the land trust, but the three new core circle members took a wait-and-see attitude. (Only Thompson was successful at maintaining relationships with all the Faerie founders.) Kilbourne, Walker's dashing acolyte, remained a loud mouthpiece. His frequent denunciations of the original movement — "Faerie is dead," "Faeries are lame" — hastened the decline of Faerie Central at La Cresta Court and the northward drift of West Coast Faerie activity. Will Roscoe recorded that "the Faerie movement itself remained healthy, vital and growing, but the land-trust, its premiere project, languished. The whole idea seemed cursed."

The spin-off organization called itself Treeroots and adapted Walker's old field of study, Jungian psychology. To adapt this practice to the gay sphere, Treeroots promoted ceremonial magic and Jungian psychological analysis. Kilhefner and Walker, the group's guiding forces, sought to identify gay archetypes based on the dreams of openly gay men. "Gay Soul-making" and "Coming Out Inside" were the names of classes they offered along with "Gay Voices and Visions" and an ongoing series of dream workshops called the "Dreamworld Descent of the Hero-shaman." Eventually, Treeroots set hundreds of men in the Los Angeles area on the "healing path," as Thompson phrased it, of its gay Jungian technique, though by the late eighties it had scaled down its level of operation as Walker, Kilhefner, and Kilbourne got their credentials and went into private practice as therapists.

(Even after Treeroots had "cleansed itself" of Harry Hay, he noted later that its troubles continued; Kilhefner, Walker, and Kilbourne refused to speak to one another for long stretches, though none resigned from the corporation. Though Walker had laid his Faerie Facism campaign on the basis that Harry was power-tripping, many people who approached Treeroots found that any criticisms they made about its handling of power were forcefully parried by being discredited as psychologically unstable.)

The resignations of Bloody Saturday wounded Harry emotionally and compromised him politically. It was the second rebellion in a year and, along with Walker's destabilization campaign, sullied Hay's reputation within the growing Faerie network. To seek solace, and perhaps as a chance to revitalize the group, Harry invited several friends to a hiking retreat in the Desolation Valley near Lake Tahoe. It was a favorite wilderness area of his, one he had visited often in the 1930s. "Young Indians long ago went [there] to discover their life's totems," he wrote in his invitation. "It might be a place for us to find renewal."

Only Roscoe and Rose accepted, and the two couples hiked ten miles to the spare, exquisite valley with its granite peaks and crystal-clear lakes. The visit launched a deep and lasting friendship between the couples. They enjoyed each other's company, and in years to come made semiannual visits together to other locales. Will and Harry became especially close and found they had much in common. Roscoe, a left-of-center gay community organizer and writer, was fascinated by the older man's ideas. For a long period, he became Harry's closest tie to the San Francisco Faeries.

The Faeries, largely oblivious to any trouble among the "heads of a hierarchy" of which many refuted the very existence, continued in their own time and on their own terms as a national movement. Harry and John attended a third annual large gathering, held in Pecos, New Mexico, in the summer of 1981, but Will and Brad, struggling with disillusionment, did not. Participants were as enthusiastic as at any gathering before, though the idea of a national gathering found some criticism as institutionalized and stale. The "quantum leap of consciousness" the founders had dreamed about was still euphorically real, especially to first-timers, but to those who had envisioned a long-term community, it seemed like a short and temporary hop. But something slowly edging into gay life began to supersede any philosophical debates: the many-headed monster called AIDS, which required a major adjustment of sexual behavior and self-definition to all gay men. As the epidemic progressed, many felt fortunate that the Faerie movement, already based in social redefinition and in values of heart over crotch, allowed them to adjust more quickly and deeply to the challenges of the AIDS crisis.

In April of 1982, Roscoe and Rose came to visit the La Cresta house for six months, staying, as would a stream of Faeries throughout the decade, in the trailer parked there which Harry called the *temenos*.* The young San

---

* *Temenos* is the Greek word for an area that is cut off or separated. Hay used it to refer to the "edge of the village" dwelling designated by ancient societies for gays. The Gay and Lesbian Community Services Center in Los Angeles adopted the term as the name of their youth outreach program.

Francisco couple, by now affectionately referring to Harry and John as their "great aunts," saw a continuation of the salon culture the older couple had cultivated at the Kent compound. Roscoe wrote that the visit was "a never-ending faerie circle," and shared insights and communion lasted around the clock, "from sunrise, with John already in the kitchen, to sunset, about when Harry got active — to midnight, when he really got warmed up."

During this visit, Harry's gay historical research had the dust shaken off it. "One night after dinner," Roscoe recalled, "while making some point about gay people in the history of civilization, Harry made a sweeping gesture toward a dark corner of the room and said, 'Of course if you really want to know about this you'll have to get into *that*.' He was referring to a haphazard pile of cardboard file boxes crammed with thousands of pages of notes from the fifties." When Roscoe returned to San Francisco the next autumn, he took four boxes of the notes with him to index and copy. He found Harry's notes impressive in their scope and detail, though to a contemporary scholar, Hay's preoccupation with the intricacies of Marxist historical materialist theory appeared dated.

Roscoe was intrigued by the fact that Hay had started with the North American Indian berdache, then researched the history of civilization as he looked for specific manifestations of that role. Roscoe decided to take up where Harry had left off and develop full empirical studies.*

A gathering held in the summer of 1982 proved to be a pinnacle of the early Faerie movement as it birthed a Faerie image and sent it into the world. Two plays were performed there, *Without Reservations,* a collaboration directed by Prince Panesi, which depicted a Faerie gathering, and *Midas Well,* by William Moritz, which showed homoerotic, nature-worshipping values triumphing over materialism. The latter play, which Moritz wrote while living at the La Cresta Court house, was all the more poignant because the natural setting of the gathering enhanced its theme that the values of antiquity are eternal and accessible. Both plays were performed later in Los Angeles.

Two Faerie films were created that summer, *Devotions,* by James Broughton and his lover Joel Singer, and *Gathering,* by Harry Frazier. These artworks were a graceful fulfillment of Harry Hay's hopes of seeing

---

* Roscoe edited *Living the Spirit,* an anthology of gay American Indian writings, and his book, *The Zuni Man-Woman,* which chronicles the life of We'Wha, a Zuni berdache famous in the nineteenth century, is scheduled for publication by the University of New Mexico Press.

this new gay consciousness take form and venture into the world. That the scene for all of this, Eagle Creek near San Diego, was owned by a gay men's leather group and had hosted S&M bike runs for years, made the Faerie magic especially miraculous.

In the early spring of 1983, Anita Hay died of cancer. For several years she had kept her illness secret from most of her friends, and a stunned Harry attended the funeral. He was viewed as "the ghost of Christmas past" by a number of former intimates, including Martha Rinaldo and Helen Gorog, whom he had not seen since the divorce more than thirty years before. Kate and Hannah also saw him for the first time in years. He felt unwelcome and defensive; several old friends snubbed him completely, he sensed, out of bigotry. He did, somewhat gruffly, reach out after that event to re-establish a few friendships with some of those who had been dear to him in a very different lifetime.

That same year, Harry's stock in the historian's marketplace rose dramatically when the University of Chicago Press published John D'Emilio's book, *Sexual Politics, Sexual Communities.* Its detailed account of the Mattachine Society in a serious historical context fixed Hay, Rowland, Jennings, and the others as the founders of the continuous modern American gay movement, and the Mattachine founders generally praised the detailed reconstruction. Since D'Emilio's interviews, interest in Hay remained. Shortly after his return from New Mexico, he was sketched by a local art collective called SPARC (Social and Political Art Resource Center), which portrayed his passing out the organizing "Call" to masked homosexuals in one scene of a massive mural in the Tujunga Wash of the San Fernando Valley.

Mitch Tuchman of the U.C.L.A. Oral History Program also requested further interviews. Oral history was a natural for Harry; Jeff Winters, an old antagonist of Hay's from Mattachine days, reviewed D'Emilio's book and ribbed, "Harry Hay curls up to an interviewer like a cat to a fire," and another writer observed simply that "Harry Hay likes to talk." Tuchman recorded seventeen and a half hours of Harry talking in great detail about the vast scope of his life, and the two-volume transcription, entitled *We Are a Separate People,* was added to the university's Department of Special Collections in 1987.

As the Faeries became stronger and more independent, Harry watched a shift in his role and a swelling of attention to more personal matters. A particularly memorable convergence was the 1983 gathering at a gay-owned cattle ranch in Napa County. Harry arrived at the Blossom of Bone gathering, as it became known, with a physical problem: Months before, a falling bookcase had injured his left ankle. He was too restless to allow it to completely heal, and by the time he arrived at the gathering it had ulcerated and he was badly hobbled. Since Harry always enjoyed pitching in with the physical labor and the driving involved in preparing for gatherings, he was miserable and unable to venture far from his immediate campsite.

Though he was a realist about his age, Harry's stamina and enthusiasm had naturally prolonged his active engagement in the thick of the Faeries. It was shocking to see the hardy elder statesman felled; he even had to be carried to circles. But his physical incapacitation gave him an opportunity to view the onset of age and the fading of power — and to ask for help. A homeopathic Faerie healer gave him a poultice of toasted cannabis seeds, which at first made the ulcers even worse, but was promised to be effective.

Harry was treated on a psychic level as well. William Stewart, a calligrapher from San Francisco, rather audaciously "adopted" the old man at one of the great circles. Stewart had seen a specific need in Harry: "I realized that this man was struggling, and needed to be 'birthed' into old age." Stewart consequently provided himself as a symbolic gentle father — one, Harry realized, that would not beat him. The next morning, Harry emotionally shared with the heart circle that he had awakened from powerful, sexual dreams about his real father and that he realized for the first time in his life that his father had truly loved him. Before leaving the gathering, Harry was the center of a healing circle whose *oms*, all focused on him, sent a strange humming through him which he compared to ultrasound treatments he once had. As the gathering ended, Hay saw that his ankle, after months, had finally begun to heal.

Will Roscoe pointed out that the Napa Gathering had produced enough of a surplus for a down payment on a piece of land, and began to promote a new model for the dormant sanctuary. The San Francisco Circle formed a nonprofit corporation with the Faerie name NOMENUS. ("No Men Us," "No Menace," and "No Menus" were among its interpretations.) NOMENUS became the phoenix from the ashes of the Gay Vision Circle, which all over again began the struggle for nonprofit status. In the Bay Area, Mica Kindman, Lloyd Fair, Cass Brayton, and Will Roscoe were already guiding the project, and Harry and John drove up frequently to participate as well, sometimes for a single meeting. Being half a state away from the main circle seemed to have a mellowing effect on Harry's relationship with the group; Roscoe characterized Hay's new role as "influence without dominance." Harry still took controversial positions and when he held the talisman he spoke passionately, but he followed the consensus of the whole. Eventually, the initial ideal of establishing an ongoing, self-sufficient community was abandoned as too ambitious for urban-based people; the new idea was to own a smaller piece of land that would be home to only a few caretakers and would host regular gatherings.

Mitch Walker and Chris Kilbourne moved to Los Angeles in 1984, and Treeroots followed. Kilbourne, Walker, and Kilhefner made an unhappy attempt to reinvolve themselves with the Faeries, with the result that Harry and John, appalled by what they felt were crude psychological confrontation tactics (with Kilbourne again acting as caustic spokesman), withdrew from planning meetings, and suffered the criticism of freshly activated Faeries who insisted that Faerie love conquer all. Hay and Burnside missed their first major gathering (at Madre Grande near San Diego), which turned out to be the most explosive in Faeriedom; those Faeries that had chided Harry for staying away told him afterward that they wished they had stayed home too.

Treeroots returned to its fifty-minute-hour politeness, and Kilbourne made it a point to attend other Faerie gatherings later with substantially toned-down rhetoric. In 1987, a low-key Don Kilhefner visited the Gold Creek gathering hosted by the Los Angeles Faeries. Still, it took long months for Harry to resume his relationship with the Faeries.

▽

Harry found a day-glow-green button that warned, "Do not Feed or Tease the Straight People." He wore it everywhere; age did not dull his social daring, nor his tongue. The more completely he immersed himself in what he often called "my real family" of gay friends, the sharper became his ripostes to straights. Two of the straight people he teased were the wives of his ex-lovers. When Will Geer died in 1974, Harry injudiciously blurted to Geer's widow, Herta, "I had him first." (To her credit, Mrs. Geer shot back, "I had him longest.") In 1983, Harry was invited to a large birthday celebration at which James Broughton shared his films and poetry in a sort of cultural love-in. Broughton introduced his former wife, the famous film critic Pauline Kael, to Harry and said, "Pauline and I have a child together."

Hay queried, "Oh really? Which one was the father?" William Moritz, who accompanied Harry on that occasion, recalled that Kael's review of Harry Hay was a withering glance and a muttered, "Son of a bitch!"

At home, Harry spent increasing hours with his massive music library, making tapes for friends and deepening his already vast familiarity with various musical styles. Then, quite suddenly, he lost his hearing. It happened in 1985 at a ceremony honoring a Faerie friend, held in a low-ceilinged hall. Harry stood in the back, between two loudspeakers at ear-level, until a pain began that swiftly grew unbearable. He left too late. "I walked in hearing and walked out deaf," he discovered. His diagnosed condition of acoustical trauma in his left ear would have healed within weeks had he been a young man, but at seventy-one improvement came slowly; he was already deaf in his right ear from early blows delivered by his father. He grappled with a fierce depression because of the loss, and wrote to Earl Robinson, "This has been such a grief because Music has been my constant companion since I was about six months old." It all sounded like toneless noise. Though he was fitted with an effective hearing aid, he never regained the full range of his hearing.

After the long wait, the dream of Faerie-owned land finally came true. In 1987, Magdalene Farm, on a forty-acre lot near Grant's Pass, Oregon, was purchased by the large NOMENUS collective. The parcel was bordered by forested mountains and by Wolf Creek, the waterway for which the neighboring town was named. It offered large meadows for circling, glades for tents of convening Faeries, and dells for dallying. An old barn on the property served as the kitchen and first-aid station. A gay man named George Jalbert had bought the land more than a decade earlier, and the *RFD* collective in nearby Golden, Oregon, expanded there. Jalbert had long been concerned with creating a gay land trust collective, an interest which, amazingly, he got through a meeting with Harry in 1975. Jalbert was a friend of Carl Wittman, and when Harry and John had dinner with them while at the height of their own land-trust fever, Jalbert caught it and wrote regularly to Hay of his search for land. When he finally found it, he invited the Circle of Loving Companions to become part of the permanent collective there. That never worked out, but when Jalbert sold the land to NOMENUS, it seemed an uncanny fulfillment of Harry's earliest vision.

"The Faeries need to come together for spiritual renewal," Hay said often, "but their work is in the world." Thus Harry was continually active in political campaigns, often as one of the few open gays and certainly as the only radical with white whiskers and a long, dangling earring. Among many other campaigns, he worked actively with Women's Strike for Peace, Resist the Draft, and the Lavender Caucus of Jesse Jackson's Rainbow Coalition. In his many speaking engagements on these various efforts, Harry wove gay consciousness into his message, always balancing coalition politics with a firm insistence on recognizing gays "as a separate people whose time has come" — a people who, he demanded, must not be "blackmailed into silence by the Left."

Phyllis Bennis, a friend from the 1980 anti-draft campaign, recalled that Harry was as effective addressing straights as he was in the gay world. "He is quite charismatic and knows how to use certain verbal techniques in winning people over to his position. I think he is tactically aware that as an older person he can command attention. He does it very shamelessly and it's great." She spoke for many when she added, "If I didn't agree with his politics, I'd probably be pissed off at how he uses power. But I do agree with him."

Bennis provided an example of Hay's determination to contribute his gay presence to coalition politics. "There was a huge blow-up between Harry and three Iranian students in the coalition. It wasn't over his being in the coalition himself, but it was voiced as a challenge to the importance of the gays and lesbians in the movement. These guys were really denigrating the significance of gays, and doing it in a very superior, macho way, all the while trying to make it sound part of the progressive struggle.

"At some point in the meeting, it turned into a screaming match. Harry went off. He launched into the most vitriolic attack on them, from the most flagrant sort of Radical Faerie style, yelling things like, 'We are a nation!' Finally he went out to take a little break, and came back after a while. These guys cooled out too. Business somehow continued — for months. The point was that Harry was willing to work in a group where he knew there were folks who had less than respect for his identity and integrity. A lot of folks would have stomped out and stayed out. Not Harry."

Harry attended countless demonstrations for progressive causes. In the 1980s, he marched against the contras, the pope, apartheid, the spraying of insecticide on urban areas, the death penalty, and the profits-over-people policies of the Reagan and Bush administrations. Harry demonstrated for nuclear disarmament, a national policy to fight AIDS, and for a woman's right to abortion. To many protests, he carried his customized all-purpose protest sign, a stick holding a pink cardboard triangle with colorful ribbons streaming from the upper corners. It read "No U.S. Intervention in Central Anywhere!" Some straight Leftists criticized the sign as too bright for the somber events of the times, but Harry was determined to protest always as a Radical Faerie. At a massive demonstration called "L.A. Rejects Reagan," shortly after the 1980 election, he worked with a group that wore all lavender and called itself "the Purple People," one more effort to liven a "straight" demonstration with refreshing Faerie sparkle.

Diverse venues continued to feature him, including the documentary film and book *Before Stonewall,* in which he described the formation of the first Mattachine Society and his years before that in the demimonde where a people without a collective identity struggled to meet. In 1986, his gay movement role was discussed in Francis Fitzgerald's book *Cities on a Hill,* serialized in the *New Yorker,* and Harry was astounded to find his interview with Jonathan Katz cited in *Citizen Cohn,* the biography of HUAC counsel Roy Cohn, Right-winger, closeted homosexual, and feared power broker; Harry Hay was the only openly homosexual Leftist of the period against whom Cohn could be contrasted. *After the Ball,* a conservative attempt to reshape the gay movement as an advertising campaign for the "product" of gay rights, blasted the obtuse style of Harry's writing. Critics notwithstanding, nis letters and ideas often appeared in the gay press, and an essay distilling many of his favorite themes was included in Mark Thompson's edited anthology *Gay Spirit, Myth and Meaning,* alongside writings by or about Gerald Heard, Walt Whitman, Edward Carpenter, Don Kilhefner, and Mitch Walker. Hay's piece, "A Separate People Whose Time Has Come," recapped his theory that gay people represent a genetic mutation of consciousness whose active fostering is now required for human survival.

As it brutishly invaded the lives of so many in the 1980s, so AIDS darkened the lives of Harry and John. The phenomenon seemed inconceivable at first, though by the middle of the decade they had lost one housemate and several dear friends to the disease, including their beloved friend Carl Wittman. Harry added AIDS-related matters to his voluminous newspaper scanning and clipping. He had long predicted that conservatives would seek revenge in a backlash against the gay movement and stated that he suspected malicious government complicity in the ethnically targeted carnage of the epidemic. At whistle-blowing, drum-beating demonstrations of ACT UP Los Angeles, Harry was there — with his hearing aid turned off. The AIDS epidemic gave new urgency to a comment that Harry had made often about gay political strategy: that gay people must explain their contribution to humanity as a whole. The heterosexual mainstream, he insisted, "has to understand why it is to their advantage to change their laws to protect us. That understanding is our only security. And we are running out of time to get that across."

John Burnside explored the Symmetricon as a therapy for people with AIDS. His instrument had gained steady attention throughout the 1970s, and was used as a special effect for several film and television projects, as well as for deep relaxation therapy. In 1987, Symmetricon performances were part of the Spiritual in Art exhibit at the Los Angeles County Museum of Art. The couple had always been curious about the impact of the moving light mandalas on the autonomic nervous system, and as the epidemic grew, Burnside built more models to make videotapes for viewing by people with AIDS.

Harry continued to receive speaking invitations from groups as diverse as the Los Angeles chapter of Black and White Men Together, gay students at U.C. Berkeley, and Georgia State University. He took his speaking engagements seriously and often stayed up night after night to prepare. Frequently, he felt he had made a new breakthrough in understanding who gays are and what, as a group, gay people needed to do next. In addressing groups outside the Faeries, Harry invariably spoke of expanding gay identity beyond his original proposal of the minority model, which he felt was no longer politically effective nor fitting to the unique natures and talents of gay people. He tended to speak at great length and dramatically, and, with techniques honed over a lifetime, he always conveyed his message.

His most prestigious invitation came in 1989 when Jacques Vandemborghe, head of the French Gay Archives, invited him to give an address at the Sorbonne, which he regretfully was unable to accept. Hay served as a featured speaker at the San Francisco Gay Pride Parade in 1982 and, with John, as grand marshall of the Long Beach Gay Pride Parade in 1986. On his seventy-seventh birthday, in 1989, the city council of West Hollywood issued a proclamation honoring Harry's lifetime of activism. Quoting Harry's own description of the spirit of the Mattachine, the council saluted his chief characteristic: "above all, audacity."

New York Heritage of Pride invited Harry to address the 1989 Gay Pride Parade in Manhattan, which proved a great adventure as well as a special honor; the occasion marked the twentieth anniversary of the Stonewall riot. In Manhattan, Harry and John stayed with Jonathan Katz. On their second night in New York, Harry went to an oral history presentation called Stonewall Revisited, featuring eyewitnesses to the riot. The existence of the New York Mattachine Society and its part in the action was mentioned, and, recalled Katz, "Someone said, 'What's the Mattachine?' I said, 'He's here, he's here.' It was very dramatic." Harry was introduced to the crowd as the man who had laid the foundations of gay activism two decades before Stonewall. He received a standing ovation, and after the presentation, dozens of people approached him. He recalled that "several came up and pressed my hand and said, 'Thank you for my life.' This was so unexpected and touching that I was suddenly at the point of tears."

Saturday, June 24, 1989, at a rally on the Great Lawn in Central Park, a huge crowd assembled to hear guest speakers, including poet Allen

Ginsberg, writer Joan Nestle, and activist Harry Hay. The sun-drenched crowd of several thousand went wild as ACT UP of New York led a contingent of nonpermitted marchers from the Village onto the lawn. "I sensed more militance than in recent years, more receptiveness to the militant messages we heard later," said Shane Que-Hee, a longtime friend of Hay's. Harry grated the audience with criticism of ACT UP's "hetero-imitative" confrontation tactics. ("Very Hay-ish!" commented Que-Hee.) A lengthy historical introduction as only Harry could give it further ruffled the crowd. But, dressed in the latest Faerie fashion — a tutu of crinoline and army camouflage — Harry gained his listeners' favor as he proposed the Radical Faerie approach of "askance" tactics, as exemplified by his costume. His remarks received sustained applause, and were reprinted in three lesbian and gay newspapers around the country.

Que-Hee felt, upon seeing Harry onstage, that he physically summarized the years of the lesbian and gay movement in the United States. He noted that "age did not bring resignation except for those physical things that age demands as its due; the mind would never bow to anyone."

In the next day's parade Harry marched with the Radical Faeries, who ran through the streets of Manhattan with a vigor and color uncommon even for them. This followed Harry's curt (and rather shocking, to those who had extended the invitation) refusal to march in the founders' section of the parade. It was not uncommon for Harry to decline just such well-intentioned civilities; he once sent a friend into convulsions of laughter by complaining that "the kids" in the movement were looking at him as "the Dinosaur Duchess." In a 1983 letter to a friend, he complained that he was "already scheduled to be a dinosaur for a gay gerontology conference, and now San Francisco Gay Pride has asked me to come up and be a dinosaur" — the same week! He requested to march in a different group.

Through the years, Harry remained true to his Marxist politics, never once becoming anti-Communist despite his own painful experience. As upheavals began in the Soviet Union, he was fascinated with Gorbachev's *perestroika* and intently watched as reforms swept Eastern Europe at the turn of the decade. "I was delighted and felt it was long overdue," he said. "And I was thunderstruck by the revelations of what had been suppressed by the bureaucracy, and by the primitiveness of the U.S.S.R. It brought back memories of the absolutely wonderful experience between 1938 and 1942 where we were actively exploring theory and practice, with regular six month evaluations and adjustments. We'd say, 'Wouldn't it be wonderful if we lived in the Soviet Union and could do this every day?' It turned out that it wouldn't have been." It saddened Hay to see people "throwing out the baby with the bath water" in completely denouncing Communism, and pronouncements of the decline of Marxism, he insisted, were premature. "Marxism needs to be revised, based on new scientific knowledge, particularly of human behavior," he said. "The underlying methodology will be proved sound." Harry was pleased in 1990 to be working with an advisory council to help facilitate that revision.

As they passed their twenty-fifth year of "walking hand in hand together," as Hay often described their relationship, the loving companions Hay and Burnside looked ever more like a couple, alike yet complementary, supportive in a thousand details by practiced instinct. Their ongoing dialogue continued with as much excitement as ever, and the vivacity and hardiness of both astonished their friends. It was their union, Harry once told a television interviewer, that gave him the will to keep going. "I had to wait until I was fifty to find out what my life was all about. And since then, it's been the most sumptuous life you can imagine."

In the spaces between their togetherness, Harry spent long nights scanning newspapers for political and scientific information, firing off letters filled with news, insights, and his ever-present opinions. Often he bent over his typewriter until dawn; depriving himself of sleep seemed only more agreeable to Harry as he grew older. As he prepared remarks for his frequent speaking engagements, he increasingly wove stories from his own life into his speeches, looking down from, as Black Elk called it, the mountain of old age. Harry recounted scenes from the Mattachine, from demonstrations in the 1930s, from his days on his uncle's ranch, all to illustrate points about freedom and community.

Even in his old age, Harry sometimes marched alone — and with substantial impact. One solo protest started innocuously, but ended up among his most newsworthy feats. It began at the 1986 Gay Pride Parade in Los Angeles, a march sponsored by Christopher Street West (CSW), in honor of the street where the Stonewall riot took place in 1969.

What became known as the "Harry Hay Incident" was actually one aspect of the multifaceted "Valerie Terrigno Incident," a complex political scenario involving the first mayor of West Hollywood, which was then ballyhooed as the world's first gay-run city. Terrigno, an open lesbian, had resigned over a scandal that Harry felt involved a "wicked miscarriage of justice." A story in the *Los Angeles Times* described the plan of CSW to block the appearance of former Mayor Terrigno in the upcoming festivity.

Harry's reaction was that "any place I walk, Valerie walks with me." Disdaining a "blatant or hetero-imitative type of confrontation," he wanted a protest that was both Faerie and specific. The result was a sandwich-board sign made out of cardboard and muslin trimmed with pinking shears. On the front of what appeared almost to be a Donna Reed apron he wrote "Valerie Terrigno Walks With Me." Choosing another gay cause that had been cast out over contested morality, he added to the back, "NAMBLA Walks With Me," thus bringing into the parade another taboo entity: the North American Man/Boy Love Association. NAMBLA, of which Hay has never been a member, advocates eliminating age-of-consent laws and has been barred from marching in the gay parades of several cities. When he learned that CSW refused to allow them to march, Harry was appalled by the hypocrisy of a self-appointed gay establishment that would declare a section of the gay community unrespectable. He could not contain his outrage.

The resulting confrontation resembled something out of a Frank Capra movie, gay-community style. The septuagenarian gay movement founder was addressed by a policeman who informed him that CSW had to approve all signs in the parade, and threatened to escort Hay out of the parade unless he removed his unauthorized messages. Hay refused to back down. When it was apparent that he intended to keep his sign and to march, he found himself surrounded by four mounted policemen. CSW public-relations officers wrung their hands. The cops glared from their horses. Harry held his ground. The impasse was broken only when an impassioned Radical Faerie, who feared that Harry would be jailed, ripped the contested sign from his neck, shredded it, and stomped on the pieces. Signless, Harry Hay marched. This episode however, was photographed and widely reported in the gay media, both locally and nationally.

CSW voted to reprimand Hay and accused him of cooking up the whole incident just to give them bad press. They shrilly (and unfathom-ably) compared Harry Hay to Jerry Falwell. Hay's response to CSW, in his letter published in a local lesbian and gay paper called *The News,* was equally sharp: "Gay pride is long out of date. How long are we going to go around saying, 'I'm proud I have blue eyes'? San Francisco and Boston have been calling it Gay Freedom Day for years: maybe it's time we had a Gay Freedom Day here too." To those who self-righteously condemned his support of NAMBLA, he told the story of Matt, his 25-year-old first love when he was only fourteen, and pointed out that "having molested an adult when I was a child until I found out what I needed to know," he had a different perspective on the issue.

The incident provides a quintessential glimpse into Hay's character. The new gay establishment was rarely challenged at that time, but with his instinct to push the agenda and stretch the status quo, Harry double-dared the gay powers that be. On sheer principle, and with a strong reminder that he was not yet through kicking, he took on the most feared and despised issues within the community, issues no one else would touch.

Whatever crossed his path was subject to that change. When Harry was asked once to speak on a panel titled "Growing Old and Gay," he refused to appear unless the name was changed. The panel in which Harry Hay participated was called "Growing Older and Gayer."

Chapter notes

▼

Personal interviews with Hay by the author provide the basis for most of this text. Over a decade of knowing Hay, I've heard many of his stories, some from public speeches, most from casual conversation. I thus collected many stray scraps of his history without formal interviews, especially between the inception of this project in late 1986 and its completion in 1990. Some information, as well, was elaborated or clarified in Hay's readings of various manuscript drafts.

Many published interviews, essays, and letters by or about Hay may be found in various organs of the gay press. Most of this material can be found at the International Gay and Lesbian Archives, the Blanche Baker Library of ONE Institute, and in Hay's personal papers, all in Los Angeles. The bulk of quotations from written sources may be found in the copious correspondence, notes, manuscripts, and family documents in Hay's personal papers.

To indicate frequently cited correspondents and collections of personal papers, initials are used for Harry Hay, James Kepner, and Stuart Timmons. Interview dates are listed at first citation. Some ongoing, informal interviews, such as with John Burnside and William Moritz, are undated.

1. From the best of families

Interviews with Hay's siblings, Jack Hay, 2/21/87, and Peggy Hay Breyak, 7/15/86. Jean Hay, letter to S.T., 6/25/87; Ronald Kirk, letter to S.T., 6/5/87; Harnish Mearns, letter to Jack Hay, undated.

Also consulted on Hay's ancestors: U.S. Government Commemorative Biography of James Allen Hardie, 1877; *Who Was Who in America, Historical Volume 1607–1896,* Marquis Publications, 1967; Allen Johnson, ed., *Dictionary of American Biography,* vol. 4, New York: Charles Scribner's Sons, 1932; Robert M. Utley, *Frontier Regulars: The United States Army and the Indian,* New York: Macmillan, 1973; Iain Moncreiffe, *The Highland Clans,* New York: C.N. Potter, 1967; Dee Brown, *Bury*

My Heart at Wounded Knee: An Indian History of the American West,
New York: Holt Rinehart, 1971; Philippe Julian and J. Phillips, *The Other
Woman: The Life of Violet Trefusis,* Harvest, London: HBJ, 1976; Brian
Roberts, *Flawed Colossus: The Life of Cecil Rhodes,* New York: Norton,
1987.

2. The example

Interviews with Peggy and Jack Hay; correspondence with Jean Hay;
Robert Balzer, letter to S.T., 7/11/87; interview with Hannah Hay Muldaven, 3/14/87.

Information on Southern California from Carey McWilliams, *Southern
California: An Island on the Land,* Salt Lake City: Peregrine Smith, 1973;
Kevin Starr, *Inventing the Dream: California through the Progressive
Era,* New York: Oxford University Press, 1985. On the Western Rangers:
Harry C. James, *A Manual For Trailfinders,* Los Angeles: Harry C. James,
1933; H. Allen Anderson, *The Chief: Ernest Thompson Seton and the
Changing West,* College Station: Texas A&M University Press, 1986. On
the Wobblies: Patrick Renshaw, *The Wobblies: The Story of Syndicalism
in the United States,* New York: Doubleday, 1967; Fred Thompson, *The
I.W.W.: Its First Seventy Years,* Industrial Workers of the World, 1967;
Charles R. Perry, *Collective Bargaining and the Decline of the United
Mineworkers,* New York: University of Pennsylvania, Industrial Research
Unit, 1984. On Wovoka: Vincent H. Gaddis, *American Indian Myths
and Mysteries,* Radnor, Pa.: Chilton Books, 1977; Will Roscoe and Harry
Hay, *A Blessing From Wovoka,* San Francisco: Vortex Media, 1988. On
Edward Carpenter: Edward Carpenter, *The Intermediate Sex: A Study of
Some Transitional Types of Men and Women,* London: Swan Sonnen-
schein, 1909; *Intermediate Types Among Primitive Folk: A Study of Social
Evolution,* New York: Mitchell Kenerly, 1914; *Edward Carpenter: Selected
Writings,* vol. 1, *Sex,* ed. David Fernbach and N. Grieg, London: Gay
Men's Press, 1984.

3. A toe in the mainstream

Interviews with Jean Hay Burke, 8/19/88; David Hawkins, 3/7/87; and
James Broughton, 10/5/86, supplied details of Hay's term at Stanford.
Hay helped secure his transcripts from Stanford University. Correspon-
dence and telephone interviews with Gerard Koskovich, Stanford's
Gay/Lesbian historian. Hay's personal correspondence from the period

from James Broughton, Smith Dawless, Jean Hay, and others was very useful. Robert Balzer, letter to S.T., 7/11/87; H.H.'s letters to Jim Kepner; an unpublished interview with Hay by William Lonon Smith; press clippings and studio biographies on John Darrow from the Margaret Herrick Library of the Academy of Motion Picture Arts and Sciences, Beverly Hills, Calif.

Jonathan Ned Katz, *Gay American History,* New York: Thomas Y. Crowell, 1976; Los Angeles High School *Blue and White,* Summer, 1929.

4. An actor's life

Interviews with Helen Gorog, 2/11/87, 4/13/87; Miriam Brooks Sherman and Al Sherman, 8/7/88; Ben Dobbs, 5/20/87; Peter Brocco, 5/9/88; Michael Furmanovsky; 3/9/89, John Cage, 3/6/87; Sally Norton, 4/8/89. John Cage, letter to S.T., 3/13/87.

On John Cage: Calvin Tompkins, *The Bride and the Bachelors: Five Masters of the Avant-Garde,* New York: Viking, 1965; Franz Von Rossum generously shared information from his forthcoming biography of Cage, 10/7/89. On Will Geer: Raymond Strait, *Star Babies: The Shocking Lives of Hollywood Children,* New York: St. Martin's, 1979; Sally Norton's unpublished Ph.D. thesis, *A Historical Study of Actor Will Geer: His Life and Work in the Context of Twentieth-Century American Social, Political and Theatrical History,* Los Angeles: University of Southern California, Drama Department, 1981. Clippings from the Margaret Herrick Library were also used for information on Geer and other Hollywood agitators. On Communism: Lester Cole, *Hollywood Red,* Palo Alto, Calif.: Ramparts Press, 1981; Joseph R. Starobin, *American Communism in Crisis, 1943–1957,* Berkeley: University of California Press, 1972; Peggy Dennis, *Autobiography of an American Communist,* Berkeley: Creative Arts, 1977; Vivian Gornick, *The Romance of American Communism,* New York: Basic Books, 1977; John D'Emilio, *Sexual Politics, Sexual Communities: The Making of a Homosexual Minority in the United States, 1940–1970,* Chicago: University of Chicago Press, 1983; McWilliams, *Southern California.*

On agitprop theater: Jay Williams, *Stage Left,* New York: Scribner's, 1974; Clifford Odets, *Six Plays by Clifford Odets,* New York: Grove Press, 1979. On Hollywood: Deems Taylor, *A Pictorial History of the Movies,* New York: Simon & Schuster, 1949; Charles Higham and Roy Moseley, *Cary Grant: The Lonely Heart,* New York: Harcourt Brace Jovanovich, 1989; Vito Russo, *The Celluloid Closet,* New York: Harper & Row, 1981.

5. Which side are you on?

Interviews with Reginald LeBorg, 5/13/88; Helen Gorog; Florence Robbins; Walter Keller, 7/2/87. Stanley Haggart, letters to H.H., 7/27/37, 10/23/37, and undated letters.

On Hollywood in the thirties: Neal Gabler, *An Empire of Their Own: How the Jews Created Hollywood,* New York: Crown, 1988; McWilliams, *Southern California;* Harry Hay, "Sister Cain," unpublished story, 1937; Harry Hay, "Flight of Quail," unpublished story, 1937; Richard Meeker [Forman Brown], *Better Angel,* Boston: Alyson, 1988.

6. Married man

Interviews with Helen and Lacie Gorog, 4/13/87; Kate Hay Berman, 3/14/87; Hannah Hay Muldaven; Bill Alexander, 7/19/86; Miriam Sherman; former C.P. colleague (name withheld by request); Stanton Price, 6/3/87; Earl Robinson, 8/12/86; Irv Niemy 7/11/86; Ben and Martha Rinaldo, John McTernan, 8/19/86; Kay Cole, 4/21/87; Joan Mocine, 1/20/89; Mary Mocine, 1/20/89; Alma Meier, 5/2/88; Jim Kepner 8/22/86; Alan Eichler, 3/14/90. Manly P. Hall, letter to S.T., 5/28/87.

Beverly Hills High School Annual, 1931; letters of Anita Hay; Harry Hay and Reginald LeBorg, *Largo,* unpublished screenplay; David Gebhard, et al., *A Guide to Architecture in Los Angeles and Southern California,* Santa Barbara: Peregrine Smith, 1977; Jay Williams, *Stage Left;* Eric Gordon, *Mark the Music: The Life and Work of Marc Blitzstein,* New York: St. Martin's Press, 1989; Larry Warren, *Lester Horton: Modern Dance Pioneer,* New York: Marcel Dekker, 1977; "Los Angeles against Gerald L.K. Smith: How a City Organized to Combat Native Fascism!" (pamphlet), Los Angeles: Mobilization for Democracy, undated (circa 1947); Otto Friedrich, *City of Nets,* New York: Harper & Row, 1896; Harry Hay, *Music: Barometer of the Class Struggle,* unpublished, 1948.

7. Changing worlds

Stewart George Rippey, *The Year of the Oath: The Fight for Academic Freedom at the University of Southern California,* Garden City, N.Y.: Doubleday, 1950; Robbie Lieberman, *My Song Is My Weapon: People's Songs, American Communism, and the Politics of Culture, 1930–1950,* Chicago: University of Illinois Press, 1989; Thoinot Arbeau, *Orchesog-*

raphy, trans. Mary Stewart Evans, New York: Dover, 1967; Enid Welsford, *The Fool: His Social and Literary History,* Garden City, N.Y.: Doubleday, 1961; J.D. Robb, "The Mattachines Dance: A Ritual Folk Dance," *Western Folklore,* vol. 20, 1961; *Grand Larousse Encyclopedique,* Paris: Larousse, 1963; Karl M. Schmidt, *Henry A. Wallace: Quixotic Crusade, 1948,* Syracuse, N.Y.: Syracuse University Press, 1960; Eann MacDonald [Harry Hay], "Preliminary Concepts," in *A Homosexual Emancipation Miscellany, 1835–1952,* ed. Jonathan Ned Katz, New York: Arno Press, 1975.

8. Mattachine

Interviews with Kate Hay Berman, Martin Block, 8/21/86; Rudi Gernreich, Summer, 1980; Helen Gorog, James Gruber, 2/4/89 and 2/11/89; Evelyn Hooker, 2/10/90; Jim Kepner, Dorr Legg, Oreste Pucciani, 5/25/90; Martha Rinaldo, Earl Robinson, 8/12/86; Charles Rowland, 7/28/86, 8/13/87, and 12/12/89; Miriam Sherman, Michael Shibley, Don Slater, Konrad Stevens, 12/12/89.

Notebook of Mattachine Society minutes transcribed by Rudi Gernreich in 1952 (papers of Oreste Pucciani); Hay's 1950s handwritten notes proposing Greek and Latin names resulting in U.S. "homophile" term remain in his papers; Ruth Bernhard, letter to S.T., undated (Summer, 1986); Hay divorce papers, Case #D-425693, Los Angeles Court Archives; Marvin Cutler [W. Dorr Legg], ed., *Homosexuals Today: A Handbook of Organizations and Publications,* Los Angeles: ONE, Inc., 1956; D'Emilio, *Sexual Politics;* Donald Webster Cory [Edward Sagarin], *The Homosexual In America: A Subjective Approach,* Greenberg, New York, 1951; Jeff Winters, "Review: *Sexual Politics, Sexual Communities,*" *Homosexual Information Center Newsletter* 37, undated (1983).

9. Collapse

Interviews with James Burford, 5/25/89; Kay Cole, Ben Dobbs, Jack Hay, Jorn Kamgren, 6/27/88; John McTernan, 8/19/86; Frank Pestana, 7/22/86 and 12/13/89; Frank Wilkinson, 12/28/89; Donald Wheeldin, 5/25/89; Sandra Gladstone, 5/26/89. Dorothy Healey, letter to S.T., 6/8/88.

"Testimony of Harry Hay, Accompanied by Counsel Frank Pestana," in *Investigation of Communist Activities in the Los Angeles, California Area,* part 1, Hearings before the Committee on UnAmerican Activities, House of Representatives, 84th Congress, 1st session, June 27–July 2, 1955, Washington, D.C.: Government Printing Office, 1955; Donald Wheeldin,

"Un-Americans Shift To San Diego," *People's Daily World,* 7/5/55; *L.A. Times,* 7/5/55; Nicholas von Hoffman, *Citizen Cohn,* New York: Doubleday, 1988; Katz, *Gay American History.*

10. Between the lines

Interviews with Kate Hay Berman, Hannah Hay Muldaven, Jorn Kamgren, Jim Kepner, Dorr Legg, Del Martin and Phyllis Lyon, 8/4/86; Don Slater, Walter Williams, 6/14/89. H.H., letter to Rudi Gernreich, undated (probably 1956).

"The Moral Climate of Canaan in the Time of Judges," *ONE Institute Quarterly of Homophile Studies,* vol. 1, no. 1 (Spring/Summer, 1958); "The Hammond Report," *ONE Quarterly: Homophile Studies,* Winter/Spring, 1963; Robert Graves, *The White Goddess: A Historical Grammar of Poetic Myth,* New York: Farrar, Straus & Giroux, 1948; Robert Graves, *The Greek Myths,* vols. 1 and 2, Edinburgh: Penguin, 1955; Robert Graves to H.H., 3/19/61; Walter L. Williams, *The Spirit and the Flesh,* Boston: Beacon Press, 1986; David King Dunaway, *Huxley in Hollywood,* New York: Harper & Row, 1989; Noel I. Garde, *Jonathan to Gide: The Homosexual in History,* New York: Vantage Press, 1964; W.H. Kayy, *The Gay Geniuses: Psychiatric and Literary Studies of Famous Homosexuals,* Glendale, Calif.: Marvin Miller, 1965; Judy Grahn, *Another Mother Tongue: Gay Words, Gay Worlds,* Boston: Beacon Press, 1984; Arthur Evans, *Witchcraft and the Gay Counterculture: A Radical View of Western Civilization and Some of the People It Has Tried to Destroy,* Boston: Fag Rag Books, 1978.

11. Loving companions

Interviews with John Burnside, Bill Fishman, Al Gordon, James Gruber, Dorothy Healey; Jim Kepner, Dorr Legg, Phyllis Lyon, Del Martin, William Moritz, Silvia Richards, June, 1988; and Don Slater, April, 1986 and June, 1989.

"Deposition of Lewis Bonham," *ONE Inc., etc., vs. Donald Rutherford Slater,* October 13, 1966, Los Angeles; "Deposition of Chet Sampson," ibid. (both in J.K. papers); Alfred Craig, "One Becomes Two: Homosexuals Split," *L.A. Free Press,* 6/18/65; Don Slater, letter to ONE subscribers, 4/18/65; *ONE Confidential,* vol. 10, no. 4 (April, 1965) (Slater); Don Slater, letter to ONE subscribers, 9/17/65; Don Slater, letter to "Friends of ONE," 9/24/65; Dorr Legg, "A Statement About ONE, Inc." (letter to ONE supporters), 8/22/66; Taylor Branch, *Parting the Waters: America in the King*

Years, 1954–1963, New York: Simon & Schuster, 1988; D'Emilio, *Sexual Politics;* "Protest On Wheels," *Tangents,* June, 1966; Paul Coates, "Problem for Army," *L.A. Times,* 4/24/66.

12. Change of scene

Interviews with Phillip Blood and Joan Blood, 5/25/89; John Burnside, John Ciddio, 8/5/86; Katherine Davenport, 4/20/87; Pat Gutierrez, 8/5/86; Sue-Ellen Jacobs, 2/3/87; Luke Johnson, 8/3/89; Jonathan Ned Katz, 4/8/90; Morris Kight, 5/28/90; Don Kilhefner, 11/1/89 and 11/8/89. Alejandro Lopez, letter to S.T., 9/18/87; Tom Dickerson, letter to S.T., 7/10/89.

"The Homosexual: Newly Visible, Newly Understood," *Time* 10/31/69; H.H., letter to editors, *Time,* 11/14/69; D'Emilio, *Sexual Politics;* Alphonso Ortiz, *The Tewa World: Space, Time, Being and Becoming in a Pueblo Society,* Chicago: University of Chicago Press, 1969; Sue-Ellen Jacobs, "Top Down Planning: Analysis of Obstacles to Community Development in an Economically Poor Region of the Southwestern United States," *Human Organization* (reprint, undated); Nancy Adair and Casey Adair, *Word is Out,* San Francisco: New Glide Publications, 1978; Edmund White, *States of Desire: Travels in Gay America,* New York: Dutton, 1980.

13. Radical Faerie

Many interviews for this chapter were conducted at Faerie gatherings between 1980 and 1989, and are undated. More formal interviews are dated. Interviews include: Albert Bell, Faygele Ben-Miriam, Betty Berzon, 7/20/89; Blue Sky Butterfly (Walter Blumoff), James Broughton, John Burnside, Joey Cain, John Callahan, Tracy Cave, Cacho, David Cohen, Craig Collins, Tom Dickerson, Dimid, Bill Fishman, Harry Frazier, Fritz Frurip, Tom Heskette, Bill Hill, Chris Kilbourne, 7/2/89; Don Kilhefner, Richard Labonté, David Liner (Sai), 8/4/86; Gene London, Lin Maslow, William Moritz, Chaz Nol, Alan Page, Will Roscoe, Bradley Rose, Dan Siminoski, Joel Singer, Stuart Szidak, William Stewart, Mark Thompson, Neal Twyford, Mitch Walker, 6/24/89; Martin Worman, 8/21/89.

Harry Hay, "Western Homophile Keynote Address," *The Ladder,* June/July, 1970; Arthur Evans, letter to S.T., 6/5/86, extensive correspondence between Harry Hay, Don Kilhefner, Mitch Walker; Circle of Loving Companions, "Who Are the Gays," and RFD staff, "Comments," *RFD,* Autumn, 1975; Evans, *Witchcraft;* Arthur Evans, *The God of Ecstasy: Sex*

Roles and the Madness of Dionysis, New York: St. Martin's, 1988; Fritz Frurip, "First Gathering Letter," unpublished, September, 1979; Mark Thompson, *Gay Spirit, Myth and Meaning,* New York: St. Martin's Press, 1987; Sharon McDonald, "Gays and Spirit, Part 3," *The Advocate,* 2/17/87; Mitch Walker, *Men Loving Men: A Gay Sex Guide and Consciousness Book,* San Francisco: Gay Sunshine Press, 1977; Mitch Walker and friends, *Visionary Love: A Spirit Book of Gay Mythology and Trans-mutational Faerie,* San Francisco: Treeroots Press, 1981.

14. Above all, audacity

Interviews with Phyllis Bennis, 8/9/86; John Burnside, John Callahan, 6/3/86; Jonathan Ned Katz, Don Kilhefner, William Moritz, Bob McNee, Shane Que-Hee, Bradley Rose, Will Roscoe, 7/1/86; Mark Thompson, 4/13/89; Martin Worman.

Stuart Timmons, "A Sign of the Times? Veteran Gay Activist Removed from Parade," *The Advocate,* 9/16/86.

Index

▼

*Alyson Publications publishes a wide variety of
books with gay and lesbian themes.
For a free catalog, or to be
placed on our mailing list,
please write to:
Alyson Publications
40 Plympton St.
Boston, Mass. 02118
Indicate whether you are interested in books for
gay men, for lesbians, or both.*